UNRAVELING
REVELATION

Hope, Wisdom, and Mystery
in John's Apocalypse

☙

LARRY PECHAWER

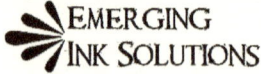

To Julie—
My loving wife of 50 years, without whom each day would
likely have been a big disappointment.

This book is a testament to her encouragement and
selfless devotion to her husband and family.

ACKNOWLEDGMENTS

Throughout the present work I have employed the abbreviations OT and NT. For me, those stand for two former professors of mine: Dr. James E. Smith (OT) and Thomas E. Friskney (NT).

With their guidance, Hebrew Exegesis and Greek Grammar came alive during my years in Cincinnati! The OT prophets and NT epistles (including Revelation) started to make sense under their tutelage. Through them and other special like-minded Bible professors, a firm commitment to the Bible as the inspired Word of God grew in me and made possible my own teaching career that spanned some four decades.

Tom Friskney spent many nights in the dorm in the 60s and 70s so that he could teach Greek at 7 a.m.! "Doc Smith" has continued to be a positive influence through his prolific writing many years into retirement. I also appreciate that he performed a special wedding in the Cincinnati Bible Seminary chapel now fifty years ago!

ABBREVIATIONS

Books of the Bible

Gen	Ezra	Hos	Mk	1Tm
Ex	Neh	Joel	Lk	2Tm
Lev	Est	Am	Jn	Tts
Num	Job	Ob	Acts	Phm
Deu	Ps	Jon	Rom	Heb
Josh	Prov	Mic	1Cor	Jas
Jdg	Ecc	Nah	2Cor	1Pet
Ruth	SoS	Hab	Gal	2Pet
1Sa	Isa	Zep	Eph	1Jn
1Kgs	Jer	Hag	Php	2Jn
2Kgs	Lam	Zec	Col	3Jn
1Chr	Eze	Mal	1Th	Jude
2Chr	Dan	Mt	2Th	Rev

English Translations

ASV	American Standard Version
ESV	English Standard Version
KJV	King James Version
NAS	New American Standard Bible
NET	New English Translation Bible
NIV	New International Version
NKJV	New King James Version
NRSV	New Revised Standard Version
RSV	Revised Standard Version

TABLE OF CONTENTS

PREFACE

The last book of the Bible was the last book I thought I wanted to focus upon at this stage of my writing efforts. However, as 2023 wound down, finishing up some work on the second coming of Christ propelled me into further research on the book of Revelation. There I intended to cobble together twenty or thirty pages from the Bible's last book as a fitting conclusion on the topic of Christ's return. Such an endeavor was difficult to avoid, especially given the nature of Revelation's focus.

A hundred and fifty pages or so later, I realized I had fallen into an "Apocalypse abyss" from which there could be no hasty escape. This book represents my feeble attempts to climb out of the hole into which I had carelessly fallen, now resolutely clawing and composing and hence carrying with me the fresh fruits and tender bruises of my labors. The last book I wanted to tackle at this point. Revelation. Really.

Massive, magisterial works on Revelation are available today along with numerous selective, specialized studies on the book. Commentaries devoted to John's Apocalypse abound. Note the Resources section below in Chapter V. The present work seeks to provide a fresh approach to the book, one that tracks my own journey in seeking to discover the basic message of the book in light of its quite fascinating original setting and to understand that message within the context of the NT as a whole (see Chapter I).

Three appendices are found at the end of the book: Appendix A, "The Man of Lawlessness"; Appendix B, "The Olivet Discourse: Jesus' 'Little Apocalypse'"; and Appendix C, "Basic Principles for Interpreting Prophecy." These provide insights into relevant issues that bind the rest of the Bible to the book of Revelation. Paul's teachings on the man of lawlessness in 2 Thessalonians 2 are frequently merged with other NT descriptions of an "antichrist" (1-2 John) and Revelation's "beast." I caution against such a merger. For some who might benefit from a basic overview of principles of interpretation, especially as they relate to key connections between the Old Testament (OT) and the New (NT), Appendix C is provided.

Body notes that involve authors with more than one work utilized in the present book will cite a keyword from the title of the appropriate work as found in the bibliographical references at the end of the book. Authors' names that are mentioned in close proximity to the body note will likely not be found within the note itself.

Abbreviations of Bible books have followed a suggested pattern offered by College Press, Joplin, MO. For the most part, the abbreviations OT and NT have been employed when referring to the Old and New Testaments. Chapter numbers for the present work, unlike those for Revelation itself, are represented with Roman numerals, e.g., "XXV" for "25". I felt that several aspects of the book made this a fitting, if subtle, choice. Another detail for readers to sort out.

English speakers are fortunate to have a multitude of Bible translations from which to study. The abundance of riches may seem daunting at times. The key distinction we must make is between a paraphrase and a more literal translation of the original text. While paraphrases like The Living Bible, The Message, and others may offer a different and fresh perspective at times, careful Bible study also needs the utilization of an actual authoritative translation, generally produced by a sizable community of recognized scholars. For dealing with difficult poetic texts like the book of Job, I have recommended that students compare translations to get the best possible results. Using the

English Standard Version (ESV) along with the New American Standard Bible (NAS) or New International Version (NIV) would be a good option.

For this book, I have chosen primarily the English Standard Version (ESV) for Scripture quotations. Other versions utilized will be so indicated. In previous publications and papers I have regularly employed the New International Version (NIV) and the New American Standard Bible (NAS). In general, I find ESV to land somewhere between NAS and NIV regarding literalness (a strength of NAS) and readability (a quality of NIV). I "grew up on King James" and still appreciate the beauty and majesty of that translation, but biblical scholarship has advanced too far and the English language has changed too much for me to recommend the King James Version as a *primary* reference for exegetical study today.

I have found the Bible to be difficult enough during my teaching career without having to look at it through a four-hundred-year-old English filter. Based upon the introductory essay by the translators in the 1611 edition of the King James Bible ("The Translators to the Reader"), readily available online, it is almost certain that they themselves, if transported to present times, would not be dependent upon the KJV today, but would opt for a newer translation more in line with contemporary English.

CHAPTER I

AS WE BEGIN: MAPPING THE JOURNEY

The book of Revelation provides challenges recognized by all. Unfortunately, John's dramatic "unveiling" (his *Apokalypsis*, the Greek term we often translate as "Revelation"), seems to offer us more questions than answers, and scholars through the centuries have debated with great fervor the exact purpose and message of this remarkable book.

In describing what lies ahead, we note a number of areas of special investigation. In light of the baggage that we all carry into a study like that of Revelation, we need to explore briefly the most relevant current approaches to Bible prophecy and to Revelation specifically (Chapters III-VI). My strong amillennial leanings will quickly become evident to some upon examination of this material. I seek to be fair if not completely objective in this overview of various takes. The reader can evaluate. Browsing the relevant mainstream conservative approaches involved in interpreting Bible prophecy may help explain how and why strongly opposing views surface when Bible students and scholars confront a book like Revelation. As noted previously, a sketch of the basic principles involved in interpreting Bible prophecy in general is provided in Appendix C.

Special attention must be given to the church's circumstances in the last half of the first century, the time of the writing of the book. These circumstances involved the church's relationship with the Jewish communities that, in their ongoing rejection of Christ as Messiah, continued to oppose the Christian message and accompanying practices even after the destruction of Jerusalem in AD 70. Complicated interactions also accompanied the dark shadow of the pagan Roman Empire that fell at times upon believers in connection with persecutions, social stigmas, and economic hardships.

Related to the early church's circumstances is the question of *theodicy*, "God's justice, justness, fairness," and how this relates to the events of the last half of the first century, events that included Rome's subjugation of the Mediterranean world and of Judean Palestine in particular, and also Rome's brutal conquest of the Jewish nation and the accompanying destruction of the Jerusalem temple complex and its ceremonial trappings. Much debated are the nature and extent of the persecutions of Christians under both Nero and Domitian in the last half of the first century. Simple answers are not available, but evidence exists that points to episodic afflictions upon Christians that varied in scope and intensity throughout this period. Was God really in charge? Revelation answers in the affirmative, yet with warnings and cautions.

A false dichotomy may exist in the minds of many with regard to interpretations of Revelation that focus upon past historical events versus predicted future developments. What some have called "pre-understandings" further the risk that weighted agendas and not measured evidence might propel the discussion. For example, dispensational premillennial theology is guided by the assumption that Revelation is talking primarily about the (now) distant-future events that will transpire *after* the "rapture" of the church. The arrival of the antichrist, the unleashing of the great tribulation, the destruction of the (modern rebuilt)

Jerusalem temple, and the fall of a modern-day Babylon are all important teachings of the book according to this perspective, teachings that involve complex future events prophesied by John.

On the other hand, the strict preterist view insists that the events prophesied in Revelation relate to first-century events such as the AD 70 destruction of the temple and the persecution of the fledgling church at the hands of the Roman Empire, and that the book, as a prophetic guide of near-future events, was written in the days of the emperor Nero preceding the fall of Jerusalem.

My own research has led me down a different path. A careful examination of the book would suggest a blending of both past and future events described by John in his visions. Revelation 12, e.g., depicts the conflict between Christ and Satan as it unfolded beginning at Bethlehem with the birth of the Messiah (Rev 12:1-5). This was followed by Christ's ascension into heaven (Rev 12:5) and the ensuing persecution of the church by Satan and his followers (Rev 12:6, 13-17). This persecution is handed over to the "beast" coming out of the sea (Revelation 13) and he and the "false prophet" (also known as the "land beast") carry on the bidding of the "great dragon." Clearly, *some* of the events in John's visions belong to the past! *Which ones* will be the key question.

The dispensational premillennial view that all of the so-called "tribulation events" in the book transpire after an alleged rapture of the church is soundly rejected in the presentation that follows. As well, the preterist view that requires an early date for the writing of the book (before AD 70, during Nero's reign), is similarly rejected. Prophetic literature in Scripture can be *predictive of future events* but also *interpretive of past and present events*. The meaning of what has already transpired can be just as important as descriptions of what will later unfold. Preaching and prognostication go hand in hand within the phenomenon of Bible prophecy. OT prophets frequently intertwine past and present circumstances with their corresponding relevant future consequences.

The "why" can be just as important as the "what." Second Kings 17, e.g., supplies a lengthy "why" as to the circumstances that brought about the destruction of the Northern Kingdom at the hands of Assyria. Past transgressions are paraded in detail. Yahweh's resulting judgments by the hands of the Assyrians are spelled out. Future judgments (e.g., captivity in Babylon) await if changes do not come about. Relevant for us here, one can accept a later Domitian dating for the book of Revelation (ca. AD 95), as the majority of scholars in fact do, while at the same time contending that many of the symbolic descriptions found can have reference to events in the past (Rome's rise to power, the fall of Jerusalem, the Messiah's advent, Nero's death, etc.).

The present work unfolds guided by the conviction that Revelation is an inspired work and belongs in the authoritative canon of Scripture. The author's interpretations presented here are not open-ended or self-contradictory speculations. Rather, they are molded by the desire to see the book as in harmony with the rest of the Bible, compatible with other NT teachings and instructive regarding how OT prophecy should be understood in light of later divine revelation.

What makes the book of Revelation unique toward the end of the first century is *not* that it is an apocalyptic work. We will discuss the significance of contemporary Jewish apocalyptic works like 4 Ezra and 2 Baruch, works comparable to Revelation in several aspects. What makes Revelation stand out is that it is an *inspired* apocalyptic work and as such presents special challenges for the modern Christian reader.

Before tackling the chapters of Revelation in sequence, the present work will proceed with a range of related overview materials involving major interpretive issues. Several chapters that take a topical slant on the book will round out this generally introductory material (topics including key second coming texts, special OT connections, etc.).

What will then follow will be the analysis of the contents of the various chapters in Revelation. Somewhat unique will be the contribution of my Chapter XII to the understanding of the historical background behind Revelation's images and descriptions. This entails background about which many late-first-century readers would have had common knowledge, but about which most Christians today are far less informed. This chapter precedes those that focus upon the Cosmic Conflict taking center stage in Revelation 12 and following (Chapter XIII, etc.) and seeks to help elucidate the at-times bewildering parade of characters, images, and events that confront us: the great dragon, the beast from the sea, the woman under attack, the false prophet, the great city, Babylon the Harlot, "666," Armageddon, etc.

Throughout the chapter-by-chapter survey of Revelation that makes up the heart of this book, nine key topics are addressed, topics that are vital to an understanding of Revelation. An attempt is made to answer important questions raised by these topics:

1. What do we make of the various cycles of seven in Revelation?

2. How are the setting and the date of the book related to its message? How does the answer aid

the interpretation of the various visions and symbols in the book?

3. How can we best understand the significance and nature of the Cosmic Conflict depicted in Revelation beginning with Revelation 12 and culminating with the defeat of the beast and the false prophet (Revelation 19) and of Satan himself (Revelation 20)?

4. With respect to the controversial millennium of Revelation 20, what are the key factors that tip the scale regarding its interpretation?

5. How should John's use of the OT guide our thinking concerning what the millennial kingdom of Revelation 20 and the new heavens, new earth, and New Jerusalem of Revelation 21-22 represent? Where does the "golden age" of OT prophecy fit in?

6. In what sense is John the seer a "new Ezekiel" and how does the answer facilitate our understanding of the imagery and message of Revelation as well as that of the book of Ezekiel itself?

7. What is at stake regarding the identification of the Great Harlot "Mystery Babylon"? What are the implications for choosing the ancient Rome or ancient Jerusalem options? What tips the scales? What are the problems with either option?

8. What is next according to Revelation's message to the church? How does the book employ the notion of "soon" regarding Jesus' return and how does that fit with the message of the rest of Scripture?

9. Finally, what special significance does the subtitle for this book with its terms Hope, Wisdom, and Mystery convey?

All of these key questions and the answers discovered in our investigations are reviewed in the concluding chapter (Chapter XXV) under the heading "need to know."

I have alluded to my work here as involving a "fresh approach" and a "different path." What exactly is meant? Perhaps I am overstating the case with such language! Much has been said by many, after all. How different and fresh can this really be? Part of the answer lies in the book's subtitle: *Hope, Wisdom, and Mystery in John's Apocalypse.* Clearly hope for the future is paramount throughout Revelation, especially as a response to the trials and tribulations facing believers at the close of the first century. A bright new creation (heavens and earth) lay ahead. The challenge to be faithful "overcomers" who would reap their rewards rings forth from the opening visions to the final exhortations of the book.

Less obvious initially is the importance of the terms "wisdom" and "mystery" for the overall message and understanding of the book. As will be developed later, challenges given within Revelation for the readers to understand the meanings of certain key terms and descriptions are central to the message of the book.

Many commentators seem to disagree with that assessment, a fact that I find puzzling. They promote whatever they view as the "big picture" from the book and eschew the "confusing, enigmatic details." But surely the call for "wisdom" to calculate the number of the beast, i.e., "666" (Rev 13:18), and the call for "wisdom" in identifying the "seven heads of the beast" and in understanding the "mystery" of Babylon the Harlot who bears a "name of mystery" (Rev 17:5, 9-11) are more than casual invitations! Rather, they lie at the heart of meaningful attempts to grasp the historical context from which many of Revelation's scenes and images derive.

Also crucial for locating the setting of the book's message is the prominent role of the "mortal wound" of the beast, a wound that heals to the amazement of the world (Rev 13:3, 12, 14). This topic dovetails with the amazement directed toward the fortunes of the beast described later in Revelation 17 (esp. 17:8). The remarkable near-demise and revival of the beast, along with the beast's desolation of the harlot that once rode upon it, are not peripheral features of Revelation, but rather lie at the core. In part, they reflect the divine hand at work in the unfolding of the early years of the church and signal that God is in control, in spite of what the church's challenging circumstances might suggest. Tribulation for the faithful will continue until Jesus returns. God's prophesied judgment upon Jerusalem fulfilled in AD 70 foreshadows final judgment upon the wicked, demonstrates His righteous wrath, and confirms His control over the course of history. And tied to the hope of believers is the promise that "soon" Jesus will return.

What to make of that? Stay tuned.

CHAPTER II

THE OLD AND NEW, THE ALREADY AND NOT YET

How the NT writers utilized the OT is a primary question for those interested in the study of Bible prophecy in general and the book of Revelation specifically. A key issue involves the distinction between what Christ accomplished at His first coming and what will occur at His second coming. We must make the distinction between the "already" and the "not yet" in regard to the fulfillment of Bible prophecy, with the NT as our infallible guide. Today we already enjoy the blessings of a kingdom and salvation made possible through Christ's crucifixion and resurrection, but we do not yet see realized the ultimate glory of the age to come. The various millennial views analyzed in the next two chapters below are based in part on these kinds of key distinctions. The debate can be quite animated at times. I believe it is possible to disagree without being disagreeable.

The Old in the New

Jesus made it clear that the OT spoke of Him (Jn 5:39; 6:45). Luke 24, the account of Jesus and those on the road to Emmaus, is particularly instructive. Jesus admonished,

> "O foolish ones, and slow of heart to believe in all that the prophets have spoken! 26 Was it not necessary that the Christ

should suffer these things and to enter into his glory?" [27]*And beginning with Moses and with all the Prophets, he interpreted to them in all the Scriptures the things concerning himself. (Lk 24:25-27)*

Jesus understood that He was to be found throughout the pages of the OT. His apostles frequently quoted messianic prophecy in their claims and arguments. We are drawn to the book of Acts, e.g., Acts 1:16; 2:16ff, 25-27; 3:18, 22-24; also 2 Peter 1:19. These are just a few of the references in the NT in which OT prophecy is applied to Jesus. We can expand that list greatly by looking at various prophecies about the establishment of the church and the promises concerning the resurrection of the Messiah and His ascension to the throne in heaven. We find recorded in Acts 13:33-35, for example, Paul's words regarding Christ's connection with the promises to David and the fulfillment of those promises in His being raised from the dead, with Paul noting Psalms and Isaiah (Ps 2:7; 16:10; Isa 55:3).

The range of citations from the OT can be somewhat puzzling. A fascinating set of questions involves exactly which prophecies were chosen and why. For example, passages from the book of Isaiah occur over fifty times in the NT in citation while the book of Ezekiel is not explicitly quoted *once* in any substantial way, even though the book of Ezekiel is a book of comparable size to Isaiah. In fact, by word count, it is even larger than Isaiah, yet there are no direct prophecies in the book of Ezekiel concerning the coming of the Messiah cited in the NT. There are certainly some texts that could have been used, e.g., prophecies about the coming of "my servant David" (Eze 34:23-24; 37:24-25) who would become a united Israel's "one king" (Eze 37:22) and "one shepherd" (Eze 34:23; 37:24).

Since we have texts that could have been utilized, the range of distribution of citations in the NT becomes an intriguing subject. However, we really cannot come to know with any degree of certainty why certain OT passages were ignored and other passages that maybe were less obvious were instead utilized. One important distinction should be made here. At times we find *allusions*, i.e., indirect or brief references, to OT passages or entities in contrast with explicit quotations. Notably, the book of Revelation frequently alludes to Ezekiel (e.g., "Gog and Magog") without quoting specific verses.

Regarding the Jewish citations of the OT as an indication of how they understood certain texts to relate to the coming of Israel's Messiah, we should note the appendix of Alfred Edersheim's book (now over a hundred years old), *The Life and Times of Jesus the Messiah*. In that appendix, Edersheim, a converted Jew, listed some 456 OT prophecies that the Jews understood to be messianic. For anyone who wants to argue that the early church made up these connections or that they saw the OT in a way that was not normal or natural, one has to explain away how the Jews themselves understood these as being messianic prophecies. Not only are many of the prophecies cited in the NT found in this list from Edersheim, but there are also additional prophecies the Jews understood as messianic that the NT does not specifically cite.

Regarding Revelation, what for many is the NT "prophecy book," noted NT scholar Bruce Metzger claims that 278 of its 404 verses contain OT allusions, i.e., brief references, either direct or indirect, rather than word-for-word citations (13). Remarkably, there are no quotations from the OT in Revelation that exceed a handful of words in length (such limited quotes can be found in Revelation 1:7; 2:27; 6:8; 10:5-6; 15:3-4). The substance and spirit of the OT are clearly found throughout the book of Revelation, just not sizable specific Scripture quotes. We find allusions to Gog and Magog from Ezekiel 38-39 (Rev 19:17-18; 20:8-9), but not direct quotations. Other allusions or references from Ezekiel include, among many, such elements as the cup of wrath, the Great Harlot, and eating a scroll (Chapter VIII).

A crucial question in this present work is how best to understand the ways the NT writers interpreted OT texts in light of the fulfillment they recognized in Jesus. As noted elsewhere (Appendix C), passages in the NT that are clear and straightforward can serve as an inspired guide for more difficult, poetic, symbol-laden OT prophetic texts. He who has ears to hear let him hear.

Already and Not Yet

Clearly, some of what the OT prophesied concerning Messiah's coming has already taken place (His "first coming") while other promises have not yet occurred (the "second coming"). Future events not distinguished chronologically in the pages of the OT are sorted out for us as we read the NT. Jesus and His apostles made helpful distinctions between promises "already" fulfilled and those that have "not yet" transpired. Be advised that the fact that there can be a "second" coming does not necessarily suggest that there must or will be two of everything: two Elijahs or two temple destructions or two falls of Babylon, etc.! The notions of "prophetic perspective" and "double fulfillment" have become crutches for some interpreters upon which to rest the heavy burdens of their particular system (cf. Appendix C). Don't like the stated fulfillment? Have another.

In his classic theological work *Christ and Time* (1950), Oscar Cullmann recognized a paradigm shift revealed and accomplished by Christ when He, through His redemptive work on the cross, created a new center point for the unfolding of God's work in His creation. For Cullmann, the beginning point for God's new age is no longer future. It is a past event, what some have called the "Christ event," a way scholars at times describe Jesus' ministry, death, resurrection, and ascension. In a sense the future is *now*; it has broken into the human arena creating both a merger and a tension between what can be designated the "already" and the "not yet."

The D-Day Analogy

When Cullmann wrote the "Foreword" to the original German edition of his work in December, 1945, the wounds of World War II were still quite fresh. It had been only seven months since V-Day (or VE-Day, "Victory in Europe Day"), and eighteen months since D-Day. VE-Day was celebrated May 8, 1945, marking the Allies' formal acceptance of Nazi Germany's unconditional surrender. But looking back, historians have pronounced that the war was effectively decided on D-Day, June 6, 1944, at which time the Allies established a beachhead at Normandy, breaking the back of the Germans. In his writing, Cullmann utilized the analogy he found in the events of the war and the celebration of "Victory Day." As Cullmann explained, the decisive battle in a war may already have occurred even though the war still continues. Christ's crucifixion and resurrection is our "D-Day" even though the final victory awaits (84).

What Cullmann and others have stressed, then, is that the battle in a real sense has already been won. Christ is the victor against Satan and the forces of darkness. He has conquered death and the grave, ushering in life and immortality. His followers are now redeemed, justified, and resurrected kingdom citizens. Christians are already "more than conquerors" (Rom 8:37).

The "already and not yet" paradigm has now become a well-worn trail in end-times studies and is certainly relevant to our study of Revelation. One of the leading spokesmen for this paradigm was the evangelical scholar George Eldon Ladd whose works on eschatology mark a high point in the scholarship of historic premillennialism in the twentieth century. One of his books, *Jesus and the Kingdom* (1964), was updated and renamed *The Presence of the Future* (1974) and remains one of the key works for engaging this topic. Ladd's contribution to the study of the second coming and related end-times topics cannot be overstated.[1]

An Unexpected Intrusion

In ancient Jewish thought, there were two successive ages set in stark contrast: the present evil age and the blessed age to come. In some fashion the coming of *mashiach*, "Messiah" (the "anointed one"), would inaugurate the glories of the age to come. Various scenarios were lined out in key Jewish sources, including the Dead Sea Scrolls, various extra-biblical works such as 4 Ezra, 2 Baruch, Enoch, and others, and the vast rabbinic literature.

What Jesus did caught everybody by surprise, including (or especially) the Jewish scholars of His day. He came to

---

[1] Other works by Ladd include *The Blessed Hope* (1950); *Crucial Questions about the Kingdom of God* (1952); *The Gospel of the Kingdom* (1959); *The Last Things: An Eschatology for Laymen* (1978); *The Pattern of New Testament Truth* (1968); and *A Theology of the New Testament* (1974). I have found the last work especially valuable.

earth to be Savior of all mankind, not just of the Jewish people. He gave His life as a ransom for many and purchased men from all nations with His shed sacrificial blood. Through His resurrection He was vindicated as the divine Son of God/Son of Man. His disciples witnessed on the Mount of Olives His ascension back to heaven, but not before He had promised that He would return some day after He had prepared an eternal home for them.

Who saw all that coming? No one, really, for even His closest companions, eyewitnesses to numerous miracles and hearers of countless parables and instructions concerning the kingdom of God, failed to fathom the divine purposes behind the angry Jewish mob and the merciless Roman cross.

On the road to Emmaus, Cleopas related to (the unrecognized) Jesus the recent events involving the crucifixion of Jesus of Nazareth. He lamented, "But we had hoped that he was the one to redeem Israel…" (Lk 24:21). In the painful retrospect of the moment, they realized they had been wrong in their hopes. But they were wrong as to *how* they were wrong.

Christ's resurrection would set in bold relief the true nature of their error. The kingdom they had long hoped for had not materialized, but the Day of Pentecost would soon be accompanied by the inauguration of a different kind of kingdom, one not of this world (Jn 18:36; Acts 2).

In the errant hopes for a restored earthly kingdom, however, violent Jewish freedom fighters would unleash their fury against the might of Rome within a single generation. Coins would be minted proclaiming "For the Redemption of Israel." Tragically, these Jews' notion of divine redemption would spell the disastrous end of the Jewish nation, their holy city, and their sacred temple. Jesus warned His generation that they had missed the time of

God's "visitation" in blessing (Lk 19:44). God's visitation in wrath would follow within a generation—the horrific consequence for Israel's ultimate act of rejection.

As Jesus explained on the Emmaus Road, the OT prophets had spoken of the events and purposes of His earthly ministry (Lk 24:25-27), just not always in clear, unambiguous language. In light of the persisting modern misconceptions and misapplications of Scripture, we should not be surprised at the ways in which the early disciples missed the mark. Not one, but *two* comings of Israel's Messiah were on the divine docket, and God's kingdom, not yet fully established and visible, had already been inaugurated in some fashion through the ministry and saving work of Jesus.

Grace would trump race as the full equality of God's new people would be experienced between Jew and Gentile—"one new man in place of the two" (Eph 2:15). The church's proclamation of the good news or "gospel" (1Cor 15:1-4) would be God's ordained way by which the world would learn the message of salvation. The believer's possession of the indwelling of God's Holy Spirit would be the down payment or "guarantee" of the promise of the future life in the age to come (Eph 1:13-14).

A Useful Paradigm

As a result of what Christ has accomplished in His crucifixion, resurrection, and ascension, redemptive time takes on a new configuration. Christians simultaneously live in both ages, sharing in the spiritual blessings of God's age to come while still persevering in the present. As Ladd has explained, through Christ's death the believer has already been delivered from this present evil age (Gal 1:4). At Calvary Christ has already defeated the powers of evil, powers that previously had brought chaos into the world (Col 2:14ff; *Theology*, 551).

As new creations, Christians have already experienced death and resurrection (Rom 6:3-4)as well as exaltation to heaven with Jesus. God has "seated us with him in the heavenly places in Christ Jesus" (Eph 2:6). Our transition from death to life is partial, incomplete, yet real. We live within the tension of experienced and anticipated eschatology. Believers are already in the kingdom (Col 1:13) yet someday will inherit the kingdom (1Cor 15:50)!

For those seeing the "already and not yet" distinction as being useful, the concept of *inaugurated eschatology* is often invoked. The kingdom of God has been inaugurated in Christ but not yet consummated. We already enjoy the indwelling of the Holy Spirit (Acts 2:38-39; 4:31; Rom 8:9-11), but our life in Christ is not fully glorified until His return. "If the Spirit of him who raised Jesus from the dead dwells in you, he who raised Christ Jesus from the dead will also give life to your mortal bodies through his Spirit who dwells in you" (Rom 8:11). We have been raised with Christ in baptism (Rom 6:4-9), but the final resurrection of our bodies awaits Christ's second coming.

The "already" aspect of the age to come, then, refers to the "inauguration stage" of the last days. The "not yet" aspect speaks to the "consummation stage" at which time Christ will return and will bring about the realization of the eternal new heavens and new earth in which righteousness dwells. As will become clear, the book of Revelation deals with both the inauguration and consummation stages of the age to come.

The Paradigm in Revelation

God's kingdom is both a present and future reality. The same is true for the term "eternal life." Life in the kingdom and life eternal often describe the same thing. More specifically, the expression "kingdom of God" in the Synoptic Gospels (Matthew, Mark, Luke) or "kingdom of heaven" (esp. in Matthew) is generally equivalent to "eternal life" in John. In the opening lines of Revelation John identifies himself as a partner in the kingdom with those to whom the letter is addressed as well as one who shared in the tribulation they were suffering for the sake of the kingdom (Rev 1:9).

Paul wrote to the Colossian church, a church not far from Revelation's Laodicea (note Col 4:16),

If then you have been raised with Christ, seek the things that are above, where Christ is, seated at the right hand of God. ²Set your minds on things that are above, not on things that are on earth. ³For you have died, and your life is hidden with Christ in God. ⁴When Christ who is your life appears, then you also will appear with him in glory. (Col 3:1-4)

"If then you have been raised with Christ"—and you have! In Romans 6, Paul links the raising of the believer from the dead to baptism (cf. Col 2:12). The churches at Ephesus and Laodicea mentioned in Revelation had earlier benefited from Paul's writings sent to that region (Col 4:16). They almost certainly knew something about the already/not yet distinction regarding eternal life and resurrection from the dead from Paul's earlier teachings.

Often the expression "kingdom of God" is a synonym for the age to come, but the present realization is also stressed. Robert Lowery, in writing on Revelation, states, "Christians are already in the Kingdom, and yet they await the coming of the Kingdom in its totality (Col. 1:13-14; Rev. 11:15)" (44).

Jesus asserted the presence of the kingdom during His earthly ministry in Luke 17:20-21: "Being asked by the Pharisees when the kingdom of God would come, he answered them, 'The kingdom of God is not coming in ways that can be observed, nor will they say, "Look, here it is!" or "There!" for behold, the kingdom of God is in the midst of you.'"

The Greek phrase *entos hymōn* can mean either "within you" (i.e., in your hearts), or "in your midst." The latter "in your midst" or "in the midst of you" seems to fit best with Jesus' overall teachings. His own presence (as king) marked the kingdom's reality.

For those for whom the kingdom of God has arrived, eternal life is now a present possession. Lowery notes that in John's writings especially we see the focus on eternal life in both the present and future sense.

> The tension between the now and the not yet is found in such passages as John 6:39, 40, 44, 54; 11:24; 12:48 and in 1 John 1:2; 2:18, 22, 28; 3:2-3. We already have eternal life, but we await the total fulfillment of eternal life (John 6:26ff.; 11:25; 12:23ff.; 14:1ff.). We already receive blessings because we belong to Christ, but we anticipate even richer blessings at his coming.

> In Revelation, John writes about the victory that Christ has won in the past (1:5, 18; 5:5-7, 9-10; 12:1-4, 7-12), as well as the final victory at the final coming (1:7; 6:12-17; 7:1-17; 11:15-19; 16:15-21; 19:1-21; 20:7-15; 22:7, 12, 20). (45)

The implications of the already/not yet paradigm for the book of Revelation are immense. Nowhere else in the

NT do we see more clearly how the blessings of the present and the joyous anticipation of the future undergird perseverance in the midst of trial. With Lowery, "John summarizes the Christian life in terms of salvation as a past fact, a present duty, and a future hope. Because Christ has saved us (1:5b) and because someday that salvation will be complete (19:1ff.), Christians must be faithful in living out the implications of their salvation" (46).

CHAPTER III

BASIC APPROACHES TO THE END TIMES
MILLENNIAL VIEWS, PART 1

Any careful study of the book of Revelation must give attention to the various end-times approaches prevalent today. In what follows my own convictions and perspectives will naturally be center stage even as I attempt to represent fairly other viewpoints. Six major views of the second coming and the end times will be briefly described. Ample resources are cited below for further in-depth analysis.

Saints down through the centuries have offered their interpretations of these sacred texts. With the passage of time, views crystallized and systems took shape. The later rise of modernism and its impact in promoting classic liberalism in the theological life of the church gave rise to strong conservative reactions. These at times have fostered views of Bible prophecy emphasizing strict literal interpretation as a barrier against the incursion of liberalism into the moral and doctrinal fiber of the church.

Such strategies can be appreciated but must be evaluated. When a staunchly conservative preacher waxes eloquent on prophetic interpretation, "God means what He says and says what He means," I get it. I just believe that the premise and conclusion here are slanted in such a way that the real truth might get sidestepped. God may use powerful, figurative language to say what He means, and His people need to be tuned in to the Bible's oft-utilized expressions of poetic, symbolic, and figurative language to understand what He says.

Not every supporter of a specific millennial view sees things the same way in all passages. Some of these distinctions are important to recognize. End-times battlegrounds often end up materializing in the most unexpected places as far as Bible texts go. That verse means *what?* Mainstream end-times debaters often have their own parade examples of prominent scholars who have done a radical about face: an amillennialist who saw the light and became a proud preterist; or a dogged dispensationalist who shocked his friends and became an avid amillennialist. Such transformations are intriguing and informative at times, if not necessarily fodder for a Hollywood movie. Yet through the years millions have been impacted by the dramatic, unexpected theological about-faces of prominent voices. Who knows? Perhaps this book will find a "convert" or two along the way.

Much of the language in this section and those following revolves around the "millennium," the term often used to describe the thousand-year reign of Christ depicted in Revelation 20 (from Latin *mille,* "thousand," and *annus,* "year"). Major views are often framed with regard to what that "millennial reign" involves and when it will occur. The figurative language encountered throughout the book of Revelation does not make the investigation any easier, to be sure!

The particular features of some of the more distinctive recent schools of thought have forced exegetes to give extra attention to certain texts and terms. Seemingly basic, seemingly straightforward words like "resurrection," "coming," "meet," "revealed," "lived," "judged," "day," "tribulation," and more are employed in a multitude of ways in promoting specific end-times scenarios. Is there one future judgment or are there seven? What are the alleged distinctions between the rapture, the return, the revelation, and the coming of Christ? How can the same Bible be employed to produce such diverse results as we regularly encounter in this field of study? Some of the answers to such questions can be surprising and enlightening. And at times frustrating.

Six viewpoints in all will be summarized here, but the bulk of consideration throughout much of the book will be given to the amillennial, historic premillennial, dispensational and preterist views in connection with how key Scripture texts are to be handled. Any serious student of the end-times and of the book of Revelation in particular must navigate the waters of these four influential major approaches especially, and of these, I believe, the amillennial view will provide the safest harbor in which to land.

Postmillennialism

Postmillennialists teach that the second coming will be postmillennial, that is, it will come *after* the "millennium." Accordingly, they view the millennium as occurring at the latter part of the church age. This millennium, in their minds, will be a period of spiritual advance and prosperity as the gospel of Christ is openly embraced by the majority (or significant minority) of people in the world. Some postmillennialists would push the exactness of the "thousand-year" time frame, others would not. They would all agree, however, that this time period will be fulfilled by a triumphant church at a time when "the earth shall be full of the knowledge of the LORD as the waters cover the sea" (Isa 11:9).

When will this supposed glorious age begin? No one can say for sure. In fact, it may have already begun. Postmillennialists would draw the analogy of the change of seasons in the year or the transition, say, between the Middle Ages and the modern era. Only in retrospect can one say with confidence that a new day has dawned. Thus, as God's people look back, they will be able to identify the time when the proposed millennium actually began. Universal peace and righteousness will characterize that glorious era.

The major problem with the postmillennial view is that there is little Scripture to support such a position. Although one must appreciate such an optimistic outlook (as some scholars have said, "Don't you *wish* it were true?"), the testimony from the Bible is ambiguous to say the least. Much of the evidence cited comes from the OT descriptions of the age to come, descriptions that in part could describe the gospel age in general (focusing on the righteous remnant of believers) but also God's new creation—Revelation's new heavens and earth and new Jerusalem, the eternal resting place for God's people. NT parables that expound the growth of God's kingdom are regularly cited as pointing to the great advance of the gospel worldwide. Of course we also see that the wheat and the tares grow together alongside of each other until the harvest (Mt 13:24-30).

Frequently theology is fashioned according to social or cultural conditions that tint our lenses and trigger our sensations of optimism or pessimism. The postmillennial outlook was quite popular in the early 1800s as that time period seemed to be pointing the way to great technological, medical, and educational advances. Great religious revivals were underway. The potential of the new American frontier was fertile ground for the postmillennial perspective. Things *were* getting better, and the best seemed yet to come!

Far fewer today, however, envision Christ's triumph over His enemies this side of the second coming. In light of two world wars, numerous regional conflicts, the Great Depression, the fearful nuclear age, ecological concerns, increased moral decay, killer viruses, the rise of fundamental Islamic terrorism—the list goes on—one can understand why such earlier optimism no longer captures man's imagination. Most feel divine intervention will be necessary. Postmillennialists have become a rare breed, although the latter years of the twentieth century witnessed some renewed interest in the approach. Neither the Bible nor current events seem to support this position.[2] Certainly the language of Revelation 20 does not.

Many postmillennialists have urged that Scripture, not current world events, should be the determining factor in our interpretation of eschatology. They have a good point, especially in view of the rapidly-changing contours of today's geopolitical landscape. I never thought that the Soviet Union would unceremoniously collapse before our eyes. Impossible. Standing on the roof of one of the World Trade Center's Twin Towers back in the nineties, I could not have imagined *their* collapse in my lifetime. A few years later they were gone. Unthinkable. Still, the optimistic postmillennial outlook is in short supply these days in view of distressing modern trends and increasing worldwide turmoil. Postmillennialism does share some features with amillennialism and that latter approach may be a better option once all the evidence is examined.

---

[2] One relatively recent postmillennial defense is Keith A. Mathison's *Postmillennialism: An Eschatology of Hope* (1990).

Preterism

In part because of the excesses of many popular futuristic schemes, including various forms of dispensationalism, another approach has gained greater popularity, that of preterism. The term "preterist" comes from the Latin for "past" and speaks to an approach where many if not all of the NT's end-times prophecies have *already* been fulfilled. The prophetic system known as "full," "strict," or "hyper" –preterism is an especially unwelcome addition to the end-times controversy, in my view.

Several books are now available featuring debates between preterists and dispensational futurists.[3] I cannot recommend such books except to serious students of the field. The approaches presented are from opposite extremes, with the middle ground being mostly ignored. The situation resembles an ancient mariner in Greek mythology having to choose between the monsters Scylla and Charybdis on opposing sides of the waterway, rather than being able to navigate a safe course well between them.

Unlike what I would consider to be the *futuristic* excesses of dispensationalism (see below), preterism teaches that second coming prophecies have *already been fulfilled* in connection with the AD 70 destruction of Jerusalem. That was when the Son of Man came "in the glory of his Father with the holy angels" (Mk 8:38). This of course is a remarkable claim! Preterists emphasize the "soon," "near," and "at hand" language in various promises of Jesus' return and claim that the only way to keep our Lord and His apostles from being discredited is to conclude that Jesus did come "soon"—in AD 70.

---

[3] Once such book is *The Great Tribulation: Past or Future? Two Evangelicals Debate the Wuestion* (1999) by Thomas Ice (dispensational) and Kenneth L. Gentry Jr. (preterist).

I taught Bible and biblical languages in Christian colleges and universities for over four decades and I do understand the preterist arguments about apocalyptic language—"stars falling," "moon turning to blood," etc.— being used at times for temporal events (e.g., the fall of Babylon, Assyria, or some other empire). But this system takes the concept beyond the limits of good sense. It is difficult to see how the Great White Throne Judgment in Revelation, or the Sheep and Goats Judgment in Matthew, or the creation of the new heavens and new earth described in 2 Peter and Revelation, or the meeting with Jesus in the clouds as described by Paul in 1 Thessalonians could have transpired in AD 70.

Those speculations take more "faith" than I am willing to invest in an interpretive scheme! Like many packages offered out there, this system can sound good initially. The siren call of preterism has an intriguing ring to it, but when the entire song is played out, something definitely seems out of key. One sure guide for testing any exotic replacement for normative doctrine is to see how the implications unfold with respect to the entirety of biblical teaching. Suspect systems in time eventually disintegrate under the bright light of Scripture. The question arises. Do these new remarkable insights support or undermine biblical consistency? Do they conform to a reasonable, mature reading of the text, or do they demand novel approach after repeated nebulous speculation?

While following the contours of the contemporary preterist landscape, I have noticed a radicalizing tendency among its spokesmen which should give rise to caution. One clear case in point must suffice for now. In order to do justice to the extent of activity described in the Olivet Discourse, especially in Matthew 24-25, some strict preterists have concluded that the "rapture" occurred in connection with the AD 70 destruction of Jerusalem. All the saints, including the apostles, were taken to heaven at this time! This is when the Sheep and Goats Judgment takes place (Mt 25:31-46). Also, the depiction of Christ's return in 1 Thessalonians 4—the *parousia* or "coming" of Christ—is describing events concurrent with Jerusalem's fall.

For some, this remarkable conclusion explains why the second and third generations of church leaders offer so little in terms of helpful advancement of theological ideas or in-depth biblical exegesis. The first-century leaders had been raptured away! In an instant the repository of Christian thought and conviction was drained nearly empty. It took centuries before the church could emerge as a dynamic intellectual resource in light of the instantaneous removal of all first-century Christian leaders. So the argument goes. This assessment of the contributions of the early Apostolic Fathers is, however, overly harsh, as most historians studying the early church would concur. The notion of a first-century rapture exhibits extreme conclusions that must be reached to provide enough oxygen for this desperate patient to breathe.

It is critical for the preterist position that all of the NT be written before AD 70, including the book of Revelation. John was still on the island of Patmos in the years immediately before Christ "returned," according to them. Therefore the battle continues to rage over whether Revelation was written around the time of Nero (several years before AD 70) or Domitian (AD 95 or so). The majority of scholars are convinced that the evidence points to the later date and I agree, as will be made evident in time. Preterists seek rather to date the book early in part to make the focus of God's judgments found there to be the fall of ancient Jerusalem, not a still future return of Christ. For them, Christ has already "returned" and so Jesus *did* come "soon," just as He promised, without any problematic delay.

However, the strict preterist solution for the problem of the "soon" language in the NT creates even bigger problems. The denial of a future return of Christ naturally has serious implications for our understanding of the Christian faith. For one thing, how can the horrible events of the fall of Jerusalem be considered as the church's "blessed hope" (Tts 2:13)? Also, I definitely do not believe that the "new heavens and new earth" (2 Peter 3; Revelation 21-22) have already come into existence! To an extent, the acceptance of hyper-preterism by some is an over-reaction to dispensationalism's hyper-literalism (see later), but full (hyper-) preterism itself also falls short of adequately dealing with the Bible's end-times teachings.[4]

A distinction must be made between the partial preterist and the full preterist views. There is a significant difference. Partial preterists like R. C. Sproul and Kenneth L. Gentry, Jr. opt for the early dating of Revelation and do believe that the fall of Jerusalem plays a large role in the prophecies of that book. The Olivet Discourse primarily describes the destruction of Jerusalem as well in their thinking (Matthew 24; Mark 13; Luke 21).

Partial preterists do believe, however, that the Bible *also* teaches the traditional second coming in most of the passages generally linked to that topic. Jesus' glorious return is a future, not past event. Partial preterist Gentry's *Before Jerusalem Fell: Dating the Book of Revelation* (1998) is commonly viewed as one of the finest books available on that topic.

---

[4] Ed Stevens, president and founder of the International Preterist Association, and John Noë, author of numerous books, e.g., *Beyond the End Times* (1999); *Shattering the 'Left Behind' Delusion* (2000), have been two of the most vocal proponents of the full preterist position.

Gentry dates the book to the reign of Nero (thus before AD 70). It would seem that dating the book of Revelation early makes one a "preterist" of some sort. Still, there is a "great wide gulf" between partial and full (strict, extreme, hyper-) preterists. In fact, partial preterists are among the most severe critics of the strict preterist view.[5]

The popular and highly influential British NT scholar N.T. Wright in his *Surprised by Hope* (2008) seems additionally surprised by the fact that anyone could confuse *him* with a preterist. He indeed describes the very notion that AD 70 was the second coming as a "bizarre position to hold" (*Hope*, 127) and affirms his own belief in an as-yet-future second coming. However, there is reason for confusion since Wright does not believe that Jesus Himself taught about the second coming! In Wright's words, "The first thing to get clear is that, despite widespread opinion to the contrary, during his earthly ministry Jesus said nothing about his return" (ibid., 125). This view is more fully explicated in his highly acclaimed *Jesus and the Victory of God* (1996).

Many have bought into this approach without carefully scrutinizing the evidence or the implications. What about John 14:3? There Jesus says, "And if I go and prepare a place for you, I will come again and will take you to myself, that where I am you may be also." Wright does not include John's evidence here. In his massive 1996 production filled with hundreds of NT citations and references, the first few verses of John 14 are nowhere to be found. Wright makes clear that his focus on Jesus comes from the Synoptic Gospels: Matthew, Mark, and Luke. But how "clear" then can we be that Jesus said nothing about His return?

---

[5] For example, Gentry and others take them to task in Keith A. Mathison (ed.), *When Shall These Things Be? A Reformed Response to Hyper-Preterism* (2004).

Selectivity often seemingly clarifies, but it also can cloud the true picture.

Wright's prolific writings on the NT are widely acclaimed, with good reason, yet I wonder if he is overzealous here in his attempts to limit Jesus' pronouncement of a day of reckoning only to those judgments poured out upon Jerusalem in the first century. In His Olivet Discourse in particular Jesus contrasts His personal return (without signs or warning) with the fall of Jerusalem (preceded by plenty of warning signs). I am convinced Jesus said a lot about His return.

Dispensationalism

At its core, dispensationalism is a form of premillennialism. According to the basic premillennial view, the second coming will be "premillennial," meaning that it will come *before* the "millennium." The church age will end with the second coming and a new age, the "millennial kingdom," will be ushered in. This will be a one-thousand-year earthly kingdom in which Christ reigns over His people. At the end of this period, Satan will be loosed for his "little season" and his armies, "Gog and Magog," will be destroyed by fire from heaven, while he himself is cast into the lake of fire (Rev 20:7-10). At this point the Great White Throne Judgment takes place (Rev 20:11-15)—an earlier Sheep and Goats Judgment (Mt 25:31-46) had supposedly occurred at the second coming *before* the "millennium." Following this final judgment at the end of Revelation 20 the "eternal state" is ushered in.

Dispensational Distinctives. It is crucial at this point to distinguish between the premillennialism described above from the view that most seem to hold today. The view briefly described above is sometimes called the "historic premillennial" view, that brand of premillennialism to which some Christians have adhered throughout the centuries. Historic premillennialism will be discussed further in our next section.

Much of modern premillennialism, on the other hand, is characterized by several distinctive newer features. This more recent viewpoint is known as dispensational premillennialism or simply dispensationalism. Although frequent reference will necessarily be made throughout the present book to the distinctive teachings of modern dispensationalism, a few remarks concerning this system need to be made at this juncture.

Dispensationalism teaches that God works with and tests man according to various divine "administrations." The popular *Scofield Reference Bible* distinguished between seven such "administrative periods" or "dispensations." Most Christians are "dispensational" to the extent that they at least recognize the distinction between the old and new covenants. Dispensationalism goes far beyond this basic distinction, however. According to dispensational premillennialism, the church age, God's current "dispensation of grace," will be replaced in the future with the seventh and final dispensation, the "millennial kingdom." Central in dispensational thinking is the Jewish nationalistic flavor of this kingdom. Christ came, it is claimed, to set up an earthly Jewish kingdom (quite similar to what many who rejected Him seemed to have been expecting!).

The Postponement Theory. When the Jews rejected their Messiah, so the view goes, the promised kingdom was "postponed" and in its place the church, a temporary stop-gap "parenthesis," was established. According to dispensational premillennialism, this promised kingdom will be established with a future Jewish generation (perhaps *already* living on earth now) after God's dealings with the church are through. Accompanying this novel approach is the idea of a secret "rapture" of the church prior to a "great tribulation" poured out against unbelievers, especially Israel.

This view seems to come from around 1830 in England and is generally credited to the Plymouth Brethren leader John Nelson Darby. Most dispensational scholars today acknowledge this basic fact, although some have strained to find earlier examples of a two-part return of the Lord in previous church writings. The rise of this distinctive approach clearly is to be connected with Darby, who found fertile soil for his novel ideas in his five or so trips to America in the 1860s and 1870s.

The eventual popularity of Darby's views was due to a great extent to the publication of the *Scofield Reference Bible* (1909) in which the text of the King James Bible was supplemented by the dispensational notes of C.I. Scofield. Unfortunately, many readers did not always clearly recognize when the Bible stopped and Scofield started! The founding of Moody Bible Institute (1886) and Dallas Theological Seminary (1924) spearheaded the rise of numerous dispensational colleges and seminaries and a strong missionary movement promoting dispensational theology worldwide thus emerged.

In the last half of the twentieth century, dispensationalism hit the mainstream through the writings especially of Hal Lindsey and Tim LaHaye. Multiple printings of Lindsey's *The Late Great Planet Earth* (1970) and related works and the enormously successful *Left Behind* series (1995-2007) created by Tim LaHaye and Jerry Jenkins have sold many millions of copies. Numerous Christians who have grown up in the church today are unaware that there is any viewpoint on the end times other than that which such contemporary popular publications have promoted.

Unfortunately, this viewpoint contains numerous problematic teachings. I would contend that it is a big deal to deny that the church was prophesied in the OT, but that is what classic dispensationalism must do. What was prophesied in the OT regarding Christ's kingdom was "postponed" when the Jewish nation rejected Christ as their Messiah. In its place the church was established as a type of "parenthesis" in between Christ's first and second comings. This approach has been labeled the "postponement theory" as well as the "parenthesis church theory."

Whichever term is used, it represents a radical departure from normative Christian theology and the church's traditional understanding of what the NT teaches. As a consequence, millions of dispensational Christians have been taught in such a way so as to miss the biblical teaching of the church's true role in God's plan.

According to dispensationalism, after the "rapture" the "great tribulation" will unfold as a prelude to Israel's salvation at the second coming. The second coming (allegedly some seven years or so after the rapture!) introduces the millennial kingdom in which converts, especially the converted Jewish people, headquartered in Jerusalem, will be ruled by Jesus Christ as He sits on the "throne of David" in that city. Christians who are either transformed or resurrected at the "rapture" technically do not participate in the earthly millennial kingdom. Their hope is different from Israel's, it is alleged. They perhaps view the millennial scene from their heavenly vantage point.

God has two distinct peoples, dispensationalism stresses. Promises to Israel are not the same as promises to the church according to this view. The hope of Israel is not the hope of the church (although Paul seems to differ—he claimed to be proclaiming the "hope of Israel" in his gospel preaching according to Acts 28:20).

The "Rapture" and the "Revelation." Earlier historic premillennialism always had those supporters who tended to emphasize Israel's role in the millennium. Excesses in this area eventually led to the birth of the dispensational approach described above. Actually, the earlier brand of premillennialism had its own set of problems and dispensationalism in part functioned to "smooth them out."

The earlier premillennial view had a problem with the "imminence" of Christ's return, since they saw so many "signs" that had to be fulfilled before the second coming. How can Christ's return be at any moment ("imminent") if there are various signs that have yet to be fulfilled? The dispensational "secret rapture" solved that problem. All the signs were now placed between the rapture and the later "revelation" (the alleged second phase of the second coming).

However, under further examination of the NT, e.g., Jesus' Olivet Discourse, many of those so-called "signs" lose their significance or disappear altogether anyway. The dispensational or pre-trib "solution" is then not even needed. (Dispensationalists view the rapture as an event that precedes and delivers Christians from the so-called "great tribulation"; cf. Rev 7:9-17.) A pre-trib "problem" looms large, however, that of attempting to carve up the NT's verses on the second coming in such a way as to present a consistent distinction between the "rapture" and the "revelation."

This distinction cannot be maintained, however, without repeatedly doing violence to the text. As will be shown, the alleged secret rapture must be smuggled into the book of Revelation. It is not an obvious teaching there.

Unlikely Distinctions. The historic premillennial view has provided a somewhat troubling depiction of who would populate the millennial earth. It generally envisions a mixed millennial society made up of both those who enter the millennium alive with their earthly, perishable bodies and those who come to life and enjoy their imperishable "resurrection" bodies at that time. Sounds like the "haves" and "have nots" to me.

Dispensationalism tidies things up a bit by shipping off the resurrected "church saints" to heaven at the rapture. Only the later "tribulation saints," both survivors and the resurrected dead, will actually populate the millennial earth according to pre-trib reasoning. In making such distinctions, however, dispensationalists have created a host of unlikely scenarios.

Their differentiation between a "rapture" to heaven and a later second coming to earth (what many call the "revelation") separated by a supposed seven-year period has given rise to a mind-boggling complex of last-days events, including a sequence of no less than seven separate judgments.

Dispensationalists seek to distinguish clearly between a "rapture" during which Christ does not "return" to earth (only meeting the church in the sky and then taking them off to heaven) and a later "return" (also termed the "revelation") in which He arrives upon a partially renewed earth (but not the final, completely renewed earth of Revelation 21-22). Upon His arrival (His "return"), Christ will establish His earthly millennial reign during which, according to their interpretation of the OT, the nation of Israel will take center stage and regain a superior standing over the Gentile believers. However, the evidence for such ideas is questionable in the OT and *absent* from the NT.

There is more. Dispensationalists distinguish between the future battles of "Armageddon" and "Gog and Magog" and then in turn conclude that, due to "problems" with the timing created by their system, the "Gog and Magog" battle of Revelation 20:7 must be a different end-times battle from the "Gog and Magog" battle of Ezekiel 38-39.One would think that one "Gog and Magog" would be enough! Clearly John in Revelation is indeed incorporating the battle of Gog and Magog imagery from Ezekiel into his depiction of the final end-times conflict and judgment (Chapters VIII, XIX).

Second Chance Theology. The dispensational brand of premillennialism has dangerous flaws in several regards.

1. Their hyper-literal interpretation leads to a bizarre, complex sequence of future events.

2. Their use of the OT often ignores the way in which the NT interprets many of the OT prophecies.

3. Their "postponement theory" teaches that Christ's church, rather than being central in God's plans, was merely an "afterthought" brought about by the Jewish rejection of the kingdom. Some critics have labeled the church "plan B" in this regard.

4. One might conclude that Christ, then, apparently failed in His mission when He came into the world, in that He allegedly came to establish the "kingdom" for Israel.

5. The separate "rapture" of the church offers a second chance for those who are "left behind" then to accept Christ and enter the "millennial kingdom."

I believe this final flaw is one of the most unbiblical and dangerous teachings of today's popular dispensational approach. If, say, a few hundred million or so Christians mysteriously vanished from the earth overnight and you were "left behind," wouldn't you get right with God in a hurry? Would you need to read a bestseller then (other than the Bible!) to figure this out? Hardly.

Does God anywhere in His Word offer such an opportunity for those today outside of Christ? The answer is No!

CHAPTER IV

BASIC APPROACHES TO THE END TIMES
MILLENNIAL VIEWS, PART 2

The most important evangelical voices speaking about the book of Revelation today come from the historic premillennial and the amillennial camps, in my estimation. These voices will be summarized here along with a somewhat recently developed dispensational premillennial compromise known as progressive dispensationalism.

Historic Premillennialism

Earlier historic premillennialism always had those supporters who tended to emphasize Israel's role in the millennium. Excesses in this area eventually led to the birth of the dispensational approach described above. Actually, the earlier brand of premillennialism had its own problems and dispensationalism in part sought to "smooth them out." The historic premillennial view had a problem with the "imminence" of Christ's return, since they saw so many "signs" that had to be fulfilled before the second coming. If Jesus could return at any moment, how could it be said that certain signs were yet to be fulfilled? The dispensational "secret rapture" solved that problem. All the signs were now placed between the rapture, which was imminent, and the later "revelation" (or "return"). More on these so-called "signs" later.

The most prominent historic premillennial spokesman of the twentieth century was no doubt George Eldon Ladd. He was joined then by other important voices such as Robert Gundry and J. Barton Payne, to name a few. Ladd was a leading voice for the "already/not yet" paradigm for NT studies, which helped make important distinctions between those prophecies already fulfilled by Christ at His first coming and those awaiting fulfillment at His second coming. Themes such as resurrection, inheritance, salvation, reigning with Christ, etc. are addressed in the discussion as to when and how these important blessings in Christ are enjoyed. Distinguishing the "already" from the "not yet" plays an important role within modern studies of the end times (Chapter II). Today we find a number of accomplished, highly regarded historic premillennial evangelical scholars. Among the voices speaking to this generation we note, among many, such NT scholars as Craig Blomberg, Ben Witherington III, Craig Evans and Douglas Moo.[6]

The historic premillennial view has presented a somewhat cloudy picture of who would actually populate the millennial earth. It generally envisions a mixed millennial society made up of those who enter the millennium alive with their earthly bodies and those who come to life and enjoy their "resurrection" bodies at that time. Again, sounds like the "haves" and "have nots" to me.

Craig Blomberg is sensitive to the issue here. In offering analogies, he observes that Jesus after His resurrection mingled with His followers for forty days. Also Matthew 27:51-53 describes a remarkable, enigmatic

---

[6] For an important scholarly overview of the issues involved, I would recommend *A Case for Historic Premillennialism: An Alternative to "Left Behind" Eschatology* (2009), Craig L. Blomberg and Sung Wook Chung, eds.

situation where a group of saints was resurrected following the resurrection of Christ. These saints appeared to many in and around Jerusalem (Blomberg, "Posttribulationism," 85).

I do not consider these parallels all that helpful. For one thing, I view the resurrection body of Jesus as described in the Gospel accounts as a special case. What we see described in the post-resurrection accounts is a far cry from what we find in the first chapter of Revelation. There we see the glorified Christ (Rev 1:12-16).

It seems to me that there was a difference in the nature of Christ's resurrected body before and after His ascension to heaven. I call this a "special case" since Jesus interacted with His disciples in Palestine for forty days teaching about the kingdom of God before He ascended to be with the Father (Acts 1:3). He did so in a resurrected body that, because of the evidential value required for proving a resurrection from the dead, resembled His earthly body before the resurrection.

Likewise, the resurrected saints in Matthew 27 were walking around on *this* earth, not on a partially glorified earth as many premillennialists seem to envision for the saints in the millennium. Would the same body be suitable for both? Would the same body be suited for the alleged millennial earth and the eternal new earth described in Revelation 21-22? Will there be stages of resurrection and glorification for the saints, perhaps separated by hundreds (or a thousand!) years? I have many other questions (and a few suggestions) here. There are significant problems with the notion of a mixed population possessing resurrected and non-resurrected bodies and sharing life in a partially restored/glorified millennial earth.

Historic premillennialists are *posttribulational*, meaning that they, like amillennial and postmillennial believers, believe in a single, unified second coming. There is no separate rapture of the church that enables it to escape the (supposed) antichrist and great tribulation. What separates premillennialists from amillennialists is the issue of a millennium following Jesus' return.

What mainly separates historic premillennialists from dispensational premillennialists is the issue of the tribulation. Historic premillennialists are posttribulational, while dispensationalists are pretribulational. Whatever the tribulation involves, the church will be involved, say historic premillennialists. It will not enjoy a pre-trib rapture, or what some call "the great escape." In his critique of pre-trib dispensationalism, Blomberg suggests that the issue of the tribulation is more important than that of the millennium. He reflects,

> What might happen if millions of Christians in the twenty-first century count on pretribulationism being true, only to have to live through this awful period? Our Christian counselors and therapists tell us that contemporary Americans may be the least theologically equipped generation in church history when it comes to dealing with personal and collective suffering and evil. ("Posttribulationism," 69-70)

Blomberg has given us food for thought. Unfortunately, there is little agreement among posttribulationists as to the exact nature and extent of the "(great) tribulation." The book of Revelation gives a sobering picture for what it means to be faithful followers of the Lamb. The suffering and martyrdom depicted there may not be tied only to first-century believers or last-days disciples, but to Christians in all places at all times.

Most informed believers would agree that the persecution and abuse of the church of Jesus Christ worldwide this past century has been unparalleled. American fundamentalism has been accused of sitting in a bubble while debating when the tribulation will start, oblivious to the degree of suffering for Christ that continues to go on in many parts of the world. Great tribulation worldwide exists *today*.

Some interpreters would tie the tribulation to the entire church age; others would link it to the time frame right before Jesus returns. The problem of this determination is directly linked to another knotty problem, that of the "imminence" of Christ's return. Dealing with this problem in depth is tied to later discussion throughout the present work.

The problem simply stated is this. If Christ's return can be at any moment (thus "imminent"), how can we believe that a number of key signs must still be fulfilled before He returns? If they have not yet been fulfilled, how can we say Jesus could return today or this very night? Good question. Answers vary, often in the form of questions. Have we understood the signs properly? Are we certain the sign has not already been fulfilled? Are such signs connected to the second coming or are they about something else (e.g., the fall of Jerusalem)? Might these signs be so immediately tied to Christ's return that they in no way could serve as a warning?

Another huge problem is the confusion some have distinguishing tribulation from wrath. The book of Revelation addresses both, but to lump them together, describing the whole pie as "the great tribulation," has created unnecessary confusion leading to many false, misleading claims. The church will not face the situation of dealing with a sea having turned to blood or stars having fallen from heaven or a host of other phenomena that are (a) linked to divine wrath, *not* the church's tribulation, and

(b) described with such figurative language that many literalistic interpreters need to step back, reassess their assumptions and recalibrate their findings. Sadly, the book of Revelation is the starting point for many end-times enthusiasts and the results often betray the lack of a proper foundation in basic principles of interpretation (Appendix C).

Progressive Dispensationalism

It is ironic that at the very time more and more church-goers are jumping on the traditional dispensational "pre-trib rapture" bandwagon (led by, e.g., Tim LaHaye, John Hagee and John MacArthur, following in the footsteps of Hal Lindsey, John Walvoord, Charles Ryrie, and others), many of the best and brightest within the dispensational fold are having second thoughts about many of the basic assumptions of that system.

A new movement known as progressive dispensationalism has sent shockwaves throughout the dispensational realm. Scholars such as Craig Blaising, Darrell Bock, Robert Saucy, Marvin Pate and many others have muddied the waters that divide dispensational and non-dispensational viewpoints, much to the dismay of the classic dispensationalists.[7]

While maintaining Israel's special role in God's future plans, progressive dispensationalists by and large reject the sharp distinction between Israel and the church and the related postponement theory regarding the kingdom. The

---

[7] Important works within this movement include Craig A. Blaising and Darrell L. Bock, eds., *Dispensationalism, Israel and the Church* (1992); Craig A. Blaising and Darrell L. Bock, *Progressive Dispensationalism* (1993); Herbert W. Bateman IV, ed., *Three Central Issues in Contemporary Dispensationalism* (1999); and Robert L. Saucy, *The Case for Progressive Dispensationalism* (2010).

church is today fulfilling OT prophecies, according to them—a view to which traditional dispensationalists have strenuously objected.

Progressive dispensationalism seems to be a "work in progress." Just where these scholars will eventually land remains uncertain in my mind. They have rejected some of the key foundations serving as the basis of the separate rapture theory. By doing so, they would seem to be in a temporary no-man's land as they move from their traditional moorings. For some time now, the leadership at Dallas Theological Seminary, a former bastion for classic dispensationalism, has been trying to tone down some of the hardline dispensational rhetoric there. A number of Dallas faculty have joined the "progressives" and criticisms from classic dispensationalists have been sharp at times.

Other variations have emerged, a testimony to the fact that even more feel that classic dispensationalism is "broken" and needs fixing. None of the newer wrinkles such as the "pre-wrath rapture" (Marvin Rosenthal) or the "mid-trib rapture" (Gleason Archer) have gained much traction. The two branches of premillennial thought most discussed in what follows regarding the book of Revelation will be historic premillennialism and classic dispensationalism. Progressive dispensationalists, if looking, will be able to find themselves between the cracks.

Amillennialism

Last, but (in our view) not least, is the amillennial view. The prefix a- indicates negation, therefore the term "non-millennial" could properly be used. However, it is not that amillennialists do not believe that such a period described as the "thousand-year reign" exists. Rather, they just do not view it as a literal thousand-year period. Nor do they view it as an *additional* period of time between the church age and the final state. The following sections provide a brief overview. Chapters XX-XXIII below will offer a more complete analysis in connection with the amillennial approach to the book of Revelation. Amillennial scholars of note among many are G. K. Beale, Jack Cottrell, William E. Cox, Anthony Hoekema, Robert A. Lowery, and N. T. Wright.

The Thousand Years: Already but Not Literal. Throughout Scripture we find several references where "thousand" serves as a symbolic number: "...with the Lord one day is as a thousand years, and a thousand years as one day" (2Pet 3:8; cf. Ps 90:4); "For every beast of the forest is mine, the cattle on a thousand hills" (Ps 50:10); "...the faithful God who keeps covenant and steadfast love with those who love him and keep his commandments, to a thousand generations" (Deu 7:9). With regard to the amillennial view, some have preferred the term "historical millennial," "ideal millennial," or better yet, "realized millennial," but the terms are a bit unwieldy, so the established term "amillennial" will be retained here.

Amillennialists do not believe that other Scriptures support the (premillennial) contention that an earthly millennium will follow the second coming. Nor do they feel, however, that such a period fits well at the end of the church age as the postmillennialists teach. They maintain that the "thousand years" symbolism of Revelation 20 logically fits into a period of time already known from Scripture. They equate the "thousand years" with the entire church age. In this view, the reign of Christ with His saints is a present reality.

Satan Already "Bound" in a Real Sense. The "binding of Satan," according to the amillennial approach, is also a present reality. Through Christ's victorious resurrection over death, and through the subsequent preaching of the gospel, Satan in a real sense is "bound." This "binding" need not be absolute, but could convey the notion of limitation. Reference to the following Scriptures will show the idea that Christ's victory over Satan has already taken place: Genesis 3:15; Hebrews 2:14-15; 1 John 3:8; Luke 10:17-18; John 12:31-32; Matthew 12:29.[8]

For example, Hebrews 2:14-15, in speaking of Christ's first coming, says, "Since therefore the children share in flesh and blood, he himself likewise partook of the same things, that through death he might destroy the one who has the power of death, that is, the devil, [15]and deliver all those who through fear of death were subject to lifelong slavery."

Similarly, 1 John 3:8 reads, "Whoever makes a practice of sinning is of the devil, for the devil has been sinning from the beginning. The reason the Son of God appeared was to destroy the works of the devil."

Note the past tense in both texts. Jesus *partook* of flesh and blood and through death *destroyed* the destroyer. The Son of God *appeared* in order to destroy the works of the devil. In a very real sense, then, Satan is now "destroyed"; his work is now "destroyed" (or "rendered powerless"). The Greek words for "destroy" are different in these two passages. At Hebrews 2:14 we find *katargeō*, to "destroy, nullify, render powerless," (at 2 Thessalonians 2:8 ESV translates it as "bring to nothing"), while the more basic word *luō*, to "loose, destroy" is found at 1 John 3:8. Both terms speak to the fact of the devil's certain doom. Satan's final, total destruction is yet future but, as Revelation states

---

[8] The Matthew passage shows the same Greek word (*deō*) for "bind" regarding Jesus "binding" the "strong man"—the devil—that we find in Revelation 20:2.

it, he is now "bound" (a vivid instance of "already/not yet").

Clearly, limitation and not absolute powerlessness is what is involved here. This approach may not resonate with the theme of books such as Hal Lindsey's *Satan Is Alive and Well on Planet Earth* (1972), but I believe that it is what the Bible teaches. In vivid, symbolic language John in Revelation reminds a beleaguered church concerning the victory that is theirs and the defeat that is Satan's.

It is a powerful reminder that helps brighten the bleak landscape of tribulation and persecution that blankets much of the book. It is also a message that resonates elsewhere in the NT: "Little children, you are from God and have overcome them, for he who is in you is greater than he who is in the world" (1Jn 4:4).

It is important to note that dispensationalists, along with historic premillennialists, have a problem themselves in dealing with the binding of Satan. According to their understanding of the events during the millennium, many millions (those allegedly born during the millennium) will reject Christ's reign, even though His visible presence will result in unimaginable blessings for all. Hordes of "closet rebels" will be chafing at the bit, and Satan's release will be a welcome development in their desire to throw off Christ's shackles. Amazingly "their number is like the sand of the sea" (Rev 20:8).

According to Revelation 20:3, Satan's binding is so that he might not "deceive the nations." A common premillennial view is that universal peace will be accomplished during the millennium by Christ's immediate destruction of any *openly* rebellious "kingdom citizens." The wicked must keep it to themselves! Apparently, Satan's being "bound" does not stop countless people all over the world from ultimately rejecting Christ's millennial reign.

How is that possible? Premillennialists struggle mightily here. Some would argue that a major purpose of the millennial reign of Christ will be to expose once and for all the evil, sinful, rebellious nature of man. But do we need a future millennium to establish that? Really?

Surprisingly, there is remarkable agreement with the amillennial understanding of Satan's doom and defeat in the present age from a number of prominent historic premillennialists. Satan *was* defeated at the cross, his power *is* diminished, Christ and those in His church *do* reign right now. But, according to them, all that is not an adequate explanation for or representation of what Revelation 20 describes. I disagree. A strong case will be made later to show that, to the contrary, the binding of Satan and the millennial reign of the saints in Revelation 20 are in fact powerful symbolic descriptions of our present reality. The millennium is now!

All amillennialists are in agreement that the second coming follows the millennium and that the "thousand years" are symbolic of the present church age. Most who hold this view would link the glorious "golden age" prophesied in the OT not to the millennium, but to the eternal state— "a new heaven and a new earth" (Rev 21:1).

Amillennialists claim that their view best allows the NT teachings to be the guiding factor. Dispensationalists, on the other hand, often tend to use overly literalistic interpretations of OT prophetic texts to serve as their basis for interpreting the NT. As a corrective, we note Floyd Hamilton's advice (see Appendix C) that "the clearest New Testament passages in non-symbolic books are to be the norm for the interpretation of prophecy rather than obscure or partial revelations contained in the Old Testament" (53-54).

I am convinced that the amillennial method of interpretation offers the best chance for a reasonable, consistent understanding of the entire revelation of God. The picture in the Gospels, Acts, and Epistles is that of a single, climactic, final return of our Lord. As well, amillennialists rightly point out the conspicuous absence of any clear promise of a future earthly Jewish kingdom anywhere in the NT.

Disagreement Without Division

Clearly there can be disagreement on the millennial issue among groups of believers, many of whom are undeniably devout followers of Jesus. Sometimes, however, the debate becomes rather heated. At times the criticisms in print can be brutal and highly personal (so-and-so's numerous divorces and you-know-who's alcoholism...). Should such harshness be the case? Should the issue of Bible prophecy be a source of division for Christians? Can this be avoided?

Of course some refuse to wear any of the above labels. At least one scholar has called himself a "pro-millennialist." He was not sure what the proper understanding of the millennium should be, but whatever it is, he was all for it! Another preferred the term "pan-millennialism." He was confident that it would all "pan out" in the end!

We are partly sympathetic with the above sentiments and do not feel that such issues should be tests of fellowship or sources of division. However, neither do we feel that one can avoid taking and maintaining a basic viewpoint. The standard options are clearly defined; the ramifications of the choices can be quite significant.

John F. Walvoord was one of the leading dispensational scholars of the twentieth century. He stated,

"The dispensational premillennial return of Christ is not an insignificant matter, but is a very important doctrine. It is the key that unlocks the great treasures of the prophetic word; it sets everything in its right perspective..." (*Return*, 46).

Walvoord certainly made it sound like a high-stakes game, this search for what the Bible says about the second coming. Unfortunately, some use dubious, long-cherished systems, rather than solid principles, of interpretation as the starting point for their search. I have found a different key from Walvoord's key. I believe it will make Scripture and Revelation in particular seem more sensible and consistent.

Chapter V

Basic Approaches to Revelation

Any commentary on the book of Revelation must deal with a number of key issues involving how to approach this important book. These same issues must be faced in any special study or survey about what the book of Revelation teaches on the second coming or end times specifically. Unfortunately the scope of this present treatment is selective and can only allow us to scratch the surface regarding many of the detailed issues and arguments stemming from the book.

We have attempted above to survey the scholarly state of affairs concerning end-times study in general. The issues discussed directly relate to how the book of Revelation is approached by many. Not all commentators agree on what the specific issues in Revelation are. Because of its extensive symbolic language, Revelation is a prime candidate for being misunderstood, a convenient repository for theories and dogmas smuggled in from preconceived interpretive paradigms and systems. Some call these "preunderstandings." As we begin our examination of Revelation, we will briefly identify some of the more important big-picture issues at hand.

Past, Present, and Future

Regarding the many works on the book of Revelation, also called the Apocalypse, we first note the great divide generally found between historical and futuristic approaches to the book. These approaches take many forms and involve many nuanced arguments and expressions. For our purposes we can only comment on the most basic, broad viewpoints commonly taken. The idea that many aspects of the book should be viewed from a historical perspective is not new. However, newer wrinkles have emerged that demand a meaningful response. Modern-day preterism, especially full or strict preterism, argues that everything in the book of Revelation belongs in the past. Language that is generally taken as a reference to the second coming is applied to the AD 70 destruction of Jerusalem by strict preterists.

The language of tribulation applies to the struggles of the church at the hands of the Roman Empire in the first century, especially in relation to the persecutions by Nero (AD 54-68). The outpouring of wrath described deals primarily with God's judgment upon the Jewish nation, culminating in the fall of Jerusalem at the hands of the Roman army. Partial preterists and not a few postmillennialists and amillennialists share in some of these views.

However, unlike full (or hyper-) preterists, they also believe that the Bible, including the book of Revelation, teaches a *future second coming* that will bring about the appearance of new heavens and a new earth along with the New Jerusalem. Strict preterism, though, maintains that the second coming is in the past and that the New Jerusalem has already arrived! As already noted, to maintain that approach does not do justice to the clear sense of many key biblical passages.

Futurists maintain that the contents of Revelation present primarily what is to take place in the days ahead. There may be an admission that the book contains several flashbacks involving past historical events (e.g. the birth and ascension of Jesus—Rev 12:1-5), but for the most part Revelation describes future events leading up to Christ's return.

Most futurists contend that the thousand-year reign of Christ in Revelation 20 is an epoch that is yet to be realized and should be interpreted literally and physically. Paradisiacal conditions will prevail on earth—"Eden" fully or partially restored—and Israel's leading role in the world will be established as a thousand years click off the clock leading up to the great rebellion of Satan and his followers described in Revelation 20:7-10. This rebellion is quashed and God then establishes His new creation—the new heavens and new earth hosting the New Jerusalem.

Not all futurists, however, agree on the events leading up to the second coming and millennial kingdom. Historic premillennialists, along with a number of amillennialists, view Revelation as describing the tumultuous events *leading up to* Christ's return. An end-time antichrist and a great tribulation, a tribulation that involves intense persecution and social and spiritual upheavals, will immediately precede Christ's coming. The church will experience this last-days tribulation according to many.

The Challenge of Imminence

But how can all the frightening events described in Revelation 6-18 unwind if the doctrine of the imminence of Christ's return is to be maintained? This is a key struggle for historic premillennialists and a number of them have either abandoned or modified the concept of Christ's imminent, i.e., any-moment return. Too many signs must be fulfilled, too many specific predictions, for Christ's return to be a surprise in any meaningful sense of the word.

The dispensational premillennial futurists have, in their minds, salvaged the doctrine of imminence by postulating two comings, the rapture and the return. In doing so they have complicated the topic tremendously. For them, most if not all of the prophecies leading up to the second coming will be fulfilled, not before Jesus comes, but after He has come to take His church back to heaven with Him. All the signs needing to be fulfilled will occur between the alleged rapture and the subsequent return or "revelation" of Christ.

The content of Revelation 6-18 describes events leading up to the second coming but, with dispensationalism, those events have little or nothing to do with the present church age. They will unfold only after the secret rapture of the church. However, Revelation itself teaches no such separate rapture. It must be imported from elsewhere. In what follows a different answer for the problem of imminence will be proposed, one that embraces a single second coming, not a complex series.

Broad-Based Approaches

Outside of the premillennial camp, many interpreters throughout history and now today approach Revelation from a more holistic perspective. One use of the term "historical" involves the notion that prophecies in Revelation point to those events that have transpired throughout the course of church history. This view has waned in popularity and its attempts to see the spread of Islam or the transgressions of the Roman Catholic papacy within Revelation's prophecies find fewer enthusiasts today.

The "idealist" approach, which is often connected to amillennialism, encourages us to find general truths in the book that apply to a variety of times and circumstances.

Faithfulness and perseverance in times of opposition and persecution have been needed throughout the history of the church and will be until the Lord returns. I believe that the idealist approach may have value when wedded to the conviction that much of the message of the book relates in particular to the initial first-century audience.

The previous chapters (I-IV) have been offered to assist the reader in recognizing key issues and distinctions regularly found in the study of Revelation (see also Appendix C). Unfortunately the book has become a repository for far-flung theories and closely-held agendas. Proceed with caution. The message of Revelation can serve as a scathing rebuke for any of a number of the modern church's shortcomings. Take your pick. Many have gladly done so.

Increasingly popular targets for contemporary "prophetic" scholars are American Christian nationalism, materialism, racism, capitalism, militarism, and any other dreaded -ism that may show up on the current hit list of claimed ecclesiastical shortcomings. While some seem to revel in pointing out alleged similarities between the ancient Roman Empire and modern America, I find the endeavor strained. Most likely a more productive application of the message of the book of Revelation lies elsewhere.

Making Sense of the Tense

Making sense of the employment of various verb tenses throughout the visions and explanations in Revelation and its role for our understanding the sequence of events described in the book is a daunting challenge. Assumptions about what will happen when and how create stumbling blocks all along the way. Of course the process of Christ giving revelation to John was a past event as John writes. He already "heard" and "saw" the images and events described in the book. However, what he heard and saw related to occurrences in the past as well as to the present and the future. Sorting out the particulars is the task.

When taken up to heaven John was told he would be shown things "that must take place after this" (Rev 4:1). But as the visions unfold it becomes clear that some pertain to past events along with others that point toward the future. In addition, the insertion of various scenes from the heavenly realm introduces a timeless quality to the whole enterprise. Has the opening of the seven seals already taken place? When did the saints worshiping before the heavenly throne arrive?

Some symbols and visions John experienced pointed to the eschatological consummation at Christ's return, while at times others revealed the significance of past events, especially those events with continuing impact. The birth, death, resurrection, and ascension of Jesus are described through signs and symbols (e.g., Revelation 12). The rise of the beast from the sea and the ensuing persecution of the church seem to reflect what Satan, the great dragon, is already up to (e.g., Revelation 12-13). The seven heads described in Revelation 17 most likely represent Roman emperors of the first century as the terms "mystery" (Rev 17:7) and "wisdom" (Rev 17:9) would suggest, a view in line with the previous call for "wisdom" for identifying the "666" cipher (Rev 13:18). More on this later.

It can be debated whether the destruction of Babylon the Harlot at the hands of the beast (Revelation 17-18) refers to the harlot Rome or the harlot Jerusalem. If the latter, then another first-century historical event is being described in apocalyptic terms and given theological, perhaps apologetic, significance. One could argue that all promised events in John's visions outside of those surrounding the second coming have already been fulfilled, perhaps even by the time of the delivery of John's vivid message. Such an approach would preserve the notion of imminence regarding Christ's return—no future events need occur before the second coming. All is ready.

A Domitian dating (ca. AD 95) may not necessarily demand an exclusively futuristic approach to the book. Some, if not many, of the events unfolding in the cosmic drama described by John could speak to *past* occurrences, occurrences now infused with new significance and meaning. Believers at the end of that first century could now look back with renewed confidence in God's purposes for the past and His plans for the future.

God's Own Apocalypse

As spelled out in the Preface, the acceptance of Revelation as a Holy Spirit-inspired work will be a guiding principle throughout. The book has an important message from God that makes sense! Revelation, then, delivers a divinely-directed message through the medium of apocalyptic literature. Unlike certain Jewish apocalyptic works contemporary with Revelation like 4 Ezra and 2 Baruch, Revelation's standing as an authoritative message from God sets it apart. Its images, symbols, promises, and warnings demand our attention. The book shares in the apocalyptic genre with other intriguing works of the time period, but as the "revelation [*apokalypsis*] of Jesus Christ" (Rev 1:1) it stands alone.

Resources for Revelation

I have found the following works particularly useful. Complete bibliographic entries are in the back of the book.

Standard Commentaries

Beale, G. K. *The Book of Revelation* (1999)

Caird, G. B. *A Commentary on the Revelation of St. John the Divine* (1966)

Hendriksen, William. *More Than Conquerors: An Interpretation of the Book of Revelation* (1967 [1939])

Ladd, George Eldon. *A Commentary on the Revelation of John* (1972)

Osborne, Grant R. *Revelation* (2002)

Smalley, Stephen S. *The Revelation to John: A Commentary on the Greek Text of the Apocalypse* (2005)

Witherington, Ben III. *Revelation* (2003)

Specialized Revelation Studies

Barr, David L. *Tales of the End: A Narrative Commentary on the Book of Revelation* (1998)

Bauckham, Richard. *The Climax of Prophecy: Studies on the Book of Revelation* (1993); *The Theology of the Book of Revelation* (1993)

Blackwell, Ben C., John K. Goodrich and Jason Maston, eds. *Reading Revelation in Context: John's Apocalypse and Second Temple Judaism* (2019)

Friesen, Steven J. *Imperial Cults and the Apocalypse of John: Reading Revelation in the Ruins* (2001)

Heiser, Michael S. *The Old Testament in Revelation* (2021)

Hemer, Colin J. *The Letters to the Seven Churches of Asia in Their Local Setting* (2001 [1986])

Hill, Charles E. *Regnum Caelorum: Patterns of Millennial Thought in Early Christianity, 2nd ed.* (2001)

Lewis, Arthur H. *The Dark Side of the Millennium: The Problem of Evil in Rev. 20:1-10* (1980)

Longman, Tremper III. *Revelation Through Old Testament Eyes* (2022)

Thompson, Leonard L. *The Book of Revelation: Apocalypse and Empire* (1990)

Wood, Shane J. *The Alter-Imperial Paradigm: Empire Studies and the Book of Revelation* (2016)

Comparative Views | Millennial Views

Bock, Darrell L. ed. *Three Views on the Millennium and Beyond* (1999)

Clouse, Robert G. (ed.).*The Meaning of the Millennium: Four Views* (1979)

Gregg, Steve. ed. *Revelation, Four Views: A Parallel Commentary* (1997)

Grenz, Stanley J. *The Millennial Maze: Sorting Out Evangelical Options* (1992)

Preterist Works

Chilton, David. *The Days of Vengeance: An Exposition of the Book of Revelation* (1987)

Gentry, Kenneth L., Jr. *Before Jerusalem Fell: Dating the Book of Revelation* (1998)

Practical, Devotional Works

Lowery, Robert A. *Revelation's Rhapsody: Listening to the Lyrics of the Lamb: How to Read the Book of Revelation* (2000)

McKnight, Scot with Cody Matchett. *Revelation for the Rest of Us* (2023)

Moore, Mark E. *How to Dodge a Dragon* (1998)

Wood, Shane J. *Thinning the Veil: Encountering Jesus Christ in the Book of Revelation* (2025)

———. ed. *Dragons, John, and Every Grain of Sand: Essays on the Book of Revelation in Honor of Dr. Robert Lowery* (2011)

Chapter VI

Answers to Basic Questions

As with the study of any Biblical book, basic questions surface that resemble the "who, what, when, where, and why" pattern for reporting news. A student of Revelation needs to come to grips with the identity of the author, the kind of book it is, the date of writing, the location of the author and audience, and the reason for the writing of the book. Each of these topics could justify extensive treatments, but for our purposes a brief overview must suffice.

Authorship

The author of Revelation identifies himself as Christ's servant "John" (Rev 1:1, 9; 22:8) and early church tradition identifies him with John the Apostle, author of the Gospel of John and of the three Johannine Epistles. The book of Revelation itself does not make those connections and it is not uncommon today for scholars to distinguish between John the Apostle (John), John the elder (1-3 John), and John the seer (Revelation). The linguistic arguments are complex and are complicated by the extensive use of the Greek OT (LXX) in historical and theological allusions throughout the book.

The equation of John the seer with John the Apostle does suggest several interesting parallels, e.g., the two resurrections of John 5:24-29 and the two resurrections of

Revelation 20:4-6, but arguments regarding the interpretation of Revelation based upon this identification of the author must remain tentative. What seems clear is that John the seer was a prophet well known to the seven churches of Asia to whom the book was written.

Genre of the Book

Much has been produced in scholarly circles concerning the literary genre of "apocalyptic" writings to which the book of Revelation belongs along with earlier biblical texts such as Daniel and sections of Ezekiel, Zechariah, and Isaiah, as well as with the Jewish writings contemporary with the book of Revelation such as 4 Ezra, 2 Baruch, and others (see, e.g., J. J. Collins; F. J. Murphy; D. S. Russell).

Apocalypticism is commonly characterized as being dualistic, climactic, and other-worldly in that two worlds, the physical and spiritual, are contrasted while the only hope for the present age is the direct, supernatural intervention of God through which a new world order will arise.

Apocalyptic literature often contains revelations mediated by angels and is generally directed toward the end of the present age. Visions of heaven may be involved, and the prophet or seer may himself be transported to the heavenly realm in the process of receiving the divine revelation. The Greek word for John's book is *Apocalypsis*, the "Revelation" or "Unveiling" (Rev 1:1). Again, what sets Revelation apart is not that it is an apocalyptic work, but that it is an *inspired* apocalyptic work.

Date

Two main approaches have surfaced regarding the date of the writing of Revelation. A common preterist view, both full and partial, places the writing of the book during the reign of Nero, most likely shortly before his death in AD 68. Most who hold this approach view the book of Revelation as focusing primarily on the destruction of Jerusalem in AD 70.

The more popular approach among contemporary scholars is to date the book to the time of Domitian and thus circa AD 95. In this approach, the coming wrath relates to the fate of the wicked at the second coming while the destruction of Babylon the Harlot may relate to ancient Rome or, in a common historicist approach, modern "Rome" as it relates to the Roman papacy. Some would identify Revelation's "harlot" with modern liberal Christian adherents while others envision a literal Babylon to be rebuilt in the Middle East and reenergized in the "anything-is-possible" future. For the Domitian dating see especially Hemer (2-12), Beale (*Revelation*, 4-27), and Wood (*Paradigm*, 110-185).

Hemer's important work focuses on the cultural and historical backgrounds of each of the seven churches of Asia to whom Revelation was addressed. The definitive work for the preterist (Nero) approach is Gentry (17ff.). The majority of scholars favor the Domitian view but a number would concede that it is not a slam dunk and that arguments for the Nero view have some merit.

There is a mediating view, one which some have acknowledged but few have actively pursued, in which the Domitian date at the end of the first century AD is accepted along with an awareness that many aspects of the book have apocalyptic references to previous historical events and are not all necessarily predictive as many assume.

As noted previously, the symbols and visions John experienced in some cases pointed to the eschatological consummation at Christ's return, while at times others revealed the significance of past events, especially those events with continuing impact. The birth, death, resurrection, and ascension of Jesus are described through signs and symbols (e.g., Revelation 12) as is the rise of the beast from the sea and the ensuing persecution of the church (e.g., Revelation 13).

The seven heads described in Revelation 17 almost certainly represent Roman emperors of the first century. It can be debated whether the destruction of Babylon the Harlot at the hands of the beast (Revelation 17-18) refers to the harlot Rome or the harlot Jerusalem. If the latter, then another first- century historical event is being described in apocalyptic terms and given theological, perhaps apologetic, significance.

There may be value in pursuing an approach to the book in which all events outside of those surrounding the second coming have already been fulfilled. Such an approach would preserve the notion of imminence regarding Christ's return—no future events need transpire before the second coming. All is ready. Regarding Revelation, then, a Domitian dating may not necessarily demand an exclusively futuristic approach to the book.

This approach should not be confused with the phenomenon described in technical terms as (Latin) *vaticinium ex eventu*, i.e., "prophecy out of the event" or "prediction after the fact." Of course, such "prophecy" is not prophecy at all. Generally we find this phenomenon in writings, sometimes apocalyptic, where a pseudonym is used by the author for literary effect or to achieve an elevated status or authority.

In extra-biblical Jewish texts such as Enoch, 4 Ezra, or 2 Baruch, writers have assumed the names of esteemed ancients (e.g., Ezra the post-exilic priest, Baruch the scribe of Jeremiah) and have then often described visions or prophecies of future events, events that in reality lie in the past and thus are known facts, not divine predictions.

I do not believe that the OT book of Daniel falls into this category although many Bible scholars have maintained that it does and assign a date of circa 165 BC for a work that claims to be much earlier—from the time of the Babylonian and Persian empires (sixth c. BC). A conservative approach lands (a real) Daniel the prophet in the courts of Babylon and Medo-Persia uttering genuine prophecies of the future, some of which point to the coming of the Messiah and even to the later destruction of Jerusalem by the Romans: Daniel's "fourth kingdom" (Chapter VIII). It is important to note that the author of Revelation identifies himself as "John" on the island of Patmos, a church leader with close ties to his initial audience, not as some earlier authority figure from the past.

A strong majority of scholars favor the late date for Revelation, and I concur that such an approach makes the most sense for the book's contents. It fits best with the descriptions of some of the churches of Roman Asia addressed at the beginning, churches that had been around for a while, not newly founded, churches plagued by false teachers such as "Balaam," "Jezebel," and the Nicolaitans, and condemned for apathy ("loss of their first love"— Ephesus; "lukewarmness"—Laodicea). A late date corresponds to the popular understanding that persecution was a growing threat for the Christians in Asia in view of the increased vitality and spread of the imperial cult during

Domitian's reign and beyond. It fits the widespread chaos, uncertainty, and fear that characterized Domitian's later years.

Most date the work 1 Clement to the 90s and it speaks of sudden, repeated misfortunes and hindrances that had fallen upon the church at Rome (1 Clement 1:1). Many see supporting evidence here for the perilous times the church at the end of the first century was facing, but not all agree on the date or relevance of this testimony.

The most cited ancient source for the late date of Revelation is Irenaeus in his *Against Heresies* 5.30.3 (ca. AD 180). There, in connection with attempts by some to identify the Antichrist by name, Irenaeus argues that if John had thought it important to communicate that information he would have done so, and notes that his apocalyptic vision (our Revelation) had been seen rather recently, toward the end of Domitian's reign.

Much of later early church testimony depends upon Irenaeus here. Others holding to the Domitian date included Clement of Alexandria, Origen, Eusebius, and Jerome. One grammatical controversy involves the expression "it was seen," in that some have argued that this could be understood as "he (John) was seen" as recently as the time of Domitian. Theoretically, some early-date enthusiasts would contend, John could have been seen in Domitian's time while his writing of Revelation could have been done earlier, in the days of Nero.

Most scholars have concluded, however, that "it was seen" makes the best grammatical and contextual sense and that Irenaeus stands firm as an early external witness for the Domitian dating (ca. AD 95) of Revelation (Wood, *Paradigm*, 112-116).

Place of Origin and Destination

John's claim that he received his revelation on the island of Patmos is questioned only by those who reject the full inspiration of Scripture. Although there is no conclusive evidence, such an exile was more likely during the reign of Domitian than of Nero (Beale, *Revelation*, 13). Persecution was more widespread in the later decades of the first century, although Nero's earlier horrific treatment of some of the Christians in Rome is well documented. Regarding the isle of Patmos, Charles Erdman notes, "This barren, rocky, sun-scorched prison stood in the Aegean Sea some seventy miles southwest of Ephesus" (41).

Important regarding the date and destination of the book of Revelation is the monograph by Colin J. Hemer cited above, *The Letters to the Seven Churches of Asia in Their Local Setting* (1986). Hemer's research led him to the conclusion that Domitian's reign was the best option for the dating of the book and not the earlier reign of Nero.

One impression that clearly derives from Hemer's book is the importance of the original audience for the message of Revelation. The dispensational approach that Revelation 6-18 describes a post-rapture generation and not the NT church is fully discredited by a reasonable survey of the message to the individual churches and of the rich imagery found later in the book that parallels that of Revelation 2-3.

The seven cities of western Roman Asia were joined by a postal route enhancing communication between communities. Three of the cities—Smyrna, Pergamum, and Ephesus—hosted provincial temples dedicated to the imperial cult, distinctions that no doubt created additional pressures for the Christian communities in those places.

Whether the early or the late date for Revelation be accepted, the influence of the apostle Paul could have been in fact significant, a reality that few commentators seem to address. Much of Paul's theology can be found in books like Ephesians and Colossians, written to cities among those of western Asia Minor. The church at Colossae was instructed to have Paul's epistles also read to the church at Laodicea (Col 4:16; cf. Rev 3:14-21) and also to read Paul's letter addressed to the Laodicean church (Col 4:16).

Much of the "already and not yet" terminology in Paul's writings, involving such topics as resurrection, inheritance, kingdom, etc. (Chapter II), would have been known to the recipients of Revelation. Paul's teachings on the second coming and on the tribulations to be expected by the church would have been common knowledge. Such a situation would make it reasonable to surmise that the Christians in western Asia were well equipped to navigate the formidable theological terrain found in Revelation.

Purpose of the Book

The contents of Revelation reveal a tone and theme unmistakably militant and uncompromising. Faced with seemingly overwhelming odds, small, vulnerable Christian communities are challenged to stand firm for the gospel and to portray a faithful witness to the world that Jesus Christ, Israel's resurrected Messiah, was the hope of the world—not Rome's emperor—and that "peace and security" (Latin *pax et securitas*) could only be realized through faith in Christ.

Other claims were illusory, including the so-called *Pax Romana*, "Roman Peace," stemming from the time of Augustus. The book is both militant *and* pacifistic! God's people are to be "overcomers," not by weapons of war but by the blood of the Lamb. They are portrayed as defeating the devil, the dragon of old, by their faithfulness. They have "conquered him by the blood of the lamb" in that "they loved not their lives even unto death" (Rev 12:11).

Victory will only come through submission. Revelation depicts scenes of victorious saints in heaven worshiping at the throne as they await the consummation (Rev 6:9-11; 7:9-17; 14:1-5; 15:2-4; 19:1-10). Meanwhile back on earth the call for faithful resistance rings out:

If anyone is to be taken captive, to captivity he goes; if anyone is to be slain with the sword, with the sword must he be slain. Here is a call for the endurance and faith of the saints. (Rev 13:10)

A frequent debate among commentators is whether or not all of the dead in Christ mentioned in the book are martyrs. The evidence is mixed, but one can make a case that the martyrs mentioned represent a larger following whose deaths may have come by various means. What is clear in Revelation, however, is that there is no safe haven for those willing to take a bold stand for their faith. "Be faithful unto death and I will give you the crown of life" (Rev 2:10).

The book of Revelation is not simply a word of encouragement to struggling churches in John's day, as some might think. Most of the letters to the churches of Asia also contained stern warnings and jarring calls to repentance (2:4-6, Ephesus; 2:14-16, Pergamum; 2:20-23, Thyatira; 3:1-13, Sardis; 3:15-20, Laodicea). False doctrines and teachers (Nicolaitans, 2:6, 15; "Jezebel," 2:20; "Balaam," 2:14) and growing apathy (2:4; 3:1-2, 15-19) are among the concerns, along with the need to hold up under persecution (2:10, 13; 3:8, 10).

As most would expect, the promise of Christ's return is a key aspect of the contribution of the book of Revelation. This promise is featured at the beginning and end of the book and resurfaces in the letters to the churches and at the end of various cycles (the sixth seal, the seventh trumpet). As well, it appears in select visions (e.g., the harvest of the earth, the Rider on a white horse from heaven, fire consuming Gog and Magog as they try to attack God's people at the end of the thousand years). The chapter immediately following will outline the impact of this topic throughout the book.

The setting of the book (date, destination, audience, contemporary circumstances) and the purpose of the book are not always closely tied together in the numerous available Revelation commentaries. This seems to me to constitute a flaw in many works.

Revelation offers numerous potential topics of interest for modern students, both casual readers and scholars: the OT background of much of the imagery and message; parallels with other biblical content, especially involving theology and ethics; numerous literary features and devices; end-times concerns and related millennial convictions (or "preunderstandings"); practical application for the modern contemporary church; encouragement for Christians under attack throughout the world; usefulness for contemporary preaching, and the list goes on. But what are the key topics from which to gain a better understanding of the book as a whole?

A Different Approach?

My approach to the purpose of Revelation sets this present work apart from most. To be sure, the importance of the OT background of the book is stressed here as in numerous treatments. Awareness of the nature of apocalyptic literature in assessing the focus and imagery of John's writings is shown to be essential. As is commonly accepted, warnings to the ancient church are understood to have enduring relevance.

What is stressed here that is lacking often elsewhere, however, is noting the importance of targeting the historical situation for the original recipients of the book. Who were these early Christians, what were they experiencing, and what concerns did they have regarding recent events and potential future developments? See especially Chapter XII, "Behind the Scenes: The Background Story." For some, Chapter XII may be the most important chapter in the present work. Commentators that focus primarily upon modern applications or upon futuristic end-times scenarios are likely missing the keys that may unlock the primary message of the book.

I believe that assigning the Domitian date (ca. AD 95) to the book of Revelation, the most popular approach taken and the one adopted here, is more important than most students of the book realize. More will be said about that choice of dates in connection with the section on the seven churches of Asia (Chapter IX). The experiences of the Christians at the end of the first century likely played a major role in their grasping prominent imagery in the book. We can learn from their *Sitz im Leben* (situation in life) and be enlightened by their setting and resultant perspectives or we can ignore such issues and stay in the dark. It may be just as simple as that.

Revelation itself highlights several key issues in bold relief. Addressing these keys is essential for the book to make sense. Among the many images and numerical expressions found throughout, certain ones demand careful attention. The calls for "wisdom" in connection with the beast with the mortal wound that amazingly heals (13:3, 12, 14), his/its number "666" (13:18), and its "seven mountains" that also represent "seven kings" (17:9-10) invite explanation. So does the label "mystery" surrounding this remarkable beast who "was and is not and..." (17:8), as well as the label "Babylon the great, "emblazoned upon the forehead of "the great prostitute" (17:1) and referred to as a "name of mystery" (17:5). These are key components of John's message that frequently get short shrift from commentators.

Many wish not to get "bogged down" with needless speculation or pursue "divisive topics" that have puzzled students of Scripture for centuries. Why bother and so miss the main point? And yet the proper identification of John's "mystery" and the correct understanding of Revelation's "wisdom" in key texts may work wonders for arriving at a satisfactory, meaningful approach to the message of the book as a whole. We may be surprised by the results. They may even help lead us to the main point!

Some of the current "big-picture" interpretations of Revelation offer numerous, broad-based contemporary applications, complete with targeted denunciations and warnings. Fine and good. Greater attention to the original setting may take us in different directions, however. I have become convinced that the nexus of three critical developments in the last half of the first century provides much of the rationale for the book. These three phenomena created consternation for the early church and demanded explanation and reassurance for faithful Christ followers. The emphasis in Revelation on addressing these paramount issues will become obvious.

1. The persecution of Christians at the hands of both Jews and Roman authorities, initial manifestations

of the promised "tribulation" for followers of Christ noted throughout the NT, created a crisis of faith for many. Revelation's exhortations to be faithful unto death were accompanied by comforting scenes of heavenly rewards for those who "conquered" by their faith.

2. The remarkable recovery of Rome from its deadly civil war following the death of Nero (AD 68-69) caused the world to "marvel." Its "mortal wound" was healed (Rev 13:3-4, 12-14) and the power of the empire grew even stronger under the Flavian Dynasty, AD 69-96 (Vespasian, Titus, Domitian). Although some of the atrocities previously committed by Nero against Christians were not repeated in Rome, there is evidence that the decades spanning the end of the first century and the beginning of the second were fraught with uncertainty and danger for Christians whose practices were brought to the attention of wary Roman authorities.

   In its message that exalted Jesus, not Caesar, as Lord, Revelation countered the beliefs of the pagan masses. Rome was not the "eternal city" and its seemingly unchallenged power would crumble ultimately as the Lamb and His followers would defeat the beast and his cohorts. Along the way God would (did) even use this pagan empire to punish adulterous Jerusalem for its rejection of its Messiah.

3. The destruction of Jerusalem and its temple were indications of God's purposes and will, not of Rome's ultimate power and dominion, in spite of the intense propaganda set forth by Vespasian and

his heirs to validate the new Flavian Dynasty, a power shift in Rome forged in part with the flames of Jerusalem's demise.

What Jesus had prophesied in the Gospels, especially in His Olivet Discourse (Matthew 24; Mark 13; Luke 21), came to fruition at the hands of God's chosen instrument of punishment, Rome, much as Israel's and Judah's previous disobedience had brought God's wrath at the hands of the Assyrians and Babylonians.

Many commentators on Revelation apparently do not see a vital connection between the above noted developments in the early years of the church and the content of John's book. I disagree, as what follows in the present work will make clear. Although Christ's second coming is certainly emphasized as the main event in God's future for His chosen, the fall of Jerusalem is also on display as a past indicator of His holiness and demands for covenant faithfulness from His people.

Jews who persist in attacking the church are members of the "synagogue of Satan" (Rev 2:9; 3:9) and are allied against God's "new Israel," the NT church (Gal 6:16). Paul had described the earthly Jerusalem of his day as being in "slavery with her children" (Gal 4:25) in contrast to the church that shares in "the Jerusalem above" (Gal 4: 26), while the book of Hebrews depicts the home of Christians as "the city of the living God, the heavenly Jerusalem" (Heb12:22). Such a distinction rings true throughout Revelation as well.

It is my conviction that within the message of Revelation we find references to the tribulations faced by the early church and the resultant messages of comfort and exhortation throughout, along with insights for navigating the challenging terrains of theodicy (the study of God's justness) as they relate to the triumphant survival of the Roman Empire from its near demise and to the horrific destruction of Jerusalem and the Jewish nation at the hands of that very empire. And through it all Christ's church is challenged to persevere as it proclaims Jesus as Lord. A lot for one book! But what a book it is.

CHAPTER VII

THE SECOND COMING IN FOCUS

The book of Revelation begins and ends with promises of Jesus that He is coming soon ("the time is near," Rev 1:3; "I am coming soon," Rev 3:11; 22:7, 12, 20). This is one of the main talking points for preterists in their argument that the AD 70 fall of Jerusalem was the "second coming" of Jesus. Although I believe that much of Revelation relates to events and individuals in the first century AD, I join the mainstream millennial views, including those of *partial* preterists (e.g., Gentry), in affirming a *future return* of Christ, regardless of what degree of importance is to be placed upon AD 70 events. But when? Apart from full preterism, if the imminence or any-moment nature of Christ's return is to be maintained, how are Revelation's "soon" promises regarding Jesus' return to be understood?

First-Century Focus

My overall approach here is based on several indicators from the text of Revelation and the NT as a whole. If John is writing to the churches of Asia Minor near the end of the first century AD, many of the things he describes have already transpired (with some perhaps still ongoing).

They include the martyrdom of followers of Christ (6:9-11); wars and the accompanying famine, pestilence, and death (6:2-8); the purchase of salvation by the slain

Lamb (5:6-10); the crucifixion of Christ, the testimony and martyrdom of Christ's two faithful, empowered witnesses, and the trampling of the Jerusalem temple by the Gentiles (11:1-10); the birth and ascension of Jesus Christ (12:1-5); Satan's being cast out of heaven in connection with Christ's triumph over him (12:7-17); the persecution and protection of the woman and her other offspring (12:6, 13-17); the beast coming out of the sea, one of whose seven heads had a mortal wound that was remarkably healed (13:1-10); and a second beast arising from the land to promote the worship of the first beast (13:11-18).

Other entities found in Revelation 6-18 likely relate to the first century as well, including the careers of the seven kings described in Revelation 17, and possibly even the fall of Jerusalem as described in Revelation 17-18, although most commentators see the fall of Rome here, a popular yet problematic interpretation.

Cycles of Wrath

If the above events have already occurred by the end of the first century, what events still remain that will unfold "soon?" The answer would seem to be those events involving the second coming of Christ and all that entails. Several aspects of Christ's return are featured throughout the book of Revelation.

In Revelation 1, we find His visible coming with the clouds in judgment (1:7). In Revelation 2-3, the messages to the seven churches of Asia involve warnings and promises relating both to Christ's return and to the believer's resultant eternal destiny. It is well recognized that Revelation contains several series or cycles of seven, including the letters to the seven churches (2:1-3:22), the opening of the seven seals (6:1-8:1), the blowing of the seven trumpets (8:2-9:21; 11:15-19), and the pouring out of the seven bowls of wrath (16:1-21). (For possible dramatic effect, the message of the "seven thunders" [?] is sealed up and not disclosed [10:4]. We are left to speculate...) Judgment is a primary component particularly in the trumpets and bowls cycles.

Most agree that key aspects of the trumpets and bowls cycles involve repetition or recapitulation. The specific events described in one cycle may be paralleled in the other. Also, many have noted that the cyclical parallels play out with increasing intensity. When the second trumpet sounds, a third of the creatures in the sea die (8:9), but with the second bowl poured out, every living thing in the sea dies (16:3). The woes connected with the seven trumpets and bowls are roughly parallel, including similar sequences, while the plagues of Egypt in Exodus 7-12 serve as the OT model or type. Parallels between the first through sixth trumpets (Revelation 8-9) and bowls (Revelation 16) include:

- ❧ the earth being harmed (8:7; 16:2)

- ❧ the sea turning to blood (8:8; 16:3)

- ❧ the rivers being made toxic (8:10-11; 16:4-7)

- ❧ the sun being affected (8:12; 16:8-9)

- ❧ the kingdom of the beast being put in anguish (9:1-11; 16:10-11)

- ❧ evil forces summoned from east of the Euphrates River (9:13-21; 16:12-16)

The seventh trumpet and the seventh bowl both bring a sense of finality, although perhaps in a different framework. The seventh trumpet signals the time of God's wrath upon the wicked and reward for the righteous (11:15-18). Similarly the seventh bowl describes the fierce judgment of God upon the harlot this "Babylon" (16:17-21). Although some have argued that the destruction of Babylon the Great occurs in connection with the second coming, the content of Revelation 17-18 would suggest otherwise. The beast and his followers destroy Babylon the Harlot (17:16-18) and they in turn at some point are conquered by the Lamb (17:14). Babylon's sudden fall is greatly mourned by its various trading partners and associates (18:9-19). The second coming does not seem to be in view here.

Visions of Tribulation and Triumph

The structure of Revelation is made more challenging by the interspersing of various visions between the cycles of judgment, some of which visions involve extensive narrative accounts. Such narrative visions include the attacks of Satan upon Christ and His followers (12:1-17); the activities of the beast and the false prophet (13:1-18); the harvest of the righteous and the wicked (14:14-20); and worship scenes involving the redeemed in heaven (7:9-17; 14:1-4; 15:2-4). The judgments connected with Christ's return seem to be represented or anticipated at or near the conclusion of the various cycles: "sixth seal" (6:12-17); "seventh trumpet" (11:15-19); and "sixth bowl" (16:12-16). As well, specific judgment scenes describe the earth being "harvested" (14:14-20) and Christ destroying his enemies in "battle" (19:11-21).

The church age, the time between Christ's first and second comings, is described as a time of both tribulation and triumph regarding God's people. It is described from two distinct vantage points: the struggles on earth at the hands of Satan's henchmen—the beast and the false prophet along with their devotees—and the resultant celebrations in heaven of those who were victorious in their faithful testimony for Christ. As noted elsewhere, debate continues as to whether all the dead in Christ in Revelation are martyrs, or whether the martyrs mentioned serve to represent the faithful dead in Christ as a whole. A sobering dispute.

Counting the Church Age

Two time frames in Revelation involving symbolic numbers are possible representations of the unfolding of the church age. Admittedly, both suggestions below are vigorously contested.

First, the "thousand years" of Revelation 20 involve both the binding of Satan and the reign of the saints with Christ and likely represent the entire church age. The number "thousand" seen this way is a *qualitative* rather than *quantitative* number. It often functions this way in the OT (Deu 1:11; 7:9; Ps 50:10; 90:4 [cf. 2Pet 3:8]; Isa 30:17). A thousand years, a thousand generations, a thousand hills— no one asks about the cattle on "hill 1,001" (Ps 50:10)! In Revelation 20 this large qualitative number views the church age in a positive light. Viewing it as a symbolic number best harmonizes with the rest of the NT and with the imagery-laden nature of Revelation itself.

Second, numbers equivalent to "three and a half" seem to be used in the book to describe the church age as a time of trial and testing. Half of seven denotes the opposite of what the "perfect" number seven suggests. The only "three and a half" actually utilized in the book is at Revelation 11:9 where the two prophets lay dead for three and a half days (Rev 11:9, 11). However, regarding the sense of three and a half years we find three obviously equivalent expressions: "forty-two months" (Rev 11:2; 13:5); "1,260 days" (Rev 11:3; 12:6); and "a time, and times, and half a time" (Rev 12:14; cf. Dan 7:25; 12:7).

What happens during this "three and a half" period? Jerusalem is trampled down by the Gentiles (Rev 11:2); Jesus' two witnesses prophesy (Rev 11:3); the "woman" (the church) is nourished by God as she struggles with Satan, the "dragon" (Rev 12:6, 14); and the "beast" is given destructive power and authority (Rev 13:5). Each of these scenes likely describes symbolically the church age viewed from the perspective of testing and tribulation (Chapter XIII).

The contents of the book of Revelation could be viewed chronologically as follows: people and events of the first century AD, those that would precede or be contemporary with the writing of the book; people and events throughout the church age; and people and events in connection with the second coming of Christ and the resulting eternal state or new creation (the new heavens and new earth). Of course there may be disagreement among the various millennial "tribes" as to what verses fit where. Perhaps we can find beneficial elements within several viewpoints, including historicist, idealist, and futurist!

Jesus' Imminent Return

How does this discussion dovetail with Revelation's claim that Jesus is coming "soon?" I believe we find ourselves exactly where we do for the rest of the NT. The warning signs that Jesus gave in the Olivet Discourse (Matthew 24; Mark 13; Luke 21) concerned the first-century fall of Jerusalem in AD 70, not the second coming (also Mt 23:37-39; Lk 19:41-44; 23:26-31).

His teaching that *did* relate to His subsequent coming in glory in the Discourse, however, emphasized that no warning signs would occur in connection with that later event. His declarations regarding "this generation" and "those standing here" related to promises for the first generation of believers (Mt 16:24-28; Mk 8:34-9:1; Lk 9:23-27).

Other teachings of Jesus involving that initial generation of believers included His prophecy regarding the death of Peter in his old age (Jn 21:18-19) and the promise of the universal spread of the gospel (Mt 28:18-20; Acts 1:8). Once the first generation of the church age essentially culminated with Jerusalem's fall (AD 70—roughly forty years after the church's birth at Pentecost), no prophecies remained needing to be fulfilled before Christ's return. His return then would be "imminent": He could come at any moment and in that sense His return would be impending, unpredictable—"soon."

The teaching of Paul maintained such an approach. Christ's return would be like a thief in the night (1Th 5:2; cf. Mt 24:43-44) and yet Paul spoke of a "man of lawlessness" who must arrive on the scene before the second coming could occur (2Th 2:1-12). I have argued elsewhere that Paul's oracle regarding this lawless figure centered around events culminating in the AD 70 destruction of Jerusalem (*Leaving*, 163-178; also see Appendix A: "The Man of Lawlessness" in the present work). Importantly, I have done so without following a preterist approach.

If Paul's man of lawlessness had to do with the fall of Jerusalem, then in Paul's mind no events beyond that horrific disaster were likely necessary leading up to Christ's return. After God's wrath had been poured out upon that generation of Jews (1Th 2:14-16; Mt 23:32-38) no signs would give future warning of Christ's imminent return. As will be further developed throughout, one might also contend that Revelation itself offers no signs needing to be fulfilled prior to Christ's return.

A late-first-century original reception of the book would have recognized many pointers to events that had already transpired. Initial audiences may well have understood themselves as living after the time of the "seven rulers" of Revelation 17:7-11 but during the time of the "eighth beast" or "eighth head" who "belonged to the seven" (Rev 17:11).

Approaches to Avoid

The second coming, then, is a major focus of the book of Revelation but commentators differ upon how the numerous elements of the book tie in with Christ's return. The "coming soon" texts are primary for the strict preterists' approach that *equates* the second coming with the AD 70 fall of Jerusalem. This focus, however, leads to a striking contradiction with many other clear texts in the NT that point to the yet-future visible, personal return of Christ to earth and therefore must be rejected. Apart from the strict preterist approach, conservative commentators on Revelation see a *future* return and deal with the "soon" texts in similar ways, apart from several important dispensational "wrinkles."

Dispensationalists tend to concede that Revelation was written to the church even if, in their minds, the bulk of the book (Revelation 6-18) is not *about* the church. They claim that the church is represented in the book as being raptured out of the world before the judgments transpire. Most see the rapture occurring at Revelation 4:1, where John is commanded "Come up here" (John, not the church!), and at Revelation 12:6 where, after Christ's first-century ascension to heaven (Rev 12:5), the "woman" (now supposedly the post-rapture tribulation saints!) is nourished in the wilderness for 1,260 days (Rev 12:6)—an obvious (to them) reference to the ominous end-times "great tribulation" (Chapter XIII).

So for them, it's one verse—the ascension of Christ (Rev 12:5), the next verse—post-rapture tribulations (Rev 12:6ff). The church age is skipped over for most of the rest of the book. How unlikely! And how at Revelation 4:1 can John represent the "raptured church" for interpreters who insist upon extreme literalism almost everywhere else?

The Eschatological "Soon"

Apart from preterism, whether the second coming is a two-stage event (with dispensationalism) or a single-stage event (with historic premillennialism, postmillennialism, and amillennialism), the mainstream views all wrestle with applying the word "soon" to Jesus' return in light of the lengthy lapse in time thus far.

Again, I believe the most helpful answer is in the concept of imminence and that Christ's return is "soon" in that it could happen at any moment: no signs or prophecies still need be fulfilled before He comes back. This is a commonly held explanation among evangelical scholars and would seem to be the best option (see also Chapter XXIV). As described in Jesus' Olivet Discourse (Matthew 24; Mark 13; Luke 21), the fall of Jerusalem in AD 70 was foreshadowed by signs of impending doom, *unlike* Jesus' subsequent return in which He would come like a "thief in the night" (Mt 24:43).

The exposition in the following chapters harmonizes well with a second coming devoid of warning signs. For the notion of imminence regarding Christ's return I suggest the label "the eschatological 'soon'."

CHAPTER VIII

JOHN AND THE SPIRIT OF PROPHECY

Revelation begins and ends with the identification of Revelation as a book of prophecy and John, Christ's "servant," as a prophet (Rev 1:3; 22:6, 9, 10, 18, 19). Here we explore the impact of the OT as a whole upon Revelation and the special role that Ezekiel in particular has upon the contents of the book. Daniel's connection with Revelation is also singled out especially regarding the imagery involving Daniel's "fourth kingdom," his "little horn" descriptions, and the possible ties with Revelation 17 and the seven heads of the beast.

An Avalanche of Allusions: The Impact of the OT

Ben Witherington III is right in saying that Revelation is not simply a transcript of John's prophetic experience. The seer reports on his visions in light of the OT and other sources (*End*, 12). What makes the book of Revelation remarkable is the extent to which the OT is utilized as well as the nature of that utilization. G. K. Beale has been a leading voice in the discussion concerning the NT's use of the OT (e.g., *Handbook*; *Revelation*, 76-99).

There is great variety in the uses of the OT by NT writers, uses involving typology, analogy, direct and indirect quotation, allusion, echo, etc. The distinction between allusion and quotation is significant regarding the study of Revelation. In quotation, we find direct citation of the OT text identified by its clear use of specific wording from an identifiable context. Many such quotes in the NT are introduced by formulas such as "as it is written" or "that the words of the prophet might be fulfilled." What is notable about Revelation is that it never utilizes such a quotation formula. As well, we do not find entire verses from the OT cited. Scholars have identified roughly three hundred separate quotations of the OT in the NT, but there are no formal quotations in the book of Revelation. What we do find are allusions—more indirect references.

These brief expressions are consciously borrowed from a specific OT passage. For a tally of allusions in Revelation, Beale notes scholarly estimates ranging from roughly four hundred up to a thousand (*Handbook*, 31)! Various criteria for identifying allusions involve the degree of word repetition, thematic suitability, likely audience recognition of the connection, repeated use of the same OT context, etc. (ibid., 31-36).

The extensive use of allusion, but not direct citation, produces the effect that John's message and that of the OT prophets are closely intertwined. John wears the prophetic mantle as one who has received extensive communication from God and thus follows in the tradition of inspired messengers like Isaiah, Daniel, and Ezekiel. Revelation does not simply utilize the OT, it absorbs it! John is not merely citing ancient authorities, he is standing in their shadow and sharing their spirit.

The choice of texts that John uses to buttress the content and explanation of his various visions and experiences is revealing. That choice should not be explained away or ignored. If premillennialists are right, then Revelation 20, the "millennium chapter," should contain Isaiah's references to the future "golden age" and earthly paradise. It does not.

Instead, those references (esp. Isaiah 60, 65) are found in abundance in Revelation 21-22, the descriptions of the eternal state *following* the millennium and involving the New Jerusalem and the new heavens and new earth. The age to come prophesied in the OT is always eternal, never millennial!

The Daniel Connection

John's use of the book of Daniel, especially Daniel 2 and 7, has been observed and analyzed by many. In several senses, Revelation is a continuation or updating of Daniel. John seems to identify the beast in Revelation with the fourth beast in Daniel 7 and the animals "leopard, bear, and lion" are used to describe the composite anatomy of the beast (Rev 13:2) while those same animals, prior to the mention of the ferocious fourth beast in Daniel 7 (Rome), describe the first three kingdoms, but in reverse order (Dan 7:3-6): lion (Babylon), bear (Medo-Persia), and leopard (Greece).

We should note that, while Daniel had been instructed to seal up the book until the time of the end (Dan 12:4, 9), John was instead told, "Do not seal up the words of the prophecy of this book, for the time is near" (Rev 22:10).

In Daniel's prophetic message, a number of extraordinary events would occur before the end: the rise of Medo-Persia, Greece and Rome; the persecutions under the Seleucid Greek despot Antiochus IV Epiphanes; the successful Maccabean revolt from Greek oppression; Herod the Great's reign (possibly); Messiah's arrival and new covenant; and Jerusalem's later destruction. For John's audience, all these were past developments. For John, the keyword now was "soon," and one could argue that for his initial late-first-century recipients no warning signs of

Christ's return were expected. They had entered the "last days" before the return of Jesus.

A *crux interpretum* for the book of Daniel is the identification of the "little horn" in Daniel 7. The "little horn" of Daniel 8 is generally recognized as Antiochus Epiphanes, a later king coming from the Greek Empire (second c. BC). The status of the "little horn" of Daniel 7, however, is not agreed upon. The small horn in Daniel 8 comes from one of the four horns springing up after the death of Alexander the Great who was the "large horn" of the Greek Empire, Daniel's "he-goat" (Dan 8:5-10, 21-24). That much seems to be clear.

The little horn in Daniel 7 admits of several possible interpretations, however, as a quick survey of Daniel commentaries would verify. For those who regard Greece as the fourth empire in Daniel, especially those who understand the book to be a pseudepigraph from the second century BC (ca. 165 BC) and thus *not* written by the prophet Daniel, the natural identification of Daniel 7's little horn with the Greek king Antiochus IV Epiphanes is made (178-164 BC). The atrocities against God and His people that Antiochus committed are therefore understood as being outlined in Daniel 7, 8, and 11 (with some adding Daniel 9's Seventy Weeks Prophecy here as well).

One can make a strong case, however, for the little horn of Daniel 7 coming out of Rome. The internal consistency of Daniel is strengthened with Rome as the fourth empire. The imagery used for Medo-Persia and Greece in Daniel 8 matches that for the second and third kingdoms in Daniel 7. The bear raised up on one side (Dan 7:5) is also the ram with one horn taller and coming up later than the other (Dan 8:3). Identified as Medo-Persia (Dan 8:20), this kingdom was initially controlled by Media but later by Persia. The leopard with four heads (Dan 7:6) and the he-goat with four horns (Dan 8:8) both represent Greece (Dan 8:21-22), the kingdom that precedes the iron kingdom (Dan 2:40, 45). The kingdom of iron is also represented as a ferocious beast with iron teeth (Dan 7:7, 19).

Josephus understood the fourth kingdom to be Rome as did the author of 4 Ezra among the Jewish apocalyptic works contemporary with Revelation and Josephus. The parallels in Revelation 13 and 17 support the Rome identification (Chapter XVIII). Jesus applies some of the "abomination of desolation" language in Daniel to the Roman period and Jerusalem's fall (Mt 24:15; Mk 13:14; cf. Dan 9:27; Lk 21:20).

With the Rome identification, a key question becomes the time frame or phase of the Roman Empire in which the little horn operates. Revelation 17 may be of help here and might be patterned in such a way as to show links with the language of Daniel, including the enumeration of kings, the destruction of the "little horn"/beast and the triumph of Christ's kingdom (Chapter XVIII).

Concerning the fourth beast's "ten horns" (ten rulers) and the addition of another with the removal of three, the 10 + 1 - 3 (= 8) progression in Daniel (Dan 7:7-8, 24) may resurface in Revelation regarding the beast's heads (rulers) as 7 + 1 (=8), with the three short-lived emperors during Rome's civil war omitted (Rev 17:9-12). The ascendance of the Flavian Dynasty (Vespasian, Titus, Domitian) and its removal of the third of three usurpers (Galba, Otho, Vitellius) brought an end to the destructive civil war (AD 68-69). As the "eighth head" (and Daniel's "eleventh horn?"), Domitian was yet said to be "part of the seven" (Rev 17:11). His end remains in the future for John's earliest readers. Both comings of Christ (the already and the not yet) may be in view. The fiery destruction of this opponent of the "saints of the Most High" (Dan 7:25) seems to be described in both books as an end-times event (Dan 7:11; Rev 19:20).

The many complexities of the book of Daniel cannot be explored here. In brief, I agree with those who recognize the atrocities against the Jews under the Greek (Seleucid)Antiochus Epiphanes, the destruction of the temple by the Romans (AD 70) and the persecution of the church (the new "Israel") at the hands of the "little horn" of Daniel 7 as being separate, distinct, yet thematically related entities found within the book.

The New Ezekiel

The frequent employment of OT references and images in Revelation can be seen especially in John's use of the book of Ezekiel.

David Chilton provides a list of obvious parallels between Revelation and Ezekiel, a list based on the work of Carrington and Goulder (Chilton, 21).

The Throne-Vision (Rev. 4/Ezek. 1)
The Book (Rev. 5/Ezek. 2-3)
The Four Plagues (Rev. 6:1-8/Ezek. 5)
The Slain under the Altar (Rev. 6:9-11/Ezek. 6)
The Wrath of God (Rev. 6:12-7/Ezek. 7)
The Seal on the Saints' Foreheads (Rev. 7/Ezek. 9)
The Coals from the Altar (Rev. 8/Ezek. 10)
No More Delay (Rev. 10:1-7/Ezek. 12)
The Eating of the Book (Rev. 10:8-11/Ezek. 2)
The Measuring of the Temple (Rev. 11:1-2/Ezek. 40-43)
Jerusalem and Sodom (Rev. 11:8/Ezek. 16)
The Cup of Wrath (Rev. 14/Ezek. 23)
The Vine of the Land (Rev. 14:18-20/Ezek. 15)

The Great Harlot (Rev. 17-18/Ezek. 16, 23)
The Lament over the City (Rev. 18/Ezek. 27)
The Scavengers' Feast (Rev. 19/Ezek. 39)
The First Resurrection (Rev. 20:4-6/Ezek. 37)
The Battle with Gog and Magog (Rev. 20:7-9/Ezek. 38-39)
The New Jerusalem (Rev. 21/Ezek. 40-48)
The River of Life (Rev. 22/Ezek. 47)

The above list serves as a good starting place, but there is no intention here to examine it point by point. Instead, we will explore major implications of the key Ezekiel connections as a means of establishing insights for the message of Revelation in light of OT parallels and foreshadowings. Numerous close connections between the prophet Ezekiel and John the seer are obvious to all. Remarkably, most of the parallels listed above occur in the same order in both books: see parallels 1-8 and 13-20 above. What to make of all this?

Calling John the "new Ezekiel" is my way of stressing the importance of the book of Ezekiel for the message of Revelation. Too often commentators have paid lip service to this obvious link without investigating sufficiently the implications. The book of Ezekiel is a landmine of difficult, controversial passages that have bewildered the church for centuries. The "valley of dry bones" (Ezekiel 37), the invasion of Gog and Magog (Ezekiel 38-39) and the restored temple vision (Ezekiel 40-48) are well-known exegetical trouble spots.

Important themes are involved here: the restoration of Israel, the eschatological battle/judgment scene vindicating God as righteous ruler, and the ultimate role of Jerusalem and the land in connection with God's people. I believe that it is critical to recognize that John in Revelation is giving us insights for these OT texts in the context of Jesus' final revelation to His church. Coherent interpretations and convincing answers are available for Ezekiel's message in view of Revelation's striking allusions to the book. Conversely, Ezekiel offers clues as to the choices of language and imagery John employs.

To the point, John employs the last-days Gog and Magog conflict of Ezekiel 38-39 to describe the great "final battle" judgment in connection with Christ's return. The allusions at Revelation 19:17-21 (Eze 39:17-20) and 20:7-10 (Eze 38:1-4, 16, 22) suggest that both passages are describing the same end-times conflict. Since the initial Gog and Magog allusion in Revelation is prior to the mention of the millennium at Revelation 20:1-6 (Rev 19:17-21) and the subsequent allusion relates to events *after* the millennium (Rev 20:7-10), one could conclude that *recapitulation* is involved at Revelation 20:1-6.

The "millennial reign" of Revelation 20 compactly and climactically revisits aspects of the church age, an age described more fully in Revelation's previous cycles and visions. The thousand-year reigns of Christ and those dead in Christ represent a powerful heavenly perspective of church-age matters. The thousand years do not *follow* the church age; they *represent* the church age, a period followed by the "Gog and Magog" (Rev 19:17-21; 20:7-10) and "Armageddon" (Rev 16:12-16) confrontations.

These two noteworthy designations actually point to a single confrontation representing judgment by means of battle imagery. Christ is portrayed as arriving from heaven on a white horse with His armies following. All the armies of the beast and the false prophet are destroyed by the sword from His mouth (Rev 19:11-21). The Armageddon conflict must also refer to the second coming since, in connection with it, Jesus warns, "Behold I am coming like a thief" (Rev 16:15)!

At the conclusion of Ezekiel, there is nothing in the restored temple vision of Ezekiel 40-48 to suggest that what is being described is in any way temporary. It follows the end-times conflict of Gog and Magog (Eze 38:1-39:29) and it utilizes language that is clearly typical or symbolic. The territorial portions for the various tribes are said each to be 25,000 cubits in length, clearly an idealized description and not one fitting anything like we know the land of Israel to be. Idealism, not literalism, best serves us here in interpretation. A glorious river flows from beneath the threshold of the temple. A thousand cubits out—more than a third of a mile (but forget the precise dimensions here)—it is only ankle-deep (talk about level!). Another thousand cubits out it is knee-deep. Yet another thousand cubits out and it becomes so deep that it is impassable (Eze 47:1-6). A remarkable body of water! The trees lining the banks of that river bear fresh fruit every month and their leaves provide healing (Eze 47:12).

In Ezekiel the temple is the focus, not the city. In fact, nowhere in Ezekiel 40-48 do we find the name "Jerusalem." It is just "the city." The exacting detail of the descriptions of the temple in Ezekiel has puzzled commentators for centuries. Much of the language seems symbolic, but why go into such detail if a literal edifice is not being described?

Elsewhere I have referred to Ezekiel as "the master of metaphor" since extended metaphors surface throughout the book (Pechawer, *Leaving*, 152-154). The figurative description of the great seaport Tyre as a mighty sailing vessel abounds with seemingly superfluous details: planks from fir trees, mast of cedar, oars of oak, deck of pines, etc. (Eze 27:1-34).

Babylon's conquest of Egypt is also given extended, hyperbolic treatment by Ezekiel. Pharaoh is a sea (or river) monster captured and slain by God's agent Babylon as the beasts of the earth gorge on its flesh (Eze 32:1-15). The resurrection of Israel's "dry bones" is perhaps the best-known metaphor (Eze 37:1-14) while Gog and Magog also, in my view, offer an extended metaphor, this one of God's final battle/judgment against His enemies (Ezekiel 38-39). Ezekiel's lengthiest, most detailed visionary experience involves the restored temple (Ezekiel 40-48).

Ezekiel concludes his lengthy descriptions at the conclusion of his book by describing the perimeter and gates of the city. He ends, "And that name of the city from that time on shall be, 'The LORD Is There' [Yahweh Shammah]" (Eze 48:15). Whatever detailed descriptions may be offered, the key is God's eternal, abiding presence.

Revelation offers both similarities with and differences from Ezekiel 40-48. John also describes a river flowing from the heart of the city, "from the throne of God and of the Lamb" (Rev 22:1; Eze 47:1-2) and pictures the tree of life on its banks bearing fruit each month and providing leaves for the healing of the nations (Rev 22:2; Eze 47:12).

He as well foresees a city of gates, twelve gates upon which "the names of the twelve tribes of the sons of Israel were inscribed..." (Rev 21:12; Eze 48:30-34). And like Ezekiel, John provides a list of the twelve tribes of Israel (Rev 7:4-8; Eze 48:1-7, 23-29), a (slightly different) list that involves symbolic features appropriate for his purposes (Chapter X).

Ezekiel is the only OT prophetic book actually to list the tribes of Israel. Unlike Ezekiel, Revelation focuses upon the city, the "New Jerusalem," and also unlike Ezekiel, John's depiction does *not* feature a temple. We are told specifically by John, "And I saw no temple in the city, for its temple is the Lord God the Almighty and the Lamb" (21:22).

We are left with one of two primary conclusions. Either Ezekiel describes a yet future earthly temple about which the rest of the Bible says nothing, or Ezekiel's temple functions as a detailed, idealized (metaphoric) picture of Israel's future, unending worship that has as its ultimate setting the New Jerusalem. The fact that John mentions the New Jerusalem alongside of the new heavens and new earth is taken by some to mean that the New Jerusalem is in essence the new creation, i.e., the new heavens and earth, the totality of God's new creation.

Importantly, the once-for-all sacrifice of Christ makes the animal sacrifices described in Ezekiel's temple vision unlikely to have literal fulfillments (Eze 43:18-27; 44:11). As an important principle of interpretation (Appendix C), with respect to typology in Scripture the (NT) antitype is always greater than the (OT) type. Along with descriptions of animal sacrifices, Ezekiel's description of the ultimate temple involves regulations for the Levitical priesthood (Eze 44:10-11, 15-31), yet there is no room in the future for such a priesthood in the literal sense, as the book of Hebrews makes abundantly clear (Heb 6:19-8:6). Whatever Ezekiel 40-48 indicates, the once-for-all sacrifice of Christ our Great High Priest (the antitype) provides the future divine accomplishment of atonement and forgiveness under Israel's new covenant. That future accomplishment is a present reality.

Other connections between Ezekiel and Revelation will be noted in passing below, including, e.g., the eating of a scroll by the prophet, the measuring of the temple, the seals on the foreheads of those being saved—these and other links could be explored. Extensive descriptions in Ezekiel 16 and 23 of Jerusalem as a wicked harlot could also play a role in the quest for the identity of Babylon the Harlot in Revelation 16-19.

More than any other prophet, with the possible exception of Daniel in the minds of some, Ezekiel served as a model and blueprint for the ministry of John in his composition of the book of Revelation.

CHAPTER IX

SPECIAL DELIVERY
FROM HEAVEN TO EARTH (REV 1-5)

The present work does not serve as an in-depth commentary for the entire book of Revelation, and no extended verse-by-verse exegesis of the book follows. Treatments contained here are quite selective, but texts are chosen with a view toward uncovering the key message of the book in light of the many expositions and suggestions out there. The importance of Revelation must not be sabotaged by the widespread disagreement persistent among interpreters. This present work attempts to identify key clues and markers that may help lead to the most likely overall approach to be taken when confronted by this powerful ancient masterpiece.

The Revealer and the Revealed (Rev 1)

As cautioned above, no detailed treatment of Revelation 1 follows here. We do find in these opening verses, however, clues for interpreting the rest of the book. The uses of "soon" (1:1) and "near" (1:3) anticipate the language at the end of the book concerning Christ's promise to "come soon" (22:6, 7, 12, 20). Readiness for Christ's return is emphasized throughout the book. John identifies with his audience, both initial and eventual, in describing himself and them as a "kingdom" and "priests to God" (1:6) and as sharing "in the tribulation and the kingdom" (1:9).

Jesus Christ received from God the Father the revelation recorded in the book and in turn made it known by sending His angel to His servant John (1:1). John then bore witness to all that he heard and saw (1:2). Behind the name Revelation is the Greek word *apokalypsis* meaning a "revealing" or "unveiling" (1:1). The readers (out loud to an audience) and the hearers (who are also obeyers) of the book will receive a blessing (1:3). The visionary nature of the book most closely aligns with the OT Ezekiel, Daniel, Isaiah, and Zechariah.

The vision of the glorified Jesus (1:12-16) recalls the heavenly figure in Daniel 10:2-9. At the beginning of each of the seven letters to the churches some aspect of the description of Jesus in Revelation 1 is repeated. The symbols and metaphors of the first chapter are thus emphasized in the letters. We find a reference to the One who walks among the seven golden lampstands holding seven stars (1:12, 16, 20; 2:1); the first and the last, who died and came to life (1:17-18; 2:8); the One with the sharp two-edged sword (1:16 ; 2:12); the One with eyes like a flame of fire and feet like burnished bronze (1:14-15; 2:18); He who has the seven spirits of God and the seven stars (1:4, 16, 20; 3:1); the One who has the keys of Death and Hades (1:18; the One who has the key of David, 3:7); and the Amen, the faithful, and true witness (1:5; 3:14). As noted below, the seven letters also each contain promises that link the churches to the fulfillments at the end of the book.

An important conversation has emerged from the wording of Revelation 1:19. Jesus said to John, "Write therefore the things that you have seen, those that are and those that are to take place after this." This verse is viewed by many as presenting a type of outline for the book.

Among numerous suggestions, we note the following. First, this verse speaks to the past, present, and future regarding things John has seen. Second, the things John has seen refer to aspects of the present and the future. Third, the words "those that are" can have the sense of "what they mean." John is to write what things he has seen and what he has been told they signify.

Regarding the third option, J. Ramsey Michaels refers to the sequence as "Vision, Explanation, and Prediction" (606-607). A literal rendering could be "Therefore write what (things) you have seen and what they are...." Involved here is the relative pronoun "who, which, what" (Greek *hos*, etc.) and the verb *eimi*, "to be." John is to write down what he sees and "what it is" (what it means) or "what they are" (what they mean).

What may be involved here, then, are explanations of the imagery related to past and present events as well as predictions of things to come. In the very next verse we are told by Jesus what the seven stars and the seven lampstands shown to John "are": they are the angels of the seven churches and the seven churches respectively (1:12, 16, 20). The seven torches of fire burning before the throne are the seven spirits of God (4:5). The golden bowls full of incense are the prayers of the saints (5:8). Other such identifications surface throughout the book pertaining to the beast's seven heads and ten horns (17:9-12), the Great Harlot named Babylon (17:16-18), the waters where she sat (17:1, 15), etc. The "fine linen" of the saints in connection with the Marriage Supper of the Lamb relates to "the righteous deeds of the saints" (19:7-9). The lake of fire is the second death (20:14).

Other explanations and identifications regarding what John is shown are given throughout the book. John was given a message to tell, one laden with images and metaphors from the distant past (e.g., OT events and personages) and the dangerous present (e.g., the beast and the false prophet). In addition to John's glimpse of future events—the things "that are to take place after this" (Rev 1:19)—the things he was also given to see concerning past and present realities were supplied with insights regarding their true meaning and significance. God's take on key circumstances and developments affecting His people differed greatly from the spin from those of John's day who thought that they were "in charge"!

The Seven Churches of Asia at a Glance (Rev 2-3)

The Greek cultural setting in Roman Asia fostered an increased threat of emperor worship. During the reign of Tiberius (AD 14-37) among the cities of the seven churches of Asia both Smyrna and Pergamum were granted provincial temples devoted to the emperor. A later provincial temple in Ephesus was then dedicated in the time of Domitian. While not a practice in the city of Rome, emperor worship was commonplace in Asia and other Greek-speaking eastern provinces. In this regard, life in the province of Asia for the seven churches addressed in Revelation was even more difficult than for those in Italy and Rome itself.

As the Greek cities in the eastern regions promoted the worship of emperors, they sought the honor of hosting temples dedicated to leaders both dead and alive. Benefits flowed in both directions as local officials honored rulers who in turn bestowed blessings to loyal subjects through a royal patron-client arrangement benefiting all concerned. Emperors shared honor with deities in these temples and thus politics and religion were intimately intertwined.

In Revelation 13 worship of the image of the beast was demanded by the false prophet (13:13-15). It will be argued later that these descriptions represent the first-century reality: Roman imperial might buttressed by the widespread imperial cult. Loyalty to the beast could often be measured by participation in the established socio-economic order, including trade guilds and other associations with ties to pagan worship. Given these structures, it likely would have been difficult for Christians in the churches of Roman Asia to hide!

The famous correspondence between the emperor Trajan (AD 98-117) and Pliny the Younger, governor of Bithynia in Roman Asia (AD 111-113), describes a life-threatening situation for Christians if they are turned in to the Roman authorities by their coworkers, neighbors, or associates. The exhortations and consolations in Revelation would seem to fit well with the end of the first century AD and the time of Domitian (see Chapter VI, "Date"). For more on the imperial cult in Roman Asia see Chapter XIV (esp. "The False Prophet").

It is beyond the scope of the present work to provide detailed arguments regarding what we know about the seven churches addressed by John in Revelation. Colin Hemer (1986) has been especially helpful in identifying potential ties between Jesus' messages to the seven churches and distinctive features or background information regarding the cities in question that would have made specific references in the book particularly meaningful. Not all alleged connections carry equal weight, but many students of Revelation have concluded that Hemer's approach is sound even if not all parallels necessarily withstand full scrutiny (regarding Hemer's "local references" see Scobie, 606-624). Several examples presented by Charles Scobie should suffice to illustrate the nature of the endeavor.

Smyrna: Jesus spoke of Himself as the One who died and came to life (2:8). The city Smyrna itself "died" circa 600 BC, destroyed by the Lydians, but was refounded circa 290 BC under Antigonus, then Lysimachus.

Pergamum: The reference to "Satan's throne" (2:13) could be a topographical reference to the shape of the hillside at Pergamum when approached from the south. The scene has been described as a "vast armchair."

Philadelphia: The odd expression regarding never going out of God's temple (3:12) may have brought to mind the constant threat of earthquakes at Philadelphia, a threat that caused many of the inhabitants to move out of the city to the surrounding countryside.

Laodicea: The language of the letter to the Laodiceans has been thoroughly mined. Regarding poverty versus prosperity (3:17-18), Laodicea was a known banking center and the city was famous for financing its own rebuilding after the AD 60 earthquake. The naked are counseled to buy white garments (3:17-18), while the city was famous for black, glossy woolen garments.

As for the reference to the blind (3:17-18), Laodicea had a medical school that featured in the first century a famous ophthalmologist, Demosthenes Philalethes. Most noted and quoted today, however, is the reference to the Laodicean Christians being "lukewarm," a state worse than being hot or cold (3:15-16). Well known is Laodicea's ancient water supply problem. Unlike the situations in neighboring cities noted for their cold-water supply (Colossae) or hot springs (Hierapolis), water brought to Laodicea upon an aqueduct was tepid, lukewarm, as it reached the city.

Numerous related connections are offered by Hemer and others. For the relevance for the date of the book see Chapter VI. The position taken in the present work is that the letters to the churches of Roman Asia were sent to Christians living at the end of the first century AD near the end of the reign of Domitian (AD 81-96).

The End from the Beginning (Rev 2-3)

One important aspect of the letters to the churches in Revelation 2-3 sometimes overlooked is that each of the letters contains imagery and symbols found in the last chapters of the book. This is an inconvenient fact for those interpreters who see little connection between the churches of Revelation and the so-called tribulation saints that are claimed to be at center stage in Revelation 6-18. The fact that various promises to the churches of Asia are seen as being fulfilled for the people of God in Revelation 19-21 makes the unified nature of the book all the more pronounced and severely weakens the dispensational argument that the church "disappears" (is "raptured") at the beginning of Revelation 4.

As the ending of the Apocalypse was read to the individual churches addressed in the book, we can imagine smiles on the faces of the congregants upon their recognition of specific promises made earlier to them at the beginning of the book. "'Eating from the tree of life'— that's us!" those at Ephesus might have exclaimed (2:7; 22:2, 14, 19). The claim by some today that the church is raptured out of the world at the beginning of Revelation 4 is even more unlikely in light of the marked continuity found in these symbolic connections. Throughout the letters promises are made "to the one who conquers." The rest of the book records the fulfillments of these promises to the church's faithful—its conquering heroes. The following list summarizes those striking connections:

Ephesus: eat of the tree of life in the paradise of God (2:7; see 22:2, 14, 19)

Smyrna: receive the crown of life; not hurt by the second death (2:10-11; see 20:4-6, 14; 21:7-8)

Pergamum: the sword from the Lord's mouth (2:16; see 19:15, 21); a new name no one knows (2:17; see 19:12-13, 16; 22:4)

Thyatira: rule with a rod of iron (2:26-27; see 19:15); receive the morning star (2:28; see 22:16)

Sardis: receive white garments (3:5; see 19:8, 14); name not blotted out of the book of life (3:5; see 19:12, 15; 21:27)

Philadelphia: a pillar in the temple of God (3:12; see 21:22-23); the name of the new Jerusalem written on them (3:12; see 21:2, 10, etc.)

Laodicea: sit with Jesus on his throne (3:21; see 20:4-6; 21:7)

Clearly in Revelation 2-3 Jesus gives the churches a sneak preview of the promises awaiting them at the end of the book. We should apply such promises at the end to the same recipients we find at the beginning of the book: the NT church. We should also apply any references throughout the book regarding the "tribulation saints" (and martyrs) to those Christ followers who were promised tribulation (*thlipsis*) throughout the NT: the NT church!

Behind the Veil: God's Throne Room (Rev 4-5)

True to its name, the book of Revelation seeks to "reveal" (*apokalyptō*) what is behind the veil of eternity. A glimpse into heaven is provided in Revelation 4-5 although naturally we are confronted with the challenge of understanding descriptions of the unseen and unknown by means of things seen and known from this life.

Several truths are highlighted in this glorious, descriptive passage. God Almighty throughout the section is referred to as "the one seated on the throne" (4:2; 5:1, 7, 13; also 6:16; 7:10; 19:4; 20:11; 21:5). Later in the book God and the Lamb are said to *share* the throne (22:1, 3). The heavenly glory described throughout is reminiscent of Ezekiel's descriptions of the divine throne chariot (Ezekiel 1; 10), including his descriptions of the four living creatures and his attempts to describe the shining splendor surrounding them and the throne. The significance of a "throne chariot" in Ezekiel became clear when, because of the sins of Jerusalem and its consequent imminent destruction, the glory of the Lord departed from the midst of the evil city (Eze 11:22-25).

In Revelation the twenty-four elders seated upon twenty-four thrones likely represent the people of God from both Testaments (4:4, 10-11), just as both Israel ("twelve tribes") and the church ("twelve apostles") are represented in the description of the New Jerusalem (21:12-14).

One of the assignments I created early in my Bible college teaching career was for students to skim the book of Revelation and look for evidence for the deity of Christ. Much can be found, including such items as Revelation's ascribing to Jesus the Lamb attributes credited in the OT to Yahweh God. Both entities (i.e., the same entity!) are described as the One "who searches mind and heart" in order to judge His people according to their "works" (Rev 2:23; Jer 17:10). Remarkable testimony to the deity of Christ also occurs here in Revelation 5 where both the One seated on the throne and the Lamb are deemed worthy of worship.

And I heard every creature in heaven and on earth and under the earth and in the sea, and all that is in them, saying, "To him who sits on the throne and to the Lamb be blessing and honor and glory and might forever and ever!" (Rev 5:13)

The scroll in the right hand of the One seated on the throne could only be opened by Christ, introduced as "the Lion of the tribe of Judah," but whose appearance was that of "a Lamb standing, as though it had been slain" (5:1-7). This brief, startling detail illustrates the book's emphasis upon the true spiritual realities present here. Christ has won the victory, not through military accomplishment, but through sacrificial death. He has already conquered, and He now challenges His church to be conquerors through Him (Rev 2-3; 12:11). The presence of the Holy Spirit is noteworthy, represented by the expression "the seven spirits of God" (1:4; 3:1; 4:5; 5:6). Worship scenes in heaven are found throughout the rest of the book and serve to help the reader/hearer appreciate God's heavenly domain (6:9-11; 7:9-17; 14:1-5; 15:2-4; 19:1-12; 21:1-22:5).

Revelation 4:1 plays a pivotal role in the book for many interpreters. A common dispensational claim is that while Revelation 2-3 refers to the church of Jesus Christ (the letters to the seven churches), Revelation 6-18 refers to the post-rapture "tribulation saints," a completely different group. It is argued that John himself represents the church when he is caught up to heaven to see what Jesus and His angels have to show him. This is quite a stretch for those who seek to emphasize the literal interpretation of Scripture!

There is no evidence for the rapture of the church in the book of Revelation and the attempt to use Revelation 4:1 as a representation of the so-called rapture merits little or no consideration (see also Chapter XIII's "A Dubious Fast-Forward").

CHAPTER X

TRIBULATION AND WRATH (REV 6-11)

Once the letters to the seven churches (Revelation 2-3) and the inspiring descriptions in the throne-room scene (Revelation 4-5) are behind us, we are now left with most of the controversial passages in the book! The disputes involved are extensive and some remain outside the scope of the present work.

Upon initial inspection, one would think that the Lamb's opening of the seven seals corresponds with the visions described in 6:1-8:5, but even that has come under question since a scroll in the ancient world typically could not be read until *all* the seals had been opened.

Some would therefore suggest that the contents of the scroll described in Revelation 5 are not presented until Revelation 10 ff. That remains for the present study an open question.

Great Wrath and Tribulation

The most important distinction in Revelation 6-18 is between the notions of wrath and tribulation. Many commentators combine the two indiscriminately. In much of this section interpreters often refer to the outpouring of God's wrath as "the great tribulation" when, in reality, much of the description involves persecution at the hands of Satan, the beast, and the false prophet, while other aspects in the description clearly refer to divine judgment,

God's wrath poured out against His enemies. To label both as "the great tribulation" unnecessarily clouds the picture. In truth, God's people are sealed or protected from God's righteous wrath (7:1-8), while at the same time they must undergo tribulation at the hands of the ungodly (7:9-17).

The destruction mentioned in connection with the "four horsemen" in Revelation 6 may well speak to the realities already experienced by the end of the first century. The warfare, famine, and death vividly portrayed easily correspond to the violent nature of the first-century Roman Empire and its many conflicts. One could argue that the devastations described do not end with the first century, and later history would favor such a position.

Many find a connection with Domitian's reign (AD 81-96)) regarding the mention of food and drink scarcity: a loud voice from heaven calls out, "...A quart of wheat for a denarius, and three quarts of barley for a denarius, and do not harm the oil and wine" (6:6b). A denarius was an average day's wage for a laborer while a quart of wheat fed only a single person for just a day, so we are encountering famine prices here! In view of a grain shortage (ca. AD 92), Domitian ordered half the vineyards in the province be cut down for the increase of grain production. The resultant outcry and political upheaval forced him to rescind the order. With the cutting down of the vineyards wine production would have been severely reduced for years (e.g., Osborne, 280-281).

With the opening of the fifth seal, martyrs for the Christian faith are depicted under the altar before God in heaven and their prayers for judgment are reported (6:9-10). The martyrs are told to rest as they will be joined in the future by other heroes of the faith who will have given their lives in the same way (6:11). They will escape God's great day of wrath, of course.

The sixth seal describes a cataclysmic finale in which the wrath of God is poured out upon the wicked. They call out for the mountains and rocks to fall upon them so as to be hidden from God Almighty and "from the wrath of the Lamb, for the great day of their wrath has come, and who can stand?" (6:16). We see here an early preview of the end. The opening of the seventh seal is delayed (8:1). Even then it serves primarily as a prelude to the sounding of the seven trumpets that comprise the next key cycle in the book (8:6).

Note that throughout the book we are left hanging after we read the descriptions of the sixth element of each of the various cycles of seven. Later regarding the sixth trumpet a demonic army crosses the Euphrates River and kills a third of mankind, leaving all still left alive completely unrepentant (9:13-21). The outpouring of the sixth bowl plague precipitates a confrontation at "Armageddon" with Christ's warning that He is coming "like a thief" for "the great day of God the Almighty." Here again, demonic forces cross the Euphrates—Rome's natural eastern border that helped prevent chaos from erupting in connection with the dreaded Parthian Empire (16:12-16). Ancient concerns for an ancient audience.

With the previous opening of the sixth seal we find the "great ones" of the earth calling upon the mountains and rocks to fall upon them and save them from the wrath of the Lamb (6:15-17). Then a visionary interlude. Prior to the subsequent opening of the seventh seal, a scene unfolds involving "144,000 sealed from wrath" and a great multitude that has come out of "the great tribulation"(7:1-17). Following a brief (ceremonial?) silence (of "about half an hour"; 8:1), seven angels blow seven trumpets (8:6-9:21; 11:15-18).

Once the sixth trumpet is sounded and a third of mankind are killed by horses breathing smoke, fire, and sulfur out of their mouths, we are told that those not slain remain unrepentant (9:18-21). At this juncture in the book we find two further interludes, one involving an angel and a "little scroll" (10:1-11) and the other containing a symbol-laden narrative featuring God's "two witnesses" who prophesy to a mostly unreceptive audience (11:1-13).

At the conclusion of these two interludes the seventh trumpet at last sounds, signaling what now seems to offer another brief preview of final judgment in which God's servants are rewarded while the wicked suffer the wrath of the "Lord God Almighty" (11:15-18). A sizable stretch of visions now follows, a stretch involving key aspects of the book: the conflict between Satan and his followers and Christ and His (12:1-13:18); the 144,000 worshiping in heaven (14:1-5); three angelic proclamations (14:6-13); and two judgment scenes involving the harvest of the earth (14:14-20).

The 144,000 Servants Who Are Sealed

Two dramatically different descriptions of God's people are provided in Revelation 7, yet, as many have suggested, the two groups may very well represent the same body of believers. Before God's outpouring of wrath upon the earth, four angels are commissioned to seal God's servants on their foreheads, the much-discussed "144,000"—12,000 from every tribe of the sons of Israel (7:1-8). That scene is followed by one in which a great multitude no one could number is described, peoples from every nation who have come out of "the great tribulation" and now live in heavenly bliss before the throne (7:9-17).

Several factors suggest that the two groups are likely the same. First, the symbolic nature of the sealing on the forehead should be recognized, especially since earlier

Ezekiel had witnessed a similar visionary scene in connection with the destruction of Jerusalem in his day (Eze 9:4-6). In Ezekiel's vision, as six divinely-sent executioners of Jerusalem set out to do their work, a man clothed in linen was commissioned to put marks on the foreheads of those who "sighed and groaned" over the abominations of the city (Eze 9:3-4). Clearly Ezekiel is given a symbolic portrayal of God's actual judgment over the apostate city, that destruction carried out by the Babylonians in 586 BC. We find something similar in Revelation as the righteous are spared from God's wrath. They receive seals on their foreheads (7:4), an action later described as having the name of the Lamb and His Father written on their foreheads (14:1). The "mark of the beast" on the foreheads of others (13:16-17) awaits later discussion.

Revelation's well-recognized practice of utilizing symbolic numbers must be noted. The dimensions of the New Jerusalem are given as 12,000 *stadia* by 12,000 *stadia* by 12,000 *stadia*, while the walls are "144 cubits" (i.e., twelve by twelve cubits) thick (21:16-17). A *stadion* measured some 600 feet, and a cubit roughly eighteen to twenty inches, i.e., the distance from elbow to fingertips (with both equivalents immaterial to the main point!). The twelve gates have the names of the twelve tribes of the sons of Israel inscribed on them (21:12) while the foundation stones have the names of the twelve apostles of the Lamb (21:14). The fact that this perfect cube theoretically would reach some 1,400 miles into space is not germane.

Instead we should focus on the imagery of a perfect cube corresponding to the OT Holy of Holies and recognize that the New Jerusalem is itself God's holy place where He embraces His redeemed ones. Therefore we find this corresponding statement that there is no temple in the

117

city, "for its temple is the Lord God the Almighty and the Lamb" (21:22).

Another clue that this listing and numbering of the tribes of Israel may be symbolic can be found in the actual names of the tribes. This list as recorded in Revelation 7:5-8 is found nowhere else in the Bible! At times in Scripture we find the listing of Jacob's twelve sons and at other times we find listings of the twelve tribes that received land (the "landed tribes," Levi the priestly tribe excluded). In the former we find Levi and Joseph mentioned while in the latter we find instead Joseph's two sons, Ephraim and Manasseh.

The listing in Revelation 7 is a mixture. We find both Levi and Joseph, but also Joseph's son Manasseh. Missing are Ephraim and Dan. One point of interest is that earlier Ezekiel (again!) had combined the mention of both Joseph and Ephraim in reference to the Northern Kingdom (Eze 37:15-19). The "stick of Joseph" and the "stick of Ephraim" are the same. Someday that stick would be joined with the "stick of Judah" in a symbol of the reunification of the Northern Kingdom and the Southern Kingdom, a clear messianic prophecy in light of the context (Eze 37:24-27).

In the OT prophets the names "Joseph" (Am 5:6, 15; 6:6; Zec 10:6) and "Ephraim" are both used of the Northern Kingdom (Hosea utilizing "Ephraim" more than thirty times in this way). The omission of Ephraim and Dan among the 144,000 sealed from wrath may speak to negative aspects of their mention in Scripture and in later tradition. The name "Ephraim" frequently represented the apostate Northern Kingdom. Perhaps less convincing is the argument from (later Christian) tradition that the alleged "antichrist" was to come from the tribe of Dan. The key here is that the uniqueness of this listing of tribes in

Revelation may speak to the symbolic nature of the groupings.

A proper understanding of the distinction between wrath and tribulation helps lead to the possible, I think likely, conclusion that the 144,000 sealed servants of God are the same as the "great multitude that no one could number from every nation" (7:9). Just as John had "heard" that the Lion of Judah had conquered (5:5) and then "saw" a Lamb standing as though it had been slain (5:6), so John "heard" the number 144,000 (7:4) but when he "looked" he saw the great multitude no one could number (7:9).

If the two groups in Revelation 7 are essentially the same, the distinction between wrath and tribulation is reinforced. Those sealed from God's final wrath are not exempt from the tribulations directed toward them by the forces of evil. Importantly, however, those who come out of "the great tribulation" are seen to exist thereafter in a state of eternal bliss (7:13-17; cf. 14:1-5).

The Plagues of the Seven Trumpets

Apart from a detailed analysis of Revelation 8-11, some key points can still be made as they relate to the focus of the book. We have already noted the parallels between the cycle of the seven trumpets and that of the seven bowls of wrath. In the trumpet cycle, the sounding of the seventh trumpet (11:15) is postponed as the contents of Revelation 10-11 unfold. The source of judgment proclaimed is God himself, a fact clearly portrayed as an angel takes fire from the heavenly altar and throws it upon the earth (8:3-5).

How does this trumpet cycle fit within the structure of the entire book of Revelation? Several views are prominent.

1. These are judgments of "the great tribulation" that will eventually follow the rapture of the church and

punish those who were "left behind." This approach, in my view, is the least helpful.

2. These are divine judgments that will play out throughout the entire church age: "woes that may be seen any day of the year in any part of the globe" (Hendriksen, 140), an unlikely view, but we should note that William Hendriksen's classic commentary *More Than Conquerors* was initially published during the horrors of World War II!

3. These are judgments that figuratively describe the events surrounding the Jewish War and the destruction of Jerusalem in AD 70. This is a standard preterist view and demands a highly symbolic, exaggerated description of first-century events. For full preterists the fall of Jerusalem *was* the second coming. Partial preterists would hold out for a future return of Christ but maintain that the focus of the descriptions of judgment in Revelation points to AD 70.

4. These are judgments (and apparently "signs") that will unfold in the days leading up to the second coming.

5. These are judgments, heavily clothed in symbolic language, that will coincide with Christ's return. None of these views are completely satisfying, and in reality, this section is one of the most difficult in the book. However, we find here guidelines that can help us with the understanding of the book as a whole, including the utilization of symbolic, especially cyclical, numbers and the close parallels between the trumpet and bowls cycles, parallels that incorporate extensive OT background and imagery. Overly literal future fulfillments of scenes

drenched in figurative language seem less likely when we do a deep dive into the imagery employed.

I disagree with those who contend that the devastations in the trumpets (and bowls) cycle are presented in Revelation as opportunities to repent. Instead the emphasis is made that, in spite of the horrific outpourings of wrath and judgment, those without God's seal on their forehead (9:4), those who bear the mark of the beast (13:16-17; 14:9; 16:2), still refuse to repent and instead curse the One who brought about their intense suffering (9:20-21; 16:9-10). These plagues are not meaningful warning signs to heed but are rather graphic depictions of the onslaught of fully deserved final judgment. Of the above views, then, I favor (5) over (4) and the rest and prefer to lump these plagues for the wicked into the fearful unfolding of the future day of the Lord.

Students of Jewish apocalyptic literature can point to works like Enoch, 4 Ezra, 2 Baruch, and others that show similar graphic, metaphoric imagery. Again, the apocalyptic nature of Revelation is not unique in its ancient setting, however, it stands alone in the NT as an example of an inspired apocalyptic work.

In addition, we might pause to consider how momentous, often catastrophic, events have been depicted by literary and artistic sources throughout history. The chiseled gypsum stone wall relief of the Assyrian conquest of ancient Judah's city of Lachish (700 BC) is now displayed in the British Museum for all to see. A must to visit!

Walking along the four walls of the rectangular room where the records of that ancient conflict are carefully mounted one can see the details of the tragic event come to light on the stone slabs that once decorated the palace walls in ancient Nineveh: children carted off into captivity;

weapons of war unleashed against the city gates and walls; leaders of the rebellion impaled upon stakes, etc. The entirety of the devastation and misery cannot be viewed all at once—it must be experienced incrementally "frame by frame" if you would.

What we see there now in the museum's Lachish Room displays the best artistic accomplishments money could buy—in King Sennacherib's day. The ancients in fact created remarkable pictorial and written records of the things that mattered. My trip to Luxor, Egypt (ancient Thebes), some twenty years ago still fills me with wonder. There and throughout Egypt are temples and tombs filled with incredible architecture, brilliant iconography, and lavish artwork—a landscape adorned with massive monuments and riveting inscriptions. No place like it anywhere in the world. Genius has flourished in all stages of technological development and artistic expression. Of course no ancient video of the second coming was possible for John the seer to capture. What he managed to produce with pen and ink under divine influence, however, has captivated the world for centuries.

John dabbled in graphic word pictures and striking symbols. The trumpets cycle in Revelation involves partial destructions, suggesting more to follow. The fraction one-third is used throughout and, again, this was a fraction utilized by Ezekiel in his descriptions of Jerusalem's 586 BC destruction: one-third would die of pestilence, one-third by the sword, and one-third by violence during their doomed attempts to escape (Eze 5:2, 12). John's language regarding the end is clearly apocalyptic and figurative: "a third of the sun was struck, and a third of the moon, and a third of the stars" so that "a third of the day might be kept from shining" (8:12).

From the bottomless pit arose smoke from which came "locusts" upon the earth that had "the power of scorpions." Their power to torment for "five months" may be a reference to the lifecycle of the locust, according to many. The pain of torment causes the wicked to long for death (9:1-6). The locusts are like horses with crowns of gold on their heads— heads with human faces featuring the hair of women and the teeth of lions (9:7)! Hardly literal, physical creatures—they seem to be demonic forces.

Locusts were one of the dreaded plagues of antiquity. Since various terrors from the ancient world would have best served John's descriptions, the power to hurt found in the tails of these monstrous locusts may be a reference to the dreaded Parthian horsemen who fired their arrows not only ahead and to the side, but also to the rear as they were speeding out of range after an attack.

Fears of the Parthian Empire across the Euphrates River to the east may have fueled the imagery involving a massive invasion that would involve three plagues—fire, smoke, and sulfur from the mouths of the horses—that would kill one-third of mankind. While some translations give the number of invaders as "200 million" (NAS, NKJV, NET), we would best be served in recognizing the nature of the Greek numbers involved.

The largest unit in Greek counting was a *myriad*, "10,000," but it could be compounded with an extender such as "twice. "Here at 9:16 the number is "a double myriad times a myriad" or "a double myriad of myriads" (cf. Daniel 7:10). ESV aptly renders: "twice ten thousand times ten thousand." In other words, take the largest base number times double that! A number symbolic of the immense threat depicted. Note that modern Chinese armies are not needed to fill in the picture here...

The troubling events described had been planned for a specific hour, day, month and year (9:15). Importantly, these do not seem to last throughout the duration of the church age. Nor are these plagues redemptive, as some suggest. I have maintained above that the focus here is upon the extent of mankind's wickedness in that those not killed by these plagues did *not* repent of their idolatry, murders, sorceries, sexual immoralities or thefts (9:20-21; cf. 16:9,11). Their judgment is more than deserved. After an important interlude (10:1-11:14), one that I believe points to *past* events, the seventh trumpet sounds and we come to the time of God's final judgment, including the reward for God's servants and wrath upon "the destroyers of the earth" (11:18). Yet there are still eleven chapters to go!

Revelation now does a reset. Following this cycle of descriptions of wrath and preceding the later parallel cycle involving the bowl plagues (15:7-16:21), we encounter the important narrative vision of Revelation 12-14 in which the cosmic conflict featuring God and Christ on one hand and Satan, the beast, and the false prophet on the other unfolds. But even before that, Revelation 10-11 presents an interlude between the sixth and seventh trumpet blasts and here the blowing of the seventh trumpet seems to describe the end: the time of God's outpouring of wrath upon the wicked and the rewarding of His faithful (11:15-18). "The kingdom of the world has become the kingdom of our Lord and of his Christ, and he shall reign forever and ever" (11:15).

As explained below, the context of Revelation 11:1-13 is not an end-times context but a church-age context. Contrary to popular belief, there is likely nothing in the passage that directly relates to the second coming. However, a brief overview of the significance of the imagery of the passage is in order. Opinions on this much-discussed text vary greatly.

CHAPTER XI

THE SCROLL, THE ROD, AND THE GREAT CITY (REV 10-11)

The shadow of Ezekiel falls noticeably upon Revelation 10-11 as it does elsewhere in the book. In an interlude leading up to the blowing of the seventh trumpet, two scenes unfold: first, John receives a scroll from a mighty angel and is commissioned to prophesy (10:1-11); and second, two supernaturally-assisted witnesses prophesy until the beast from the abyss slays them, witnesses who, after "three and a half days," are resurrected and translated to heaven (11:1-13).

The Little Scroll

The commissioning of John and his reception of a scroll from an angel in Revelation 10 parallels the account found in the book of Ezekiel. Ezekiel was handed a scroll and told to eat it and then to speak to the house of Israel. When he ate it, it was "sweet as honey" in his mouth (Eze 2:8-3:3). John centuries later was commanded to take a scroll from the hand of a mighty angel and was instructed to eat it with the promise that it would be "sweet as honey" in *his* mouth (Rev 10:8-10).

John reported that indeed it was sweet as honey in his mouth, but it in turn made his stomach bitter (10:10). Ezekiel had earlier related that, having consumed the sweet scroll given him, he was lifted up and taken by God's Spirit "in bitterness in the heat of my spirit" (Eze 3:14). Both prophets, then, were given a scroll to eat and as a consequence experienced both sweetness and bitterness.

The proclamation of God's goodness and good news is not always a welcome message. Ezekiel was frequently warned and reminded of the rebellious nature of his audience in exile (Eze 3:26; 6:8-10). John would subsequently record the martyrdom of the two witnesses whom God had ordained for the proclamation of the gospel (Rev 11:4-10). John seems to combine elements from both Ezekiel and Daniel in that the mighty angel described in Revelation 10 closely resembles that of Daniel 10 (and Daniel 12).

An element of intrigue is added when the mighty angel calls out and the "seven thunders" sound. John is commanded *not* to write down what he had heard from these seven thunders (10:3-4)! We are thus deprived of the content of another cycle of seven, but the fact that there were indeed seven thunders adds to the stylized imagery of the message of the book.

We are also alerted to the cyclical and retrospective nature of the book since the sounding of the seventh trumpet would signal that "the mystery of God would be fulfilled" (10:7; cf. 11:7-18). Yet after the triumphant statement that punishments and rewards, along with the beginning of God's unopposed reign, followed the sounding of the seventh trumpet (11:15-18), a fresh visionary sequence commences.

This sequence features the birth of Israel's Messiah and Satan's attempts to destroy Him and His followers (the church). These attempts would include enlisting the various efforts of the "beast" from the sea aided by the "beast" from the land (12:1-13:18), with the latter beast also being designated the "false prophet" (16:13; 19:20: 20:10). Thus the sounding of the seventh trumpet brings us to "the end," but not to the book's final description of "the end." More to follow.

A Brief Preview?

The remarkable account in Revelation 11 is viewed by some as an abbreviated summary of the rest of the book: Jerusalem under Gentile control (11:1-2); the proclamation of the gospel with divine authority and supernatural assistance (11:3-6); the martyrdom and subsequent resurrection of these powerful witnesses (11:7-12); resultant judgment upon the wicked city where Christ had been crucified (11:1-2, 8, 13); and the apparent conversion of many who witnessed these things (11:11-13).

Revelation 11:1-13 is a highly condensed account brimming with figurative language and symbolism directly tied to OT imagery and events. Unless we ascribe to the view that the "two witnesses" here will come on the scene after the church has been raptured to heaven, and I do not, we are left with a densely packed summary of past events. This summary describes, among other things: the conflict, both spiritual and physical, that occurs during the church age; the supernatural power available to God's witnesses; the martyrdom of Christ's witnesses, not unexpected in view of their Lord's earlier crucifixion; the opposition and hatred of the unbelieving world toward those who follow Christ; the vindication of the "two witnesses" by their ascension to heaven; and a great devastation upon "the great city" in which thousands die and others come to glorify God through these events.

The Measuring Rod

In another parallel to Ezekiel, John was given a measuring rod and told to measure the temple of God, the altar, and those worshiping there (11:1; cf. Eze 40:3ff; Zec 2:1-5). The most likely significance of this measuring is positive; an indication of what God values and protects. The outer court of the temple is not to be measured, however, but is left to be trampled by the Gentiles for a "forty-two-month" period, a time-frame elsewhere indicating the tribulation aspect of the church age (esp. Chapter XIII).

The "trampling of the holy city for forty-two months" (11:2) seems to correspond to Jesus' language in the Olivet Discourse where He said "Jerusalem will be trampled underfoot by the Gentiles, until the times of the Gentiles are fulfilled" (Lk 21:24). Thus the AD 70 destruction of Jerusalem may well be in view here at 11:2 as it is in Luke's Gospel. It would seem that the church age and the "times of the Gentiles" are roughly equated. The same time period, described later as an equivalent "1,260 days" of prophecy or testimony, would suggest that the ministry of God's "two witnesses" is also tied to the activities of the church age (11:3,7). The term *naos*, "temple," throughout Revelation speaks of the temple proper, not including the outer court, and regularly refers to the heavenly abode of God and His people.

The Two Witnesses

The language describing the "two witnesses" is multi-layered, all from the fabric of the OT. The two olive trees and lampstands "that stand before the Lord of the earth" have power to shut off rain from the sky and power to turn the waters into blood and strike the earth with every kind of plague (11:6). The lampstand/olive tree imagery suggests a connection with Zerubbabel and his contemporary, the high priest Joshua, leaders in Judah's return from exile (Zec 4:1-14). This return (sixth to fifth c. BC) would pave the way for the coming of Israel's Messiah and a deeper spiritual restoration.

Images of Moses and Elijah also come to the fore. Their presence at the Transfiguration in the Gospels speaks to their prominence as OT figures (e.g., Mt 17:1-13). The OT emphasizes the value of having two witnesses (Deu 7:6; 19:15) and the testimony of the two here may represent the collective witness of God's people of both covenants. It has even been suggested that the two witnesses are the combined testimony of the OT and NT prophetic revelation.

The rising of the beast from the "bottomless pit" (or "abyss") anticipates the career of the beast in Revelation 13-19. Opposition to the gospel testimony of these witnesses is intense, a fact further reflected by the rejoicing and merriment of the "earth dwellers" when the two witnesses are killed (11:10). The language "make war on them and conquer them and kill them" might suggest a larger, corporate target (the church) involved, not just two individuals (11:7).

The Great City

Importantly, both expressions "the holy city" (11:2) and "the great city" (11:8) seem to represent Jerusalem here. Outside of this chapter, Jerusalem is called "the holy city" only twice in the NT, both times in Matthew (Mt 4:5; 27:53). It may be significant that in both contexts in Matthew reference is made to the temple and thus the "holy" nature of the Jerusalem of Jesus' day could be loosely claimed (Mt 4:5; 27:51).

Notably the temple is also singled out at the beginning of Revelation 11 in connection with "the holy city" (11:1-2). Here the imagery seems mixed. The inner sanctuary that is "measured" and is therefore precious or valued may speak of God's true people (the church), while the outer court, trampled down and defiled, likely points to unbelieving Israel and its punishment for rejecting its Messiah. In His Olivet Discourse Jesus had earlier spoken of the Gentiles trampling down Jerusalem during the church age (Lk 21:24).

The qualifier "where their Lord was crucified" (11:8) has been explained away as being generic or even somehow tied to Rome, but the intent is almost certainly Jerusalem, which is here called "Sodom" (11:8) as it is in Isaiah's condemnations of the apostate Jerusalem of his day (Isa 1:9-11). According to Ezekiel, the whoring Jerusalem of his own day was worse than Sodom (Eze 16:46-50)! Another suggestive Ezekiel connection. The fact that the book's initial reference to "the great city" here clearly refers to Jerusalem calls into question the insistence of some that the same term later in the book (16:19; 17:18; 18:10, 16, 18, 19, 21) must refer to Rome (Chapter XVIII).

Christians at the end of the first century could have had a number of individuals in mind who had been murdered at the hands of the Jews, including Stephen (Acts 7:54-60), James the brother of John (Acts 12:1-3), and James the brother of Jesus—the James mentioned as the leader of the Jerusalem church in Acts (Acts 15:13-21; 21:17-26; Gal 1:18-19; 2:9-12) and the author of the NT book of James (also known as "James the Just": Josephus, *Antiquities* 20.199-201).

Paul recounted his own role in the persecuting and even killing of Jewish Christians prior to his conversion (Acts 8:1; 9:1-2, 13-14; 22:19-20; 26:9-11; Gal 1:13; Php 3:6). As well, church tradition describes the execution of both Paul and Peter at the hands of the pagan emperor Nero, while the accounts of violent conflict between Paul and his Jewish antagonists throughout Acts might suggest that strident Jewish opposition in Rome played a part in Paul's martyrdom there.

The city described as devastated by an earthquake in which seven thousand are killed probably points to Jerusalem and the events involved in the Jewish War (AD 66-70). The number seven thousand may very well be a "remnant in reverse": seven thousand slain, not spared (cf. Rom 11:4; 1Kgs 19:18). Some of those who were spared would have come to recognize the righteous wrath of God in this disaster. The fall of Jerusalem was presented by early church leaders as evidence for the veracity of Jesus' claims and predictions. We should note in passing that the devastation of "the great city" here is accompanied by "a great earthquake" as is the destruction of "the great city" described later and labeled "Babylon the great" (Rev 11:8, 13; 16:18-19). Are the two "great city and great earthquake" passages highly symbolic descriptions of the *same* significant event? I believe so.

The cycle-ending sounding of the seventh trumpet brings us again to the judgment of the end (11:15-18; cf. 6:12-17 and the sixth seal). But the end is not yet the end! What follow in the text, though not in elapsed time, are events describing the "cosmic conflict" in which Satan, the "great dragon," along with his demonic underlings, the "beast" and the "false prophet," wage war against Christ and His church. This war, in a sense already won through the blood of the Lamb (12:11), will culminate in Christ's return from heaven, final judgment, and the establishment of an eternal new creation, the new heavens and new earth.

Much of the rest of Revelation offers a symbolic description of this cosmic conflict. Before engaging that, however, we need to look behind a different kind of veil than we did above in Chapter IX. We now will explore those historical, political, and social backgrounds that are intimately connected with the mindset and experiences of John's original audience, backgrounds not always at the forefront of the thought of modern readers.

Yet without a solid understanding of events and circumstances leading up to the close of the first century, one's prospects for grasping Revelation's message are bleak. I believe that this next chapter is foundational for most for the rest of what follows.

Chapter XII

Behind the Scenes:
The Background Story

In Revelation 4-5 we were given a glimpse behind the veil of eternity into the very throne room of Almighty God, a not unexpected opportunity within the parameters of ancient apocalyptic writing. Such glimpses into the heavenlies characterized the genre. However, before pursuing an analysis of the cosmic conflict and its resolution in Revelation 12-22, we now need to look behind a different kind of curtain, a move that may greatly assist us in our attempts to unravel the cascade of symbols and characters described in the last half of the book. Among the troublesome entities introduced are the beast, the false prophet, the "great city," Babylon the Harlot, the "mortal wound," the "fallen kings," Armageddon, and of course, the "thousand years" during which Satan is bound and Christ and His saints reign.

Paramount in the discussion will be the issue of how the Christians in late-first-century Roman Asia would have understood the images and actions paraded before them. Here is where I insist we must start. To begin instead with the modern religious, political, or international scene and its potential implications for interpreting Revelation in my view would lead (and indeed has repeatedly led) to unlikely and unwarranted conclusions.

Whether we choose the "early" (AD 63-68) or "late" (AD 92-95) date for Revelation, numerous elements in the book were past or present realities for the original recipients: Christ's birth, death, resurrection, and ascension; the martyrdom of Christians; the ravages of war; Satan being cast out of heaven; the beast rising from the sea, etc. Since such contents likely were known past events, other aspects of the book's narrative may also have occurred already. A common dispute between preterists and futurists is whether or not the book of Revelation contains references to the AD 70 destruction of Jerusalem. Futurists often claim that the descriptions of catastrophic judgment all relate to Jesus' future coming (or, with dispensationalism, *plural* comings—both rapture and return), while preterists argue that many or all of these descriptions point to the wrath poured out by God upon the city of Jerusalem in AD 70.

Past, Present, and Future

The above dispute may contain a fallacy. The book could refer to *both* the second coming *and* the destruction of Jerusalem, corresponding to the situation we find regarding Jesus' Olivet Discourse (Matthew 24; Mark 13; Luke 21—see Appendix B). Another fallacy would be that any references to the fall of Jerusalem in the book need to be predictions of the future and not descriptions of the past.

If we were to compare Revelation to apocalyptic works contemporary with it, such as 4 Ezra and 2 Baruch, we would find that such books indeed contained apocalyptic narratives regarding past events. Fourth Ezra, for example, contained descriptions of the first-century Roman Empire including its succession of emperors. We find a description of an eagle (Rome) that came up from the sea (cf. the beast of Rev 13: 1) that had twelve wings and three heads (*4 Ezra* 11:1).

The focus in the vision concerning the three heads makes it clear that the Flavian Dynasty is in view: Vespasian, Titus, and Domitian. For the author of 4 Ezra, these emperors were a matter of public record, not instances of true prediction, even though he may have claimed them as such and even used a pseudonym ("Ezra" or Greek "Esdras") to mask his true identity. Voices from the distant past often had an aura of authority and importance attached and thus fostered for some the desire to utilize pseudonymity as a tool to garner acceptance and respect.

In Revelation, on the other hand, John identified himself as "John." No drama there! John offered a varied fare: predictions of the future centering around Christ's return; descriptions and interpretations of past events; and applications of such for the present (including John's "present") to guide and fortify John's audience(s) for the ongoing struggle of faith.

Much debate has ensued regarding the seven emperors ("kings") of Revelation 17, but the use of the word "mystery" (17:5, 7) and the call for "wisdom" (17:9) suggest a puzzle for the original recipients to solve in light of their experiences and knowledge (cf. 13:18 regarding "wisdom" in connection with "666"). It is probable that the seven kings mentioned in Revelation 17 had already come on the scene by the last half of the first century. It would not be a matter, then, of predicting the future here in this case as much as it would be of understanding the past and its significance. Today's interpreters who assume that John's call for "wisdom" to solve his "mystery" was directed only toward themselves many centuries after the book's original recipients lived have their own reward.

The Need to Look Back

As modern readers of the Bible, we sometimes lack specifics regarding ancient historical events and personages that may have played a role in shaping the thought and language patterns of the inspired authors of Scripture. As a primer for a survey of Revelation's message, it would be helpful for us to touch upon key events and individuals that may have impacted both the author and initial audience of the book. The closer we can come to the thought world of John and other first-century believers, the better chance we have of overcoming a multitude of chronological and cultural barriers. He or she who has ears to hear let him or her hear.

Imagine you are a leader in the church at Ephesus at the end of the first Christian century. A Jewish Christian in western Roman Asia, you are fluent in Greek, conversant in Latin and Hebrew, and know a smattering of Aramaic. A former reader in the synagogue, as a believer you now meet with the local body of Christ. Relations with the Jewish synagogue and its community are strained. You have available to you scrolls containing most of the NT books, including all four Gospels, Acts, and all of Paul's letters. You have access to the Greek OT or "Septuagint" (LXX), as well as to various Hebrew OT scrolls. You are even aware of the history of the Jewish War written by Josephus circa AD 75-81, originally written in Aramaic but now available in Greek as well.

Since Ephesus is part of Roman Asia where Greek culture and literature still prevail, you function primarily in a Greek-speaking and Greek-thinking world. Your knowledge of the past is framed heavily by Greco-Roman culture and literature and by the Jewish faith and its traditions. You are also most certainly aware of the storyline below.

The Jews Under the Greeks

After the close of the writing of the Hebrew Scriptures and following the conquests of Alexander the Great, Palestine came under the control of Greek rulers, initially the Ptolemies of Egypt and then the Seleucids of Syria.

Under the Seleucid King Antiochus IV Epiphanes the Jews in Judea suffered severe religious persecution that led to their revolt against the Greeks, an uprising championed by Judas Maccabeus (Judah "the Hammer") of the Hasmonean family, subsequent founder of the Hasmonean dynasty.

Under Antiochus IV, the Jewish Scriptures were sought out and destroyed and the holy temple was desecrated. Utilizing guerrilla tactics, the Jews ultimately defeated the Greek occupation and the Jerusalem temple was cleansed in 164 BC. The celebration of Hanukkah (the "Feast of Dedication," also the "Festival of Lights") memorialized that victory (see 1 and 2 Maccabees in the Apocrypha).

In connection with these events, Rome's growing influence and power in the region is well documented. Initially the Jews viewed the Romans as friends, the Greeks being a common enemy, but the arrival of Pompey and his capture of Jerusalem in 63 BC signaled the end of Jewish independence and the beginning of Roman control of the region.

Rome Takes Control

In the protracted hostilities and struggles following the assassination of Julius Caesar (March 15, 44 BC), Mark Antony, along with the Egyptian queen Cleopatra, opposed Octavian, the adopted heir of Julius Caesar, in the struggle for control. In the naval Battle of Actium in 31 BC Octavian achieved a resounding victory and the suicides of Antony and Cleopatra would soon follow.

Herod the Great, appointed King of the Jews earlier by the Romans, had backed the losing side, but he was able to preserve not only his life but also his royal station by convincing Octavian that he would be a loyal friend to him just as he had been to Antony. Octavian viewed Herod's administrative skill, political and military experience, and hard-won connections to be assets too valuable to be summarily discarded. Herod would rule the Jewish people for another quarter century until his death in 4 BC.

After years of civil war and violent upheaval following the assassination of Julius Caesar, the emergence of Octavian as "Caesar Augustus" was a welcome development. Ancient listings considered Augustus as either the first or second Roman emperor of the Julio-Claudian dynasty, a dynasty that would include Augustus, Tiberius, Gaius (Caligula), Claudius, and Nero. Julius' dubious status as "emperor" and the lengthy hiatus between his rule and that of Augustus has caused some not to view him as the first emperor, granting that distinction rather to Augustus.

Remarkably none of the rulers of the Julio-Claudian dynasty were succeeded by sons. Things would change with the later Flavian Dynasty in which Vespasian (AD 69-79) was succeeded by his son Titus who, after a short reign (AD

79-81), was succeeded by his younger brother Domitian (AD 81-96).

The lack of succession in the earlier Julio-Claudian dynasty fueled its unpredictable progressions. The lengthy rule of Augustus was hailed as a triumph of order and security (27 BC-AD 14), while the reigns of Gaius (AD 37-41) and Nero (AD 54-68) came to be known as reigns of intrigue, terror, and indulgent neglect. Many died at the hands of these later murderous, brutal dictators, especially men of high rank who posed potential threats, such as Rome's numerous senators. The memories of both Gaius (Caligula) and Nero were later damned by the Roman senate. Consequently, the two were not divinized by the senate as others of the dynasty were following their respective deaths. With the lengthy reign of Claudius (AD 41-54), the emperor during much of the Apostle Paul's ministry, there was some return to the "peace and security" (1Th 5:3) that characterized the days of Caesar Augustus.

Persecution and Hostilities

The events of AD 64-73 would have been deeply etched into the psyches of Christians, especially Jewish Christians, living in the last quarter of the first century AD. A great conflagration broke out in Rome in AD 64, a fire many blamed on Nero himself. It would result in a massive, lavish building program orchestrated by Nero, with projects including his glorious "Golden House" and a 120-foot-high statue of himself. Likely as a deflecting of blame for the fire, Nero chose the Christian community in Rome as his scapegoats, condemning many of them to horrific punishments and deaths.

The Roman historian Tacitus describes the events in detail and notes that even those who, like himself, despised the unfortunate Christians eventually felt pity upon them because of Nero's personal vendetta and resultant brutality. Some Christians were condemned to the gladiatorial arena, others crucified and lit as human torches to illuminate Nero's gardens. Numerous other atrocities are also recorded (Tacitus, *Annals* 15:44).

Long-standing Christian tradition places the martyrdom of both Paul and Peter either during or soon after this initial persecution. In addition, continued antagonism between leading Roman officials and the Jews in Palestine ultimately led to a catastrophic result there. The neglect of the provinces worsened during Nero's reign of terror. The string of ineffectual and even hostile procurators appointed over the Jews in Judea eventually resulted in the cessation of Jerusalem's daily sacrifices on behalf of the emperor in AD 66, a virtual declaration of war.

After initial Roman military setbacks in Judea that only encouraged the Jews toward further rebellion, Nero commissioned the general Vespasian to lead the quashing of the uprising. A capable leader, yet one with an undistinguished pedigree, Vespasian was an ideal choice for the needful but insecure Nero. Highly successful and popular generals always posed a threat. Vespasian lacked such standing, but in his new role, he flourished and quickly subdued most of the region in rebellion apart from Jerusalem itself and a few key fortresses.

Problems came for Nero from the west, however, where Roman legions fomented an uprising and the Roman senate subsequently recognized the general Galba as their new emperor. Rather than facing a worse fate, Nero committed suicide June 9, AD 68. Nero's funeral was a small, private affair and that led to suspicions that Nero really had not died but had escaped to the east, specifically to Parthia east of the Euphrates River, and now planned a future triumphant return and conquest of Rome. The Parthian Empire was a much-feared threat at this time for Rome.

Over the next several decades more than one pretender played the role of Nero "revived" or "restored" and created turmoil in the process for the eastern provinces. This *Nero reditus* ("Nero returning, returned") or *Nero redivivus* ("Nero revived, resurrected") tradition may have found some representation in Revelation where a threat from east of the Euphrates is mentioned (Rev 9:13-19; 16:12-14).

I believe that Revelation possibly utilizes this well-known tradition as background for a symbolic frightful, end-times threat, but not as a literal, future political or military development. For John, if Nero lived on, it was only symbolically through the later Flavian tyrant Domitian (AD 81-96), whose despotic tendencies and deadly inclinations became all too obvious. Early church fathers fittingly labeled Domitian as a "Second Nero."

Upon hearing the news of Galba's rise to power, Vespasian suspended all activities on the Judean front until confirmation of the new emperor's wishes. Importantly, what happens next probably relates to the language in Revelation involving a time when the beast "is not" (Rev 17:8, 11) and when the beast receives a "mortal wound" that amazingly heals (Rev 13:3, 12, 14).

Further unrest among the Roman legions resulted in the suicide of Galba just seven months after taking the throne, with another general, Otho, instead acclaimed by the legions and the senate. Otho's failure a few months later to fend off other legions committed to their own leader, Vitellius, led Otho also to take his own life. He viewed that act to be the honorable thing to do rather than creating the bloodbath that would follow his further resistance. Otho had reigned a little over three months. Vitellius, however, was soon in trouble himself as legions of the east decided that their formidable representative, Vespasian, was a more worthy recipient of ultimate power.

Vespasian was acclaimed Imperator by the Egyptian and Syrian legions in July 69. Soon, forces near Rome loyal to Vespasian captured, tortured, and assassinated the pitiful Vitellius. He had reigned but eight months. Thus concluded what modern historians of ancient Rome have labeled "The Long Year" or "The Year of the Four Emperors."

Rome's Revival

Ancient historians like Josephus and Tacitus viewed the recovery of the empire as nothing short of remarkable. Josephus speaks of Rome suffering calamities on all sides (*War* 4.585) and notes that Vespasian's rise to power accomplished "the unexpected deliverance of the public affairs of the Romans from ruin" (*War* 4.657). Regarding the "Year of the Four Emperors," Tacitus spoke "of a period rich in disasters, terrible with battles, torn by civil struggles, horrible even in peace" (*Histories* 1.2).

To borrow John's language, the seeming "mortal wound" was "healed" by the accession of Vespasian and the prospects of a continuing dynasty through his sons Titus and Domitian. Meanwhile, the Jewish rebels had been encouraged and empowered by Rome's troubles, but soon reality set in as Vespasian commissioned his son Titus to finish the Judean campaign and capture Jerusalem and the few other areas yet to be conquered.

The Jewish historian Josephus, an eyewitness to the conflict, records the horrors of the conquest of Jerusalem by the Romans and also the internal strife and violence that occurred among the Jewish factions that resisted. Many

Jews were assassinated by fellow countrymen, especially by militant Zealots and also by so-called *Sicarii* (Latin, "dagger-men"). Fellow Jews were murdered sometimes because of their wealth and position, sometimes because of suspected collaboration with the Roman enemy, and sometimes both.

Propaganda, Politics, and the Jewish Defeat

The destruction of the Jerusalem temple in August 70 along with the sack of the city effectively concluded the Jewish Revolt. Several strongholds held out for a time. The Herodian fortress at Masada near the Dead Sea was finally captured in AD 73. Josephus relates the remarkable tale. Some 960 Jewish soldiers and family members committed suicide rather than allowing the Romans to have their own way (*War* 7.275-406). Following the conquest of Jerusalem and the defeat of the revolt, a Roman triumph honoring both Vespasian and Titus was held in Rome AD 71. Josephus' description is the most extensive of any Roman triumph recorded in history (*War* 7.122-162).

The upstart Flavian Dynasty welcomed the credibility and prestige that the suppression of the Jewish Revolt brought. Vespasian took every opportunity to promote his accomplishment: inscriptions on coins (e.g., *IVDAEA CAPTA*, "Judaea captured"); the building of his Temple of Peace in which spoils from the Jerusalem temple were on display; and the construction of the Roman Colosseum, finished during the reign of Titus (AD 79-81) and accomplished in part with the spoils of the Jerusalem conquest.

The Arch of Titus, completed by Domitian, still features carvings of the triumphal procession in which Jewish captives carried the temple's seven-candled *menorah* and the table of shewbread. In the minds of many scholars, the concerted propaganda efforts of the Flavian Dynasty initially hindered any hope for the rebuilding of the Jerusalem temple, a hope that was further diminished by the Christianization of the Roman empire following the conversion of Constantine.

Twice in Revelation we read that the whole world "marveled" (*thaumazō*) at the wounded beast seemingly brought back from the dead (Rev 13:3), the beast that "was and is not" and yet returned (Rev 17:8). These remarkable events surrounding the fall of the Julio-Claudian Dynasty and rise of the Flavian Dynasty are most likely in view in John's words here.

Who's Really in Charge?

This triumph of Rome became for some a topic of *theodicy*, "God's justice." Just as the OT prophet Habakkuk struggled with the idea that a brutal power like ancient Babylon would be used by God to punish His people Israel and His holy city Jerusalem, both Jews and Christians over the last quarter of the first century wrestled with the issue of God's justice in bringing about both Jerusalem's fall and Rome's virtual resurrection. For those wondering "Who's in charge?" seeming answers could be jarring.

The Jewish historian Josephus concluded that God had given Rome center stage and dominion for a time. Jewish apocalypticists roughly contemporary with the writing of Revelation submitted that Rome's power to destroy Jerusalem and the temple had been given it by God in response to the sins of His people (sins those Jewish writers could not always clearly identify!).

Christians were instructed by the Olivet Discourse that contained Jesus' predictions of Jerusalem's destruction within a generation (Matthew 24; Mark 13; Luke 21). And here the sins were clearly spelled out. Israel would be punished because of its wholesale rejection of Jesus as Messiah and Deliverer. The Early Church Fathers would emphasize Christ's words in their defense of the Christian faith and in their attacks against Judaism's continued claims.

The Original Recipients

John's message for the seven churches of Asia addressed, it would seem, some of the issues that events noted above had caused. Was the fall of Jerusalem and destruction of the temple a sign of the inferiority of the God of the Bible? Not at all.

Did Rome's survival from its near collapse AD 68-69 signal the invincibility of the Empire? It did not, but the stark warning in Revelation was that a choice would need to be made. The eternal perspective through faith would need to be exercised in the face of then-current political realities. The mark of the beast led in one direction; God's seal upon the forehead provided a glorious alternative path.

The Greek setting in Roman Asia fostered the increased threat of emperor worship and greater consequences for the refusal by Christians to fully participate. Smyrna was granted the first provincial temple devoted to the emperor (26 BC) and Pergamum the second (AD 23).

The later provincial temple in Ephesus was dedicated in the time of Domitian. Emperor worship was not a practice in the city of Rome, but it was commonplace in Asia and other Greek-speaking eastern provinces. In some ways, then, life in the province of Asia for the seven churches addressed in Revelation was even more difficult than for those in Italy and Rome itself. The exhortations and consolations in Revelation would seem to fit well with the end of the first century AD.

Students of prophecy who envision Revelation's focus to be a post-rapture tribulation involving a future antichrist and future worldwide persecution are not all that interested in the historical survey above. For them "we all know" that Revelation is an "end-times book" and whatever symbols may be involved point to the future and not the past. And yet such assumptions have led the church into a great season of confusion and controversy.

Perhaps an awareness of the historical survey above can provide an aid to the interpretation of the book of Revelation in its teaching on the second coming and related matters. At least we can become better aware of what the late-first-century church was thinking. That cannot but help.

CHAPTER XIII

THE COSMIC CONFLICT (REV 12)

With Revelation 12 the main narrative of the book unfolds, presenting what some have labeled the "cosmic drama" or "cosmic conflict" featured in the book. A great conflict is described, one in which the audience of the book must participate, whether wishing to or not. The great dragon is now introduced with his two prominent henchmen: the beast (sea beast) and the false prophet (land beast).

Much of what follows in Revelation focuses upon the activities and final destruction of these two characters or characterizations. In contrast to the dragon, a designation devoted to a single entity, Satan himself, both the beast and the false prophet likely represent a plurality of individuals involving a sequence presented by John especially in Revelation 17.

Christ and Satan in Conflict

Even if the heads of the beast in Revelation 17 represent various Roman emperors as discussed previously and below, the true enemy of the church as depicted in Revelation is not Rome and its leaders. Rather, Satan is singled out in John's visions as the great opponent of Christ and His church. The overarching theme of Revelation 12-22 is the cosmic conflict between Christ and Satan that culminates in Christ's second coming, the punishment of

Satan and his followers, and the establishment of God's new creation: His new heavens and new earth.

Satan's role in Revelation continues that described elsewhere throughout the NT, including the teaching that he is a defeated foe because of Christ's redemptive work on the cross and His victory over death (e.g. Heb 2:14-15; 1Jn 3:8). Through Christ's atoning death His followers have conquered Satan already (Rev 12:10-11).

Both here and at Revelation 20 Satan's full complement of titles is expressed: the great dragon, that ancient serpent, the devil, Satan, the deceiver (12:9; 20:2-3). The term "devil" comes from the Greek *diabolos*, which means the "accuser," while the name "Satan" comes from the Hebrew *satan*, which indicates "adversary." In the Greek OT *diabolos* is also sometimes used to translate the Hebrew *satan*. There is a thin line between accuser and adversary.

Back to the Beginning (Bethlehem and Beyond)

In light of the emphasis in the NT that Christ conquered Satan at His *first* coming (see "The Fall of Satan" below), it is noteworthy that the cosmic conflict between Christ and Satan depicted in Revelation 12 begins with the birth of Christ and the great dragon's attempt to destroy Him.

I have friends who have insisted upon placing a toy dragon within their Christmas nativity scenes! I support their theology, if not necessarily their praxis. The description proceeds from the birthing scene to the male child's ascension to heaven (12:2-5), repeating the Biblical refrain that the child would rule the nations with a rod of iron (12:5; 2:27; Ps 2:9).

The dragon's extensive description includes the phrase "that ancient serpent," a designation that reminds the reader of a commencement of conflict much earlier than Christ's birth at Bethlehem. In Genesis 3 we find what has been labeled the Protevangelium, the "first gospel promise," in connection with the sin of Adam and Eve and the curse upon them and especially upon the serpent (Gen 3:14-19).

In longstanding church tradition the bruising of the heel of the "seed of woman" points to the crucifixion of Jesus, while the bruising or crushing of the head of the serpent himself speaks to Christ's resurrection and victory over the one who (had) had the power of death (Heb 2:14; Rom 1:4; 8:34-39; 16:20). Reference to the "serpent of old" in Revelation seems to take us back to Genesis 3 and the victory over Satan depicted there in the Protevangelium.

The victory over Satan is stressed two ways in Revelation 12: first, the woman is nourished by God during the time the dragon pursues her (12:6, 14-16); and second, even if their faithful testimony leads to death, the church overcomes Satan, the accuser, "by the blood of the lamb and by the word of their testimony" (12:11). In the first half of the book especially we find reminders of Christ's victory accomplished through His resurrection (1:18; 2:8; 3:21) and His death or blood (1:5, 7, 18; 2:8; 5:6, 9, 12; 7:14; 11:8; 12:11).

Revelation stresses that for believers death and resurrection will be the path for overcoming as well, with special mention of the path of martyrdom (2:10; 6:9-11; 7:13-14; 11:7; 12:11; 13:7, 10; 15:2; 16:6; 17:6; 19:2; 20:4-6).

A Dubious Fast-Forward

Dispensationalists who relegate much of Revelation to a post-rapture literal "three-and-a-half-year" tribulation period must explain away the clear message of Revelation 12. After the birth and ascension of Christ (the male child), the woman who has given birth now flees to the wilderness for a time of nourishment, described as both "1,260 days" (12:6) and "a time, and times, and half a time" (12:14).

Just as a putative rapture of the church is inserted at Revelation 4:1 by dispensationalists in connection with John's being caught up to heaven, an insertion that, in effect, separates the seven churches in Revelation 2-3 from the rest of the book, here both the entire church age and the alleged pretribulational rapture would now seem to be awkwardly inserted between 12:5 and 12:6 at a place where Christ's ascension after His resurrection is immediately followed in the text by the 1,260-day period of nourishment for God's people. Their desired result: the church age is completely bypassed!

This presumed fast-forward by pretribulational dispensationalists is absolutely unwarranted. The fact that in the text the 1,260 days *immediately follow* the ascension of Christ to God's throne strongly suggests that this numerical representation (along with "a time, and times, and half a time" and "forty-two months") represents the church age in its entirety from the perspective of tribulation or opposition as well as, in this case, protection from such.

Putting things in plainest terms, the text says that the male child (Jesus) was caught up to God's heavenly throne (the ascension) and the woman (the church) fled into the wilderness. It does not say (or suggest) that the male child (Jesus) was caught up to God's heavenly throne (the ascension) and, after the church age was over and the church had been raptured from the earth, the woman (the post-rapture tribulation saints) fled into the wilderness.

Key finding here? The 1,260 days of tribulation in Revelation do not *follow* the church age: they *coincide* with the church age!

The Fall of Satan

Revelation 12 depicts the defeat of the dragon and his angels by Michael and his angels in a war fought in heaven (regarding Michael in the OT, cf. Dan 10:13-14, 21; 12:1). Consequently heaven no longer has a place for them and the great dragon and his angels are thrown down to earth (12:7-9). Three realities result from this remarkable development:

1. The throwing down of Satan from heaven involves the establishment of God's kingdom and the authority of His Messiah (12:10).

2. In connection with this, the saints have conquered Satan by the blood of the Lamb and by the word of their testimony (12:11).

3. Having been cast down to earth, the devil is full of great wrath for he knows his time is short (12:12).

In addition, 12:10 seems to suggest that the devil, having been cast out of heaven, no longer can function as the accuser who accuses (or rather had accused) God's people day and night before God's throne. We seem to find Satan's role as accuser several times in the OT (Job 1:9-10; 2:4-5; Zec 3:1-10). His attacks against Job are well-known. From a later time, within the context of Satan's accusations against Joshua the high priest (a sixth c. BC post-exilic leader and an OT type of Christ), God promises the sending of a future servant called the "Branch" (a messianic title). We read, "… I will remove the iniquity of this land in a single day. In that day … every one of you will invite his neighbor to come under his vine and under his fig tree" (Zec 3:9-10). A future day of deliverance will signal the dawn of the messianic age and the defeat of Satan the accuser.

In the Gospels, when the seventy-two returned to Jesus after their mission in which even the demons submitted to them as they employed His name, Jesus affirmed, "I saw Satan fall like lightning from heaven" (Lk 10:18). In the hours between His Triumphal Entry and arrest, Jesus spoke of His impending crucifixion as a triumph over Satan: "Now is the judgment of this world; now will the ruler of this world be cast out. 32 And I, when I am lifted up from the earth, will draw all people to myself" (Jn 12:31-32).

John adds, "He said this to show by what kind of death he was going to die" (Jn 12:33). At Christ's crucifixion and resurrection, the serpent's striking the heel of the seed of woman would trigger the crushing of its own head by that very seed of woman, Jesus the Messiah (Gen 3:15). As the "already and not yet" paradigm emphasizes (Chapter II), the great cosmic conflict is yet being fought, but is already won!

The Bible's teaching on the fall of Satan is not easy to untangle. Much less is found on the devil in the OT than most realize. Revelation adds to our supply of data but also to our level of confusion. Painting in broad strokes, we can present a basic, if sketchy, portrayal.

Although found present in the garden of Eden (Genesis 3), Satan apparently at that time still had access to the heavenly throne and functioned as the accuser (see above). The supernatural promoter of human sin against God, more and more the devil would become "the ruler of this world" (Jn 12:31), or even, as Paul put it, "the god of this world" (2Cor 4:4).

As angels throughout the Bible illustrate, access to the heavenly realm and to the earthly landscape are not mutually exclusive. Through his redemptive work on the cross Jesus effected the casting out of Satan from heaven as both the Gospel of John and the Revelation from John indicate (Jn 12:31-32; Rev 12:7-13). The casting out of demons during His public ministry signaled Christ's authority, one that even the demons themselves recognized (Mt 8:28-32) and one that resulted in laying waste Satan's domain by Christ's "binding the strong man" (Mt 12:25-29; cf. Rev 20:1-3).

The picture throughout many of the NT epistles and sermons (Acts) presents Satan as a now-defeated foe (Eph 4:27; 6:1; 1Tm 3:6; 2Tm 2:24-26; Heb 2:14; Jas 4:7; 1Jn 3:8; also Acts 10:38; 13:10-12; 16:16-18; 19:12-17; 26:18). This a formidable list of texts!

Even Peter's oft-cited description of the devil as a prowling, devouring lion concludes with the call to resist and the promise that those who do will be called into eternal glory (1Pet 5:8-10). They win! Satan loses. Sounds like Revelation's hope for the faithful who conquer through Christ (Rev 2:7, 11, 17, 26; 3:5, 12, 21; 12:10-11).

Escape from death is not the promise in Revelation but rather conquering through death or in spite of death. Jesus challenged, "Be faithful unto death, and I will give you the crown of life" (Rev 2:10). John warns, "If anyone is to be taken captive, to captivity he goes; if anyone is to be slain with the sword, with the sword must he be slain. Here is a call for the endurance and faith of the saints" (Rev 13:10). The key here is recognition of Satan as a fallen foe. He cannot win.

Strong connections exist between the language of Revelation 12 and Revelation 20. The same designations for the devil are listed in the same order: dragon, serpent ("that ancient serpent"), the devil, Satan (12:9; 20:2). In Revelation 12 the dragon is defeated by Michael and his angels and thrown (*ballō*) down to earth (12:8-9) while in Revelation 20 the dragon is bound by an angel and thrown (*ballō*) into the pit (*abyssos*, "abyss" or "bottomless pit") for a thousand years (20:1-3).

The question to be answered later is whether Revelation 12 and 20 describe events separated by several thousand years, involving both the first coming (12:1-17) and the second coming of Christ (20:1-3), or instead offer complementary yet distinct descriptions of the *same* remarkable developments: the de facto defeat of Satan through Christ's redemptive work and Satan's resultant status in which his power both to accuse and to deceive are now limited.

According to amillennialism, just as in Revelation 12 a "defeated" dragon continues to make war with the saints (12:8, 11, 17), so also in Revelation 20 a "bound" and "imprisoned" dragon no longer can deceive the nations in the way he once did, and yet his influence in the world is still very real (20:2-3; 13:1-2).

Under Attack "Three and a Half Years"

In the midst of the description of the dragon's pursuit of the woman who had given birth to the male child, we are told that the woman, now the persecuted church, is nourished in the wilderness "for 1,260 days" (12:6) or "for a time, and times, and half a time" (12:14). As previously noted (Chapter VII), numbers equivalent to three and a half (years) seem to be used in the book to describe the church age as a time of tribulation, trial, and testing. Half of seven denotes the opposite of what the "perfect" number seven suggests.

In Revelation we find these three equivalent expressions: "forty-two months" (11:2; 13:5); "1,260 days" (11:3; 12:6); and "time, times, and half a time" (12:14 cf. Dan 7:25; 12:7). While the woman is nourished and protected (spiritually!) by God, times of conflict and struggle unfold "1,260 days" (12:6) or "a time, times and half a time" (12:14). Jerusalem is trampled down by the Gentiles "forty-two months" (11:2); Jesus' two witnesses prophesy "1,260 days" (11:3), are killed, and are raised back to life and ascend to heaven (11:7-12); and the "beast," promoted and assisted by the "false prophet" (13:11-14; 16:13; 19:20), persecutes the church "forty-two months" (13:5). Each of these scenes likely describes symbolically the entire church age viewed from the perspective of testing and tribulation.

The mention of Satan having only a "short time" (*oligon kairon*) at 12:12 raises several questions. Is this "short time" the same as the "little while" (*mikron chronon*) that follows Satan's release from his prison (20:3)?

That is unlikely.

Might it instead be a reference to the "three and a half" period of testing present throughout the church age?

This seems more to the point, especially when we consider that the battle fought is not over the masses but for the individual soul. Satan wins or loses the conflict one person at a time. The Bible teaches us to "number our days" for "they are soon gone" (Ps 90:10-12).

Our time is short. The devil knows this already; his intentions toward us are unwavering and time-sensitive. John warns of his great wrath and fury (12:12, 17).

CHAPTER XIV

THE RISE OF THE BEAST (REV 13)

As the transition from Revelation 12 to Revelation 13 shows, Satan's opposition to the church utilizes a human element, one involving pagan rulers and authorities. In Revelation 13 we are introduced to two entities, the beast from the sea and the beast from the land, the latter also being referred to as the "false prophet" (16:13; 19:20). Both Greece and Rome were identified by the Jews as empires from the sea. At Daniel 11:30, the expression "ships of Kittim [Cyprus]" is used to describe the Romans. The Dead Sea Scrolls employ such designations also, e.g., in the Habakkuk Commentary.

Daniel 7 describes a vision in which four great beasts come out of the sea, beasts representing world empires, while the description in Revelation 13 presents a single beast incorporating various elements of Daniel's previous symbolic descriptions (leopard, bear, lion).

If Rome indeed is the fourth beast of the book of Daniel as Josephus believed (*Antiquities* 10.208-210, 276), the Jewish author of 4 Ezra believed (*4 Ezra* 12:10-30), and most conservative Christian interpreters have maintained, it would make sense for Revelation to present the Roman Empire as a composite beast, one that had incorporated elements of the previous ones described in Daniel (Babylon: lion; Medo-Persia: bear; Greece: leopard).

The connections with Daniel strengthen the likelihood that Revelation's beast was a phenomenon emerging in the first century, not a post-church-age, post-rapture entity as dispensationalism would maintain. As well, the link with Revelation 12 suggests that the church is center stage in the conflict even as the dragon enlists the beast from the sea in attempts to destroy the people of God.

Satan's Henchman Arrives

The description of the dragon in Revelation 12 ends with, "And he stood on the sand of the sea" (12:17). Translations vary here as some would place the last few words of 12:17 instead at 13:1. In addition, more importantly, KJV reads, "And I stood on the sand of the sea" (13:1), while most modern translations follow the best manuscript evidence in reading that "he stood on the sand of the sea," referring to the dragon. This preferred reading strongly suggests that the dragon standing at the edge of the sea summoned the beast up from out of the sea, not that John ("I") was standing at water's edge watching.

The words "sea" (*thalassa*) and "abyss" (*abyssos*) are closely connected and often equated in antiquity, frequently with ominous overtones, and the beast is described as coming out of both the abyss (11:7; ESV "bottomless pit") and the sea (13:1). The previous mention of the beast at 11:7 seems to anticipate the conflict narrative that commences at Revelation 12.

The Beast's Rise, Fall, and Rise and Fall

The introduction of the beast in Revelation 13 contains four noteworthy elements.

1. The beast derives his power from the dragon, and that power allows him to "conquer" the saints (13:7), even though, in the spiritual realm, the saints

have already conquered the dragon by the blood of the lamb, even in death (12:11).

2. The remarkable survival of the beast from its "mortal wound" takes center stage (13:3 [two times], 12, cf. 14 "wounded by the sword and yet lived"), a survival that causes "the whole earth" to marvel (13:3-4; cf. 17:8).

3. The call for wisdom in identifying the ruler with the number "666" suggests a challenge likely intended for the book's initial first-century audience, not just one for distant future generations. A similar call for wisdom is echoed by John at Revelation 17:9-11 where the riddle of the seven kings and seven mountains is presented. Discernment of past and present events and their significance is likely what is needed here, not clever prognostication of the future.

4. The other beast, the land beast, also labeled the "false prophet" (16:13; 19:20), demands the people's worship of the beast from the sea. Emperor worship was prevalent during the early years of the Roman Empire, especially in the eastern (Greek) provinces.

As suggested in Chapter XII, Nero's reign and death and Rome's survival of its resultant civil war are the best loci for deriving a meaningful setting for key aspects of Revelation's content. The healing of the mortal wound and the time when the beast "is not" likely speak to the near-demise of Rome in connection with its civil war and "Year of the Four Emperors" following Nero's downfall and suicide.

The Number of the Beast: 666

Current speculations about the number "666" abound and include linking it with numerous villains from the past and present. Modern candidates have included Hitler, Khrushchev, and many others. I have not yet investigated derivatives of Putin's name in light of current events at the time of writing. Please stay tuned.

While on a tour of Beverly Hills some thirty years ago, our group was informed by the tour guide outside of one of Ronald Reagan's homes that the home's address "668" we were viewing had been altered from an original "666" at the request of Nancy. I couldn't blame her!

The phenomenal impact of the Internet upon the world has spawned a popular theory. Combining the abbreviation www (World Wide Web) with the fact that the Hebrew letter *w* (*waw*) represents the number "6," one gets the equation Internet = 666. I am just the messenger on this.

Among the candidates from antiquity, the emperor Nero is most mentioned. The name Nero(n) Caesar, if written in Hebrew (also Aramaic) letters (*nrwn qsr*), provides the total numerical value of 666. An inscription from near the Dead Sea shows this precise spelling of Nero's name.

The alternate spelling *nrw qsr* without the final letter *n* (*nun*) totals 616, which, interestingly, is found as an alternative in various Greek manuscripts of Revelation. In addition, the Greek word for "beast" (*thērion*), if spelled with Hebrew letters, gives us *trywn*, another "666!" Thus Neron Caesar = 666 = "beast." That works as well as anything, perhaps. Multiple speculations have surfaced throughout the centuries.

At the end of the day, I do view the Nero connection as a possible component here, although the substitution of

Hebrew equivalents for Greek or Latin letters in the computation process seems somewhat dubious. The Jewish-Christian makeup of much of the initial audience could help explain the suitability of the phenomenon.

The use of numerical equivalents of Hebrew letters in conveying connections or messages is called *gematria*, a popular Jewish interpretive practice. For the use of Greek letters in a similar way the term is *isopsephy*. A famous wall graffito from Pompeii reads "I love her whose number is 545." Concerning Nero, the letters of his name also spell out for some a grim accusation by its Greek numerical value (1,005), "He killed his own mother!"

Regarding further possible significance of the number 666 in antiquity, scholars have proposed a connection with the phenomenon of triangular numbers. For example: Ten is the triangular number of 4. That is, 4+3+2+1 = 10.

Thirty-six is the triangular of 8, which is 8+7+6+5+4+3+2+1 = 36. And 666 is the triangular of 36, thus a triangular of a triangular (36+35+34 ... +3+2+1 = 666).

The significance of 8 as a doubly triangulated number is then connected by some to the "eighth head" (which is both *from out of* and *in addition to* the "seven heads") at Revelation 17:11. Sound complicated? For a thorough discussion of this and related phenomena see Richard Bauckham (*Climax*, 384-407; also David Chilton, 347-350).

I am skeptical of the value of this whole line of reasoning. On another sidenote, one advanced by Chilton, at the height of his glory, Solomon received 666 talents of gold in a year (1Kgs 10:14; 2Chr 9:13). Might this number then have later suggested apostasy? Probably a bit of a stretch. Of course much has been written about the number "six" being one less than the "divine number seven" and therefore a symbol of imperfect, sinful humanity. This goes on and on...

In connection with ancient options, I venture to make one observation not generally offered in the literature that involves the Roman numeral system (but see Bruins, Sanders, Watt for discussion). That counting system was somewhat unique in its representation of numbers, although the suggestion has been made that the prevalence of "5" within it ties in with the use of the fingers of the hand for counting (not shocking).

Many today are familiar with the basic numbers: D (500), C (100), L (50), X (10), V (5), and I (1). There was no zero.

One key feature was that various combinations with some element of "four" in them ("49" [40 + 5 +4], "96" [50 +40 +5 +1]) could not exhibit a fourfold repetition (with rare exceptions) and instead various "1" elements [100, 10, 1] were positioned *before* the appropriate symbols, so we see IX, "9," not VIIII. Thus "49" became XLIX ("10" from "50" plus "1" from "10") and "96" turned into XCVI. As a further example, CLVII = 157, but 159 would be CLIX.

The letter M should be excluded from the discussion for our purposes since it was not normally employed until centuries later and was not a part of the standard ledger of symbols used every day at the time Revelation was written.

Later, along with the growing use of M, the multiplier 1,000 was often indicated by a horizontal line called a *vinculum* above another number. Thus, 5,000 would have been V with a horizontal line above it. The earliest examples of the symbol for 1,000 itself were represented by a circle with a vertical line through it (looking something like CIƆ or Φ). Earliest forms may have employed an additional horizontal line across the middle. Larger numbers involving tens of thousands, hundreds of thousands, and beyond were indicated by various circle/line combinations. For a remarkable discussion of ancient numbering systems, including ancient Roman, see Karl Menninger (1957-58; transl. from German 1969).

During the first century, six basic numerical symbols represented by Roman letters were utilized in the empire (borrowed and adapted mostly from the neighboring Etruscan civilization). Proceeding left to right in descending order with the six symbols generally utilized in Roman numerical records, including tax and commercial, we are left with the list DCLXVI, which, if read as a single number, would be 666.

Dealings throughout the empire required the repeated use of these six symbols in various combinations. Perhaps this was John's (or the angel's) somewhat cryptic way to point to the distinctive Roman counting system and its ubiquitous employment throughout the Roman Empire's financial dealings (note the context of "buying and selling"; Rev 13:17). Perhaps just a coincidence, but I wonder...[9]

---

[9] Depicted in various Roman artifacts and architecture were the human "recorders" or "calculators," each with his hand-held *abacus*. This was generally a small, metallic plate with engraved lines into which small pebbles were placed as counters. The adroit sliding of pebbles into their appropriate configurations to arrive at accurate mathematical assessments was an essential function in the ancient Roman commercial world. Roman numerals would record the results of such calculations.

As Menninger has documented, the *abacus* played a role for centuries and was likely borrowed by the Chinese (their *suan pan*) and then in turn by the Japanese (their *soroban*). Marco Polo and the court of Kublai Kahn have been mentioned as a possible link, but a healthy trade industry between the Roman Empire and China already existed by the time Revelation was written at the end of the first century. More recently, competitions sponsored right after World War II pitting the Japanese *soroban* against Western electronic machines surprised many when skilled Japanese *soroban* experts achieved faster calculation times than their Western counterparts.

The phrase "the number of a man" (13:18) could also be rendered "a human number"—neither *arithmos*, "number," nor *anthrōpou*, "of (a) man" has the article ("the") in the Greek. Note Revelation 21:17 where "144 cubits by human measurement" (lit. "by measure [*metron*] of man [*anthrōpou*]") offers a useful parallel. Perhaps what is involved at 13:18 is that the number 666 encapsulates the number system employed in the everyday financial bustle of human endeavor in John's day, the system introduced to the Mediterranean world and its environs by the Roman Empire and its head, a (human!) beast.

As noted previously, the mark on the hand or forehead may be symbolic or non-literal (13:16-17; cf. 14:9, 11; 7:3-4; 14:1; Eze 9:4-6) but the DCLXVI (666) here may represent markings (financial records) that were all too visible for those "in business" with the beast and his system.

To be clear, the actual terms used in Revelation are the three Greek words "600" (+) "60" (+) "6," spelled out: *hexakosioi hexēkonta hex* (alternately represented by the Greek numerals χ [600] ξ [60] ς [6]).

However, the everyday reality of 666 visualized in the Roman world would have been the numerical inventory DCLXVI. "Mystery" solved?

The "Mortal Wound" and the "Is Not" Phase

John's mention of the "mortal wound" most likely relates to the beast as a whole, namely the Roman Empire,

---

Also depicted in ancient artwork were larger "counting tables" upon which even more involved calculations could be achieved. The ancient Roman abacus, along with its more recent counterparts, was held in the left hand as the right hand (the one "marked" in Revelation!) performed the necessary calculation.

since the individual emperors are also viewed by John as heads upon the beast (17:3, 7, 9). The mortal wound of the empire coincided with the death of the emperor Nero and its chaotic aftermath.

As noted later in Chapter XVIII, I take Nero to be the fifth king who was fallen, followed by the brief "is not" phase of the empire, i.e., the frightful ensuing civil unrest and political turmoil (17:8-11). Vespasian (the sixth king) and his sons (kings seven and eight) healed the wound, restoring and revitalizing the empire, and the Roman world "marveled." John explains, however, that the revival of the beast is temporary: the beast will rise only to go to its destruction (17:8, 11). There is only one "eternal city" and it is not Rome.

Regarding the land beast or "false prophet" (16:13; 19:20; 20:10), Revelation 13 here depicts the practice of emperor worship that increased dramatically in the last half of the first century in the eastern, Greek-dominated sector of the empire centered in Roman Asia (Asia Minor). This region was the location of Revelation's "Seven Churches of Asia." The following section briefly examines the importance of the Roman imperial cult for the book of Revelation.

The False Prophet

Many modern commentators point to the burgeoning imperial cult in the eastern provinces of the first-century Roman Empire as the historical reality behind the actions of the false prophet or beast from the land. Much has been written about this so-called imperial cult (e.g., Friesen, Hemer, Thompson, Wood). It goes too far to suggest that the focus of Revelation is anti-imperial or anti-Roman. Shane Wood has offered the term "alter-imperial" (*The*

Alter-Imperial Paradigm: Empire Studies and the Book of Revelation). As Wood had noted throughout his work, the focus of Revelation is not the destruction of the Roman Empire, but the creation of an alternate empire, the kingdom of God. Rome is not the primary enemy in the book. Satan is.

The Greek cities of the eastern portion of the empire promoted the worship of emperors and they sought the honor of hosting temples dedicated to leaders both dead and alive. As previously noted, benefits flowed in both directions as local officials honored rulers while rulers bestowed blessings to loyal subjects through a royal patron-client arrangement. Backs were scratched in both directions.

In addition, emperors shared honor with deities in these temples and thus politics and religion were intimately intertwined. Among the seven churches of Asia in Revelation, Smyrna, Pergamum, and Ephesus stood out as hosts of provincial temples devoted to the honor of Roman emperors.

Worship of the image of the beast from the sea was demanded by the false prophet, also designated as the beast from the land (13:11-15), and loyalty to the (sea-)beast could also be measured by the subjects' participation in the established socio-economic order, including trade guilds and other associations in which ancillary pagan worship would have been prevalent and expected. Little agreement has been reached regarding any literal, historical basis for the mark on the right hand or forehead required for one's "buying and selling" in the market place (13:16-17; cf. 7:3; 14:1).

The mark on the forehead described in a vision in Ezekiel 9, a vision in connection with the 586 BC destruction of Jerusalem, seems to have been spiritual, not physical. Less certain is the nature of the markings described in these enigmatic words from the "new Ezekiel" in Revelation. What is clear in Revelation is the sharp distinction between those marked in this manner (14:9-11) and those who bear the seal of God on their foreheads (7:3; 14:1; 22:4).

A much-discussed question is whether the descriptions of persecution in Revelation fit best with the time of Nero or that of Domitian. The descriptions in fact could fit either. However, the intense persecution under Nero was limited in both time and scope, primarily involving Nero's brutal attacks that made the Christians in Rome scapegoats for the devastating fire of AD 64. The memory of these atrocities against Christians would have lived on for decades, so an audience during either emperor's time is possible.

Widespread persecutions are not spelled out in the ancient records involving Domitian's reign, but clues do exist for such a circumstance of intense tribulation and opposition. Domitian encouraged a culture of fear, promoting the actions of spies and informants against his various targets, as numerous ancient historians relate after his death.

The famous correspondence between the emperor Trajan (AD 98-117) and Pliny the Younger, governor of Bithynia in Roman Asia (AD 111-113), describes a slightly later situation in which Christians are in grave danger if they are exposed to the Roman authorities by their coworkers, neighbors, or associates (for excerpts see Barr, 166-169). The emperor's instructions emphasize that there is not to be an organized, official attempt at rooting out the Christian elements in society, *but* if certain individuals are brought to the attention of those in charge and if such individuals are unwilling to deny Christ and offer worship to the emperor, they are to be summarily executed.

To be clear: the penalty for any accused of being Christians who did not deny such charges was death! This precarious situation had existed apparently for several decades and very possibly had been initiated during the time of Domitian. A picture of danger and persecution around the end of the first century and soon after is strikingly painted, therefore, but the details are fuzzy. Any claim that Revelation could not have come from the time of Domitian since there was no intense persecution at that time should be dismissed.

Conditions described in the correspondence between Trajan and Pliny were sobering for the Christian community, one at great risk. The impression from the exhortations in Revelation is that, whatever had transpired by the time of writing, more was to come.

The Identity of the Beast Revisited

Both the beast and the false prophet are cast into the lake of fire at Christ's second coming (Rev 19:20) and thus apparently have continued their efforts throughout the church age (as the eighth head of the beast [17:11] and its religious support system?). Governments and false religions will bolster one another throughout this entire period; opposition to the Bible and the gospel will come from both until Christ's return. So how do we best wrap our heads around Revelation's (sea-) beast?

Appendix A will develop the thesis that the designation "man of lawlessness" in 2 Thessalonians 2:1-12 described the Jewish leadership in connection with the Jewish Revolt of AD 66-70. In harmony with Jesus' teachings in the Olivet Discourse concerning the destruction of Jerusalem and its temple (Matthew 24; Mark 13; Luke 21), Paul affirms that Christ will not return until the lawless one who takes control of the Jewish temple arrives on the scene. This evildoer will seek to manipulate his Jewish followers through various signs and wonders.

Jesus had prophesied that the destruction of Jerusalem would occur within a single generation (e.g., Mt 24:32-35). Paul's words allow that as well since no timeframe is given by him for the arrival of the man of lawlessness. All Paul affirms is that this evil personage must come before the return (*parousia*, "presence, coming") of Jesus as described throughout the Thessalonian letters. How much before is not stated. If Paul's words in 2 Thessalonians 2 are understood as an oracle in reference to the AD 70 fall of Jerusalem, then the arrival of the man of lawlessness and the subsequent second coming of Christ have in fact been separated by a significant period of time.

It should be noted that John's teaching on the "antichrist" had little in common with Paul's teaching on the man of lawlessness. In the books 1 and 2 John we find references to the antichrist and, more specifically, the spirit of antichrist. Involved here is no military conflict or acute persecution of the church, but rather a theological heresy in which some denied that Jesus had come in the flesh or that Jesus was in fact God's Messiah (1Jn 2:22; 4:2; 2Jn 7).

In spite of the majority opinion (or assumption) of Bible teachers and preachers, Paul's man of lawlessness and John's antichrist are separate, mostly unrelated entities. As well, Revelation's beast shows little similarity to either Paul's man of lawlessness or John's antichrist figure!

The oft-assumed equation "antichrist" = "man of lawlessness" = "beast" needs rethinking. A number of commentators, including prominent, highly-regarded scholars, regularly use the terms interchangeably. A discussion about the beast of Revelation is assumed to be a discussion about the antichrist or the man of lawlessness ("man of sin" KJV).

However, a closer look suggests little about the beast of Revelation that corresponds with either the man of lawlessness or the antichrist. The beast is no theologian or heretic and never set up headquarters in the Jerusalem temple (*naos*, i.e., holy place or holy of holies). The antichrist is not said to have any political or military connections or supernatural miraculous powers. His domain of influence is church doctrine and belief.

Paul's man of lawlessness sits in the temple of God and brings about the destruction of those who mistakenly follow him. No church doctrine is debated. In fact in 2 Thessalonians 2:1-12 there is no mention of the church at all, persecuted or otherwise. Consequently, the above assumed three-fold equation may actually refer to three entities that have little in common with one another. Broad assumptions and speculations have long taken center stage in the discussion concerning the man of lawlessness, the antichrist, and the beast.

The general conclusion here is that the beast refers to human governance that opposes God and His righteous kingdom. Demonic influence may certainly be involved. The beast arrives as an opponent of the church with the rise of the Roman Empire and the title "beast" refers generally to the empire as a whole. The individual rulers of Rome, such as Augustus and Nero, are the heads. The "eighth head" mentioned by John suggests that the "seven-headed beast" is complicated indeed!

The eighth head in some sense belonged to the seven and would go to destruction, apparently at Christ's return. Before then, however, the beast (Rome under Vespasian?) destroys the Great Harlot (Jerusalem?) and thus carries out

God's purpose in the matter (17:16-17). Room is left here in John's visionary computation for an eighth head, a future manifestation of the beast, one that derives from the seven but will ultimately be destroyed by God's power and purposes in due time.

Does this eighth head represent a single ruler (Domitian?) or could it comprise a sequence or series of rulers, Roman or otherwise (Domitian and successors?)?

Since the beast and the false prophet are destroyed at Christ's return, it would seem that the manifestation of these anti-Christ forces began with Rome's antagonism and that the ancient empire's opposition to the church was but the initial stage of a continuing spiritual conflict that awaits final resolution at the second coming.

The entire church age is in view, as already suggested in previous mentions of the symbolic "three-and-a-half" (year) period of opposition and protection—the "forty-two months," "1,260 days," and "time, times, and half a time"—that seems to span the time between Christ's first and second comings.

Chapter XV

The Harvest of the Earth (Rev 14)

Following the introduction of the beast and the false prophet, Revelation turns to a series of scenes involving the 144,000 who were sealed from wrath, three angels flying overhead with distinct announcements concerning God's judgment, and two scenes of judgment utilizing the metaphor of a great harvest. These are followed by a worship scene (Revelation 15) that transitions into the description of the outpouring of the seven bowls of God's wrath (Revelation 16).

144,000 Redeemed from the Earth

Revelation 7 earlier introduced 144,000 sealed from the tribes of the sons of Israel who escaped the outpouring of God's wrath announced by the seven trumpets. It was suggested above that the 144,000 servants of God with the seal of God represented symbolically the same group mentioned immediately afterwards, a great multitude no one could number from every nation, tribe, people, and language. This multitude that stands before the throne and the Lamb and worships God had come out of the "great tribulation" and now serves God before His throne in heaven.

The further description of the 144,000 in Revelation 14 would seem to support the notion that the two groups mentioned in Revelation 7 are the same. In Revelation 14, the 144,000 who have the name of the Lamb's Father written on their foreheads sing before the throne in heaven a new song (14:1-3). These 144,000 had been redeemed from the earth. They are pure and undefiled, blameless (14:5), and had been redeemed as "first fruits for God and the Lamb" (14:4).

The mention of the fact that they are "virgins" has been explained in several ways. It is perhaps best to understand that, in light of the overarching theme of spiritual warfare present in the book, the 144,000, likely mustered in Revelation 7 as a military force (corresponding to the common OT purpose for a census), are engaged in "holy war" and thus are to abstain from sexual relations (Deu 23:9-11).

In another vein, Jesus had said that in the resurrection the redeemed would be like the angels, neither marrying nor given in marriage (Mt 22:30; Mk 12:25; Lk 20:34-36). Perhaps the contrast is being offered here between the purity of the 144,000 and the improper sexual behavior of the fallen angels mentioned in popular apocryphal Jewish texts like the book of Enoch.

Either way, the key parallel for our purposes is that both the unnumbered multitude from every nation in Revelation 7 and the 144,000 mentioned again at Revelation 14 worship before the throne and follow the Lamb (7:9-12, 15-17; 14:1-4). They are redeemed by the blood of the Lamb, sealed from divine wrath, and are faithful overcomers in tribulation.

These 144,000 are offered in stark contrast to those who follow the beast and the false prophet. While the wicked bear the mark of the beast ("the name of the beast or the number of its name"; 13:17), the 144,000 have the Lamb's name and His Father's name written on their foreheads (14:1). The former will face God's outpouring of wrath in judgment (14:9-11); the latter have been redeemed from the earth (14:3).

Three Angelic Messages

Three angels flying overhead address the theme of judgment from several vantage points (14:6-11). In view of God's impending judgment upon the world, the first angel proclaims "an eternal gospel" to all who dwell on the earth. The hope is that all will respond by giving God glory (14:6-7; cf. 11:7; 12:11). A second angel announces the fall of Babylon: "Fallen, fallen is Babylon the great, she who made all nations drink the wine of the passion of her sexual immorality" (14:8). This is the first of six mentions of Babylon in Revelation (14:8; 16:19; 17:5; 18:2, 10, 21). In all references apart from 18:10 we read the words "Babylon the great." At 18:10, we read, "Alas! Alas! You great city, you mighty city, Babylon! For in a single hour your judgment has come."

In Revelation 17, we learn that the fall of Babylon the Great will come at the hands of the beast and its ten horns. They will come to hate the prostitute who is named "Babylon the great" and in their destroying her will carry out the purposes of God for divine judgment (17:16-17).

Since this Babylon will be destroyed by the beast and his armies while the beast himself, along with his armies and the false prophet, is subsequently destroyed by Christ riding a white horse and leading the armies of heaven at His return (19:11-21), it seems apparent that the fall of Babylon is not a part of the second coming but rather precedes it in an earlier historical outpouring of judgment. While many commentators point to ancient Rome as the Great Harlot of the book of Revelation (Chapter XVII), I will make a case for Jerusalem as that figure (Chapter XVIII).

The third angel returns to the topic of final judgment with an emphasis upon the wicked. Those who follow the beast will drink the wine of God's wrath (14:9-10). Their torment will be endless (14:11). The debate regarding eternal suffering versus some form of annihilation as being taught in Scripture has been ongoing and vigorously contested. Committed conservative Christians can be found on both sides of the issue.

A detailed investigation is beyond the scope of the present work. Arguments involve how to understand various terms translated "destruction" and "punishment," and expressions like "eternal" and "forever." Relevant texts illustrate the complexities of these and related issues (Mt 8:12; 22:13; 25:30, 46; Mk 9:43-49; Lk 13:28; 16:19-31; Isa 34:8-12; 66:22-24; Jude 7). "Weeping and gnashing of teeth" is a frequent refrain in the Gospels.

It is true that the term "destroy" does not always mean "annihilate," but it is also true that "eternal punishment" may not necessarily indicate unending conscious torment. The key text in Revelation 14 is replete with symbols that depict a horrific reality for those who follow the "beast," a reality that will likely be shared by other unconverted "earth dwellers" through the ages. One might assume that followers of the beast here represent all who ever reject Christ, but that is not completely clear.

And another angel, a third, followed them, saying with a loud voice, "If anyone worships the beast and its image and receives a mark on his forehead or on his hand, ¹⁰he also will drink the wine of God's wrath, poured full strength into the cup of his anger, and he will be tormented with fire and sulfur in the presence of the holy angels and in the presence of the Lamb. ¹¹And the smoke of their torment goes up forever and ever, and they have no rest, day or night, these worshipers of the beast and

*its image, and whoever receives the mark of its name." (Rev
14:9-11)*

We note arguably figurative elements involving
receiving a mark on the hand or forehead, drinking from
the cup of wrath, tormented with fire and sulfur, the eternal
smoke of torment, etc. Any potentially figurative
descriptions of eternal punishment do not cancel out the
realities involved, but they may serve to warn us about
being overly literal in our perception of matters. Related
language elsewhere may suggest a more nuanced
understanding of specific images and descriptions. What
does Jude 7 signify when it states that ancient Sodom and
Gomorrah serve "as an example by undergoing a
punishment of eternal fire?" Similar language was employed
by Isaiah in describing the destruction of the kingdom of
Edom, a destruction with extensive, long-lasting
consequences but not one that could in any way be taken
as literally "eternal."

*For the Lord has a day of vengeance, a year of recompense for
the cause of Zion. ⁹And the streams of Edom shall be turned
into pitch, and her soil into sulfur; her land shall become
burning pitch. ¹⁰Night and day it shall not be quenched; its
smoke shall go up forever. From generation to generation it shall
lie waste; none shall pass through it forever and ever. ¹¹But the
hawk and the porcupine shall possess it, the owl and the raven
shall dwell in it. He shall stretch the line of confusion over it,
and the plumb line of emptiness. ¹²Its nobles—there is no one
there to call it a kingdom, and all its princes shall be nothing.
(Isa 34:8-12)*

Edom did not burn "forever." As has been repeatedly
noted, "forever" language in Scripture, often involving the
expression "unto the age" in both Hebrew (*le°olam*) and

Greek (*eis ton aiōna*), along with related expressions, frequently conveys an understood limitation. The OT priesthood, land promises, and temple all involved "forever" language that came to be understood as conditional and/or tied to the relevant dispensation under consideration (e.g., Ex 40:15; Num 25:13; Gen 13:14-17; 2Chr 7:16). Regarding the nature of divine punishment in Scripture both prophetic and eschatological texts carry enough warning signs concerning the need to distinguish between literal and figurative language or at least to recognize the potential presence of either (also see Appendix C). Note Beale's thorough assessment of the evidence regarding 14:9-11 (*Revelation*, 758-765).

In Revelation 14, John (or the angel) adds that this message calls for endurance and faithful obedience (14:12). No one would want the fate of those who worship the beast. A further voice from heaven offers encouragement and comfort in a blessing upon all who die in the Lord from that point forward (14:13).

Two Harvest Scenes

The theme of harvest is a common metaphor in Scripture for judgment (Jer 8:20; 51:33; Hos 6:11; Joel 3:13; Mt 9:38; 13:30-39; Jn 4:35). The nature of the distinction between the two harvest judgments described in Revelation 14 is debated. It is unlikely, most agree, that both of these accounts are describing the same thing.

One distinction often made is that the first harvest account describes the harvesting of the righteous. This harvest is done by one sitting on a cloud looking "like a son of man" with a "golden crown on his head" and a "sharp sickle in his hand" (14:4). This one "like a son of man" is told to reap the earth for the harvest is fully ripe. He who sits on the cloud swings his sickle across the earth and the earth is reaped (14:15-16). The language describing this figure brings to mind the messianic "one like a son of man" language of Daniel 7:13 and naturally has prompted the popular conclusion that this is Christ Himself in Revelation 14 and no mere angel.

Another angel with a sharp sickle is then called upon to reap a harvest as well. This angel is said to have "authority over the fire" of the altar and his harvest involves gathering grape clusters from the vine of the earth "for its grapes are ripe" (14:17-18). This great harvest of grapes is thrown "into the great winepress of the wrath of God" (14:9). The grape harvest, therefore, is seen to be a harvest of judgment upon the wicked.

Although the great winepress of judgment described here could have reference to final judgment, as does the judgment of the righteous described immediately above, a number of commentators, especially those who espouse some form of preterism, argue that here we have a description of the AD 70 destruction of Jerusalem. AD 70 is seen elsewhere in Revelation by both preterists and some non-preterists. For non-preterists AD 70 could be viewed as a judgment that has *already* occurred, along with other past events described in some of John's visions. This past judgment upon ancient Jerusalem is possibly found, e.g., at Revelation 11:13; 14:8, 17-20; 16:17-21; 17:1-19:2. Opinions differ greatly on this. Passages need to be analyzed on a case-by-case basis.

Here at Revelation 14 the wrath of God results in blood flowing from the winepress which was trodden "outside the city." The mention of "outside the city" is suggestive of Jerusalem. Hebrews notes that in bringing about eternal redemption Jesus suffered "outside the gate"

(Heb 13:12) and "outside the camp" (Heb 13:13). In Jesus' day criminals were crucified outside the city.

John further writes that the blood "flowed from the winepress, as high as a horse's bridle, for 1,600 stadia" (14:20). The dimension 1,600 stadia (approx. 184 miles) may be an approximation of the length of Palestine, or Israel's territory, as perhaps measured from the coastal city of Tyre in the north to the border of Egypt in the south (Beale, *Revelation*, 782). The graphic reference to blood as high as a horse's bridle is figurative and has close, numerous parallels in Jewish apocalyptic and rabbinic literature (Bauckham, *Climax*, 40-48).

It is possible that both the announcement of the second angel regarding "Babylon the great" and the second description of harvest/judgment "outside the city" in Revelation 14 (14:8, 17-20) have reference to AD 70.

Chapter XVI

The Seven Bowls and Plagues (Rev 15-16)

A worship scene featuring the victorious redeemed in heaven transitions into the outpouring of wrath performed by seven angels with seven golden bowls (Rev 15:1-8). As God's wrath is poured out of these bowls, one of the angels proclaims the just nature of these divine judgments. Those who have shed the blood of saints and prophets deserve their miserable fate (16:5-7).

Parallel Plagues

The parallels between the plagues of the seven bowls (Revelation 16) and of the sounding of the seven trumpets (Revelation 8-9) have been previously noted (Chapter X). Here it can be observed that the similarities between these outpourings and the previous plagues of Egypt in Exodus 7-12 are enhanced by the reference to the saints' singing "the song of Moses" (Rev 15:3; Ex 15:1-18) and the reference to "the tent of witness" located in heaven (Rev 15:5; Acts 7:44).

Clearly the trumpet plagues of 8:6-9:21 transpire *after* the events of Revelation 11-13 (events involving, among other things, the arrival of the beast), as do the later bowl plagues, but the extent of time between the seven trumpet plagues and the seven bowl plagues of 16:1-21, if any, is unclear.

On one hand, the intensity of plagues seems to increase from the trumpet plagues to the bowl plagues but, on the other hand, the nature and ordering of the plagues are quite similar. For example, the sixth trumpet plague involves a terrifying threat from across the great Euphrates River (9:13-21) as does the sixth bowl plague (16:12-16). The Parthian Empire east of the Euphrates was one of the greatly feared entities during the early Roman Empire. The Euphrates to the east was a protective barrier against upheaval and chaos. Massive armies crossing it signaled a worst-case scenario.

An overlooked common feature of the two series of plagues is the emphasis upon the unrepentant nature of the sufferers. In Revelation 9 in connection with the sixth trumpet we read,

The rest of mankind, who were not killed by these plagues, did not repent of the works of their hands nor give up worshiping demons and idols of gold and silver and bronze and stone and wood, which cannot see or hear or walk, 21nor did they repent of their murders or their sorceries or their sexual immorality or their thefts. (Rev 9:20-21)

Revelation 16 continues the theme. After the pouring out of the fourth bowl of wrath we are told, "They did not repent and give him glory" (16:9); and after the fifth bowl's being poured out we read, "They did not repent of their deeds" (16:11). Often commentators speak about the redemptive purpose of these plagues but I believe this is misguided. The emphasis is not upon the opportunity to repent but upon the fact that, in spite of these displays of God's wrath, those who are the objects of that deserved wrath are unwilling to change, unrepentant to the end.

The plagues accompanying the blowing of the seven trumpets and those accompanying the pouring out of the bowls of wrath are at the heart of what is perhaps the most confusing aspect of the imagery in Revelation. Some would carve out a three-and-a-half-year or even seven-year interval during which these plague sequences might occur.

Traditional historicists have tried to locate these plagues within the history of the church, while strict preterist scholars attempt to connect all of these judgments with the AD 70 destruction of Jerusalem. Tied to this whole issue is the topic of imminence. Can Christ return at any moment ("soon") or must certain dramatic signs unfold before the second coming? How can there be extensive, repeated warning signs if Jesus is to come like a thief in the night?

By way of review, in Revelation, Christians are not protected from experiencing the tribulation of persecution but rather from the outpouring of God's wrath upon non-believers. It is greatly confusing when some use the term "tribulation" or "great tribulation" to describe God's wrath toward the wicked. John shared in the "tribulation" with the recipients of his message (1:9) and much of the NT stresses the importance for the faithful to persevere under tribulation (*thlipsis*).

Paul spoke of the tribulations believers must endure (1Th 1:6) and of "the wrath to come" awaiting unbelievers (1Th 1:10). The key question for us to consider briefly here is the general nature and timing of the two major cycles of seven in the book: the seven trumpets and the seven bowls. How do they fit in regarding the future?

The descriptions of those suffering the effects of the plagues in connection with the trumpets and the bowls offer some clues. The picture in Revelation 7-9, 11:15-19, and 15-16 is of the judgment of the wicked. God's servants are protected from the coming wrath (7:1-8), and others who are not are either killed in the plagues or, as is emphasized throughout, refuse to repent (9:20, 21; 16:8, 11). The key here is that believers are not affected by these plagues, only the unrighteous "destroyers of the earth" (11:18).

How much time elapses between the beginning of the plagues and the actual return of Christ? The answer does not come from these texts directly. The concern stated in the text is more the frightful fate of the "earth dwellers" who have chosen to follow the beast and not the Lamb.

The only indication within the descriptions of the plagues that a significant time sequence may be involved is the mention of the tormenting "for five months" by locusts that seem like scorpions. However, many commentators suggest that this imagery builds upon the length of the lifecycle of the locust and that the power to "hurt people for five months" should not be taken literally (9:10). That makes sense. The very descriptions of the locusts direct us to a non-literal approach: their looking like horses; the appearance of crowns of gold on their heads; human faces with women's hair and lions' teeth; breastplates resembling iron; the sounds resembling chariots and horses rushing into battle (9:7-9). Scary and bizarre—right in line with much of ancient apocalyptic literature.

Other symbolic numbers in Revelation point us to realities behind the numerical imagery, as already noted. We find instances and multiples of twelve (12) in connection with the New Jerusalem: 12 tribes, 12 gates, 12 foundations stones, the 12 apostles, dimensions for the length, width, and height of the city as 12,000 stadia each, the city wall of 144 (12-by-12) cubits, and 12 kinds of fruit on the tree of life. Also we see the use of seven (7) and its multiples throughout the book: e.g., the Lamb has 7 horns and 7 eyes and these eyes are the 7 spirits of God, which in turn represent the Holy Spirit. There are 7 churches, 7 seals, 7 trumpets, 7 thunders, 7 bowls poured out; 7,000 die in connection with the fall of the great city symbolically called "Sodom." The symbolism of three and a half (half of 7) has been discussed at length above. The mention of "a thousand years" in Revelation 20 has been alluded to frequently and will be focused upon later regarding that chapter.

The need to interpret the expression "five months" literally, then, is not based upon the general impression gleaned from Revelation's vision imagery. The same is likely true for the "ten days" tribulation that Christians at Smyrna are told some will suffer (2:10), the "single day" (18:8) or "single hour" (18:10, 17, 19) in which "Babylon" falls, or the "half an hour" of silence following the opening of the seventh seal (8:1).

The book of Revelation contains numerous references to the second coming, and the trumpet plagues and bowl plagues likely fit into the book's picture of the end. Whatever events transpire leading up to or in connection with the visible return of Christ, once they begin it will be too late for them to serve as any kind of warning. Perhaps the closest to what we find in Revelation comes from Luke's account of Jesus' teaching in the Olivet Discourse regarding Christ's return:

> *And there will be signs in sun and moon and stars, and on the earth distress of nations in perplexity because of the roaring of the sea and the waves, [26]people fainting with fear and with foreboding of what is coming on the world. For the powers of the heavens will be shaken. [27]And then they will see the Son of Man coming in a cloud with power and great glory. [28]Now when these things begin to take place, straighten up and raise your heads, because your redemption is drawing near. (Lk 21:25-28)*

Whatever impact these developments will have, followers of Christ have been sealed and are safe from the outpouring of God's wrath upon the world. The present heavens and earth are stored up for fire that will be unleashed when God judges the world and destroys the ungodly (2Pet 3:7). The faithful await life upon a new earth, however that new earth may come into being and however God may purge the old of all impurity (2Pet 3:11-13). However long it will take.

Disaster at "Armageddon"

The sixth bowl of wrath involves the final conflict with the dragon, the beast, the false prophet, and their followers (16:12-16). The fact that this is not a true battle at all, but rather a metaphoric expression of divine judgment, is confirmed by the parenthetical words of Jesus: "Behold, I am coming like a thief! Blessed is the one who stays awake, keeping his garments on, that he may not go out naked and be seen exposed" (16:15). Being ready for what comes is the focus. Note that the conflict anticipated at 16:12-16 is the same second coming "battle" that is described in Revelation 19:11-21 and likely also in 20:7-10.

The name "Armageddon" has prompted much debate and discussion but, again, there is no literal battle that takes place there, wherever "there" is! The name seems to come from Hebrew *har Megiddo*, the hill of Megiddo, and refers to a city that occupied a strategic spot in ancient Palestine. The main road for any major movements, especially those including armies and their supplies, went past Megiddo in order to reach the wide, open Valley of Jezreel connecting east from west in the region. Control of that overlook of this key road connecting Egypt with much of the rest of the world was crucial.

Egyptian Pharaoh Thutmose III (fifteenth c. BC) celebrated a famous victory there. According to him, "Taking Megiddo is like capturing a thousand cities!" In other words, an extremely strategic site! Also, good King Josiah was tragically killed at Megiddo in a battle with Egypt (2Kgs 23:28-30).

Revelation's choice of terminology here makes perfect sense. Battle imagery was common prophetic language employed for divine judgment (e.g., Joel 3), especially since God time and again actually used warfare to punish His people for their unfaithfulness, as repeatedly evidenced in the book of Judges and later experienced at the hands of major powers like Assyria and Babylon—see, e.g., Hosea, Amos, Jeremiah, Habakkuk.

Devastation of the "Great City"

At the pouring out of the seventh bowl (16:17) the greatest earthquake ever causes "the great city" to split into three parts. In this event "God remembered Babylon the great" by pouring out His wrath (16:18-19). Great hailstones "about 100 pounds each" fell from heaven on people and they cursed God because of this plague of hail (16:21). The Greek term translated "about 100 pounds each" is *talantiaios*, "weighing a talent." The same term is used by Josephus in describing the huge stones hurled by the catapults of Rome's tenth legion against Jerusalem (*War* 5.269-274). Initially the stones, having a bright white appearance, could be spotted by the Jews and be avoided. Eventually, the Romans darkened the stones so that they would be less visible and more deadly.

The city being split into three parts suggests another Ezekiel connection in that God spoke to Ezekiel of the fate of Jerusalem's inhabitants in his day thus: a third part of

Jerusalem would die of pestilence and famine; a third part would die by the sword during the Babylonian invasion; and a third part would be scattered to all the winds where the sword would still find them (Eze 5:12). Preterist commentators on Revelation often point to three rival factions that comprised and as well compromised Jerusalem's defenders during the AD 66-70 Jewish War. These factions participated in brutal, self-destructive infighting that Josephus described in detail.

In Zechariah 13 we may have another possible use of a "third" in reference to Jerusalem's fall. At the beginning of Revelation we find an allusion to Zechariah 12 (Rev 1:7): the inhabitants of Jerusalem, God remarkably says, will "look on me, on him whom they have pierced" (Zec 12:10). A few verses later in Zechariah we read of a fountain opened for the house of David and Jerusalem "to cleanse them from sin and uncleanness" (Zec 13:1).

Zechariah continues with descriptions of a Shepherd being stricken whose sheep are then scattered, a clear prophetic reference to Christ and His followers (Zec 13:7; Mk 14:49-50). Then in the land "two thirds shall be cut off and perish, and one third shall be left alive" (Zec 13:8). This remaining third is being tested and refined to prove its worth. As a result, God promises, "They will call upon my name, and I will answer them. I will say, 'They are my people'; and they will say, 'The Lord is my God'" (Zec 13:9).

Not all will embrace God's Shepherd. Israel's rejection of Him will spell the doom of Jerusalem and the nation. According to Zechariah, at some future juncture "two thirds" will be cut off as God's hand is turned against them (Zec 13:7-8).

It may seem odd that the sixth bowl brings us to the confrontation at the second coming while the seventh bowl may offer a figurative description of the fall of Jerusalem in AD 70. And yet the scene depicted in the sixth bowl is anticipatory. (Its eventual realization would come "soon" as would Jesus' return.) The awaited climactic "battle" at Christ's return does not occur until Revelation 19. Earlier the seventh trumpet brought us to final judgment as well (11:15-19) but several narrative interludes intervened.

Of the ten uses of the term "Almighty" (Greek: *pantokratōr*) in the NT, eight are found in Revelation. Two of them are clearly connected to the second coming. Revelation 16:14 calls that coming "the great day of God the Almighty." Revelation 19:15 speaks of "the wrath of God the Almighty" in connection with Jesus' arrival from heaven on a white horse to destroy His enemies.

In warning of that great day of judgment at the "battle of Armageddon," Jesus reminds "Behold, I am coming like a thief..." (16:15). This will be no typical "battle"! The "Jesus on the white horse" battle (19:11ff) and the "enemies assembled at Armageddon" battle (16:14-16) are the same climactic, symbolically expressed confrontation marking God's judgment of evildoers. In contrast, the extended description of judgment upon "Babylon the great" (16:17-18:24) seems to describe an outpouring of wrath *prior to* and *separate from* the events surrounding the second coming.

How so? A big clue is that the merchants of the world do not express fear for their own immediate safety but rather chagrin over the extensive revenues lost now because of the Great Harlot's demise (18:11-19). Such financial reversals would be meaningless in connection with Christ's return.

What is this outpouring of wrath bemoaned in Revelation 18 if it is not connected with the second coming? Many point to the fall of Rome in the fifth century

(AD 410 or 476?), while others suggest the fall of Jerusalem in the first century (AD 70). We will give particular attention to the Jerusalem option in what follows (esp. Chapter XVIII).

Chapter XVII

Babylon and the Beast (Rev 17-18)
Part 1: Identifying the Great Harlot

Revelation 17 serves as a stumbling block for many interpreters. Extremely important for the overall understanding of this great book, however, are the identifications of the "great prostitute" called "Babylon the great" and the "beast" with seven heads and ten horns that carries the harlot. It might make sense to some to "skip over the hard parts" and focus upon the more basic ideas of the book.

However, just as the saying "The devil's in the details" can ring true, the details can also serve the divine, helping Christ's church better grasp His message to them. Distinguishing important, informative details from eye-catching apocalyptic "window dressing" is no easy matter and clues along the way are welcome. Granted, it may be easy to lose the "big picture" when wrestling with striking, sometimes shocking, symbols and images. What is the important thing here, the key message?

For me, one guiding principle for the ensuing discussion is simple. Extensive details accompanied by a call for "wisdom" should not be glossed over (17:9; 13:18). These highlighted details are in fact part of the "big picture." They may very well be a key component.

Introductory Matters

Revelation 12 begins the narration of the conflict between the dragon and the Lamb while Revelation 13 shows the dragon summoning the beast from the sea to carry on his warfare with Christ and His church begun in the previous chapter. The links between Revelation 13 and Revelation 17 are many and are critical for understanding the overall message of the book. The beast suffers a "mortal wound" and yet lives. The healing of the mortal wound causes the whole world to marvel (13:3, 12). The mark of the beast and the identity of the beast are connected to the number 666.

John says that the identifying of this individual or entity "calls for wisdom" and involves some kind of calculation or insightful recognition (13:18). Another call for wisdom occurs at Revelation 17:9. The content of this later chapter involves a "mystery" regarding both the harlot and the beast (17:7).

Modern or Future Babylon as the Great Harlot

The need to take "Babylon" in Revelation as the literal city of Babylon is felt especially within dispensational circles. The Bible says what it means and means what it says, so it is argued. The problem of course is that Revelation is full of symbols and metaphors and we find, e.g., "Sodom" and "Egypt" as apparent designations for Jerusalem, "where their Lord was crucified" (11:8).

Interest in Babylon in Iraq held sway during the years Saddam Hussein kept power but has lessened in more recent years for obvious reasons! The future is always full of surprises, but the future ascendancy of Babylon in the Middle East to a position of eventual world domination, as

191

some today envision, represents a future difficult to embrace. Any such "faith" position needs to be grounded in clear Bible teaching, not just in overly charged speculation.

The Papacy (Ancient, Medieval, and Modern "Rome") as the Great Harlot

One popular view among many Protestant commentators has been the "papacy view" in which the Roman pope is equated with the end-times antichrist of Revelation (remembering that Revelation never uses the term "antichrist," but rather the "beast").

From Martin Luther and the Protestant Reformation, and even earlier, some form of the "papacy view" has persisted. In more recent years, however, it has diminished in appeal. Such a view represents a common element of an "historicist" approach in which the emergence of the Roman Catholic Church, the rise of Islam, the growth of modern ecclesiastical liberalism, and other developments are viewed as foreseen in John's visions.

The candidates regarded as fulfillments of Bible prophecy throughout the Christian era are seemingly endless. This alone should warrant caution. Fewer and fewer more recent commentaries, especially technical ones, embrace the view that the papacy is being targeted in Revelation. The overall historicist approach in general has been in steady decline.

Ancient Rome as the Great Harlot

A popular view today regarding Babylon the Harlot in Revelation 17-18 is that ancient Rome, or the Roman Empire, is the harlot who "rides the beast" (17:3). This view is held among conservative and liberal scholars alike. The arguments for this view are persuasive, especially in light of the importance of Rome in connection with the rise of persecution against Christians, a major focus of the book.

Whether we think of the atrocities against Christians in Rome at the hands of Nero or the climate of opposition and persecution that was surely present during Domitian's reign, Rome's persecution of Christians was a first-century reality, one that would persist and increase in the several centuries that followed.

As previously suggested, Rome or Roman hegemony makes the best candidate for the beast that rose out of the sea (13:1). And with respect to compelling imagery, the conceptual transition from the city goddess Roma to the prostitute "Babylon" is admittedly effortless. The immoralities, idolatries, and brutalities of the Roman Empire make it a logical candidate as the deserving recipient of the outpouring of God's wrath. This might very well be the correct approach, but some have voiced concerns regarding this identification.

I have strong reservations that will be explained below. One viable option is to equate ancient Jerusalem with the Great Harlot of Revelation 17-18. With this view, riding the beast suggests collaboration with the beast and certainly such collaboration was true of the Jewish leadership in Jerusalem, especially among the Sadducees and Herodians. The Jerusalem view will be explored following the critique of the Roman Empire view below.

In Revelation 17, an angel invites John to see the judgment of the Great Harlot but much of the "mystery" involved actually relates to the scarlet beast upon which the woman rides, not to the woman herself (17:5, 7). As noted earlier, that beast, like the great dragon (12:3), has seven heads and ten horns (13:1), and it bears blasphemous names

(17: 3). John is told that "a mind with wisdom" is needed for understanding the identities of the seven heads, which were seven rulers (17:9-11). Not inconsistent with apocalyptic imagery are the complexities involved.

The angel explains that the seven heads not only represent seven rulers but also seven mountains, mountains that almost all agree describe the ancient city of Rome. The problem that many seem to ignore is that since the Great Harlot rides upon the seven-headed beast, how can she be identified with Rome? Is not Rome or the Roman Empire itself the beast persecuting the church?

Perhaps the strict equation of the beast with Rome needs rethinking. The description of seven heads certainly presents its own interpretive challenges. Some would identify the beast as a demonic being who dwells in human rulers, and such an approach has some merit (e.g., McKenzie). And yet the empire itself seems to be a "beast." Perhaps the empire is only a beast when a particular ruler is controlled by this supernatural entity.

After the beast and his followers destroy the Great Harlot, the beast lives on (in some form) and ultimately will be destroyed by the Lamb at the second coming (17:14-17; 19:19-22). This would suggest that the beast is an entity not strictly limited to the activities of Rome or the Roman Empire, but one that will endure throughout history, perhaps taking on various manifestations. We might best view the beast in general as the demonic force or personage(s) behind anti-God human government in its various forms. The kingdom(s) of the beast and the kingdom of God are in direct conflict. One might argue that once the beast has finished his purposes for Rome, he allies himself with others (e.g., the Vandals, the Goths), later barbarian forces that overwhelm the increasingly vulnerable western Roman Empire.

With this approach, the beast could be perceived as an ongoing reality throughout the church age, summoned by the dragon in connection with his war against the righteous "woman" (the church) at the onset of the battle (12:1-13:4).

Apart from dispensationalism's alleged, unwarranted gap before 12:6 (skipping the church age!), the text seems to portray an ongoing conflict that began with the incarnation of Christ. The dragon's summons of the beast was a past event with continuing impact (12:17-13:8). Revelation makes clear the danger for Christians the beast presents (13:7-10).

That danger continues to this day. The church must be vigilant. There is no rationale from Revelation itself for placing the career of the beast in a post-rapture, post-church-age setting, no matter how appealing such a view might be to some. There is no escapism in John's message to the seven churches.

Having said the above, I do find the identification of the Great Harlot as Rome awkward. In what sense is Rome riding the beast? Apocalyptic language can be disorienting: an obscene woman rides upon a beast with seven heads, heads that represent the seven hills of Rome. The woman is said to be "drunk with the blood of the saints, the blood of the martyrs of Jesus" (17:6), while the beast, John earlier writes, "was allowed to make war on the saints and to conquer them" (13:7).

In other words, both the harlot and the beast are persecutors of the church. Pertinent questions would be whether or not these are separate entities and in what sense might they be related. The uncertainty involved is perhaps the uneasy product of the phenomenon of apocalyptic imagery, but questions persist.

A problem little discussed by commentators is the inappropriateness of the fall of ancient Rome as a fulfillment of the oracles in Revelation (16:19-21; 17:1-19:3). As will be outlined below, ancient Rome fell in the fifth century AD, and much had happened by then regarding Rome's relationship with the church.

The message from heaven to John was that the great city Babylon would be destroyed "in a single hour" (18:10, 17, 19; "in a single day," 18:8). Revelation's description of Babylon's violent fall emphasizes a deserved, catastrophic event and the description "in a single hour" describes a level of suddenness and finality. How does the fall of Rome fit in with such a description? Not very well, as we will now see.

The barbarians who sacked Rome were known by designations such as Vandals and Goths. We get our word vandalism from the former! The Goths, located in eastern Europe, were divided into the western Goths, the "Visigoths," and the eastern Goths, the "Ostrogoths." The Visigoths under their chieftain Alaric sacked Rome in AD 410. This attack marked the first arrival of a foreign army at the gates of Rome since Hannibal 625 years earlier. Soon after, in 412, Augustine of Hippo began writing his enduring classic *City of God*. In his work Augustine felt the need to explain that Rome did not fall in 410 because it had become Christianized, a claim made by some of the pagans of that time. More on that in a moment.

The Vandals who had earlier settled in Spain attacked North Africa and were laying siege to Hippo while Augustine lay dying there in 430. The Vandals took control of the western Mediterranean and in 455 they sacked Rome, plundering it worse than the Visigoths had 45 years previously (North, 112-114). But that was not all. German mercenaries led by Odovacar took over Rome in 476 and this is the oft-cited traditional date for the "fall of Rome." Jim North comments, "Actually little changed. Roman administration had been collapsing in the West for some decades...." (116).

Jaroslav Pelikan has provided a stimulating account of the fall of Rome and how both ancient writers and modern historians have approached the topic. [10] Highly recommended.

Among the works of ancient Christian authors those by Tertullian, Jerome, and Augustine will be briefly touched upon here. Tertullian was representative of those who viewed the welfare of Rome and of the world in general as intimately connected. Based on his understanding of the "man of lawlessness" in 2 Thessalonians 2 (but see Appendix A), Tertullian, labeled the first theologian of the Latin West, championed the view that the "restrainer" delaying the arrival of the "antichrist" was the Roman empire itself and he understood that the fall of Rome would signal the arrival of this antichrist. Thus Tertullian urged prayer for Rome to stave off "a mighty shock impending over the whole earth—in fact, the very end of all things..." (Pelikan, 47).

The great fourth-to-fifth-century biblical scholar Jerome held similar views. The end was being retarded only by Rome's continued existence. Rome, then, "was all that stood between the human race and the end of the world" (ibid., 46). Jerome's views of Rome had changed over the years. He could no longer gleefully cite Revelation 17 identifying Rome as Babylon the Harlot upon Rome's fall to Alaric in 410. He would acknowledge that in fact Rome "with the confession of Christ blotted out the blasphemy written on her forehead" (ibid., 51).

---

[10] See Jaroslav Pelikan, *The Excellent Empire: The Fall of Rome and the Triumph of the Church* (1987). Pelikan's work offers valuable insights concerning the relationship of the early church to Rome's fall.

Augustine, learned contemporary of Jerome in North Africa, penned his work *City of God* in the aftermath of Rome's 410 fall. Augustine's grief over the fall of Rome was profound. Part of his motivation in writing was to explain that Rome's fate was not the result of its acceptance of Christianity. He notes the remarkable fact of Alaric's sparing Christians who took refuge in the shrine of Peter and views such unprecedented restraint in warfare as a triumph of Christ and the church (ibid., 93). Roughly a century before Alaric's conquest of Rome, Constantine had converted to Christianity and upon becoming emperor transformed the dynamics of the empire's approach to that religion and to paganism.

Jim North estimated that in the century prior to the 410 sack of Rome the percentage of the Roman Empire that was Christian grew from about 10 percent to about 90 percent of the population (North, 69). A common view is that the number of Christians in that span grew from roughly three to four million to thirty million or more or roughly half of the empire's population (e.g., Ehrman, *Triumph*, 104, 170-173, 287-294). Whatever the precise number, the growth of Christianity in the Roman Empire during the years between Constantine's conversion and the 410 sack of Rome was remarkable.

All this is to say that the nature and timing of Rome's fall with respect to the prophecy regarding the fall of Babylon the Harlot is odd at best and troubling at worst. Of what benefit was the destruction of Rome over 300 years later when, in reality, it had now become a major center of Christianity and Christian influence in the ancient world? (I am not attempting here to specify what makes one a Christian.)

I concur with North that Constantine's conversion was genuine. Following his conversion, Constantine never again offered a sacrifice and he suppressed the attempt by the imperial cult to offer sacrifices to him (North, 63). I find little discussion in most conservative Christian commentaries about the awkwardness of such a delayed fulfillment of Revelation's condemnation of the Great Harlot.

As emperor, Constantine convened church councils to settle divisive theological issues (e.g., Nicaea, AD 325). The success of the church mattered deeply to him. His founding of Constantinople in the east in 330 as the new capital of the empire greatly diminished Rome's *political* significance. However, one thing that Rome had that Constantinople did not was its apostolic foundation and prestige in the Christian Mediterranean world. An eastern capital of the empire was created with Constantinople, in part, to allow Constantine fuller expression of Christian promotion as displayed in the many churches and shrines erected.

In advocating a reformed Rome's demise as an example of God's righteous wrath, some might suggest "too little, too late" regarding Rome's transformation—the die was cast—but one of the problems for theologians and historians regarding the fall of Rome must be the applicability of such a delayed destruction as a fulfillment of judgment in light of the transformative events that had occurred in regard to the church and Rome to that point.

In light of the remarkable changes the century previous, heaven's "Hallelujahs" in response to the fall of a fifth-century Rome ring a bit hollow for me (19:1-5). Additionally, as will now be further developed, if Rome's fall was a necessary precursor of Christ's return, the notion (doctrine) of imminence regarding Christ's coming goes out the window.

CHAPTER XVIII

BABYLON AND THE BEAST (REV 17-18)
PART 2: ANCIENT JERUSALEM AS
THE GREAT HARLOT

In spite of the issues outlined in the previous chapter, numerous commentators view the Great Harlot Babylon as ancient Rome. However, the view that Babylon the Harlot is Jerusalem also has its adherents and proponents, including strict preterist David Chilton, partial preterist Kenneth Gentry, and critical scholars such as Margaret Barker and J. Massyngberde Ford.

The following overview addresses the possibility of Jerusalem being the Great Harlot in light of the nature of the references to Jews, Israel, and Jerusalem seen throughout Revelation, in light of parallels in Ezekiel's prophecies and in other OT oracles of doom, and in light of the overall trajectory of Revelation 17.

This involves the "mystery" and "wisdom" related to the arrival, disappearance, and reappearance of the beast and its seven (also eight!) heads (17:7-11) and the tie-in of this with "the judgment of the great prostitute" (17:1, 16-17; 16:19-21).

The Name "Jerusalem"

The fact that the name "Jerusalem" is found only three times in Revelation is both surprising and potentially significant. In all three instances the reference has to do with the eternal New Jerusalem, not with the former Jewish capital (3:12; 21:2, 10), another fact worth noting. Within the storyline found in Revelation 11 the ancient earthly city Jerusalem is designated "the holy city," yet one trampled down by the Gentiles (11:2), and "the great city," yet one in which Jesus had been crucified (11:8).

The low esteem held for it in this vision is evidenced not only by the description of the evil perpetrated within it (11:7-12), but also by the dubious nomenclature granted it: "Sodom and Egypt" (11:8)! The prophet Isaiah had opened his magisterial work with a description of Jerusalem as a whore whom he called "Sodom" (Isa 1:10). And Ezekiel (him again!) reminded Jerusalem and Judah that their whorings had begun long ago in, you guessed it, Egypt (Eze 23:19-21, 27).

We find only sporadic references to Jerusalem as "the holy city" in both the OT (e.g., Neh 11:1, 18) and NT (Mt 4:5; 27:53; Rev 11:2) and several cases in Revelation where the New Jerusalem is termed "the holy city" (21:2, 10; 22:19). Referring to the despicable city described in Revelation 11 as "the holy city" may seem a bit odd since the same city is described as "the great city that symbolically is called Sodom and Egypt, where their Lord was crucified" (11:8). Perhaps the mention of the temple and its outer court played a role here in its designation (11:2; cf. Chapter XI).

Of greater interest is the fact that "the holy city" is also described here as "the great city." This initial use of that term in the book is followed by seven more (11:8; 16:19; 17:18; 18:10,16, 18, 19, 21). It is at least likely that the eight references to "the great city" all refer to the same city in Revelation. And that would be Jerusalem.

The book of Hebrews speaks of "the heavenly Jerusalem" as the present (as well as future) home of the redeemed, "the assembly of the firstborn who are enrolled in heaven" (Heb 12:22-23). In a sense, then, Christians "already" have a home in "Jerusalem." When Revelation speaks of Satan's final efforts to destroy God's people it describes an attempted attack upon "the camp of the saints and the beloved city" (20:9). These designations almost certainly refer to the church.

The extensive harlotry imagery employed in the OT prophets regarding Jerusalem (esp. in Isaiah, Jeremiah, Hosea, and Ezekiel) makes more than plausible the notion that John (our "new Ezekiel") might designate the apostate Jerusalem of his generation Babylon the Harlot. That idea is enhanced further by the intriguing fact that first-century Jerusalem is never designated "Jerusalem" in Revelation. Such a lacking aids the suggestion that in Revelation the unfaithful Jewish capital bears the special title "Babylon the great."

For Paul writing to the Galatians, the apostate Jerusalem of his day corresponded to Hagar the slave woman and to Mt. Sinai, both images reflecting Jerusalem's failure to embrace God's new covenant with His people (Gal 4:25). The son(s) of the slave woman persecuted the children of promise (Gal 4:29). Calling first-century Jerusalem "Babylon" in Revelation might not be that much of a stretch.

The Name "Israel"

In reviewing Revelation's approach to Israel and Jerusalem as a whole, it may further surprise some that the name "Israel" also occurs only three times in the book (2:14; 7:4; 21:12). One occurrence (2:14) is in reference to the pagan OT prophet Balaam son of Beor (Num 22-24; 31:8, 16); another describes the twelve gates of the New

Jerusalem as having the names of the tribes of the sons of Israel inscribed upon them (21:12). John also describes twelve foundations stones in the New Jerusalem bearing the names of the twelve apostles on them (21:14).

At Revelation 7:4, we find the name "Israel" in connection with 12,000 from each of the twelve tribes, thus 144,000. The debate continues as to whether these 144,000 refer to Israelite believers or to the followers of Christ in general. As previously noted (esp. Chapters X, XV), I take the latter view. I also hold that these 144,000 who are servants of God with seals on their foreheads are likely the same group described in the next few verses as a "great multitude" from all nations who come out of "the great tribulation" (7:9-14).

Here and elsewhere in Revelation we must distinguish between the wrath of God in judgment and the tribulation suffered at the hands of evildoers. The 144,000 are sealed from the effects of the wrath of God, while the great multitude may very well have suffered martyrdom in the tribulation promoted by the beast and the false prophet. Spiritual deliverance and physical suffering or death may be in contrast here, all pertaining to a single group. John says that he "heard the number of the sealed" (7:4) but that he *saw* the great multitude (7:9). Earlier, John had heard that the Lion of the tribe of Judah had conquered and was worthy to open the scroll and its seals, but when he looked, he saw a Lamb standing as though it had been slain (5:5-6).

Very possibly the 144,000 from "Israel" provide a military metaphor and the numbering serves as a census for God's army of faithful followers. Later in Revelation 14 the 144,000 are described as standing with the Lamb worshiping, singing a song that can only be learned by them. These 144,000 are described as having been "redeemed from the earth" (14:3). They have been "redeemed from mankind as first fruits for God and the Lamb" (14:4). The language here sounds a universal tone and suggests that the 144,000 represent the people of God as a whole, Jew and Gentile.

The Name "Jews"

The mention of the Jews in Revelation is instructive as well. The term "Jews" occurs but twice, each time in the letters to the churches (2:9; 3:9). Both references are strongly negative in that each Jewish synagogue mentioned is described as "a synagogue of Satan." Those in the synagogue who say they are Jews are lying. How so?

Some suggest that the Jews involved had harmed their fellowship with their synagogue through the violation of certain Jewish restrictions, but most likely they are involved with the persecution of the Christians in Smyrna and Philadelphia. The language of Revelation 3:9 contains an OT allusion involving reversal: what the OT promised that the Gentile world would eventually do for Israel, Jesus now tells the church that the Jews will someday do for them. "...behold, I will make them come and bow down before your feet, and they will learn that I have loved you" (3:9).

Revelation builds on Isaiah here. In vivid language Isaiah promised that in the future those who had afflicted Israel would pay homage to Israel (Isa 45:14; 49:23; 60:14). At Revelation 3:9, those who afflict God's people "Israel" are the Jews themselves, since the besieged church represents God's new "Israel." The role reversal outline is striking. Thus, the tone is set quite early in the book of Revelation regarding Christ's rejection of the false claims of Jews who had rejected Him as Messiah and Lord.

Revelation 11

Later chapters provide possible references to Jerusalem's judgment. The trampling of the holy city for forty-two months (11:2) seems to correspond to Jesus' language in the Olivet Discourse where He said "Jerusalem will be trampled underfoot by the Gentiles, until the times of the Gentiles are fulfilled" (Lk 21:24). At Revelation 11:13 we see a description of a great earthquake from which the "city" fell, likely Jerusalem (cf. "the holy city" [11:2]; "the great city" where Christ was crucified [11:8]).

Seven thousand are killed in the earthquake, a seeming reversal of the remnant concept in the OT in which seven thousand (a symbolic number) are left or spared (1Kgs 19:18; Rom 11:4). Here, however, it is the seven thousand, a partial representation, that are destroyed. Others seem to repent (cf. Chapter XI).

Revelation 14

Elsewhere, in a description of judgment involving a grape harvest, the wrath of God results in blood flowing from the winepress which was trodden "outside the city" (Chapter XV). The blood "flowed from the winepress, as high as a horse's bridle, for 1,600 stadia" (14:20).

The city mentioned here is very possibly Jerusalem, while the dimension 1,600 stadia (approx. 184 miles) is often viewed by commentators as an approximation of the length of Palestine or Israel's territory, perhaps measured from Tyre to the border of Egypt (Beale, *Revelation*, 782). The reference to blood as high as a horse's bridle is figurative and has numerous close parallels in Jewish apocalyptic and rabbinic literature (Bauckham, *Climax*, 40-48).

Revelation 16

At the pouring out of the seventh bowl (16:17) the greatest earthquake ever causes "the great city" to split into three parts. In this event "God remembered Babylon the great" by pouring out his wrath (16:18-19). Great hailstones "about 100 pounds each" fell from heaven on people and they cursed God because of this plague of hail (16:21).

The Greek term translated "about 100 pounds each" is *talantiaios*, "weighing a talent." As noted in Chapter XVI, the same term is used by Josephus in describing the huge stones hurled by the catapults of Rome's tenth legion against Jerusalem (*War* 5.269-274). Also consult Chapter XVI for the important connections with Ezekiel and especially Zechariah.

In Revelation 16, Jesus warns of that great day of judgment to transpire at the "battle of Armageddon" while reminding "Behold, I am coming like a thief..." (16:15). Strange battle! Clearly the language here is pointing to God's final judgment of evildoers at the second coming (16:14-16; 19:11ff.).

In contrast, the extended description of judgment upon "Babylon the great" (16:17-18:24) seems to describe an outpouring of wrath prior to and separate from the events surrounding the second coming. In connection with the giant "hailstones" falling from the sky (from catapults?) we read "...and they cursed God for the plague of the hail, because the plague was so severe" (16:21).

Such language perhaps could apply either to the destruction of Jerusalem or to the second coming "plagues" (cf. 16:1-11). However, later in the text the merchants of the world do not express fear for their own immediate safety but rather chagrin over the extensive revenues lost because of the Great Harlot's demise (18:11-19). This seems an unlikely statement in connection with the second coming.

What is this outpouring of wrath bemoaned in Revelation 18? Many point to the fall of Rome in the fifth century (AD 410? 476?), while others suggest the fall of Jerusalem in the first century (AD 70).

It should be noted here that the "Rome" option regarding the fall of Babylon would seem to lessen any notion of an imminent (at any moment) second coming. If we insert the identification of Babylon as Rome into the mix, both the AD 70 fall of Jerusalem (Olivet Discourse) and the fifth-century fall of Rome would be necessary precursors of the second coming. Another weakness in the Babylon as Rome option (Chapter XVIII).

Babylon the Great

If "Babylon the great" at 16:19 refers to Jerusalem, then obviously that is the identity of Babylon the Harlot in Revelation 17-18 as well. Does the language of Revelation 17-18 support such a possibility?

Commentators often point to the ending of Revelation 17 as clear evidence that Rome is the intended city, not Jerusalem. The last verse in particular needs to be addressed and will be below (17:18). From there we will offer two key arguments from the language of Revelation 17-18 that point to Jerusalem as the intended city.

First, we need to revisit the likelihood of Ezekiel's imprint upon John's own words here, especially in view of Ezekiel's extended, provocative descriptions of OT Jerusalem as a wicked harlot (Ezekiel 16, 23).

Second, we need to examine the "mystery" and "wisdom" aspects of John's description of the seven-headed beast: its arrival on the scene, its temporary demise, its return on the scene, and its ultimate destruction. In the midst of all this, the beast and the "ten kings" turn against Babylon the Harlot to destroy her. The merchants of the world weep at their lost revenues. Who are the players in this drama and when is it played out? Answers to those questions will help us identify Revelation's "Babylon the great."

Ezekiel 16 and 23 make tough preaching from the pulpit. Frankly, I have not attempted it! Ezekiel describes the whoredom of Jerusalem in vivid language that tends to make most modern readers squirm (cf. Isaiah 1; Jeremiah 3; Hosea 1-4).

We must keep in mind, however, that the explicit sexual language is for the most part metaphoric. Harlotry, sexual promiscuity, and the like are metaphors of unfaithfulness describing the reality of Judah's idolatry and wickedness. In making the case for Jerusalem being identified as the Great Harlot of Revelation 17-18, one could argue that John mimics to some extent Ezekiel's lewd descriptions of Jerusalem leading up to its earlier destruction by Babylon in the sixth century BC.

Of course, as Jesus Himself noted (Mt 23:29-38), the Jerusalem of the first Christian century would be guilty of the death of Israel's Messiah Himself. What level of condemnation could one expect for that? In the OT, the harlot metaphor is applied to Jerusalem (frequently), Nineveh (Nah 3:4-7), and Phoenician Tyre (Isa 23:15-17), but not actually to Babylon itself, although that ancient city certainly did fit the unsightly mold. However, the one ancient city for which the metaphor would involve more precisely the notion of unfaithfulness or a broken covenant relationship would, of course, be Jerusalem.

The focus of Revelation 17 would seem to favor the identification of Jerusalem as the harlot destroyed by the beast. Our earlier survey of historical background information comes to bear here. The angel promises to show John the judgment of the great prostitute (17:1). In his doing so much attention is paid to events involving the fall and rise of certain heads of the beast (17:7-11).

Leading up to the fall of Jerusalem in AD 70 the Roman Empire experienced a terrifying upheaval that resulted in a "mortal wound" being healed to the amazement of the world (13:3, 12, 14). We earlier described the tumultuous "Year of the Four Emperors" as a perilous episode for Rome after Nero's suicide (Chapter XII). I am convinced that the "mortal wound" phase of the beast is the "is not" phase mentioned at Revelation 17:8, after which there is a recovery, one described in two conflicting ways.

From the divine perspective, the angel states that the beast will rise from the bottomless pit and then go to destruction (17:8a), while instead the world marvels because it thinks the beast "was and is not and is to come" (17:8b). Those who worship the beast do not realize its ultimate defeat. Its "resurrection" will not stand. Unlike the Eternal One sitting on the throne who is described repeatedly with slight variation as "the One who was and is and is to come" (1:4, 8; 4:8; 11:17; 16:5; see Baukham, *Theology*, 28-30), the beast will not endure. His days are numbered.

For the much disputed 17:10, I would therefore argue the following. Nero was the fifth king and he had "fallen." His death in AD 68 and the consequent turmoil that nearly brought Rome to its knees was the "mortal wound" that was remarkably "healed." If Nero was the fifth ruler, then Augustus would have been the first, even though most other ancient sources list him as second following Julius Caesar (so we have 1-5 = Augustus, Tiberius, Gaius,

Claudius, Nero versus Julius, Augustus, Tiberius, Gaius, Claudius).

Yet a civil war broke out after the death of Julius that was not settled for more than a dozen years. No ongoing dynasty was yet in place until Octavian (now "Augustus") took absolute control. Questions are raised as to whether Julius was the first actual "emperor" anyway. Also, perhaps most importantly, we should consider that from the perspective of the early church Rome's role as the beastly opponent of Christ and the church would have begun with Augustus (27 BC-AD 14), not Julius Caesar.

Most Roman and Jewish sources do list Augustus as second but Revelation 12-13 pictures the beast arriving on the scene in connection with Satan's initial attacks upon the incarnate Christ and His church. Augustus fits that time frame best. (As Luke's Christmas story unfolds, "there went out a decree from Caesar Augustus..." [Lk 2:1]). Jewish works like 4 Ezra do portray Julius as the first ruler, the "first wing" upon the "great eagle," using that work's metaphor for the early Roman Empire. Since in *4 Ezra* 11:13-17 the "second wing" reigns twice as long as any of the others, that wing must represent Augustus.

However, we should note that the Roman conflict with Jerusalem and Judea had begun earlier, highlighted by the capture of Jerusalem by Pompey in 63 BC and by his blatant desecration of the temple in his entering the Holy of Holies. Julius Caesar perhaps fits best as the first ruler for the author of 4 Ezra, but Augustus Caesar fits best for Revelation's symbolic survey.

After the "is not" days in connection with the Roman Civil War (17:8, 11), the "one is" would be Vespasian and the one "not yet come" who will remain only "a little while" would be Titus (17:10), who reigned but two years (AD 79-81). The eighth beast/head is Domitian who is alive at the time Revelation is written. He is an "eighth" but he "belongs to the seven" and goes to destruction (17:11). As the eighth, he importantly represents an element *beyond* the seven but he has similarities to one of the seven, namely Nero. Again, Domitian was commonly regarded as a "Second Nero."

The relevant well-known historical events above lead up to the judgment of the harlot, and John emphasizes that God had placed into the heart of the beast and the ten horns the desire to carry out His purposes "until the words of God are fulfilled" (17:17). Two important conclusions derive from these words: (1) Jerusalem's fall was the work of God while (2) Rome was His instrument of judgment. God used the beast to punish His own (now apostate) people! Sounds familiar to students of the OT (including, of course, the book of Ezekiel).

The view above sees these specific descriptions in Revelation not as predictive but as interpretive of recent events, events in which the hand of God was at work. In this reconstruction, the one "who is," according to the angel, is the one who is the head of the beast when the beast desolates the Great Harlot, namely Vespasian. Correspondingly, it is his remarkable rise to power that heals the beast's "mortal wound." The emergence of the Flavian Dynasty (Vespasian, Titus, Domitian) causes the world to marvel.

The ten horns of the beast are symbols of earthly power and serve here to describe broadly the ancient, fluid coalition of kingdoms at Rome's beck and call. Numerous nations played a role in the destruction of Jerusalem and their cooperation with Rome's forces was fueled by a widespread, deeply seated disdain for the Jewish people and their practices.

The future demise of the beast at Christ's return is also said to involve these "horns," worldly anti-Christian forces then present who will share in the trauma of Christ's defeat and destruction of the beast (and false prophet) whom they serve (17:12-18; 19:17-21).

Outside of Revelation, the NT provides several unflattering portrayals of first-century Jerusalem. In his arguments against the troublesome Judaizers described in Galatians, Paul contrasts earthly Jerusalem, the chief domicile of the unbelieving Jews of his day, with the heavenly Jerusalem, the home of those who had embraced Jesus as Lord and Savior. In his jarring contrast between Hagar/Mt. Sinai/the slave woman/the present Jerusalem and the "free woman" (Sarah)/the "mother" of believers/Jerusalem above, Paul describes earthly Jerusalem as in bondage, enslaved under the old covenant (Gal 4:21-31). Elsewhere he speaks of the persecution of believers in Judea at the hands of unbelieving Jews whose impending (or unfolding) punishment from God would be deserved (1Th 2:14-16).

In his highly influential *Jesus and the Victory of God* (1996), the British scholar N.T. Wright concluded that OT imagery regarding ancient Babylon, despised enemy and oppressor of Yahweh's chosen, is actually applied to first-century Jerusalem by Jesus Himself! How so?

In the Olivet Discourse, Jesus uses terminology found in the OT prophets regarding the fall of Babylon and the warning to flee the city before it is destroyed (e.g., Isa 13:6, 9-11, 19; 48:20; 52:11-12; Jer 50:6, 8, 28; 51:6-10,45-46, 50-51, 57). We read from the prophets, "Go out from Babylon, flee from Chaldea ... say, The LORD has redeemed his servant Jacob" (Isa 48:20); "Flee from the midst of Babylon; let everyone save his life!" (Jer 51:6); "Go out of the midst of her my people! Let everyone save his life from the fierce anger of the LORD" (Jer 51:45). "Day of the LORD" language is employed to mark the devastation of Babylon, the oppressor of God's people (e.g., Isa 13:6). In 539 BC, the Babylonian Empire fell to the Medes and Persians allowing many, including the Jews, to return to their homelands.

Wright and others have written much about the spiritual "return from exile" envisioned and accomplished by Jesus in His messianic role. According to many, the "new Israel" was announced and founded through Christ's redemptive work, a work opposed by Satan and by Jerusalem and its religious hierarchy.

Satan, not Rome, is the enemy Jesus singles out in His teachings, and it is Jerusalem, not Rome, that plays the role of Babylon the oppressor. Jesus warns His followers (the true Israel now) to flee from their oppressor, "Babylon," i.e. Jerusalem, when it is attacked by God's agent of judgment, Rome's armies. All three versions of the Olivet Discourse warn Jesus' followers to flee from Jerusalem (spiritual "Babylon") when it faces imminent destruction (Mt 24:15-25; Mk 13:14-23; Lk 21:20-24; see Wright, *Victory*, 356-360).

The Dominion of Jerusalem

And the angel said to me, "The waters that you saw, where the prostitute is seated, are peoples and multitudes and nations and languages. ¹⁶And the ten horns that you saw, they and the beast will hate the prostitute. They will make her desolate and naked, and devour her flesh and burn her up with fire, ¹⁷for God has put it into their hearts to carry out his purpose by being of one mind and handing over their royal power to the beast, until the words of God are fulfilled. ¹⁸And the woman that you saw is

the great city that has dominion over the kings of the earth."
(Rev 17:15-18)

Revelation 17:18 is key for the argument of many that the harlot of Revelation 17-18 *cannot* be Jerusalem, but rather, *must* be Rome. Although previously John seemed to use the term "the great city" to describe Jerusalem itself (Rev 11:8), most commentators see no reasonable way in which Jerusalem can be described as having "dominion over the kings of the earth." However, a solid argument *can* be made for such a designation.

When the Jewish philosopher and statesman Philo arrived in Rome as part of a delegation to petition the Roman emperor Gaius (Caligula), it was discovered that the emperor was planning to erect a colossal statue of himself as Zeus in the Jerusalem temple. Philo describes in detail the intense grief and anxiety this news brought.

In response to the news, the emperor's dear Jewish friend, Herod Agrippa, wrote a lengthy, impassioned letter seeking to dissuade his friend from his intended actions. Historians may debate to what extent Philo's account of the content of Agrippa's letter represents Philo more than Agrippa himself, but the wording of the letter speaks to the importance given to Jerusalem in the middle of the first century AD by influential Jewish leaders. The importance of the wording requires the following lengthy quote. After Agrippa assures Gaius of the fact that the Jews "love their Caesar," he writes:

As for the holy city, I must say what befits me to say. While she, as I have said, is my native city she is also the mother city not of one country Judaea but of most of the others in virtue of the colonies sent out at divers times to the neighboring lands Egypt, Phoenicia, the part of Syria called the hollow and the rest as well and the lands lying far apart, Pamphylia, Cilicia, most of Asia up to Bithynia and the corners of Pontus, similarly also into Europe, Thessaly, Boeotia, Macedonia, Aetolia, Attica, Argos, Corinth and most of the best parts of Peloponnese. And not only are the mainlands full of Jewish colonies but also the most highly esteemed of the islands Euboea, Cypress, Crete. I say nothing of the countries beyond the Euphrates, for except for a small part they all, Babylon and of the other satrapies those where the land within their confines is highly fertile, have Jewish inhabitants. So that if my own home-city is granted a share of your goodwill the benefit extends not to one city but to myriads of the others situated in every region of the inhabited world whether in Europe or in Asia or in Libya, whether in the mainlands or on the islands, whether it be seaboard or inland. It well befits the magnitude of your great good fortune that by benefiting one city you should benefit myriads of others also so that through every part of the world your glory should be celebrated and your praises mingled with thanksgiving resound. (Philo, *The Embassy to Gaius*, 281-284 [LCL])

The Greek root *myriad* means "ten thousand," and although it is used hyperbolically here ("myriads of others"), the point is made. Countless cities in the Roman sphere and beyond were impacted by what impacted Jerusalem. She was the "mother city" for many regions or countries within the empire in that they were populated by many thousands of Jewish settlers and entrepreneurs. Both the islands and the mainlands were "full of Jewish colonies."

According to Agrippa, Jerusalem was the "mother city" of most of the countries within the Roman Empire in that numerous Jews had settled into those various regions and their ties to Jerusalem were strong. The NT makes mention of the extensive pilgrimages of Jews to Jerusalem for the festivals (Acts 2:5-11; 20:16; 21:17 ff.). The coffers in Jerusalem bulged from the vast resources delivered via the "temple tax," a financial obligation for the Jews throughout the Jewish Diaspora and thus throughout Rome's empire that, prior to the temple's destruction, substituted for offerings to the Roman deities.

Jerusalem's "dominion" within the Roman Empire was unsurpassed by any city save Rome itself with the possible exception of Alexandria, Egypt.

The Beast That Now Is

The angel's call for a "a mind with wisdom" (17:9) can best be answered if the apologetic controversies involving Rome's role and Jerusalem's role in connection with the Christians and Jews of the first century be kept in mind.

Among the issues with which the late-first-century Christians likely struggled were:

1. Why has God allowed a pagan empire to persecute His people, the church?

2. Did the miraculous recovery of Rome following AD 68-69 indicate the supremacy of the Roman state and its deities and the inevitability of its success?

3. Did Rome's conquest of the Jewish nation and destruction of its holy city and temple indicate the superiority of Rome and its gods over the God of Israel?

4. What is God's view of the Jews' current standing and their attempts to undermine His purposes for the church?

At the heart of the storyline in Revelation 17 are the events surrounding the rule of "the one who is" and the previous brief, tumultuous rules of those in the dramatic interlude involving the time when the beast "is not." Nero was the last of the five who had fallen (17:10) and the chaos subsequent to his death was described as a mortal wound that was miraculously healed (13:3, 12-14).

The tumultuous "Long Year" or "Year of the Four Emperors" was the "is not" phase for the empire or the beast. The "resurrection" of the beast raised the obvious question for the Mediterranean world: "Who is like the beast, and who can fight against it?" (13:4). Answer? No one! Or so it seemed.

The rise of the Flavian Dynasty involving Vespasian, Titus, and Domitian was a remarkable turn of events, one that the new dynastic leaders sought to buttress and exploit whenever possible. A significant part of that strategy involved the ongoing emphasis upon Rome's defeat of Jerusalem and the god of the Jews. A glorious Roman Triumph in AD 71, the production of coins celebrating the defeat of the Jews, the display of the items confiscated from the Jerusalem temple before its destruction, etc., all played their role in the promotion of Flavian supremacy, indeed inevitability.

Rome was back, the Jewish nation was destroyed, the church remained vulnerable, and questions lingered. I believe that John's Apocalypse was produced in part to answer or at least address key questions like those noted above. The reign of Vespasian ended the "is not," civil war phase of Rome's struggles, and his efforts and those of his son Titus accomplished the destruction of Jerusalem that effectively ended the Jewish Revolt.

The Fall of "Babylon"

The sudden demise of "Babylon" elicits great sorrow and mourning from her various trade partners. Merchants who had gained great wealth from business with the harlot weep and mourn aloud: "Alas, alas, for the great city that was clothed in fine linen, in purple and scarlet, adorned with gold, with jewels and with pearls! [17]For in a single hour all this wealth has been laid waste" (18:16-17).

Shipmasters and merchants of the sea throw dust on their heads as they lament, "Alas, alas for the great city where all who had ships at sea grew rich by her wealth! For in a single hour she has been laid waste" (18:19). A mighty angel tosses a great stone into the sea saying "So will Babylon the Great city be thrown down with violence, and will be found no more; and the sound of harpists and musicians, of flute players and trumpeters, will be heard in you no more..." (18:21-22a; cf. Jer 51:61-64).

The language above and in the rest of the chapter is strongly suggestive of a catastrophic event imbedded in the pages of ancient history, not entwined with the second coming and its accompanying circumstances. Turning to Ezekiel once again, we find perhaps the closest parallels to the language of Revelation 18 in the description of the fall of Tyre to Nebuchadnezzar and the Babylonians in Ezekiel 27. There merchants and mariners grieve over the fall of that prominent trade center on the eastern edge of the Mediterranean.

In an extended metaphor, Ezekiel describes Tyre as a great trading vessel that sank during a powerful storm into the heart of the sea (Eze 27:26-27). Tyre's merchant partners weep bitterly over her loss: "They cast dust on their heads and wallow in ashes; [31]they make themselves bald for you and put sackcloth on their waist, and they weep over you in bitterness of soul, with bitter mourning" (Eze 27:30b-31).

The language applied to ancient Tyre here describes the collapse of a great economic power and center of international commerce. The best candidates for such descriptions in Revelation would be Rome or Jerusalem in light of previous arguments above.

The language at Revelation 18:16 deserves further comment. The luxuriant adornment of the great city at 18:16 is a repeat of the language at 17:4 where the harlot's arrayment is described. G. K. Beale joins others in noting that the listing of precious items here corresponds to the raiment of the high priest in Israel, utilizing the same terminology as that found in the Greek OT (Ex 25:3-7; 28:5-9, etc.). The same precious materials are found in the cargo list at 18:12-13 (*Revelation*, 912-13).

The OT scholar Iain Provan has called into question the common assumption that the trade depictions in Revelation 18:9-19 describe Rome's exploitation of its considerable leverage over various trading partners. Such exploitation is read into the text by interpreters guided in part by their understanding that Rome is the Great Harlot and that greed and the lust for power are key aspects of the harlot's evil. Understandable.

The listing of trade items in Revelation 18, however, could simply be indicative of typical ancient commercial enterprise as practiced in OT times (as depicted by Ezekiel in Ezekiel 27). As Provan has noted (85-88), Revelation 18 actually makes no mention of economic exploitation and its inclusion of horses and slaves (18:13) and even chariots (18:13), e.g., corresponds to the realities found in various

OT texts (including Ezekiel 27:13-14 regarding slaves and horses). The mention of chariots may speak to the oft-cited conditions in Solomon's time (1Kgs 4:26-28) and need not depict the circumstances of Rome's first-century trade practices.

Comments below, coupled with previous discussion, suggest that Revelation's extensive connections with the book of Ezekiel make more likely the identification of the Great Harlot as Jerusalem, "the great city" (Rev 11:8; 16:19; 17:18; 18:10,16, 19, 21). As well, OT prophets like Isaiah, Hosea, and Jeremiah, along with Ezekiel, utilized graphic harlotry imagery in describing Jerusalem's unfaithfulness to God.

It seems right to contend that Jerusalem's ultimate act of unfaithfulness to the God of Israel would have been its rejection of the Messiah Himself in the person of Jesus of Nazareth. The "revelation of Jesus Christ" given to John the seer could be expected to match the words of Jesus earlier in which Jerusalem would be left desolate because of its rejection of Christ (Rev 1:1; Mt 23:37-38).

Jerusalem the Harlot

For students of the OT, the identification of the Great Harlot in Revelation 17 as the city of Jerusalem may make a lot of sense. Repeatedly the prophets of Israel addressed the nation with such terminology. The book of Hosea is based upon the painful analogy between the faithlessness of Hosea's wife Gomer and that of the Israelite nation whose "husband" was Yahweh God (esp. Hosea 1-3). Throughout the book, God's people are accused of "playing the whore" as depicted by their attraction to pagan gods and practices (Hos 1:2; 4:10-19; 5:3-4; 6:10; 9:1).

Isaiah opens his majestic work with a series of accusations against Judah and Jerusalem. "How the faithful city has become a whore, she who was full of justice! Righteousness lodged in her, but now murderers" (Isa 1:21). The names "Sodom" and "Gomorrah" are applied by the prophet to the faithless residents of Jerusalem (Isa 1:8-10; cf. "Sodom and Egypt," Rev 11:8).

Jeremiah begins his imposing book with similar accusations. He proclaimed, "You have played the whore with many lovers... (Jer 3:1). Both Israel and Judah "played the whore" (Jer 3:6-9). As for Israel, "She went out on every high hill and under every green tree and there played the whore" (Jer 3:6). Judah followed suit (Jer 3:8-10).

Especially relevant, in light of our characterization of John as the "new Ezekiel," are descriptions in Ezekiel 16 and 23 of Jerusalem as a lewd, uncontrollable whore. The language is strikingly graphic and violent. Awareness of Ezekiel's metaphoric language regarding Jerusalem's harlotry or whoredom makes Revelation's application of the expression "Babylon the great" in Revelation 17 to rebellious first-century Jerusalem more plausible. Again, the ministry and book of Ezekiel, more than the efforts of any other prophet, served as a model and blueprint for the ministry of John in his writing of Revelation.

In John's day, Jerusalem had played the harlot with Rome ("riding on the beast," Rev 17:3-11) much as she had with both the Assyrians (Eze 16:28; 23:11-13) and the Babylonians (Eze 16:29; 23:14-18), and, even before that, with the Egyptians (Eze 16:26; 23:3-4, 19-21). In turn, God would use the Babylonians (586 BC) and later the Romans (AD 70) to punish apostate Jerusalem. As Revelation states, when the beast and its ten horns destroy the harlot, they carry out God's divine purposes (Rev 17:16-17). The fact that Yahweh God is in charge here, not Rome, addresses several of the deep concerns that John's contemporaries had regarding God's purposes and plans for His people.

CHAPTER XIX

BEAUTIFUL BRIDE OR BUZZARD BAIT? (REV 19)

The final chapters of Revelation depict Christ's return, the defeat of Satan and his followers, and final judgment—including the lake of fire, also labeled as the "second death." John describes a new heavens and new earth within which is featured the eternal New Jerusalem. As with the previous chapters in John's book, symbolism abounds and connections with the rest of Scripture are of utmost importance for the interpretive task.

What Lies Ahead

As Revelation began, so it ends: with a focus upon the church of Jesus Christ. The church is described as "the Bride, the wife of the Lamb" (Rev 21:9) and is also equated with the New Jerusalem (21:10, 27). Along with that found within the rest of the book of Revelation, symbolism and figurative language predominate in such images as Satan's being "bound," the "first resurrection," the "second death," the millennial (thousand-year) reign of the saints, paradise restored, etc. We need to follow the commonly accepted principle of interpreting the unknown by means of the known when dealing with these highly controversial chapters.

Revelation ends with Christ's promise that he is returning "soon" (22:7, 12, 20). As stressed previously, the "soon" coming of Christ involves imminence rather than immediacy. He *could* come at any moment. No future sign-events are necessary before Christ's return.

The following topics are of particular concern for the closing chapters of Revelation:

- ☙ The timing of the millennial reign in Revelation 20 in relation to the return of Christ described in Revelation 19

- ☙ The meaning and timing of the "binding of Satan"

- ☙ The nature of the "first resurrection" and "second death"

- ☙ The connections between Revelation 19-22 and the OT

- ☙ The nature of the "loosing" of Satan following the millennium

- ☙ The imagery involved in the descriptions of the New Jerusalem

- ☙ The nature of the eternal state

- ☙ The meaning of Jesus' promise that he would come "soon"

- ☙ Selected NT descriptions of the day of the Lord

The topics listed will be covered below, although not necessarily in the order described above. Earlier we sought to provide an overview of the basic issues encountered and of the primary approaches today with respect to questions regarding Revelation and the end times.

A careful examination of the key relevant texts at the end of Revelation now follows in these last chapters.

Striking Contrasts of Imagery

The imagery of the marriage of the Lamb to His bride the church (Rev 19:1-10) is in striking contrast to what has preceded in Revelation 17-18, namely the destruction of the Great Harlot at the hands of the beast and its supporting cast. The beast and its followers ("ten kings," 17:12-13) are said to be the unwitting instruments of God's judgment upon the harlot (17:17). The identification of this harlot with Jerusalem and not Rome (Chapter XVIII) has the advantage of conforming to what the rest of the NT says concerning the imminence of Christ's return.

In light of Jesus' teaching in His Olivet Discourse (Matthew 24; Mark 13; Luke 21) and Paul's concerning the man of lawlessness in 2 Thessalonians 2 (Appendix A), a pattern may be suggested: following Jerusalem's fall in AD 70, a signature event in Bible prophecy, no other predicted signs or events are necessary leading up to Christ's return.

Four shouts of "Hallelujah!" ("Praise the Lord!") resonate in Revelation 19, three in connection with the judgment against the Great Harlot (19:1, 3, 4), and one pertaining to the marriage supper of the Lamb (19:6). The transition from the one reason to rejoice to the other is marked by the words, "Then I heard what seemed to be the voice of a great multitude, like the roar of many waters and like the sound of mighty peals of thunder, crying out..." (19:6).

What is *not* indicated is the temporal progression, the space of time between the destruction of the Great Harlot and the coming of Christ. From previous comments provided above the best answer would seem to be that, after the Great Harlot's demise, Christ will come (the eschatological) "soon"!

Attempts to link the doom of the Great Harlot with events directly tied to the second coming are not supported by the language of Revelation 17-18, especially that of Revelation 18. Additionally, efforts to identify the Great Harlot with the ancient Rome destroyed in the fifth century AD undermine any notion of imminence regarding Christ's return that seems to be indicated in "thief in the night," "lightning flashing," and other NT depictions.

Some early church leaders held that antichrist would not be unleashed upon the world until Rome fell (Chapter XVII). Then Christ would return. But how can the notion of imminence be maintained with such an approach?

Another striking contrast unfolds in Revelation 19. In addition to the jarring juxtaposition of desolated Babylon the Harlot with the glorious, victorious bride of the Lamb, John now replaces the anticipated arrival of the Lamb of God for His bride with the startling appearance of Jesus the Divine Warrior with the armies of heaven.

> *Then I saw heaven opened, and behold, a white horse! The one sitting on it is called Faithful and True, and in righteousness he judges and makes war. 12His eyes are like a flame of fire, and on his head are many diadems, and he has a name written that no one knows but himself. 13He is clothed in a robe dipped in blood, and the name by which he is called is The Word of God. 14And the armies of heaven, arrayed in fine linen, white and pure, were following him on white horses. 15From his mouth comes a sharp sword with which to strike down the nations, and he will rule them with a rod of iron. He will tread the winepress of the fury of the wrath of God the Almighty. 16On his robe and on his thigh he has a name written, King of kings and Lord of lords. (Rev 19:11-16)*

Previously we had anticipated seeing the Lion of Judah open the scroll in heaven but instead were shown a Lamb looking as if it had been slain (Rev 5:3-7). This later reversal here now is also striking. The Lamb is eagerly expected but the heavenly Warrior arrives! The two-sided coin employed in Revelation's message continues to highlight contrasting images.

Battle Imagery in Revelation

The creative title introducing this present chapter comes from a sermon by my former OT professor James E. Smith ("Doc Smith") and speaks to the dark contrast between the rewards of the righteous and the fate of the wicked within Revelation.

The term "beautiful bride" needs little explanation in light of the NT's description of the church as the bride of Christ (Eph 5:25-32) and especially of Revelation's identification of the bride with the New Jerusalem (Rev 19 6-9; 21:9-10; 22:17). The "buzzard bait" designation stems from the description in Revelation19 of Christ's coming on a white horse with His armies and defeating the beast, the false prophet, and their followers. Once the beast and the false prophet are thrown into the lake of fire, the rest are slain by the sword coming from Christ's mouth. We are told that "all the birds were gorged with their flesh" (Rev 19:21). Hence, buzzard bait.

As demonstrated in additional OT prophetic texts (e.g., Joel 3; Micah 5; Zechariah 14), one of the prevalent powerful metaphors for God's judgment upon the wicked is that of battle or the battlefield. In a judgment scene in Joel 3 we see a reference to the "Valley of Jehoshaphat," meaning the valley of "Jehovah (or Yahweh) has judged," and a description similar to that of Ezekiel's Gog and Magog campaign in which God summons His (and Israel's) enemies to engage in warfare against Him (Joel 3:9-12). This summons to attack is a summons to their destruction!

Along with battle imagery for judgment, we also see in Joel 3 the metaphor of harvest (Joel 3:13). Elsewhere we find the metaphor of a sacrificial feast or offering (Eze 39:17-19; Zep 1:7-8).

Such metaphors for divine judgment are found elsewhere in Scripture, especially in Revelation (e.g., Rev 12:7-17; 13:7; 14:14-20; 16:12-16; 17:14; 19:11-21; 20:7-10). Jesus spoke of the harvest in connection with the salvation of souls (Mt 9:38). In contrast, the grape harvest specifically can serve as a metaphor for condemnation (Rev 14:17-20; cf. Joel 3:13).

In the opening lines of Revelation Jesus is described as the One with the sharp two-edged sword (1:16; 2:12; cf. 2:16) and now that sword is utilized for the destruction of His enemies. Perhaps it is significant that the beast and false prophet are not slain as their human armies are but are directly cast into the lake of fire (19:19-21). The designations beast (sea-beast) and false prophet (land-beast) seem to encompass more than single individuals and may suggest supernatural or demonic associations.

Various commentators, especially those of postmillennial persuasion, identify the sword coming out of Jesus' mouth as the Word of God containing the life-saving gospel used to convert the nations. Surely that is not the case here! Christ's enemies are slain by the sword and the birds of the air converge and eat their flesh (19:21).

This speaks of utter defeat, not salvific opportunity! Connections with Ezekiel's Gog and Magog descriptions are made immediately below and in the next several chapters.

Gog and Magog

The great climactic confrontation in Revelation 19 is referred to as "the great supper of God" (19:17) as the birds flying above are invited to gorge themselves upon the flesh of the wicked: "the flesh of kings, the flesh of captains, the flesh of mighty men, the flesh of horses and their riders, and the flesh of all men, both slave and free, both small and great" (19:18). Importantly, this language seems to be drawn from Ezekiel 39:17-20 in its description of the Gog and Magog invasion.

> *"As for you, son of man, thus says the Lord God: Speak to the birds of every sort and to all beasts of the field: 'Assemble and come, gather from all around to the sacrificial feast that I am preparing for you, a great sacrificial feast on the mountains of Israel, and you shall eat flesh and drink blood.* [18]*You shall eat the flesh of the mighty, and drink the blood of the princes of the earth—of rams, of lambs, and of he-goats, of bulls, all of them fat beasts of Bashan.*[19]*And you shall eat fat till you are filled, and drink blood till you are drunk, at the sacrificial feast that I am preparing for you.* [20]*And you shall be filled at my table with horses and charioteers, with mighty men and all kinds of warriors,' declares the Lord God." (Eze 39:17-20)*

This end-times judgment of the wicked also seems to correspond to Revelation 20:7-10 which again contains language parallel to Ezekiel (Eze 38:21-22) and which actually employs the label "Gog and Magog" (Rev 20:8). If Ezekiel's Gog and Magog account is utilized both at Revelation 19 in a description of the second coming and at Revelation 20 in a description of Satan's final doom, it becomes even less likely that those two descriptions of judgment are separated by a thousand-year kingdom on earth.

Rather, they speak of the same thing. If so, recapitulation is involved here, with Revelation 20 describing the church age in a condensed, colorful, and climactic fashion.

The Day of the Lord: The Big Picture

When we come to the last half of Revelation 19, we arrive at a graphic description of the second coming and the judgment of the wicked as depicted in a gruesome battle scene. Again, warfare or battle functions as a frequent metaphor for divine judgment in Scripture.

I believe that in Revelation 19 we have arrived at the final, climactic battle scene, a scene that is mirrored in several other passages. The next three chapters will focus upon the contents of Revelation 20. Importantly, in the amillennial approach to Revelation 20, the thousand years during which Satan is bound and the saints reign with Christ are a figurative measurement of the church age and these years possibly represent the duration of the intermediate state for the Christian martyrs, their (conscious) state between death and the final resurrection.

In this regard, the final "battle" of Revelation 20:7-10 is then viewed as a recapitulation of the climactic defeat described in Revelation 19. In Revelation 20, Satan is cast into the lake of fire after his attack upon God's people fails, while in the previous chapter both the beast and the false prophet are cast into that lake of fire after their battle efforts come to naught.

If Revelation 19-20 are sequential, as many do believe, then the beast and the false prophet are cast in the lake of fire a thousand years before Satan is, but if Revelation 20 represents recapitulation (as in the amillennial view), then all three are cast into lake of fire at roughly the same time.

This makes better sense in my view. As a chiastic literary structure (A:B::B:A), [Satan]:[beast-false prophet]::[beast-false prophet]:[Satan], the presentation of Revelation's cosmic conflict by John ends as it began, with the devil featured in violent opposition (Revelation 12 and 20). He opposes God and His kingdom to the bitter end.

A brief overview of key NT texts regarding the themes surrounding the "day of the Lord" is now given in order to complement Revelation's teaching on the subject. Revelation was not produced and presented in a theological vacuum, especially if the late (Domitian) date for the book is held. Paul's epistles were likely known, especially those addressed to the regions and cities in close proximity to the seven churches of Asia (e.g., Ephesians, Colossians, also a letter to Laodicea [Col 4:15-16]).

Universal Transformation

> *But the day of the Lord will come like a thief, and then the heavens will pass away with a roar, and the heavenly bodies will be burned up and dissolved, and the earth and the works that are done on it will be exposed. ¹¹Since all these things are thus to be dissolved, what sort of people ought you to be in lives of holiness and godliness, ¹²waiting for and hastening the coming of the day of God, because of which the heavens will be set on fire and dissolved, and the heavenly bodies will melt as they burn! ¹³But according to his promise we are waiting for new heavens and a new earth in which righteousness dwells. (2Pet 3:10-13)*

Peter's teaching on the day of the Lord contains several critical elements. That day will be unexpected, "like a thief," and therefore unaccompanied by warning signs. Also, this thief-like intrusion will bring about the dissolution of the present created order and will result in "new heavens and a new earth in which righteousness dwells" (cf. Revelation 21-22). This reads like a preview of John's promises in his Apocalypse. The premillennial view struggles here since Peter specifies that the *present creation* will be destroyed at this time (2Pet 3:7). This is important, for there is no room here for a thousand-year transition between the second coming and the arrival of the new heavens and new earth.

A Thief in the Night, A Day of Wrath

The unexpected nature of Christ's coming (or the "day of the Lord") is described by Jesus, Paul, and Peter as being like the arrival of a thief in the night (Mt 24:43-44; 1Th 5:2; 2Pet 3:10; Rev 3:3; 16:15). Rapture enthusiasts are hard pressed to find a separate "pretribulational rapture" of the church in Revelation (note Chapters IX, XIII), and are also forced to admit that the "thief in the night" label cannot refer to the coming of Jesus at the so-called rapture since elements of divine wrath are associated with it.

This last point is obviously not very well spelled out in dispensational teaching on the subject, nor is the fact that the "left behind" language in the Gospels also cannot refer to the dispensational "rapture" but rather to their later "return" of Christ. Paul's words below make clear that wrath and judgment are essential parts of the future day of the Lord that will arrive like a thief in the night.

> *Now concerning the times and the seasons, brothers, you have no need to have anything written to you. ²For you yourselves are fully aware that the day of the Lord will come like a thief in the night. ³While people are saying, "There is peace and security," then sudden destruction will come upon them as labor pains come upon a pregnant woman, and they will not escape. ⁴But you are not in darkness, brothers, for that day to surprise you like a thief. ⁵For you are all children of light, children of*

*the day. We are not of the night or of the darkness. ⁶So then
let us not sleep, as others do, but let us keep awake and be
sober. ⁷For those who sleep, sleep at night, and those who get
drunk, are drunk at night. ⁸But since we belong to the day, let
us be sober, having put on the breastplate of faith and love, and
for a helmet the hope of salvation. ⁹For God has not destined
us for wrath, but to obtain salvation through our Lord Jesus
Christ, ¹⁰who died for us so that whether we are awake or asleep
we might live with him. (1Th 5:1-10)*

A Glorious Return

*But in those days, after that tribulation, the sun will be
darkened, and the moon will not give its light, ²⁵and the stars
will be falling from heaven, and the powers in the heavens will
be shaken. ²⁶And then they will see the Son of Man coming in
clouds with great power and glory. ²⁷And then he will send out
the angels and gather his elect from the four winds, from the
ends of the earth to the ends of heaven. (Mk 13:24-27)*

In His Olivet Discourse. Jesus made a discernible
distinction between events surrounding the AD 70 fall of
Jerusalem and those in connection with the second coming.
The verses directly above are in reference to the latter.

An Eternal Separation

*Then he left the crowds and went into the house. And his
disciples came to him, saying, "Explain to us the parable of the
weeds of the field."³⁷He answered, "The one who sows the good
seed is the Son of Man. ³⁸The field is the world, and the good
seed is the sons of the kingdom. The weeds are the sons of the
evil one, ³⁹and the enemy who sowed them is the devil. The
harvest is the end of the age, and the reapers are angels. ⁴⁰Just
as the weeds are gathered and burned with fire, so will it be at*

the end of the age. ⁴¹The Son of Man will send his angels, and they will gather out of his kingdom all causes of sin and all law-breakers, ⁴²and throw them into the fiery furnace. In that place there will be weeping and gnashing of teeth. ⁴³Then the righteous will shine like the sun in the kingdom of their Father. He who has ears, let him hear." (Mt 13:36-43)

In the parable of the Wheat and the Weeds, Jesus explains that the judgment of souls awaits the end of the age when He will send out His angels to gather up the wicked ("sons of the evil one") and throw them into the fiery furnace. The oft-used metaphor of harvest here also points to the painful separation that one day will transpire.

The contrast between the condemned and the redeemed could not be more vividly portrayed. Satan's role in sowing suffering and destruction is highlighted, but not all will succumb to his wiles. In God's kingdom "the righteous will shine like the sun."

A Climactic Upheaval

Perhaps the end-times chaos depicted in various scenes in Revelation is most closely approximated in Luke's version of the Olivet Discourse where frightful upheavals in the natural order are described in connection with Christ's return.

And there will be signs in sun and moon and stars, and on the earth distress of nations in perplexity because of the roaring of the sea and the waves, ²⁶people fainting with fear and with foreboding of what is coming on the world. For the powers of the heavens will be shaken. ²⁷And then they will see the Son of Man coming in a cloud with power and great glory. ²⁸Now when these things begin to take place, straighten up and raise your heads, because your redemption is drawing near... ³⁴But watch yourselves lest your hearts be weighed down with dissipation and drunkenness and cares of this life, and that day come upon you suddenly like a trap. ³⁵For it will come upon all who dwell on the face of the whole earth. ³⁶But stay awake at all times, praying that you may have strength to escape all these things that are going to take place, and to stand before the Son of Man. (Lk 21:25-28, 34-36)

The signs mentioned by Jesus here are not warning signs. Rather they are signals that the end has come. For the believer they are signs of redemption, for unbelievers indicators of deserved wrath that has overtaken them. The upheaval will be worldwide: none can escape save those for whom Christ comes in triumph. The heavens, the seas, the land—all will be affected in connection with the second coming. Distress, fainting, fear, foreboding—all experienced by those who do not know Christ; glory and redemption—promises for the redeemed.

Righteous Judgment, Fiery Return

In his letters to the Thessalonians Paul also depicts both sides of the second coming: righteous wrath, fiery vengeance, and eternal destruction, along with the glorification of those who have believed.

This is evidence of the righteous judgment of God, that you may be considered worthy of the kingdom of God, for which you are also suffering— ⁶since indeed God considers it just to repay with affliction those who afflict you, ⁷and to grant relief to you who are afflicted as well as to us, when the Lord Jesus is revealed from heaven with his mighty angels ⁸in flaming fire, inflicting vengeance on those who do not know God and on those who do not obey the gospel of our Lord Jesus. ⁹They will suffer the punishment of eternal destruction, away from the presence of the

Lord and from the glory of his might, [10]when he comes on that day to be glorified in his saints, and to be marveled at among all who have believed, because our testimony to you was believed. (2Th 1:5-10)

Christians will be saved from wrath on the day of God's wrath (1Th 1:10), a promise that not all second coming passages emphasize. The fact that in some passages Paul does not focus upon the judgment of the wicked at Christ's return does not mean that he is speaking of an earlier, separate coming for his church, a coming that does not involve wrath but only salvation.

Not all texts should be expected to portray both sides of the second coming. Actually, given dispensational parameters in which the alleged rapture of the church *cannot* involve judgment upon the wicked, there are in reality very few possible "rapture texts" in the NT (including perhaps Jn 14:3; 1Cor 15:51-52; Php 3:20-21; 1Th 1:10; 2:19; 3:13; 4:14-17; maybe one or two others). And, of course, none of these need to be texts regarding a separate rapture of the church. These just represent the only *possible* (if unlikely) options for that approach.

CHAPTER XX

THE MEANING OF THE MILLENNIUM
(REV 20), PART 1

Any in-depth discussion about the second coming, the book of Revelation, or the end times inevitably becomes a debate regarding the nature of the "millennium," the thousand-year reign of Christ as described in Revelation 20. Unfortunately, any attempt to describe what the Bible says about the second coming often migrates into a discussion about what the Bible does not say! As indicated earlier, the differences between the millennial views can be significant and they are important. A primary issue regards whether the millennial kingdom described in Revelation 20 has reference to a future age following Christ's return or to the present age, the church age, which much of the NT claims is itself a fulfillment of many of the glorious promises to God's people.

The Controversy Continues

As noted in some detail in Chapters III and IV, the major end-times views today are articulated in terms of the nature of the "millennium" of Revelation 20. Specific designations have been coined to describe the relationship between Christ's return and this millennial kingdom: premillennialism—Christ will return *before* the millennium; postmillennialism—Christ will return *after* the millennium; amillennialism—no distinct millennial age exists, but rather the term refers to an era already established within NT teaching: the church age.

As amillennialist William Hendriksen explains, Revelation 19 carries us to the very end of history, to the day of final judgment, while with Revelation 20 we return to the beginning of the present dispensation (221). Thus for amillennialism Revelation 20 involves recapitulation, a retelling of the story previously told, but with different features in focus.

An ongoing debate involves the nature of the early church's views of the millennium. A common claim among historic premillennialists and dispensationalists is that many of the Early Church Fathers, including Irenaeus and Tertullian, held premillennial views and that it was basically not until the more allegorical approach of Origen (third c.) and the influential fourth- and fifth-century scholars Augustine and Jerome that the amillennial view held sway. In other words, amillennialism was a later development within the NT church and premillennialism initially was preferred.

This whole approach has been extensively researched and found wanting, however, as shown in the important work by Charles E. Hill, *Regnum Caelorum: Patterns of Millennial Thought in Early Christianity* (2001). Hill does not deny that the premillennial view was held among various early church scholars, but he lists numerous other early scholars within the church who clearly held to a non-millennial perspective, including Clement of Rome, Ignatius of Antioch, Polycarp of Smyrna, Hermas, Melito of Sardis, Athenagoras, and others (75-108).

As displayed throughout Hill's work, the term "millennialism" can be replaced by "chiliasm," from the Greek word *chilia*, "a thousand." Premillennialism then is "chiliasm" and amillennialism becomes "non-chiliasm."

(The Greek letter *chi* [*ch*] has a harsh or aspirated "k" sound.)

Two important results from Hill's research include explanations for the premillennial preferences of scholars like Irenaeus. One of the major threats to the early church that Irenaeus exposed (in his *Against Heresies*) was Gnosticism, a view that held that all physical, material things were inherently evil and that only the non-material, "spiritual" realities were good.

Consequently, the rejection of a physical millennium on earth could have been viewed as a step toward Gnosticism and so belief in the millennium could have been viewed as a hedge against heresy. Forms of Gnosticism contained the dangerous teaching that the (OT) God of the creation of the world (the "Demiurge") and the (NT) God who was the Father of Christ were two different beings. Also, Christ, the spirit being, was said to have departed from Jesus, the physical being, before the crucifixion.

One can see how eschatological views that tended to turn one toward a Gnostic or non-material approach might have been avoided. However, this may be another case of throwing out the baby with the bathwater.

Another connection Hill made in his research was that the vast majority of early premillennialists also held to a subterranean view of the intermediate state. In this approach, the dead in Christ were taken to the underworld awaiting their earthly millennial hope.

Early amillennialists, on the other hand, believed that upon death believers were taken to heaven to be, as Paul put it, "with Christ" (Php 1:23). This latter view has prevailed as orthodox Christian doctrine. Hill shows that some of the theological tendencies among early Christian premillennialists were a possible byproduct of connections with early Jewish eschatology such as that found in books like 2 Baruch and 4 Ezra (45-68).

The true nature of the biblical teaching on the millennium depends neither upon ancient views within the early church nor upon more recent scholarly speculations, but upon what the Bible actually teaches in view of the full scope of its content. In our proceeding from the known to the unknown and interpreting difficult, unclear texts in light of clearer ones, we need to make sure that our views of Revelation's content are in conformity with what the rest of the NT teaches. The debate concerning literal versus figurative often boils down to the question of what best conforms to the total NT teaching on the subject at hand.

Two prominent features of Revelation 20's teachings concern the binding of Satan and the reigning of the saints with Christ. They are both said to extend for "a thousand years" and almost all interpreters agree that the same thousand-year period, whatever it signifies, is in play here. The exact nature of the Bible's teaching on the binding of Satan and on the reigning of the saints with Christ will be explored below. Strong opinions accompany these topics, but it is best to keep strict dogmatism at bay. The difficulties involved in Revelation 20 are the source of much of the theological debate that occupies today's Christian writers and speakers.

The Binding of Satan

In connection with Revelation 12 we have examined the topic "The Fall of Satan" (Chapter XIII). The emphasis here will be upon the specific terminology "the binding of Satan." As noted above, the NT stresses Christ's victory over Satan at His crucifixion and resurrection and even in His preliminary exploits in connection with His casting out demons during His public ministry, at which time He "bound the strong man" (Mt 12:22-30: Mk 3:22-27).

The evidence will be further developed in what follows in several ways: key NT texts that emphasize Christ's victory over Satan (e.g., Heb 2:14-18; 1Jn 3:8; Mt 12:22-30; Mk 3:22-27); problems with the premillennial approach; other ancient Jewish references to the "binding of Satan" as demonstrations of God's power over him; and possible connections with the Roman Triumph in which captive enemy leaders were imprisoned (and bound) awaiting execution (see Chapter XXII, "Satan Released Yet Still Bound: God's Triumphal Procession?").

Satan's Binding in the NT

Regarding key NT texts, Hebrews 2:14-15 and 1 John 3:8 stand out along with texts in the Gospels where Jesus describes his victories over Satan's demons as "binding the strong man" (Mt 12:22-30; Mk 3:22-27). The passages in Matthew and Mark show the same Greek word (*deō*) for "bind" regarding Jesus "binding" the "strong man"—the devil—that we find in Revelation 20:2.

The "binding of Satan," according to the amillennial approach, is a *present* reality. Through Christ's victorious resurrection over death, and through the subsequent preaching of the gospel, Satan in a real sense is "bound." This "binding" need not be absolute, but could convey the notion of limitation. Various Scriptures show the idea that Christ's victory over Satan has already taken place: Genesis 3:15; Hebrews 2:14-15; 1 John 3:8; Luke 10:17-18; John 12:31-32; Matthew 12:29; Mark 3:27.

For example, Hebrews 2:14-15, in speaking of Christ's first coming, says, "Since therefore the children share in flesh and blood, he himself likewise partook of the same things, that through death he might destroy the one who has the power of death, that is, the devil, [15]and deliver all those who through fear of death were subject to lifelong slavery."

Similarly, 1 John 3:8 reads, "Whoever makes a practice of sinning is of the devil, for the devil has been sinning from the beginning. The reason the Son of God appeared was to destroy the works of the devil."

Note the past tense in both texts. Jesus *partook* of flesh and blood and through death *destroyed* the destroyer. The Son of God *appeared* in order to destroy the works of the devil. In a very real sense then, Satan is now "destroyed"; his work is now "destroyed" (or "rendered powerless"). Both texts speak to the fact of the devil's certain doom. Satan's final, total destruction is yet future but, as Revelation states it, he is now "bound," limited in a real sense.

According to Revelation 20:3, Satan's binding was "so that he might not deceive the nations any longer." Hebrews 2:15 may shed light here when it states that Christ's purpose through His death and resurrection was that He might "deliver all those who through fear of death were subject to lifelong slavery."

Hopelessness in the face of the harsh reality of death is one of Satan's deceptions that no longer holds sway when confronted with the truth of the gospel. The great lie has been exposed, the falsehood promulgated by the one who has been a liar and deceiver from the beginning. Christian hope extends beyond the grave! Death will be destroyed forever through Christ's resurrection power (1Cor 15:20-26). The deceiver's influence has been reduced for those washed in the blood of the Lamb (Rev 12:11), death's veil has been "swallowed up" (Isa 25:7-8), and the nations now stream to "the mountain of the house of the Lord" (Isa 2:2).

Some point to the sinful condition of our fallen world and ask how Satan could possibly be "bound" today. For them the painful evidence shouts otherwise. In response, we can point to texts like Hebrews 2:14-15 and 1 John 3:8 above. How have the devil's works been "destroyed" by Christ's *first* coming? How did Jesus, by becoming human, destroy the one who had the power of death, Satan himself? If these verses can ring true, why cannot verses proclaiming the "binding of Satan" as a present reality, verses found in a highly symbolic apocalyptic work, also represent a spiritual truism?

The imagery of the great dragon as a defeated accuser of God's people cast from heaven to earth in Revelation 12 has morphed into that of a great dragon imprisoned and bound as a defeated deceiver of the nations in Revelation 20. The devil's great wrath and his status as defeated foe coexist today, even as followers of the Lamb can conquer Satan through their testimony and yet in the process may in fact experience martyrdom (Rev 12:11).

Through Revelation's vivid, symbolic language John reminds a beleaguered church concerning the victory that is theirs and the defeat that is Satan's. It is a powerful reminder that helps brighten the bleak landscape of tribulation and persecution that blankets much of the book. It is also a message that resonates elsewhere in the NT: "Little children, you are from God and have overcome them, for he who is in you is greater than he who is in the world" (1Jn 4:4). Even when the devil is described as roaming around like a roaring lion that is "seeking someone to devour" (1Pet 5:8), the firm, accompanying promise is that those who faithfully resist will, after suffering a little while, enter into eternal glory (1Pet 5:10).

Paul explained to King Herod Agrippa II that God had sent him to open the eyes of the Gentiles (or "nations,"

Greek *ethnē*) "so that they may turn from darkness to light and from the power of Satan to God, that they may receive forgiveness of sins..." (Acts 26:17-18). Through the gospel the binding of Satan's power, his deception, was now in progress. This spread of the gospel may have been incremental and not effectual for all, but this gospel was nonetheless powerful—in Paul's words, "the power of God for salvation to everyone who believes, to the Jew first and also to the Greek" (Rom 1:16).

Yes, the power of deception still played its role in Satan's schemes. Yes, the false prophet deceived many to worship the beast, resulting in their demise (Rev 13:11-14; 14:11; 19:20-21). And yes, Satan is called "the deceiver of the whole world" in connection with his being cast down to earth from heaven (12:10). But there is, in fact, much more to the story.

Removed from access to the heavenly throne, Satan's power to accuse is held in check and he is conquered by the blood of the Lamb and by the testimony of believers, some of whom are slain for their faithful word (12:7-11). The bound Satan will eventually be released from prison, not in triumph but in utter defeat. He and the wicked he has influenced, those deceived from the nations (20:8), will be cast into the lake of fire. This as the result of a so-called "battle" that will be fought, a battle that actually serves as a metaphor for judgment. There is no final battle. We must not forget that!

John's mention of the nations (or Gentiles) here dovetails with Paul's emphasis upon the gospel's power and reach. Through the message of the cross the nations now have opportunity to respond to the grace of God in a new and vibrant way. With a touch of hyperbole Paul could claim (to believers in close contact with Revelation's "Seven Churches") that in his time the gospel was bearing fruit "in the whole world" (Col 1:6) and had been proclaimed "in all creation under heaven" (Col 1:23). The devil's realm of influence was under attack! See below for Jewish parallels to the notion of Satan being "bound," limited in his power and effectiveness.

Premillennial Problems

Contrary to what some might assume, premillennialists have problems themselves in dealing with the binding of Satan. In the premillennial understanding of the events during the millennium, many millions will reject Christ's reign (particularly those allegedly born during the millennium!), even though His visible presence will result in unimaginable blessings for all. Hordes of "closet rebels" will be chafing at the bit, and Satan's release will be a welcome development in their desire to throw off Christ's shackles. Amazingly "their number is like the sand of the sea" (Rev 20:8).

According to Revelation 20:3, Satan's binding was so that he might not "deceive the nations." And yet millions are deceived in the premillennial version of things! A common premillennial stance is that universal peace will be accomplished during the millennium by Christ's immediate destruction of any *openly* rebellious "kingdom citizens." The wicked must keep it to themselves!

Apparently, Satan's being "bound" does not stop countless people all over the world from ultimately rejecting Christ's millennial reign. How is that possible? The ugly picture that accompanies any premillennial understanding of a future millennium on earth is exposed by Arthur H. Lewis, *The Dark Side of the Millennium: The Problem of Evil in Rev. 20:1-10* (1980).

Surprisingly, there is remarkable agreement between the amillennial understanding of Satan's status in the present age and the view of numerous historic premillennialists. Satan was defeated at the cross, his power is diminished, Christ and those in His church do reign right now. But according to the standard view of premillennialism, these facts are not an adequate explanation for what Revelation 20 says. Satan has not yet been bound in the way Revelation describes. For premillennial interpreters an additional thousand years on earth must still follow.

Satan's Binding in Jewish Literature

Much discussion and debate exists about the various names and roles of Satan found in ancient Jewish literature. Some of that discussion actually involves the imagery of Satan being "bound."

In the OT itself, we find along with the designation Satan terms like Belial (sixteen times; also in Paul: 2Cor 6:15) and of course the serpent of Genesis 3. In the Gospels the name Beelzebul ("Lord Prince" or "Baal the Prince") is found as a designation for the devil (seven times).

In extra-biblical Jewish texts the identifications and functions of the head of the demonic world were multiplied. Names such as Samael and Azazel, along with Satan and Belial, can be found. In the book of Jubilees, stemming from the second-first century BC, we see the name Mastema, a word that is linguistically connected to the Hebrew term Satan ("Adversary") but is only found twice in the OT, there as a noun signifying "hatred" (Hos 9:7, 8).

The relative absence of extra-biblical Jewish terms and entities throughout the book of Revelation is rather remarkable. Revelation leans heavenly upon the fabric and framework of the OT world, not upon the realm of later Jewish thought. (The recent work edited by Blackwell,

Goodrich, and Maston seeks to highlight connections between Revelation and Jewish literature from the same general time period: *Reading Revelation in Context* [2019]. Such connections have often proved to be complex and ambiguous.) One possible connection with Jewish literature does involve the "binding of Satan" theme as presented in the book of Jubilees.

It should be noted here that Jubilees was apparently a popular book within first-century Judaism. We find evidence among the Dead Sea Scrolls of more than ten copies of Jubilees, all represented in fragments. Jubilees was originally written in Hebrew, copied into Greek, and then the Greek text was translated into Ethiopic, the ancient Semitic language from Ethiopia also known as Ge\[c\]ez. Our only complete copy of Jubilees is in Ethiopic.

Jubilees shares a number of features with an even more popular intertestamental Jewish work, the book of Enoch, including references to fallen angels who have relations with human women, angels known in both Enoch and Jubilees as the "Watchers." (The "sons of God" in Genesis who take human women as they please are often viewed as fallen angels, especially in ancient sources, but they could also refer to evil human dynastic rulers, "the great men of old" [Gen 6:1-4]. "Great" in power and influence. Immediately following this text in Genesis we read that God saw man's wickedness and determined to blot him out [Gen 6:5-7]. This could suggest that the aforementioned "sons of God" in Genesis were wicked humans, not fallen angels.)

The role of Mastema in Jubilees mirrors and expands that of Satan in the OT. Just as Satan counseled God to test the integrity of Job, so Mastema counseled God to test Abraham in connection with offering up his son Isaac (*Jubilees* 17:15-16). It was then Mastema who aided the

Egyptian priests in their attempts to oppose Moses, and it was Mastema whose powers were connected with the deaths of the firstborn of Egypt.

The book of Jubilees covers Genesis 1 through Exodus 12 and embellishes Satan's (Mastema's) role in the events of Israelite history. Important for our discussion here is the repeated use in Jubilees of the expression "bind" or "bound" in reference to God's limitation placed upon Mastema and his hosts.

The following texts in Jubilees mention the binding or loosing of Mastema and/or his demonic forces: *Jubilees* 10:5-7; 18:2; 48:13-16; 49:2. Noah's prayer in Jubilees asked God to "imprison" the evil spirits descended from the "Watchers" and to hold them fast in the place of condemnation so they would not bring destruction upon mankind (*Jubilees* 10:5). If imprisoned, they would not be able to rule over the spirits of the living and they would not have power over the sons of the righteous (*Jubilees* 10:6).

Note the ominous warning offered regarding these powerful demonic forces: if not imprisoned, they would have domination over mankind, including the righteous. There seems to be no middle ground. In regard to Mastema's accusations resulting in the testing of Abraham in connection with his son Isaac, an angel intervened and told Abraham not to kill his son and, as a result, "Prince Mastema was put to shame (and was bound by the angels)" (*Jubilees* 18:12). Here the defeat of Mastema is referred to as a "binding."

Concerning Mastema's role in connection with Israel's struggles in leaving Egypt we read,

On the fourteenth day and on the fifteenth and on the sixteenth and on the seventeenth and on the eighteenth days, Prince Mastema was bound and imprisoned and placed behind the children of Israel so that he might not accuse them. [14]On the nineteenth day we let them (Mastema and his demons) loose so that they might help the Egyptians pursue the children of Israel. ...[16]On the fourteenth day we bound him that he might not accuse the children of Israel on the day when they asked the Egyptians for vessels and garments... (*Jubilees* 48:13-14, 16; Lumpkin, transl.)

A number of times we find that the metaphor of "binding" is employed. Significantly, Mastema's inability or ability to accuse Israel or to help the Egyptians pursue Israel is described as his being "bound" and/or "imprisoned" on one hand, and being "loosed" on the other. When Mastema is free or "loosed," he has the power to kill the firstborn in the land of Egypt (*Jubilees* 49:2).

We acknowledge the sizeable differences between the inspired book of Revelation and the fanciful, imaginative expansion of biblical revelation found in the book of Jubilees. And yet the literary parallels are instructive. Noteworthy is the emphasis in Jubilees upon the imagery of "binding" and "loosing" in connection with God's power over the forces of evil, highlighted in the references to Mastema. Also of note, when Mastema (Satan) is bound and imprisoned, he is unable to accuse God's people. He wields no power over them.

When Mastema and his forces are "loosed," havoc ensues. Sounds a bit like Revelation 20. Once Satan is "bound" and "imprisoned" he is unable to deceive the nations (20:3). Of course, in Revelation Satan is not only the "deceiver" (12: 9; 20:3, 8, 10), but he is also the "accuser" (12:10). In Jubilees, the "binding" and "loosing" of evil Mastema represent an ongoing, fluid theme, oft repeated. In Revelation, in contrast, Satan's role as accuser and deceiver are forever diminished through Christ's once-for-all redemptive sacrifice and His subsequent resurrection. Hallelujah!

The differences between Jubilees and Revelation are striking, to be sure, and yet the popularity of Jubilees and its teachings may likely have found awareness and even familiarity from Revelation's initial (probably mostly Jewish Christian) audience, if not from its later readers. Comparisons with ancient books like Jubilees may help the modern reader better navigate a book like Revelation, one rich in ancient Hebrew imagery and contemporary with other well-known Jewish apocalyptic works. Those who insist that Satan cannot be viewed as "bound" today in light of his destructive influence throughout the world might want to reconsider their reasoning.

That position seems to undermine Scripture's teaching on Christ's victory over Satan as a *fait accompli*. The battle is won ("already"). The devil now awaits his final ("not yet") defeat as a bound prisoner. Parallel imagery and strikingly similar language found in ancient Jewish literature like Jubilees regarding Satan (or Mastema) seem to be instructive.

CHAPTER XXI

THE MEANING OF THE MILLENNIUM (REV 20), PART 2

Coinciding with the binding of Satan is the reign of resurrected saints. Both are said to last for a thousand years. But when and where? The basic premillennial approach sees this reign as occurring on (a partially renovated) earth *following* Christ's second coming. The amillennial view sees this as a reign in heaven of the dead in Christ during the church age *before* Christ returns.

In considering these options the use of the terms involving resurrection and life in the NT will be examined and Revelation's employment of OT imagery regarding Israel's glorious future "golden age" will be explored. Is this "golden age" best connected with the thousand-year period highlighted in Revelation 20 or with the eternal new heavens and new earth (and New Jerusalem) of Revelation 21-22? A key question to answer.

Connected to all this is the overarching inquiry: does the content of Revelation 20 follow in chronological order the content of Revelation 19, which in fact describes the second coming, or does Revelation 20 take us back to Revelation 12 and the inauguration of the church age and the conflict between Christ and Satan, thus offering a condensed, targeted recapitulation of developments described previously in the book?

A final consideration will involve the connections between Revelation 20 and the letter to the church at

Smyrna (Rev 2:8-11). Distinctive linguistic characteristics point to a strong connection and perhaps a key to interpreting the symbolic language found in both.

The Reigning of Resurrected Saints

The issues arising out of the wording of Revelation 20:4-6 are complex and to aid in exposition the passage is quoted in full below:

> *Then I saw thrones, and seated on them were those to whom the authority to judge was committed. Also I saw the souls of those who had been beheaded for the testimony of Jesus and for the word of God, and those who had not worshiped the beast or its image and had not received its mark on their foreheads or their hands. They came to life and reigned with Christ for a thousand years. ⁵The rest of the dead did not come to life until the thousand years were ended. This is the first resurrection. ⁶Blessed and holy is the one who shares in the first resurrection! Over such the second death has no power, but they will be priests of God and of Christ, and they will reign with him for a thousand years. (Rev 20:4-6)*

A number of questions surface from this text. How many groups are described here? Are all the souls mentioned here martyrs? How is their "reign" described and what distinctions may be involved? Who are "the rest of the dead" who do not come to life until after the thousand years? In what sense do these souls "come to life?" What kind of resurrection is this?

The first two questions above go together. Likely not all those mentioned in Revelation 20 are martyrs for the faith. Some who did not worship the beast may have died by other means. Hence the "first resurrection" probably includes more than martyrs, instead representing all the dead who are faithful unto death. (As well, not all martyrs were actually beheaded as the text describes. Some faced other forms of execution.)

Another difficult distinction is that involving those seated on thrones with authority to judge and those who experience the first resurrection and reign with Christ for a thousand years. The same or different groups? "Sitting on a throne" and "reigning" would seem to be two ways of describing the same thing.

In the letters to the seven churches such actions as conquering, having authority, ruling, wearing a crown, and sitting on Christ's throne all describe the same basic triumphant reward (2:10-11, 26-27; 3:21). The image of saints reigning can also be viewed in Paul's letters as well as elsewhere in Revelation (Rom 5:17; 2Tm 2:12; Rev 5:9-10; 22:5). Paul reminded Timothy, "If we have died with him, we will also live with him; [12] if we endure, we will also reign with him" (2Tm 2:11-12). Resurrected and reigning: two important outcomes of endurance for believers.

In Revelation 4 we see twenty-four elders seated on thrones with crowns on their heads. Do these represent the entirety of the saved human population? Probably not. They are mentioned along with or in addition to the martyrs from the great tribulation (cf. Rev 7:13-17).

We seem to need room for the possibility or even likelihood of some overlap in the heavenly visions offered. The same entities could be described in varying ways. Also, the same imagery could be directed toward separate entities. Not all who "reign" or have been "resurrected" in Revelation are pictured as seated on thrones or wearing crowns. Serving the One seated on His throne is also a powerful image depicting those wonderfully redeemed and resurrected (7:13-17).

After the introduction of the Lion/Lamb in Revelation's initial throne room scene, we read,

And they sang a new song, saying, "Worthy are you to take the scroll and to open its seals, for you were slain, and by your blood you ransomed people for God from every tribe and language and people and nation, ¹⁰and you have made them a kingdom and priests to our God, and they shall reign on the earth." (Rev 5:9-10)

Noteworthy is the fact that, although "Israelite" language like "kingdom and priests" is employed here, those so addressed represent peoples "from every tribe and language and people and nation." Clearly God's "new Israel," the church, is in view. The promise "they shall reign on the earth" is no proof-text for an earthly millennium, as some claim. The "new earth" of Revelation 21-22 will be eternal.

The reference to "the rest of the dead" noted above very possibly involves only the unsaved, those who do not experience the first resurrection and therefore those whose names are not found written in the book of life (20:15). The books that are opened, books containing the deeds of the dead standing before the throne, signal the final judgment for those not in Christ, those whose names are not written in the book of life (20:12-15).

Paul's earlier statement that "we must all appear before the judgment seat of Christ" to be judged according to our works (2Cor 5:10) is clarified here in the sense that those found in the Lamb's book of life are reckoned as righteous in Christ, justified through His blood. The decisive "work" (action) involved in response is knowing Christ Jesus as Lord!

The resurrection language of Revelation 20 demands the extended discussion that follows. To begin, "coming to life" likely describes the experience immediately after death for those in Christ, those who will at that time enter into the presence of Christ in heaven (Php 1:21-23). It may make the best sense to view judgment as instantaneous upon death. (Can't God's deliberation be at least as fast as the latest supercomputer?) Viewed another way, the fact that "the dead in Christ" will rise at Christ's coming to join those still alive would seem to indicate that they have *already* been judged as being "in Christ" (1Th 4:16)!

The First Resurrection

John's designation "the second death" (Rev 2:11; 20:6, 14; 21:8) alongside "the first resurrection" (20:5, 6) in Revelation is suggestive. Clearly the second death relates to the eternal, spiritual death also designated as "the lake of fire" (19:20; 20:10, 14, 15; 21:8). Revelation makes no mention of a "first death" or a "second resurrection," but one is tempted to fill in between the lines: the first death would signify physical death while the second resurrection would then refer to the final "physical" resurrection, that which occurs at the second coming and that some would designate the general resurrection.

Again, no such designations "first death" or "second resurrection" occur in Revelation, but the spiritual nature of the two terms that *do* occur, first resurrection and second death, should be evident.

Premillennial interpreters tend to resist this conclusion and insist that the first resurrection occurs at the beginning of the millennium while the later, general resurrection occurs at the end, and *both* are physical in nature. The difference between "first" and "second" is more a matter of time than essence for them. It is strongly urged by premillennialists that the word "resurrection" here must refer to a physical one, since that is the meaning of the Greek word *anastasis*, "resurrection," elsewhere in the NT. Also, they insist that since coming to life at the end of the millennium at 20:5 involves physical resurrection (for all the dead), the nature of the resurrection described at 20:5, 6, that designated the "first resurrection," must also be physical.

This insistence is odd for two reasons. First, the symbolic, visionary nature of the descriptions throughout Revelation should caution us from pigeonholing terms into fixed slots. The fact that the term "death" in Revelation can speak to both a physical and a spiritual phenomenon should elicit caution. Eternal (the "second") death will follow physical death for many. The book speaks often of physical death (2:10, 13; 6:8, 9, 11; 9:11, 15, 18; 11:7, 19; 12:11; 13:10; 14:13; 16:5; 19:2, 21; 20:4, 9, 13).

Second, Jesus earlier had spoken about life and death and resurrection in ways that were veiled yet powerful. Jesus told Martha the sister of Lazarus, "Whoever believes in me, though he die, yet shall he live, 26 and everyone who lives and believes in me shall never die..." (Jn 11:25-26). In this short statement utilizing the words "live" and "die," Jesus covers the gamut: physical death, spiritual life, physical life, absence of spiritual death. Believers shall never die, but though they die they shall live. Got it?

To argue that the term *anastasis*, "resurrection," must indicate physical resurrection in Revelation (where it occurs only twice) seems odd, especially when the repeated expression "second death" (spiritual!) opens up a range of possibilities.

G. K. Beale offers ample NT evidence that the Greek verb *zaō*, "live, come to life," and noun *zōē*, "life," can be used for both physical and spiritual life and, of particular relevance here, for the existence of believers in the intermediate state—the state after death and before the general resurrection (*Revelation*, 1008-1011). Paul referred to dying (dead to sin) and living (alive to God) with Christ spiritually (Rom 6:4-13), while John relates that Jesus spoke of the believer passing from death into life in a spiritual sense followed still by a "resurrection of life" at the general resurrection (Jn 5:24-29).

In connection with the intermediate state, Jesus quotes Moses in speaking of God as the God of Abraham and the God of Isaac and the God of Jacob and then describes those individuals as *presently living*: "Now he is not God of the dead but of the living, for all live to him" (Lk 20:37-38; cf. Mt 22:31-32; Mk 12:26-27). Here Jesus is describing the patriarchs as being alive during their intermediate states, the time between their physical deaths and the general resurrection from the dead.

Premillennial approaches to the "first resurrection" suffer on several counts. The insistence on a physical resurrection is questionable, as noted above. Also, regarding dispensational premillennialism, if the first resurrection occurs at the beginning of the millennium, i.e., at the second coming (or Christ's "return" or "revelation") what should be made of the glorious resurrection described by Paul in 1 Corinthians 15?

This resurrection, in dispensational thinking, occurs for the church at the rapture, an event preceding the second coming and its "first resurrection" by seven years or so. One would think that this alleged earlier resurrection, a resurrection also supposedly spotlighted in 1 Thessalonians 4 by Paul, would be the "first," so how does that all work out?

For dispensationalism there is a resurrection at the rapture, a resurrection at the second coming (or "return"), and a resurrection following the subsequent millennial reign (at the Great White Throne Judgment). Lots of resurrections. With dispensationalists, the second of these seems to be the "first"! Combining the first two above, two allegedly separate resurrection events, into a single conceptual entity, the "first resurrection," seems awkward. Dispensational scholars generally struggle here. Their "first resurrection" is actually their second.

An oddity from premillennialism in general is the notion that the beast and the false prophet experience the lake of fire, the "second death," immediately prior to the "first resurrection." It cannot be proven, but it is commonly assumed that the lake of fire (*Gehenna*, "hell") does not yet exist or at least that no one will be thrown into it until the last day, what John describes as the Great White Throne Judgment (Rev 20:11-15).

In premillennial thought, however, the beast and the false prophet experience the lake of fire a thousand years before Satan does and before his other, later ("Gog and Magog") followers do. This seems off to me. Rather, I would suggest, in a chiastic ("mirror image") literary structure (A:B::B:A), Satan is introduced first (Revelation 12), preceding the entrance of the beast and false prophet (Revelation 13) and then terminated last (Revelation 20), following the demise of the beast and false prophet (Revelation 19).

Previously Satan, the beast, and the false prophet were all mentioned together as having demonic spirits issuing forth from their mouths, demons who assemble together the forces of evil at Armageddon for the final conflict (Rev 16:13-16) designated as the "battle on the great day of God the Almighty" (16:14). In amillennial thought, all three—the dragon, the beast, and the false prophet—suffer the same fate in connection with that "conflict" (which is battle imagery for final judgment). At approximately the same time.

The amillennial camp offers two primary suggestions for the nature of the "first resurrection" enjoyed by believers. Augustine and others have maintained that this expression describes the spiritual resurrection occurring at conversion. Paul pointed to baptism as the moment when believers are "raised up" with Christ and "made alive" together with Him (Col 2:12-13; cf. Rom 6: 3-11). Followers of Christ have been "born again" and enjoy new life in Christ. Eternal life is something now ("already") enjoyed, not just something to be anticipated (1Jn 5:11). However, although appropriate and powerful NT terminology for conversion, the above designations actually may not be the focus in Revelation's expression "first resurrection."

The other prominent amillennial answer is that the first resurrection represents the inauguration of and participation in the intermediate state of each believer, that state immediately following physical death and continuing until Christ's return and the accompanying general resurrection (see esp. Hill, 220-248).

In Revelation 6:9-11 those "slain for the word of God" call upon God to enter into His final judgment; however, they are comforted ad encouraged to "rest a little longer." There is no "soul sleeping" here. These martyrs are actually given (temporary? anticipatory? mostly metaphoric?) "white robes" as they each await the consummation. The fact that the world is still full of the wicked after Christ's millennial reign (20:7-9) makes it more likely that the thousand years in question describe the church age, not a paradisiacal earthly reign of Christ from Jerusalem as commonly envisioned in premillennial reconstructions. This dovetails with the view that the intermediate state for the dead in Christ is represented here, the totality of which coincides with the church age.

The language in much of the NT suggests that saints who have died in Christ are "made alive" immediately after death. Paul speaks of being "with Christ" after his "departure" (Php 1:23). After death ("away from the body"), Paul explains, believers are "at home with the Lord" (2Cor 5:8). In one sense they "have fallen asleep," i.e., have died (1Th 4:14), but, in a fuller sense, they now abide in Christ's presence.

The book of Revelation strongly affirms such an understanding. Four parallel scenes stand out.

1. As noted above, at Revelation 6:9-11 we see martyrs under the altar in heaven calling out for divine judgment upon the wicked dwelling on earth. The general resurrection at Christ's return lies ahead following the martyrs' "intermediate state."

2. Revelation 7:8-17 describes worship before God's throne by followers of the Lamb prior to the opening of the seventh seal (8:1). The intermediate state is in view.

3. At Revelation 15:1-4, prior to the unleashing of the seven bowl plagues (Revelation 16), those who had conquered the beast sing in worship in heaven, dead yet very much alive! Again, the intermediate state.

4. Further, at Revelation 19:1-9 we find a great multitude in heaven celebrating in anticipation of the triumphal marriage supper of the Lamb. Still yet another glimpse of the intermediate state for the dead in Christ.

Why is it surprising to some that the righteous dead repeatedly described in Revelation as actively worshiping and interacting with God prior to the general resurrection upon Christ's coming could be said to have been "made alive" or to have experienced a "resurrection to life"(a "first resurrection")? Here the book of Revelation seems to explain itself for those willing to allow it to do so.

Hence in Revelation 20 we offer an additional scene describing the intermediate state:

5. At Revelation 20:4-6 the dead in Christ "reign for a thousand years" leading up to Christ's return, the final judgment, and the creation of the new heavens and new earth. This reign is in heaven, not on earth. A common-sense approach to the term "first resurrection" favors an amillennial understanding of the thousand-year reign of Christ and His saints in Revelation 20.

The Missing Connection

The problems with the premillennial understanding of Revelation 20 are legion. One of the most challenging is the missing connection between the OT descriptions of the future "golden age" and the actual description of the millennium in Revelation 20. Importantly, Revelation's allusions to the key OT golden age texts in Isaiah 60 and 65 are found in Revelation 21-22 in the context of the arrival of the New Jerusalem and the new heavens and the new earth, an arrival depicted in Revelation as *following* the millennial kingdom of Revelation 20, whenever and whatever that may be. The attempts to confiscate the descriptions of the eternal state in Revelation 21-22 and smuggle them into the descriptions of the millennium in

Revelation 20 are misguided and telling—desperate attempts to salvage a suspect system.

On the other hand, the so-called millennium of Revelation 20 contains no observable parallels with the OT's descriptions of a future golden age or kingdom age for God's people. There is no mention of Christ (Israel's Messiah) reigning on the earth, let alone in Jerusalem. Also, there is no mention of Israel whatsoever!

This seems strange in light of the many claims made by premillennialists about the future of Israel upon the so-called millennial earth. Instead, the scene in Revelation 20 seems to be in heaven where martyrs for Christ come to life and reign with Christ for a thousand years (20:4). Remember that reigning with Christ is a key promise given to the church earlier in the book for those who overcome or "conquer" (2:10, 26-27; 3:11, 21).

For a chapter that is the Bible's lone source for the claim of a thousand-year reign upon the earth, Revelation 20 is remarkably uncooperative! The scene seems to be set in heaven, not on earth. The church, not physical Israel, is the obvious focus. Satan's role as a defeated foe seems paramount, paralleling earlier claims in Revelation about his being conquered by Christ's faithful ones even as he is cast down from heaven to earth (12:7-12). Revelation 12 portrays conditions playing out in the church age and that would seem to be the case for Revelation 20 as well.

Descriptions of the millennium in Revelation 20 do not pertain to events that follow the church age but rather to events in connection with the church age. Revelation 20 begins a new, compact, climactic, visionary sequence in the book that commences with Christ's victory over Satan in connection with His first coming. It then goes on to describe the final defeat of Satan and his followers, the final judgment before God's throne, and the descent of the New

Jerusalem from heaven to earth signaling the commencement of the eternal state—events tied to the second coming. The use of Ezekiel's language regarding the final climactic battle (involving "Gog and Magog") points to the second coming at both 19:17-21and 20:7-10, further supporting the conclusion that the millennial reign of 20:1-6 is a visionary recapitulation reinforcing truths revealed throughout the book and is not the beginning of a new chronological sequence of events.

Recapitulation Recap

For many, the key question for Revelation is the relationship between Revelation 19 and Revelation 20. Is the second coming battle described in Revelation 19 followed by a millennial reign on earth as supposedly described in Revelation 20, or is Revelation 20 presenting a recapitulation of previous content involving the cosmic conflict between Christ and Satan? Premillennialists strongly urge that the only possible understanding of Revelation 20 is that it follows chronologically the climactic battle described in Revelation 19. Below are nine key issues involved with my take on each.

1. The figurative use of the expression "a thousand years" in Revelation 20 has strong support from other biblical texts utilizing the number "thousand" in a figurative or symbolic way and from the rest of the book of Revelation in its use of symbolic numbers throughout, a use documented thoroughly in the present work (e.g., Deu 7:9; Ps 50:10; 90:4; 2Pet 3:8; Chapters X, XIII, XV).

2. Both the binding of Satan and the reigning of the saints with Christ are said to be a thousand years in duration, while both realities are described throughout the NT as being present to some extent within the church age itself. The "already and not yet" paradigm described earlier (Chapter II) recognizes Satan's current status as a defeated foe and that of the church as already victorious over him, while at the same time presenting the devil as a dangerous, powerful force for evil in the world and the church as experiencing various forms of tribulation and opposition. It has been suggested above that Revelation 20 focuses upon the triumphant saints in heaven during the church age (involving the "intermediate state" of those who have died in Christ and now reign with him) and not upon an earthly kingdom of sorts.

3. It has been stressed that there is no mention of Israel or even Jerusalem specifically and no utilization of OT "golden age" texts within Revelation 20 and its description of the so-called millennium. Instead the saints of the NT church, God's "new Israel," are the focus.

4. The "golden age" passages in the OT prophets are instead employed in Revelation 21-22, chapters that describe the new heavens and new earth along with the New Jerusalem that *follow* the thousand years of Revelation 20, whatever those may describe (Chapter XXIII). Isaiah 60 and 65 especially are utilized extensively by John here and only by vigorous sleight-of-hand can interpreters seek to make the millennium of Revelation 20 a fulfillment of the descriptions in Isaiah 60 and 65. Only with a pair of millennial sunglasses tinted toward a future thousand-year reign can John's use of the OT be seen to incorporate a millennial kingdom prior to the establishment of the New Jerusalem.

5. Both Revelation 19:11-21 and 20:7-10 borrow imagery and language from Ezekiel's Gog and Magog accounts in Ezekiel 38-39. The battle metaphor is utilized to describe divine judgment and both the reference to fire from heaven and the reference to the birds of the heavens eating the flesh of the slain are utilized by John from Ezekiel (Chapter XIX). John actually uses the names Gog and Magog in his description of Satan's followers (20:8) and it is almost inconceivable that the two battles John depicts here are not one and the same (leaving the possibility that the second one is a reenactment of the first as a part of God's "triumph" over Satan—Chapter XXII).

6. The great final battle is anticipated in Revelation 16:12-16 and described at 19:11-21 and 20:7-10. The end-times battle awaited at Revelation 16:12-16 involving the dragon, the beast, and the false prophet seems to be broken down in later chapters. The encounter against Christ and his heavenly forces involves the beast, the false prophet, and their armies (19:19-21), while Satan's attack after his release from prison will end with fire descending from heaven to destroy his followers (20:7-9). The first encounter described ends with the beast and the false prophet being cast into the lake of fire while the second encounter depicts the devil himself cast into the lake of fire. Are these climactic engagements separated by a thousand years or are they two descriptions of the same final encounter? I am convinced that the latter is the case.

7. Some interpreters have noted that in these above three passages the Greek word for "battle" or "war" (*polemos*) has the Greek article (thus *ho polemos*). Generally, but not always, in English translations the Greek article will be represented by the English definite article "the." Thus, regarding the above instances, we could expect to find: Christ's enemies are assembled "for *the* battle of the great day of God the Almighty" (16:14); the beast and his forces are gathered to engage in "*the* battle against the One seated upon the horse" (19:19); Satan gathers his followers "for *the* battle" (20:8).

Greek scholars and Bible translators continually wrestle with how best to interpret and translate the Greek article. (Unlike English, Greek has no indefinite article, so *logos* could be rendered either as "word" or "a word.") In many ways usage of the Greek article parallels that of the definite article in English, but in other cases not so much. Here, as with other linguistic issues, translators of the NT regularly traverse the poles of literal accuracy and literary nicety.

Taking care to be precise and trying to offer a reading that is optimally understandable for a given audience are not always readily compatible tasks. Evaluating translations in regard to such issues becomes complicated. Sometimes what "sounds right" replaces a less polished but more precise translation. And important distinctions are at times lost. That may be the case here.

A number of scholars have suggested that the Greek articles found at Revelation 16:14, 19:19, and 20:8 point to one specific end-times conflict (Beale, *Revelation*, 834-837; Kistemaker, 244-245; White, 545-547). In contrast, the term *polemos*, "war, battle," without the article (six times in Revelation) regularly points to the *ongoing* war waged throughout the church age by Satan and the beast against God's people and not to the "final battle" (11:7; 12:7, 17; 13:7; cf 9:7, 9).

If indeed the three articular forms in Revelation point to the same end-times battle, as I believe they do, we find another argument for the view that Revelation 20 involves a recapitulation of the events of Revelation 19 and earlier chapters. Thus the battles summarized in Revelation 19 and 20 (along with that anticipated in Revelation 16) each describe the final conflict that brings us to final judgment and the establishment of the new heavens and new earth.

Not surprisingly, English translations do not always make this clear regarding these three instances. For example, ESV reads "assemble them for battle" (16:14); "gathered to make war" (19:19); and "gather them for battle" (20:8). None of these readings help the reader to recognize that a specific battle, the *same* specific battle, is involved in all three passages.

In contrast, both NAS and NET do provide the (definite) article at 16:14 and 20:8, but not at 19:19. KJV and NIV give us a rendering of the article only at 16:14. Smoothness of translation is often a consideration, of course, and the insertion of the English definite article may render the wording unwieldy, as it may here, especially at 19:19.

In this case, however, I believe that correct interpretation and theological uniformity could have been aided by the insertion of the definite article in the appropriate spots above. Such an insertion could have helped clarify that the same singular conflict, *the* coming battle, is involved in all three relevant texts and that therefore the battle in Revelation 20 is a recapitulation of that in Revelation 19.

Greek scholars and translators would rightly caution us concerning matters of idiom and context. Armies are "assembled for battle" to "make war," not "assembled for war" to "make battle". I should note that I am not aware of any standard translation that renders the Greek text "the battle" in all three passages mentioned here. On the other hand, since we are dealing with a metaphor for final judgment in these passages, therefore a distinct (metaphoric) "battle," not a protracted war, is involved. The same final battle. Emphasized through recapitulation.

8. A prominent feature of this recapitulation involves the parallels between Satan being cast out of heaven and down to earth in Revelation 12 and his being bound and cast into the abyss in Revelation 20. Adding to the impression that these two sections are closely linked is the fact that both display a comparable inventory of titles for the evil one: the great dragon, that ancient serpent, the devil, Satan, the deceiver, the accuser (12:9-10); along with the dragon, that ancient serpent, the devil, Satan (20:2).

Satan's role as *accuser* is thwarted when he is cast down to earth and loses access to the heavenly throne (12:10). His role as *deceiver* is greatly hindered by his being cast into the abyss, bound and imprisoned, while the life-imparting gospel spreads throughout the earth (20:2-4). Appreciation for the imagery in both of these pivotal passages is hindered by an attachment to wooden literalism, an attachment particularly unwise in light of the overall metaphoric nature of the book of Revelation.

9. Repeatedly in Revelation we encounter cycles that bring us to the end only to find that we are in some sense back to where we started. The sixth opened seal brings us to the arrival of the great day of the wrath of the Lamb and of the One seated on the throne (6:16-17). But hold on. Instructive interludes along with destructive demonic plagues still await.

The blowing of the seventh trumpet signals the arrival of judgment: wrath for the wicked and the rewarding of the saints (11:18). The sixth bowl of wrath finds God's enemies assembled for the final battle at Armageddon (16:12-16). Parallel cycles (the trumpets and the bowls) are both interrupted and intensified with various visionary interludes, some recounting the past with others pointing to the future.

In light of what has transpired leading up to Revelation 20, it would not be surprising to find one final reset in which promises made earlier to the seven churches are highlighted (Chapter IX) and Satan's ultimate defeat is described.

The binding of Satan and the reigning of the saints in heaven in Revelation 20 are best understood as representing a condensed recapitulation of much of what the book has already introduced and developed. The alternative approach, one in which Revelation 20 is viewed as chronologically sequential to what has preceded, is a heavy burden to bear for those who seek meaningful harmonization with the rest of the NT. The insertion of a thousand-year earthly kingdom following the second coming creates incredible challenges for the student of NT eschatology.

Issues like these should not be tests of fellowship but they certainly deserve our careful attention. A view that promotes careful, contextual exegesis and the realization of the unity of biblical theology throughout Scripture is to be preferred over one that leaves us grasping for straws and piling up untenable solutions.

The Smyrna Link

Few commentators on Revelation have stressed the remarkable literary connection between Revelation 20 and Jesus' letter to the church at Smyrna in Revelation 2:8-11. In my view, this connection underscores the symbolic nature of the "thousand-year" binding of Satan and the spiritual nature of the "second death."

And to the angel of the church in Smyrna write: "The words of the first and the last, who died and came to life. ⁹I know your tribulation and your poverty (but you are rich) and the slander of those who say that they are Jews and are not, but are a synagogue of Satan. ¹⁰Do not fear what you are about to suffer. Behold, the devil is about to throw some of you into prison, that you may be tested, and for ten days you will have tribulation. Be faithful unto death, and I will give you the crown of life. ¹¹He who has an ear, let him hear what the Spirit says to the churches. The one who conquers will not be hurt by the second death."' (Rev 2:8-11)

In the letter to Smyrna we find a number of elements corresponding to those mentioned in Revelation 20: the devil, the casting of someone into prison, tribulation ten days (versus reigning a thousand years), the crown of life for those faithful unto death, and conquerors unharmed by the second death. In Revelation 2 the devil casts (*ballō*) believers into prison (*phylakē*), while in Revelation 20 the devil himself is cast (*ballō*) into his own prison (*phylakē*), also called the "abyss," or "bottomless pit" (2:10; 20:3, 7).

In Revelation 2 Christians will suffer tribulation "ten days" (2:10), while in Revelation 20 they will reign for "a thousand years" (20:4, 6) and the devil himself will be bound and imprisoned for "a thousand years" (20:2). In Revelation 2 the crown of life is promised, while in Revelation 20 coming to life through resurrection is experienced (2:10; 20:4-6). In both Revelation 2 and 20-21 and nowhere else in Scripture we find the distinctive term "second death," a term used as a reference to spiritual, eternal death (2:11; 20:6, 14; 21:8).

The parallels (and contrasts) are striking. I am convinced that those to whom Revelation was initially sent would have grasped the implications and thus would have understood the symbolic nature of the language especially used in Revelation 20. For the Christians at Smyrna, their "ten-day" period of suffering would pale in comparison to their "thousand years" of reigning with Christ!

The evil one behind their imprisonment for their faith had himself been chained and imprisoned. The death they might experience would end in their receiving a crown of life. The lake of fire, the "second death," awaited their persecutor, the devil.

The letter to the church in Smyrna in Revelation 2 anticipates the imagery found later in Revelation 20. The connections emphasize further the symbolism employed there in its climactic, condensed summary of the church age and intermediate state of believers. Once again Revelation functions as a two-sided coin (cf. esp. 5:5-6; 7;4, 9; 19:6-16): Satan imprisons/is himself imprisoned; ten days/a thousand years; faithful death/crown of life; first resurrection/second death.

All clues for properly understanding Revelation 20 are most welcome. I am drawn to the approach that sees this chapter as being explained by the rest of Scripture, not by any system that views it as a doctrinal outlier or innovator because of which commonly accepted biblical truths and teachings must be modified or minimized.

Chapter XXII

Satan's Final Doom (Rev 20)

The eternal destruction of Satan and his followers is recorded at Revelation 20:7-15 and includes a description of Satan's "last stand" against God's kingdom and of the ensuing Great White Throne Judgment for those whose names are not written in the "book of life." The duration of Satan's release from prison is called "a little while" (20:3; KJV "a little season").

The close of Revelation's "cosmic drama" in Revelation 12-20 is controversial and challenging to interpreters. Revelation 20:7-10 reads,

> *And when the thousand years are ended, Satan will be released from his prison ⁸and will come out to deceive the nations that are at the four corners of the earth, Gog and Magog, to gather them for battle; their number is like the sand of the sea. ⁹And they marched up over the broad plain of the earth and surrounded the camp of the saints and the beloved city, but fire came down from heaven and consumed them, ¹⁰and the devil who had deceived them was thrown into the lake of fire and sulfur where the beast and the false prophet were, and they will be tormented day and night forever and ever. (Rev 20:7-10)*

The "Little Season"

A "little season" ("little while," ESV) is described as a necessary time following the thousand years during which

Satan has been bound (20:3). The interpretation of this time period can go in several directions. Taking this as a dramatic vision and not a chronological documentary, one could argue that the loosing of Satan is primarily a literary device. He is loosed in anticipation of his demise. Despite Satan's final, desperate efforts, he and his followers are destroyed while God's beloved are completely unharmed, those described as "the camp of the saints and the beloved city" (20:9). The description of a final battle here is, as elsewhere in Revelation, not a picture of a battle at all but rather of divine judgment.

The "little while" here is not the same time period as the "short time" of Revelation 12:12. The latter expression likely pointed to the duration of Satan's opportunity during the church age to tempt and destroy the "woman and her offspring" (the church), expressed as a time of tribulation and divine protection lasting "1,260 days" or a "time, times, and half a time" (both = "forty-two months" as equivalents to three and a half [half of seven] years). See especially Chapter XIII.

The amassing of an ungodly horde following a supposed millennium during which Christ reigns in glory over the earth on a throne in Jerusalem is a problem for the premillennial view and diminishes the likeliness of that view. The notion common among premillennialists that the purpose of the millennium is to demonstrate once and for all the full extent of mankind's evil ways has little merit. Several decades into the twenty-first century do we really need any more proof of the pervasive presence of sin in the world?

The massive march over the face of the earth results in the surrounding of "the beloved city" and "the camp of the saints," designations that seem to point to a spiritual reality, the church, rather than a physical city. Again there is no battle; instead fire comes down from heaven consuming the wicked (Rev 20:9).

Rather than being a second of two separate "Gog and Magog" encounters as premillennialism would seem to require, this destruction of the wicked at 20:9 mirrors that at 19:21 where, in connection with the beast and the false prophet being thrown into the lake of fire, all who follow them are slain by the sword coming out of Christ's mouth at His second coming. At 20:9 the evil combatants are simply consumed by fire. Both of the descriptions in Revelation 19-20 portray the outcome anticipated in Revelation 16 where these forces are "assembled at Armageddon" for the final conflict (16:16).

Satan is depicted as a relentless foe on the offense even unto the bitter end, although it is clear that his fate is sealed. Perhaps it is significant that he is not depicted as a helpless captive hurled into a fiery lake but rather as an active opponent of God and His righteous followers. As with the beast and the false prophet, Satan's doom occurs in connection with his aggressive opposition to God.

Translations differ in how they express the timing of the casting of the beast and the false prophet into the lake of fire in conjunction with the casting of Satan himself into that lake. Again, I would argue that the mention of Satan's doom last is for literary and dramatic effect as part of a chiasm (A:B::B:A; a "mirror image") and not so much as a chronological indicator.

In Revelation's cosmic drama Satan, the great dragon, is introduced first (Revelation 12) followed by the beast and the false prophet (Revelation 13). At the end, the beast and the false prophet are cast in the lake of fire (Revelation 19) and that description is followed by the description of Satan's destruction in the lake of fire (Revelation 20).

In the premillennial system, the beast and the false prophet are thrown into the lake of fire a full thousand years before Satan is. But is that what Revelation actually teaches? Is their doom basically simultaneous with that of their leader Satan or are the two already in the lake of fire for a lengthy time before Satan joins them?

A comparison of translations at 20:10 shows a variety of treatments regarding the sequence: "where the beast and the false prophet were" (ESV); "where the beast and the false prophet had been thrown" (NIV); "where the beast and the false prophet are too" (NET); "where the beast and the false prophet are also" (NAS); "where the beast and the false prophet are" (KJV). What is the issue here?

If the events of Revelation 19 precede those of Revelation 20 by a significant period of time, then the beast and the false prophet are already in the lake of fire and Satan eventually joins them. If Revelation 19 and Revelation 20 both are describing the same second coming, however, then the casting into the lake of fire of the beast and false prophet is basically simultaneous with that of Satan.

How does the Greek read? What is the tense of the Greek verb at 20:10? The answer is that there is no Greek verb! Often in the Greek NT the verb "to be" in its various forms can be understood (represented in English by "is, are, was, were," etc.). Therefore in such a case, contextually-based theology, not grammar, must decide the issue. Both ESV and especially NIV suggest a chronological sequence in which the beast and the false prophet were already in the lake of fire. Such a translation choice would seem to favor a premillennial approach. NET, NAS, and KJV, however, put the verb in the present tense, therefore "are," not "were." This allows the amillennial understanding that Satan, in the unfolding of Revelation's scenes, joins the beast and the false prophet whose demise has already been described, but he does not necessarily chronologically follow them in their fate.

In essence we have the same event described from two vantage points. By our approaching the scenes in Revelation as often complementary, and not necessarily chronological, we can appreciate that the combination of visions and explanations brings into vivid focus the realities being described. The book itself offers numerous indicators that the scenes often are not in chronological sequence (e.g., Christ's birth and ascension to heaven halfway through the book at Revelation 12). Repetition and recapitulation are strategies employed to convey the book's message.

Trying to fit in the events of Revelation 20:7-10 is a challenge for all. Both historic premillennialists and classic dispensationalists seem to have two periods of future tribulation, apostasy, rebellion, etc., one before an earthly millennial kingdom and one after. A major difference here between dispensationalists and historic premillennialists is that dispensationalists argue that the church is raptured out and therefore avoids this terrible time (or these terrible times) of tribulation.

Many premillennialists seem to agree in general, however, that there are two distinct future rebellion/tribulation periods outlined in Scripture, one immediately preceding the second coming and the other following the millennium, setting the stage for the Great White Throne Judgment. Some historic premillennialists may also view the entire church age, or much of it, as a tribulation (or even "great tribulation") period. In contrast, dispensational premillennialists place the rapture between the church age and the alleged three-and-a-half-year "great tribulation" that leads up to Christ's return (their "second coming" that, by their configuration, is really a third!).

Many amillennialists see an outbreak of evil at the end of the millennium, i.e., the end of the church age, and connect the "little season" of 20:3, 7-10 with it. For most amillennialists, Satan's rebellion and attack upon "the camp of the saints" is a recap of the previous confrontation described in Revelation 19:11-21 and, for many, also a reiteration of the theme of an end-times tribulation and persecution of the church found earlier in the NT. Several questions arise here, however.

Since the Revelation 20 description of Satan's final stand says nothing about persecution or about Christians suffering tribulation or Christians departing from the faith, does this later text really speak about the same thing earlier texts are said to describe? There seem to be no casualties for God's people as the book winds down, only judgment for Satan's hordes.

An even bigger question involves the broader assumptions surrounding an end-times tribulation and persecution of the church. Paul's writings to the Thessalonians and to Timothy are often used in support for the notion of a major latter-days apostasy. Such assumptions are open to debate. Especially relevant here is my discussion regarding the man of lawlessness found in 2 Thessalonians 2: 1-12 (Appendix A).

As I argue there, Paul's use of the Greek *apostasia* is best rendered "rebellion" or "revolt," and not "falling away" or "apostasy," and refers to the Jewish Revolt against Rome (AD 66-70), not to an end-times falling away ("apostasy") from the Christian faith. If Paul's enigmatic "lawless one" played his part in the first-century destruction of Jerusalem and does not have the future role most assume, much of the scholarly steam pent up concerning an end-times tribulation is released. Also important is the previous observation that much of Revelation 6-18 is *not* about end-times tribulation poured out upon believers through Satan's machinations but rather about end-times wrath poured out upon unbelievers by God (Chapter X).

As stressed in Appendix A, my views on the man of lawlessness do not depend upon a strict preterist view that links the AD 70 fall of Jerusalem to the second coming. Paul's teaching in 2 Thessalonians 2 has long puzzled interpreters and I offer here an approach that helps avoid many of the common failed assumptions and conclusions in dealing with this enigmatic text.

Open to debate as well are Paul's words in 1 and 2 Timothy where Paul warned Timothy about "last-days" or "latter-days" apostates who introduce false teaching. These passages are given more weight than they perhaps deserve and are often identified with a more distant situation than perhaps Paul was describing. Regarding such "last-days" evildoers, Paul warns Timothy to avoid such people (2Tm 3:5). One might therefore surmise that such individuals had already arrived!

Paul states that "the Spirit expressly says that in later times some will depart from the faith," a departure involving false teaching and devotion to the teachings of demons. Abstinence from marriage and adherence to certain dietary regulations would be involved (1Tm 4:1-3). This sounds both like the Gnostic heresy that threatened the early church and like other early deviations that have continued throughout history, and not necessarily strictly end-times developments.

At the end of the day, interpreters are left with several less-than-satisfying solutions as to what is involved in the "little season" at Revelation 20:3. It might be best simply to regard the description in Revelation 20:7-10 as a figurative, symbolic reenactment of what Revelation has already described: Christ's triumphant return and the doom of His enemies. The use of "Gog and Magog" imagery lends credence to that. Just as the OT prophets described the final confrontation between God and His enemies with battle terminology, so does John (the "new Ezekiel") in Revelation. As in Ezekiel, in Revelation fire from heaven destroys God's foes (Eze 38:22; 39:6; Rev 20:8-9) even as they are gathered for battle and are defeated (Eze 38; 21; 39:3-4; Rev 19:17-19, 21; 20:8-9). Less satisfactory, in my view, is the notion that a further alleged "end-times" tribulation is now announced, a brief time closing out or following the inaugurated millennial kingdom (the church age) during which Satan's powers hold sway. There is one other intriguing possibility that should be explored.

Satan Released Yet Still Bound: God's Triumphal Procession?

Since compelling treatments of Revelation 20:7-10 are few and far between, perhaps we should look in a different direction, one that recognizes the "already and not yet" aspects of Satan's defeat (Chapters II, XIII) and the feature of recapitulation as it relates to the imagery of Revelation 20. Also potentially important in the equation are the socio-political as well as religious phenomena in play at the end of the first century AD.

In his valuable treatments of this controversial passage, Shane Wood has presented an intriguing paradigm that deserves consideration (*Paradigm*, 189-216; "Release," 181-191; *Veil*, 154-172). Wood sees great importance in the fact that, following his imprisonment, Satan is said to be released but not unbound. Key to his discussion is the existence of the highly significant phenomenon during the Roman Empire (and earlier Republic) known as the Roman Triumph. Commanders victorious in Rome's military conflicts were often given a "triumph" in honor of their achievements. More than three hundred such triumphs are recorded regarding ancient Rome.

The most extensive, detailed description of the Roman Triumph from antiquity is found in the *Jewish War* by Josephus, a description of the triumph celebrated in Rome following the AD 70 destruction of Jerusalem (*War* 7.116-157). Perhaps the closest thing for American sensitivities regarding the grandeur of the event would be Macy's Thanksgiving Parade or perhaps Mardi Gras or a Super Bowl celebration (*sans* the violence and bloodshed of the ancient Roman event).

Josephus describes the extravagant display of massive floats, the parade of wartime prisoners, and the opulent and often exotic displays of the spoils of war, complete with elaborate reconstructions of relevant fortifications and topographical features, along with reenactments of the glorious accomplishments of the victorious Roman legionary forces. The most impressive prisoners were commandeered for the roles of defeated, doomed foes. Roman soldiers marched in triumph to the crowd's delight. Still seen today on the Arch of Titus in Rome is a depiction of treasures being carted off from Jerusalem, including the temple's golden menorah.

As with other triumphs, the one Josephus described ended with the execution of various prisoners and particularly the enemy leader. The Jewish general Simon bar Giora was viewed by the Romans as the key military leader in Jerusalem's rebellion and was accordingly executed at the conclusion of the parade to the gleeful shouts of Rome's onlookers. (As noted in Appendix A, "The Man of Lawlessness," the despotic Jewish rebel John of Gischala, who was only exiled by Rome, played a larger role in the early stages of Jerusalem's revolt.)

Most prisoners who were not executed were sent to slave camps. Each Roman Triumph signaled the incomparable power and influence of the Roman Empire and its leaders. The *Pax Romana* ("Roman Peace") was repeatedly propped up through violent exercises of military domination.

In anticipation of a triumph, the defeated enemy leader was chained and incarcerated awaiting his eventual execution, the official culmination of the Roman victory. Such an imprisonment could last for months or even years. The celebrated execution of the chief enemy was a highlight in the minds of the Roman conquerors and the unfortunate death or, at times, suicide of such a leader before the triumph was deeply regretted. Octavian (Augustus) had a mannequin made of Cleopatra to be exhibited during his triumph since she had committed suicide.

Also relevant to note is that Domitian, the emperor when Revelation likely was penned, participated in the triumph Josephus describes that followed the Jewish Revolt. He rode on a single white horse accompanying Vespasian and Titus, his father and brother, as they rode in a *quadriga*, a splendid four-horse chariot that became standard equipment for those honored in such triumphs.

In addition to the general familiarity with the Roman Triumph for early Christians in the empire, we might note the likelihood that a copy of Josephus' *Jewish War*, written circa AD 75, would have been available in the library in Ephesus and/or in libraries of other cities of Roman Asia. The library at Pergamum was said to be second only to that in Alexandria. Previously Paul himself had used imagery from the Roman Triumph in his powerful metaphor involving following Christ in "triumphal procession" as a prisoner, triumphant even in the face of death (2Cor 2:14-16).

A key feature of the Roman Triumph was the reenactment of the victorious military campaign. Wood suggests that John's description of Satan's release from prison describes God's triumph, part of which is the final destruction of the enemy leader, Satan himself. Wood emphasizes the fact that Revelation describes Satan as being released from prison but not being unchained or unbound.

His "leading his army," then, may not be the initiating of a new confrontation but merely the reenactment and final resolution of the old one, a confrontation in which the devil had already been defeated—cast out of heaven and down to earth and then cast into the bottomless pit in chains awaiting his destruction (Rev 12:7-12; 20:1-3, 9-10). Satan's release from prison will therefore pave the way for his taking center stage one last time, not for a dramatic comeback but for his decisive defeat, in order to imitate that which took center stage in typical Roman Triumphs when defeated, bound enemy leaders were paraded to their execution.

The ancient "open-air" altar at the temple of Domitian in Ephesus, viewable in the museum of Ephesus today, depicts imagery of a triumph, including the scene of two figures, a Roman soldier raising his weapon and looking down upon a the other figure: a bound captive sitting down awaiting execution (Wood, "Release," 190). For Christians in Ephesus near the end of the first century, this prominently located altar and its artwork may have been a familiar sight.

More significant still was their familiarity with the ongoing political and cultural imprint of the Roman Triumph upon Roman society. Once the church's chief enemy is described in Revelation as bound and imprisoned, John's initial audience could easily have connected the dots regarding Revelation's message: Satan, already defeated and bound, will experience his ultimate defeat at God's grand triumph.

The above approach may not answer all questions, but it provides a plausible explanation of the imagery involved with respect to Satan's being imprisoned and then released while yet chained or bound. Satan was indeed "bound" at Christ's first coming and he is already depicted in the initial verses of Revelation 20 as a defeated prisoner of war. His intended attack against the "camp of the saints" upon his release may reflect what had been described earlier in Revelation after he had fallen from heaven and sought out to destroy the church (Rev 12:7-17). Revelation 20:7-10 may very well offer a triumphal reenactment of Satan's previous failed campaign.

The Great White Throne Judgment

John's description of the Great White Throne Judgment is notable both for its succinctness and for its vivid imagery (20:11-15). Again God is described as the One sitting on the throne and the dissolution of the present heavens and earth in His presence is affirmed (20:11; cf. 2Pet 3:7, 10-13).

The merism "great and small" represents the idea of everyone (all relevant parties) standing before the throne (20:12). John makes an important distinction between the fact that "books were opened" and the fact that another single book, "the book of life," is rather the key. On one hand, the dead are "judged by what is written in the books" (20:12); on the other hand, the only book that matters is the book of life: "And if anyone's name was not found written in the book of life, he was thrown into the lake of fire" (20:12, 15).

Although the word "resurrection" is not used by John here, the general resurrection of the dead seems to be in mind (cf. Jn 5:28-29). The dead come from Death and Hades and the sea (20:13). It is difficult to determine whether the judgment scene here involves all of the dead or only the unrighteous dead. A case could be made either way, although the latter is more likely.

The battle described in Revelation 19 seems to serve as a striking metaphor for God's judgment of the wicked, but how do matters actually unfold? One could best argue that the wicked will all be slain at Christ's coming and then subsequently raised to face final condemnation. Some interpreters have suggested, however, that there will be survivors from that battle so that the alleged millennium on earth could be populated by some of the wicked. This is misguided reasoning.

According to John, aside from the beast and false prophet who are cast into the lake of fire, "the rest were slain" (19:21). Clear enough. And how can followers of the beast survive this battle if indeed the battle imagery here represents final judgment? For such to happen the battle/judgment metaphor would be mangled, beyond just mixed!

A personification is involved in connection with "Death and Hades" in which both of them are cast into the lake of fire. They are enemies now vanquished. John describes the lake of fire as "the second death," a term used in the Bible only in this context (20:6, 14; 21:8) and earlier in the letter to the church at Smyrna (2:11).

The Smyrna connection at the end of Revelation 20 is highlighted by parallel and contrastive imagery involving the letter to the Smyrna church (Rev 2:8-11) and the description of the millennium throughout Revelation 20 (Chapter XXI). At the conclusion of this scene, Satan, the beast, and the false prophet are joined by their followers (all the unrighteous) in the lake of fire (19:20; 20:10, 15; also 21:8). The contrast between scenes here and those that follow in Revelation 21 could not be greater.

Various judgment scenes in Scripture do not so much depict multiple judgments as they rather describe multiple facets of judgment. At times the righteous are in view, at times the wicked. Regarding the fate of the wicked in the NT we read of the "lake of fire," "outer darkness," "weeping and gnashing of teeth," a "great wide gulf," etc. I am convinced that the Great White Throne Judgment (Rev 20:11-15), the Sheep and the Goats Judgment (Mt 25:31-46), and appearing before the Judgment Seat of Christ (2Cor 5:10) all refer to the same final judgment, not separate events (cf. Jn 5:28-29; Acts 17:31; Rom 14:12; Heb 4:12-13; 2Pet 3:7; Jude 14-15; Rev 11:17-18; 14:14-20).

From an amillennial perspective the final battle scene of Revelation 19:11-21 is followed by the Great White Throne Judgment of Revelation 20:11-15 without an intervening millennium.

Chapter XXIII

New Heavens and New Earth (Rev 21-22)

One of the surprising results from the comparison between the language of the OT prophets and the descriptions in the book of Revelation is the near absence of any OT connection with the "millennium chapter," Revelation 20, in contrast to the repeated OT parallels with Revelation 21-22, chapters depicting the New Jerusalem and the new heavens and new earth. The close parallels between Isaiah 60, 65 and Revelation 21-22 are numerous and obvious. In my view, premillennialists are "one chapter off" in their assigning of important OT-NT parallels here. The OT golden age sees its fulfillment in Revelation 21-22, not in Revelation 20.

Where to Start?

Revelation 20 is the wrong place to begin an end-times study, for several reasons. One, it contains highly symbolic language that should be interpreted in light of clearer passages.

Two, there is no agreed-upon interpretation of when and where the thousand-year reign of Christ and His saints occurs. Is it present or future? Does it occur on earth or in heaven? Using standards of extreme literalism, some have arrived at a complex picture of the millennium into which they have forced other passages to fit, with dubious results.

Three, a big problem is the lack of exact parallels from the OT. Israel is not mentioned in Revelation 20. No prophetic texts depicting a future golden age are utilized there. The only thing that jumps out is the mention of Gog and Magog, but even *that* is a problem. Dispensationalism actually teaches that this Gog and Magog invasion in Revelation 20 is not the same as that in Ezekiel 38-39! If it were, their complex timeline and insistence on the literal interpretation of certain time spans go out the window (where to fit the "seven years," Eze 39:9; the "seven months," Eze 39:14?). Confusion reigns.

Revelation 21, on the other hand, is the ideal place to begin. It is true that this description of the new heavens and new earth contains numerous symbols and figures of speech. Consequently, the basic principle for interpreting Scripture that states in effect that we should proceed from the non-symbolic to the symbolic seems to be violated. However, what makes Revelation 21 so ideal is that there has been widespread agreement regarding what it describes.

Revelation 21-22 depicts the eternal state, using figurative language to describe spiritual realities in term of earthly entities. The value of the passage becomes apparent. It serves as a kind of "control text." Since such symbolic language is clearly used to describe the eternal state in this passage, when identical or at least similar language is used elsewhere, such as earlier in Isaiah, it should be viewed as also referring to the eternal state, unless compelling evidence dictates otherwise.

Specific insights may be gained by noting close parallels found in the OT prophets. The striking parallels between the language of Revelation 20-22 and Isaiah 60 and 65 are displayed later below. Regardless of the figurative nature of Isaiah's wording, John's dependence upon Isaiah is undeniable. Since Isaiah's "new heavens and new earth" promise is applied by John to the eternal state, can there be any claim that Isaiah's promise originally referred to a future, temporary earth, renovated or otherwise? Certainly not a convincing one.

Contrasted Millennial Approaches

For premillennialists, Revelation 20 continues chronologically the description of events found in Revelation 19, and so the millennial reign of Christ follows the second coming. (Thus the second coming is pre-millennial.) This alleged "natural" reading of the text places undue strain upon the rest of the eschatological teaching of the NT. Fitting in this thousand-year reign between Christ's return and the realization of the new heavens and new earth is extremely awkward. There is no apparent room in the NT picture outside this single chapter.

The telling words of influential scholar John F. Walvoord illustrate the faulty application of OT promises to the closing chapters of Revelation. He and other dispensational premillennialists have persisted in applying the language of Isaiah 60 and 65, e.g., to a supposed thousand-year earthly kingdom even though John in Revelation sees these texts fulfilled in the eternal new heavens and new earth. For the record, Walvoord has referred to Isaiah 60:1-17 as a description of "the lesser role of Gentiles in the millennium" (*Kingdom*, 303) and to Isaiah 60:21 as describing the righteousness to be manifested "in the millennial reign of Christ" (307).

In a book on the messianic kingdom comprising over three hundred pages, he reserved his description of the new heavens and new earth for the last two pages of the book! His loaded statement that "very little description is given of this in Scripture" (333) indicated that he would not visualize any connection with Isaiah 60 (or 65). In his brief discussion of the eternal New Jerusalem, not one OT passage was offered as parallel!

And yet, Walvoord spent several hundred pages linking numerous OT prophecies with an alleged millennial kingdom (including a millennial Jerusalem). With Walvoord, who is representative of numerous dispensational scholars, the "forever" promises of the OT have been transformed into "millennial" promises—a clear case of the Scriptures being sacrificed at the altar of the system.

In the amillennial approach, Revelation 19 concludes a series of visions with a description of the second coming in which battle imagery is employed to describe Christ's victory over his enemies. Revelation 20, then, commences the brief, climactic series (or final sequence) of events that ends in the description of God's "forever": the eternal state, described as the new heavens and new earth containing the New Jerusalem that comes down from heaven.

Revelation 20-22 features recapitulation to open and begins that with Christ's defeat of Satan (Satan's being "bound" and "imprisoned"), while then describing the intermediate state of the dead in Christ (designated "the first resurrection") that coincides with the church age on earth. Satan's final doom is pictured, perhaps incorporating imagery from the Roman Triumph in which the enemy leader was ceremoniously executed following a period of being bound and imprisoned. The physical resurrection of Christ's fallen foes is followed by a scene of general judgment in which Death and Hades and all not found written in the Lamb's book of life are cast into the lake of fire, the "second death."

For the redeemed, the New Jerusalem appears in the new creation God has prepared for those who belong to Him.

The Isaiah Connection in Focus

Upon his entering the examination room to give me my diagnosis, my orthopedic surgeon-to-be made a dramatic pronouncement: "You've been lied to!"

For a moment, I was taken aback. Huh?

A decade previous I had blown out my right knee in an ill-advised pickup game of basketball on a carpeted gym floor and had been told by a local surgeon that "at my age" (only mid-40s at the time!) it would be best just to manage with an expensive knee brace.

After more than ten unsatisfactory years trying to compensate, I was ready for a second opinion. I got it, got the ACL surgery, and got some of my life back. Older and wiser. No more pickup ball games, carpeted floor or otherwise.

It is tempting to begin the following discussion on the "New Jerusalem" of Revelation 21-22 in light of Isaiah 60 and 65 with the same startling claim my surgeon offered, but I choose a calmer approach. Yes, sometimes Bible interpreters may stack the deck in a way conducive to the acceptance of their particular schemes and systems.

Truth be told, at some point we all wrestle with how to treat biblical texts that do not seem particularly favorable to our manner of interpretation on a specific issue. I have my set of favorite passages stressing the deity of Christ while ardent Jehovah's Witnesses have their bundle of texts that show clearly in their minds that Jesus is not, as they might put it, "God Almighty." I am convinced, of course, that my collection of texts trumps theirs, and I have good reasons (sticking with Revelation, e.g., at Revelation 5:11-14 both the Lamb and the One seated on the throne of heaven receive the same worship!).

Strong differences can also surface when Christians debate eschatological issues and millennial views. Unfortunately, circular reasoning often comes into play, as does the practice of picking favorites—favorite texts with which to begin the exegetical argument.

A good case in point would be the handling of Isaiah 65:17-25. The amillennialist stresses the fact that Revelation 21 borrows Isaiah's imagery in describing the eternal new creation, while most premillennialists argue that the language of Isaiah must be taken as literal and therefore must apply to a more earthly, imperfect, temporary setting. The chart on pages 300-301 displays the close parallels between Isaiah and Revelation in their descriptions of the new heavens and ne earth. But before that is shown, some explanation of the figurative language in much of Isaiah's description is in order.

"For behold, I create new heavens and a new earth, and the former things shall not be remembered or come into mind. [18]But be glad and rejoice forever in that which I create; for behold, I create Jerusalem to be a joy, and her people to be a gladness. [19]I will rejoice in Jerusalem and be glad in my people; no more shall be heard in it the sound of weeping and the cry of distress. (Isa 65:17-19)

The prophets of ancient Israel heralded the future manifestation of a "golden age" for the people of God. Life as they then knew it would be gloriously transformed as they shared God's blessing and presence in a way they never had previously. Peace and prosperity would be the endless themes. Two questions, however, immediately surface: *when* will this golden age transpire, and *who* will share in it? The

Bible does answer both questions, but with answers that are quite different from some of the popular views today.

One pervasive approach in end-times study today is to equate such descriptions with the future earthly millennium championed by the various camps of premillennialism. According to Walvoord, "the wolf and the lamb will feed together" in the millennium, indicating that at that time "the curse which creation has endured since Adam's sin will be in part suspended as even animal creation will be changed" (*Kingdom*, 318).

The other distinct approach, that followed here, is that the golden age describes the eternal state itself, a time when truly "No longer will there be anything accursed..." (Rev 22:3). The present world order will be replaced by a far more glorious existence on God's "new earth." Which then is it: the "millennium" or the "new heavens and new earth?" The evidence below points to the latter.

Posing the question another way, who are the recipients of the "golden age" promises of the prophets: the faithful of all generations throughout God's redemptive history or just a final generation of believers at the close of the church age? To answer that only a final generation of the faithful is involved would seem to make irrelevant much of the prophetic message for its original audiences. The future they are shown is not for them, it would seem, but just for that one, final generation. The promised someday is not their day, but a distant another's. Thus, a skewed end-times focus here does injustice to the message of hope for the numerous generations keeping faith with their faithful God.

Other verses in Isaiah 65 continue to describe the future blessing in God's New Jerusalem. But controversy still simmers. The descriptions Isaiah gives are very "physical" or "earthly" sounding and do not seem to match exactly what the NT describes. However, this is not the problem it might seem. The key to the language we are about to note is that the OT prophet is describing God's "new creation" in terms of "ideal existence" as the ancient Israelites would have envisioned it. A key element is the "reversal of fortune" or the freedom from the invasions and captivities that plagued Israel in Isaiah's time and in the days of Jeremiah and Ezekiel, among others. An analysis of the remaining verses should paint the picture more clearly.

No more shall there be in it an infant who lives but a few days, or an old man who does not fill out his days, for the young man shall die a hundred years old, and the sinner a hundred years old shall be accursed. (Isa 65:20)

Throughout the OT long life is viewed as God's blessing (Deu 6:2; 22:7; 1Kgs 3:14; Ps 91:16; Prov 3:16). In the new age to come life spans will be incredible. The hundred-year-old will be but a babe! Since no one will actually be "accursed" in the New Jerusalem, not one will actually fail to reach age one hundred. That milestone is just the starting point. The days of God's people will be "like the days of a tree" (Isa 65:22). Some of the giant Sequoia trees existing today have been around several thousand years!

What about "the sinner a hundred years old?" Many commentators and translations have taken a different tack here. The Hebrew word "sinner" is *chote*, from a verbal root meaning "to miss the mark." Therefore, instead of the translation "sinner" here (e.g., KJV, NKJV, ASV, RSV, ESV), many have suggested "one who fails," in the sense that the one who fails to reach a hundred years old shall be thought accursed (NIV, NAS, NET). This latter understanding is to be preferred.

Some might be puzzled as to how this description could reference the eternal state when it talks about people dying! The answer lies in the figurative nature of the description. Ideal existence is being described in terms to which OT Israel could easily relate.

One example of an ideal picture of life is provided in descriptions of Solomon's reign: "And Judah and Israel lived in safety, from Dan even to Beersheba, every man under his vine and under his fig tree, all the days of Solomon" (1Kgs 4:25). In one messianic prophecy describing the glorious future kingdom, Zechariah employs language reminiscent of the "ideal" Solomonic age: "In that day, declares the LORD of hosts, every one of you will invite his neighbor to come under his vine and under his fig tree" (Zec 3:10).

The known is used to portray the unknown. In Isaiah, the ideal picture given is in stark contrast to the ordeals that Israel as a nation was facing. The message is clear that in God's future plans for His people they need never again fear the horrors of foreign invasion and slaughter.

Death, therefore, will no longer be violent or premature. But there is more. The picture presented is that death need not be feared at all! The picture far transcends the ideal known existence (among the limited OT references to eternal life, cf. Job 19:25-27; Ps 49:15; 73:24).

Technically speaking, death is really not in the scene depicted by Isaiah. The Hebrew says literally: "For the youth will die the son of a hundred years," therefore, at the age of a hundred (Isa 65:20). Since in fact no "youths" will apparently die in the New Jerusalem (since there will be no sorrow!), this statement is purely hypothetical.

If one were to die at age one hundred, he or she would be but a child. In similar fashion, since no one will ever be "accursed" in the new city, no one will fail to reach the age of a hundred. Age one hundred, far beyond any reasonably hoped-for life span in Isaiah's day, will just be the starting point in the new heavens and new earth!

Clearly the language of Isaiah does not stress limitation of life but the absence of limitation. The emphasis is not upon death, but upon abundant life. The parallel to Isaiah's "no more shall be heard in it the sound of weeping and the cry of distress" (65:19) found in Revelation 21:4 adds the reason why: "...and death shall be no more..."(cf. Isa 25:6-8).

> They shall build houses and inhabit them; they shall plant vineyards and eat their fruit. 22They shall not build and another inhabit; they shall not plant and another eat; for like the days of a tree shall the days of my people be, and my chosen shall long enjoy the work of their hands. 23They shall not labor in vain or bear children for calamity, for they shall be the offspring of the blessed of the LORD, and their descendants with them. (Isa 65:21-23)

What about all this reference to "building and planting?" Does this mean there will be work in heaven? Well, in a sense there could be! Certainly the idea of sitting around playing harps all day is not overly appealing to most. Ideal life in the mind of the ancient Hebrews was not the idea of idleness, but of satisfying work. The first thing we learn about Adam's activity after creation was that God put him in the garden of Eden "to work it and keep it" (Gen 2:15).

However, the key involved here is the reversal of such curses as found in Deuteronomy 28 concerning the threat of invasion and captivity: "...You shall build a house, but you shall not dwell in it. You shall plant a vineyard, but you shall not enjoy its fruit" (Deu 28:30). As the curse is reversed, the absence of death in God's new creation will be accompanied by the absence of calamity, loss, and misfortune.

It is in this same context of building and planting that the reference to "bearing children" must be understood. Does this indicate that there will be "maternity in eternity?" Not really! Rather, the contrast from the horrors of seeing innocent children slaughtered in warfare is being made.

Deuteronomy predicted the atrocities that would accompany siege warfare, atrocities fulfilled in Babylon's capture of Jerusalem. Most horrifying to imagine, loving mothers, half-crazed by starvation, would eat their own children (Deu 28:53-57; Lam 2:20; 4:10)! The references to "not bearing children for calamity" and the expression "their descendants" should be viewed as ideal symbolism, not as literal. Peace, not war, will be the eternal theme. Life without calamity awaits God's chosen. This Isaiah passage, by the way, is a main premillennial proof text for the idea that babies will be born during the millennium after Christ returns! Parallels with the language in Revelation 21-22, however, indicate that we are viewing here an eternal, not a millennial, state.

> *"Before they call I will answer; while they are yet speaking I will hear.* [25]*The wolf and the lamb shall graze together, the lion shall eat straw like the ox, and dust shall be the serpent's food. They shall not hurt or destroy in all my holy mountain," says* the LORD. (Isa 65:24-25)

The perfect prosperity and peace of the New Jerusalem will be enhanced by God's presence and intimate communication. In that city there will be no need of a sanctuary, for God Himself will be the temple (Rev 21:22). The imagery of peace is further highlighted by the reference to the animal kingdom—natural predators along with their prey will dwell in mutual security and bliss (cf. Isa 11:6-9).

Truly the "curse" will be removed! Paradise will be restored. Some hope that such a text promises that animals will indeed be in heaven, but that debate will not be engaged in here.

Not all is well in paradise, however. Many interpreters are forced to reject the entire approach given above. Because of a dogged insistence upon literalism some cannot accept that Isaiah's language is actually a description of the eternal state. One can certainly appreciate their concern. If our approach is correct, the references in Isaiah 65 to "building and planting," "the wolf and the lamb," etc., present a figurative description of the eternal new heavens and new earth. Importantly, should not similar language elsewhere in the OT then be expected to refer to the same ultimate fulfillment? If Isaiah's words here describe the eternal state, then what OT "paradise" terminology must refer to a future "millennial earth?" In effect, the premillennialist's rationale for a "millennium" is seriously weakened.

The dispensational solution to the problem is strained. The dispensational approach commonly employed here could be labeled the "cut-and-paste method," a method in which context is often ignored to buttress the validity of a particular system. Here is a graphic case in point. Since Isaiah's words *cannot* actually be referring to the eternal state (because of dispensationalism's literalistic standards), there must be a break in the passage. Isaiah 65:17 and its mention of the creation of a new heavens and new earth is correspondingly divorced from words following at Isaiah 65:18-25.

Thus, for example, C. I. Scofield, in his highly influential dispensational *Reference Bible*, states: "Verse 17 looks beyond the kingdom-age to the new heavens and new earth, but verses 18-25 describe the kingdom-age itself"

(769). In other words, the content of Isaiah 65:18-25 belongs before that of Isaiah 65:17. Overly strict literalism often involves rearranging verses to make them fit the system. Hence, cut and paste—one example of "rightly dividing the Word of Truth" dispensational-style.

A careful look at the passage in question, however, should convince the unbiased reader that no break in the passage can be maintained. To argue that the verses following the mention of creation of the new heavens and new earth are in fact descriptions of "millennial" life before that very creation is strained. It is based upon an attempt to salvage the notions of a pre-conceived system, not upon sound principles of exegesis. In the words of amillennialist Anthony Hoekema, "One will see a millennium here only if he has previously put on his millennial glasses" (176)!

Two major disconnects stand out here. If the thousand-year reign of Christ mentioned in Revelation 20 is supposed to be the fulfillment of the many OT prophecies of a golden age, why are there no clear connections in Revelation 20 with the OT except for the mention of Gog and Magog which, ironically, many premillennialists reject as being the same Gog and Magog from the OT (Ezekiel 38-39)?

Israel is not even mentioned in Revelation 20, nor is the land, nor is Jerusalem specifically. The absence of OT imagery in Revelation to describe an alleged, much-anticipated millennial kingdom is inexplicable. The other major disconnect is the remarkable fact that the extensive OT descriptions of the golden age, including the New Jerusalem and the new heavens and new earth, are cited in Revelation as being fulfilled in the eternal state that follows the millennium, whatever the millennium is.

Isaiah 60 and 65 especially contain striking language parallel to Revelation 21-22. The following chart shows the specifics.

Revelation 21:1, 2, 4, 23, 24, 25-26; 22:5

Isaiah 65: 17-19; 60:19, 3, 11, 20-21a

Then I saw a new heaven and a new earth, for the first heaven and the first earth had passed away, and the sea was no more. (Rev 21:1)

For behold, I create new heavens and a new earth, and the former things shall not be remembered or come into mind. (Isa 65:17)

And I saw the holy city, new Jerusalem, coming down out of heaven from God, prepared as a bride adorned for her husband. (Rev 21:2)

But be glad and rejoice forever in that which I create; for behold, I create Jerusalem to be a joy, and her people to be a gladness. (Isa 65:18)

He will wipe away every tear from their eyes, and death shall be no more, neither shall there be mourning, nor crying, nor pain anymore, for the former things have passed. (Rev 21:4)

I will rejoice in Jerusalem and be glad in my people; no more shall be heard in it the sound of weeping and the cry of distress. (Isa 65:19)

And the city has no need of a sun or moon to shine on it, for the glory of God gives it light, and its lamp is the Lamb. (Rev 21:23)

The sun shall be no more your light by day, nor for brightness shall the moon give you light; but the Lord will be your everlasting light, and your God will be your glory. (Isa 60:19)

24 By its light will the nations walk, and the kings of the earth will bring their glory into it,	And nations shall come to your light, and kings to the brightness of your rising. (Isa 60:3)
25 And its gates will never be shut by day—and there will be no night there. 26 They will bring into it the glory and the honor of the nations. (Rev 21: 24-26)	Your gates shall be open continually; day and night they shall not be shut, that people may bring to you the wealth of the nations, with their kings led in procession. (Isa 60:11)
And night will be no more. They will need no light of lamp or sun, for the Lord God will be their light, and they will reign forever and ever. (Rev 22:5)	20 Your sun shall no more go down, nor your moon withdraw itself; for the Lord will be your everlasting light, and your days of mourning shall be ended.
	21 Your people shall all be righteous; they shall possess the land forever… (Isa 60:20-21a)

The above parallel columns make obvious that Isaiah's "golden age" is eternal, not millennial, since the prophet's descriptions are applied by John not to the millennium of Revelation 20 but to the new heavens and new earth of Revelation 21-22. Numerous parallel themes emerge:

⅓ The creation of a new heavens and new earth (Isa 65:17-19; Rev 21:1-2) ß The appearance of the New Jerusalem (Isa 65:18-19; Rev 21:2)

ß The removal of all weeping and mourning (Isa 65:19; Rev 21:4)

ß No sun or moon will be needed; the Lord Himself will be their light (Isa 60:19; Rev 21:23)

ß Nations and kings will come to the city's light (Isa 60:3; Rev 21:24)

ß The wealth of the nations will be brought into the city (Isa 60:11; Rev 21:26)

ß The city's gates will never be closed; there will never be night (Isa 60:20; Rev 22:5)

The fact that John utilizes Isaiah in his descriptions of the eternal state cannot be denied. Again, the eternal state, *not* a millennium. Commonly within premillennial thought, Revelation 21-22's descriptions of the New Jerusalem are said to be descriptions of a millennial Jerusalem positioned within the overall descriptions of the eternal new heavens and new earth. This claim is an act of desperation. It goes beyond ignoring context, it defies it.

The book of Revelation in no way supports the notion of an earthly millennial kingdom and John's use of Isaiah's words from Isaiah 60 and 65 in describing the eternal New Jerusalem in God's new heavens and new earth speaks volumes. Again, the common premillennial approach here starts with assumptions about what the language of Isaiah must (literally) mean, rather than about what the NT shows it to mean. Revelation's use of Isaiah instead should guide us to the conclusion that Isaiah's new heavens and new earth (and New Jerusalem) are descriptions of an eternal state, not a temporary, transitional one.

The notion that somehow an alleged millennial earth will just morph into the eternal earth (the new heavens and new earth) is shown to be incorrect in light of Peter's description of the day of the Lord: "But the day of the Lord will come like a thief, and then the heavens will pass away with a roar; and the heavenly bodies will be burned up and dissolved, and the earth and the works that are done on it will be exposed" (2Pet 3:10).

Peter also warned that "the heavens and earth that now exist are stored up for fire," fire kept for judgment day (2Pet 3:7). Let's be clear. Peter says that *the earth that now exists* will be destroyed by fire. On the day of the Lord. This present earth. Again, no room for an earthly millennial paradise here.

The City of God, the People of God

The focal point of Revelation's description of the new heavens and new earth is the New Jerusalem. One fascinating aspect of the usage of "city" imagery here is that two pictures are actually being developed. One picture is that of an actual city into which people enter: a city of walls, gates, and streets (21:12-26). But the other picture presented is that the city actually *is* the redeemed people of God.

The New Jerusalem coming down out of heaven from God is introduced twice, the second time apparently from a closer vantage point (21:2, 9-10).In both cases the term "bride" is used to describe it (21:2, 9). John writes, "And I saw the Holy City, new Jerusalem, coming down out of heaven from God, prepared as a bride adorned for her husband" (21:2). An angel describes the New Jerusalem to John as "the Bride, the wife of the Lamb" (21:9).

Scripture elsewhere identifies the church as the bride of Christ (Eph 5:32). Revelation 19 earlier describes the marriage of the Lamb for which the bride, Christ's church, had made herself ready (19:6-9). The New Jerusalem, therefore, is the wife of the Lamb, the redeemed saints clothed "with fine linen, bright and pure" (19:8).

Further elements in the imagery reinforce this people-city equation. The walls of the city contain twelve gates, each gate having the name of one of the twelve tribes of Israel written on it (21:12). The walls also have twelve foundations upon which are the names of the twelve apostles of the Lamb (21:14). The combination of Israel's tribes and Christ's apostles is a way to describe the totality of God's people, both OT and NT saints. A temple structure is replaced by the personal presence of God Himself (21:23).People and fellowship replace buildings and property in the eternal city of God (21:3).

The absence of night enables the gates of the New Jerusalem to be open "round the clock" (21:25), a picture of peace and security (cf. Neh 7:3). The striking reference, "and the sea was no more" (21:1), seems to signal the elimination of all that which was dark, dangerous, mysterious, and foreboding, especially in light of the earlier mention of the sea "giving up its dead" (20:13-14).

The description of the city and its wall is to be viewed as clearly symbolic. The dimensions of the city are those of a perfect cube, being 12,000 stadia (equivalent to about 1,400 miles) in length, width, and height. Imagining a structure stretching from Dallas to New York City misses the point. The picture is one of strength and perfection. Very possibly the imagery is based on the Holy of Holies in the former Jerusalem temple which was also a perfect cube. Now the entire city is most holy ground!

To envision a literal cube-shaped community would be a mistake, in my estimation. This would also be true of the symbolic nature of the size of the walls—144 (twelve-by-twelve) cubits thick (about seventy-two yards by literal dimensions). The use of symbolic numbers serves to strengthen the idea of perfection. Some have suggested instead a pyramid or mountain, rather than a cube, with God's throne at the pinnacle. Either way, symbolic language is operating here.

Paradise Regained

A final glimpse within the heavenly city reveals the existence of the garden of God—paradise regained. Or more importantly, full fellowship with God restored. G. K. Beale and others have furthered the view in which Eden represented a park-like sanctuary where God dwelt (with the worked garden adjacent to it) and that one important aspect of man's commission was to extend the boundaries of Eden to fill the entire creation. In the OT and later Jewish thought the temple served as a microcosm of all of heaven and earth as many of its fixtures and designs suggested. In the future, it was anticipated, the temple would encompass all the world. The absence of a separate temple in the New Jerusalem may speak to that hope and expectation (Beale, *Revelation*, 1109-1111; "Eden," 5-31).

While the early chapters of Genesis record man's banishment from Eden and his separation from the tree of life, Revelation's last chapter pictures man's complete restoration to fellowship with God. The tree of life, the leaves of which are for "the healing of the nations," is in full view, positioned next to a river of the water of life flowing down from God's throne (22:1-2; Eze 47:12). The "curse" will be forever removed (22:3). Eternal life, light, and joy will be the lot of the redeemed. But perhaps the most glorious promise of all is found in the simple statement, "They will see his face..." (22:4).

CHAPTER XXIV

FINAL WORDS (REV 22)

Revelation begins and ends with the promise of the imminent return of Jesus ("the time is near," Rev 1:3; "I am coming soon," Rev 3:11; 22:7, 12, 20). Again, this promise is a main pillar for the strict preterist view that the AD 70 fall of Jerusalem *was* the "second coming" of Jesus.

I am not a preterist (as noted repeatedly), but I do believe that *parts* of Revelation relate to events and individuals in the first century AD, including the arrival and activities of the beast and likely the AD 70 fall of Jerusalem. Contrary to strict preterism, throughout the present work I have argued for a future return of Christ, regardless of what degree of importance is to be placed upon AD 70 events.

Also, unlike N. T. Wright, e.g., I would contend that Jesus, in His teaching ministry, predicted both the destruction of the Jerusalem temple standing then and His subsequent return "like a thief in the night" (cf. Wright, *Hope*, 125-127). Although he rejects any association with strict preterism, throughout his extensive writings, works in which he rightly holds to a still-future second coming of Christ, Wright has famously argued that in the Gospels Jesus never spoke of the second coming (with Wright conspicuously ignoring John 14:1-3), a view that must be rejected. Wright's approach here exhibits a selective sifting of the evidence.

In broad terms, scholars have frequently pointed out parallels between the language of the Olivet Discourse (esp.

Matthew 24) and the words of Paul in 1 and 2 Thessalonians. Paul clearly incorporates Jesus' lively terminology (thief in the night, coming in the clouds, angelic hosts, etc.). If Jesus intended that language only to describe the fall of Jerusalem to the Romans, how can we reconcile that with the apparent reality that Paul repeatedly borrows it for his descriptions of the future second coming? Any claim that Jesus never spoke of His second coming is difficult to accept when the full testimony of the NT is laid out.

Still Coming "Soon"

Still the question remains. Apart from strict preterism and its insistence that the AD 70 fall of Jerusalem *was* the second coming, if the imminence or any-moment nature of Christ's return is true, how are the "soon" promises regarding Jesus' return in Revelation to be understood now, centuries later?

All attempts at date setting must be abandoned. Jesus Himself acknowledged that as the Son of the Father He did not know the day or the hour of His own coming (Mt 24:36), but He did know that He would leave and subsequently return. His return would be sudden, unexpected, and also imminent—it could happen at any moment, as the rest of the NT contends. Nowhere in the four Gospels does Jesus actually say that He would return "soon" (*tachy*) or "quickly" (*en tachei*), but He does so in the book of Revelation (here and Chapter VII). At Luke 18:6-8, however, we read that God's righteous judgment can be rendered "speedily" (*en tachei*) in some fashion, even if Christ's return does not occur in the near future.

In connection with Luke 18:6-8, Darrell Bock discusses the term "soon," what I suggest could be labeled the "eschatological 'soon.'" In his helpful words,

> Jesus is not promising that God will come soon—that is, in a short period of time; otherwise God's people would not have become discouraged, which seems to be the assumption behind Jesus' second point. Rather, his coming is soon in that it is next on the eschatological calendar. Prophetic texts often foreshorten the timing of events to show their sequence (for example, Is 61:1-2 and the two comings of Jesus). God has not forgotten the elect. Next on the calendar is his bringing their vindication in justice. Until the vindication comes, it seems a long way away, especially in the midst of persecution, but after it comes and is established for eternity, it will not seem so delayed. (*Luke*, 295)

What is next on the eschatological calendar, to use Bock's words? Christ's return in glory! It is important to consider ways in which terms like "soon," "speedily," "near," and even "immediately," can be understood in light of the obvious lengthy lapse of time since the promises were made. It has been suggested that the Greek expressions in question (e.g., *tachy, en tachei*) primarily mean "quickly, suddenly," involving *kind* of action, more than "soon, without delay," expressing *time* of action (e.g., Witherington, *End*, 25-26). And yet the full range of meanings can be found in the NT. In Paul's words to Timothy about his travel plans, we seem to find the sense of "soon" or "without delay": "I hope to come to you soon [*en tachei*], but I am writing these things to you so that, [15] if I delay, you may know how one ought to behave in the household of God..." (1Tm 3:14-15).

309

This sense is certainly the case when Festus speaks of his intentions to leave Jerusalem and return to Caesarea: "Festus replied that Paul was being kept at Caesarea and that he himself intended to go there shortly [*en tachei*]" (Acts 25:4). The ESV "shortly" is apt here. Festus was apparently leaving "soon" or "without delay," and probably not "rushing back" at a fast pace to Caesarea and his palace. The sense of "quickly" may be the case in other instances, however.

The notion of "suddenness" regarding Christ's return does have its expression in the NT. Christ speaks of His coming as being like the arrival of a "thief in the night" (Mt 24:43-44; cf. 1Th 5:2; 2Pet 3:10; Rev 16:15). As well, He describes His return as being like the lightening that flashes across the sky, producing an image that conveys two aspects: suddenness and visibility to all—no one will miss it (Mt 24: 26-27; Lk 17:24).

The best approach here? The "eschatological soon" is a "soon" made possible by the fulfillment of all signs and promises that were given regarding events needing to occur before the second coming of Christ. If such fulfillments have already occurred, then the return of Jesus is truly "imminent," it could happen at any moment but it need not happen immediately. Some have spoken of possible or potential imminence versus necessary imminence. The difference there is between the idea of "will" or "must" (necessary) versus the idea of "could" or "might" (possible). The words "It could be today," have never been truer, but it would be mistaken to state "It *will* be today."

We should keep in the back of our minds Peter's reminder that God's time and our time are kept differently. Peter writes,

But do not overlook this one fact, beloved, that with the Lord one day is as a thousand years, and a thousand years as one day. ⁹The Lord is not slow to fulfill his promise as some count slowness, but is patient toward you, not wishing that any should perish, but that all should reach repentance. ¹⁰But the day of the Lord will come like a thief, and then the heavens will pass away with a roar, and the heavenly bodies will be burned up and dissolved, and the earth and the works that are done on it will be exposed. (2Pet 3:8-10)

Peter stresses the sudden nature of Christ's return but the question of how soon is left up to God's timetable. And with God a day (or even "a watch in the night," i.e., a few hours, Ps 90:4) is like a thousand years. What is His definition of "soon?" And how could we label Him "slow?" He will of course be right on time!

Doubtful Takes on Imminence

1. The strict preterist take on imminence dates Revelation to the time of Nero and views the book's references to Christ's "soon" coming as being fulfilled within a few short years by Rome's destruction of Jerusalem. There is then no yet future return of Christ. All is fulfilled by AD 70. But can the fall of Jerusalem bear the full weight of the many NT promises of Christ's glorious return? Does such an event represent what Paul described as the "blessed hope" of the church (Tts 2:13)? Not without bending the natural meaning of words beyond recognition! This would also be true of the imagery and symbolism in Revelation's portrayals of judgment and wrath, portrayals that seem to be far greater in scope than the fall of first-century Jerusalem.

2. The dispensational approach regarding imminence, on the other hand, is to take all the signs pointing to events leading up to the second coming and place them after an alleged rapture of the church. The signs, then, have nothing to do with the church, but rather with the later post-rapture tribulation saints converted in the midst of great tribulation (actually "the great tribulation" according to them). Any assumed signs or predictions pointing to Christ's return have to do with the later return of Christ following the alleged seven years following the rapture and not with any events preceding the rapture itself.

For dispensationalists the rapture is impending and no signs need be fulfilled prior to that event; it is imminent and therefore "soon" in the eschatological sense. The "signs" given by Jesus in the Gospels, then, for them point to post-rapture events that will unwind during the so-called "great tribulation," events that will involve the desolation of a yet future Jerusalem temple, a future antichrist figure coming to power, etc.

Once those who embrace this approach start to read the fine print, however, the problems begin to multiply. Teachings of Jesus that obviously related to the destruction of first-century Jerusalem (Matthew 24; Mark 13; Luke 21) are twisted beyond recognition by pretribulational dispensationalism. According to many dispensationalists, Luke is said to be talking about first-century occurrences (which he is!), while the parallel (and often identical!) accounts in Matthew and Mark are speaking about post-church-age, post-rapture events involving an alleged future antichrist persecuting post-rapture tribulation converts. Such an approach renders the Bible almost unintelligible.

Since dispensational scholars incorrectly view the troubling events foreseen in the Olivet Discourse (esp. Matthew 24; Mark 13) as post-rapture abominations and tribulations, the familiar "thief in the night" designation for Christ in His coming must, by careful dispensational reasoning, refer to the later return of Christ following the great tribulation and not to the rapture itself.

Read that sentence again.

Let me then restate it.

According to standard dispensational assumptions, their "rapture of the church" *cannot* be the "thief in the night" coming, in spite of what their popular books and movies say. Few premillennial pulpits pound home that point today! Nor do they emphasize that the "left behind" language in the Gospels cannot refer to the alleged rapture (Mt 24:40-44; Lk 17:34-37), for the same reason. If the events of the Olivet Discourse *follow* the rapture and occur during the subsequent "great tribulation," as the dispensational system teaches, then the warnings and promises that follow those events ("left behind," "thief in the night") must relate to the later second coming (dispensationalism's "return" or "revelation"), not the alleged rapture.

Top dispensational scholars have actually concluded that John 14:1-3 is the only rapture text to be found in the Gospels (Walvoord, *Blessed*, 92-93; Toussaint, 122, 131). For obvious reasons, that conclusion is not being communicated by many dispensational preachers either. And, of course, there is no good reason to attach John 14:1-3 to the notion of a separate rapture of the church. The pre-trib rapture of classic dispensationalism is an endangered species in the Gospels!

3. More broadly speaking, the assumed necessity for further signs to be fulfilled before the second coming has led to the denial of imminence by some. For them, Christ cannot come until certain scenarios in human history unfold. This frank denial of imminence leaves one uncomfortable, puzzled by the seeming mixed messages in Scripture on this theme. There are those who would contend that the nature of the relevant signs is vague enough to hinder the confident identification of such signs and any accompanying fulfillments. Thus imminence becomes an option more than a promise for some interpreters.

Interpreting Revelation in Light of Imminence

My contention is that all relevant signs needing to be fulfilled preliminary to Christ's return have been fulfilled and in fact were fulfilled in events in the first century, especially those connected with that first generation of believers in Jesus as Lord and Messiah. These include Jesus' prediction regarding Peter's martyrdom in old age (Jn 21:18-19), His proclamation regarding the universal spread of the gospel (Mt 28:18-20; Acts 1:8; cf. Col 1:6, 23), and His predictions concerning the destruction of Jerusalem and the temple (Mt 23:37-39; Lk 19:41-44; 21:21-24; 23:26-31). A proper interpretation of the Olivet Discourse is crucial in this regard (Matthew 24; Mark 13; Luke 21).

Importantly as well, a major stumbling-block in the discussion is removed with the identification of Paul's "man of lawlessness" as an antagonist in connection with the Jewish Revolt and the subsequent destruction of

Jerusalem, rather than as an end-times "antichrist" figure (Appendix A).

It has been argued previously that numerous visionary scenes in Revelation could have depicted events that had already occurred by the end of the first century. What events then still remain that will unfold "soon?" They are those events occurring in connection with the second coming of Christ. They include His visible coming with the clouds in judgment (Rev 1:7), His victory in the great Last Battle (Rev 19:11-21), the Great White Throne Judgment (Rev 20:11-15), and the casting of Satan, the beast, and the false prophet into the lake of fire (Rev 19:20; 20:10). The highly figurative and stylized trumpet plagues and bowl plagues would seem to attach to the second coming matrix of events as well (Rev 8:6-9:21; 11:15-19; 16:1-21).

We note that both plague sequences involve the enumeration "seven"; they offer closely parallel language generally in sequence; they each borrow imagery from the OT plagues in connection with the Exodus from Egypt; they both lead up to the second coming itself; and both sequences stress the deserved nature of the plagues and the lack of repentance on the part of all affected.

In contrast with the statement to Daniel that his prophecies were sealed up until the time of the end (Dan 12:9), John is instructed, "Do not seal up the words of the prophecy of this book, for the time is near" (Rev 22:10). Daniel's visions were in part preliminary, containing events that would unfold in the subsequent years leading up to God's establishing His messianic kingdom (events such as the return from Babylon, the persecution under Antiochus Epiphanes, the rise of future empires including Greece and Rome, etc.).

For readers of Revelation, the emphasis is not upon events that must still transpire leading up to the climax of human history, but upon what has *already* happened and continues to happen as God's people are called to faithful obedience in the face of tribulation. Actually Daniel had relatively little to say about the second coming—Christ's first coming being more the focus—while Revelation repeatedly singles out that later key event on the horizon of God's future for His people.

It should be noted from previous chapters that my identification of Babylon the Harlot with Jerusalem, not Rome, supports the notion of imminence as presented throughout the rest of the NT. Conversely, the common view that ancient Rome was the harlot John spoke of severely weakens the argument that the entire NT, including Revelation, teaches an imminent return for Christ. If Rome had to be destroyed first, as it eventually was in the fifth century AD, the notion of imminence falters. The metaphoric thief in the night of the NT had to remain a yet future threat as long as Rome stood.

The AD 70 fall of Jerusalem marked the end of the first generation of the church, approximately, while the fall of Rome occurred centuries later (410? 476?), and, in fact, a century or more after the conversion of much of the Roman Empire to Christianity. The time for punishing the pagan persecutor of the early church had long since come and gone. A consistent NT doctrine of Christ's imminent return fits well with identifying the Great Harlot of Revelation as first-century Jerusalem, destroyed by Rome in AD 70 according to God's stated divine purposes.

The imminence doctrine does not fit well with equating that ancient prostitute with Rome, a city destroyed in the fifth century, long after it had become Christianized. To be sure, identifying the Great Harlot of Revelation as ancient pagan Rome—with all its lewd, brutal, deplorable practices and values—seems to satisfy best the sensitivities of most modern commentators. For many, any alternative would be unthinkable (but see Chapter XVIII).

Still, their view creates the awkward conclusion that the beast, identified as Rome, destroys the harlot, who is also Rome! Can you ride the beast if you are the beast? Ancient apocalyptic imagery can be confusing, certainly, but I wonder if proponents of the "Rome" identification have muddied the waters here with their questionable assumptions. They have certainly compromised any notion that Revelation presents a view of imminence regarding Christ's return.

Closing Promises

What would unfold for Christ's faithful overcomers in the future? The final chapter answers: entrance into the New Jerusalem (22:19); access to the tree of life (22:19); drinking freely from the water of life (22:17); worship before the divine throne (22:3); seeing God's face (22:4); and reigning with God forever and ever (22:5). Jesus reiterates the judgment motif found throughout the book: "Behold, I am coming soon, bringing my recompense with me, to repay each one for what he has done" (22:12).

Solemn words from Jesus close out the book:

> *I warn everyone who hears the words of the prophecy of this book: if anyone adds to them, God will add to him the plagues described in this book, ¹⁹and if anyone takes away from the words of the book of this prophecy, God will take away his share in the tree of life and in the holy city, which are described in this book. (Rev 22:18-19)*

Although many over time have attached the warning here to the Bible as a whole, in its original setting it applies to John's Apocalypse specifically, and yet the spirit of the cautionary prohibition rings true for all of Scripture. The prayer from commentators should be that they (we) can convey accurately the intent of the message of this great book that closes the pages of God's Word. The book concludes like a more traditional NT epistle: "The grace of the Lord Jesus be with all. Amen" (22:21).

Jesus' final promise that He is coming soon is closed by John's ardent prayer: "Amen. Come Lord Jesus!" (22:20). We join countless other students of God's prophetic word and of the book of Revelation in particular in adding our "Amen" to that ancient, heartfelt request.

CHAPTER XXV

CONCLUSION

With the ending of the book of Revelation tough questions remain. At this concluding juncture I would like to summarize the initial motivating factors involved in my writing the present work and how those have been addressed throughout. The significance of a number of key texts in Revelation will be reiterated, texts with content that helps guide us in our search for the purpose and meaning of much of what John wrote. To be sure, it is hard to escape the conclusion that this is a complex ancient work. It is filled with extensive allusions and rich symbolic imagery related to other parts of the Bible itself, as well as to the socio-historical setting of Roman Western Asia near the end of the first Christian century.

The level of controversy that continues to confront the modern evangelical church in its attempts to understand Bible prophecy in general and various end-times teachings in particular can be disheartening at times.

It is hoped that the present work has shed some light on these important topics as it has sought to "unravel Revelation." In addition, our prayer is that contemporary readers will be motivated to dig even more deeply into the riches of Scripture and its teachings on the important matters addressed here.

I am calling this my "Conclusion," but in light of the complexities of what has been traversed throughout, I have fashioned it into somewhat of a "recapitulation," altogether fitting in light of how much that term has been discussed and promoted within. I find myself here rehashing arguments and supplying a few extra crumbs for the offering along the way. All for the best, I hope.

Uneasy Alternatives

No doubt by now the present reader has become quite aware of my eschatological leanings in regard to the various mainstream millennial views and arguments. The strongest concerns registered throughout have been in response to the modern dispensational premillennial position and to the tenets of modern hyper-preterism.

Both approaches intersect with the study of Revelation in numerous significant and complicated ways. Both approaches, in my view, have failed in their primary attempts to integrate convincingly their distinctive views with Scripture in general and the book of Revelation in particular (Chapter III). A key motivating factor for the present work has been the desire to offer an interpretation for John's Apocalypse that avoids the pertinent dispensational and preterist excesses while providing a conservative Scriptural analysis true to the original intent of the book.

(1) The Dispensational Alternative

Dispensationalism struggles with any notion that the NT church is the focus of the book. Such a focus, in light of Revelation's extensive use of OT allusions and terminology, renders the dispensational distinctions between Israel and the church less and less tenable. And yet the repeated close ties between the promises to the seven churches in Revelation 2-3 and the ultimate descriptions of the blessed fate of believers toward the end of the book would seem to make that focus abundantly clear (Chapter IX).

In dispensational thinking, much of Revelation 6-18 applies to the "tribulation saints" on earth after the alleged rapture of the church. Some unbelievers "left behind" become part of the new, redeemed remnant on earth who are converted after the rapture, perhaps by the two witnesses of Revelation 11, or by the 144,000 servants with the seal of God on their foreheads (Revelation 7), or by the angel flying overhead proclaiming an eternal gospel (Revelation 14), etc. Many tribulation saints die at the hands of the beast and his followers (Chapter X).

On the plus side, with dispensationalism the oft-proclaimed imminence (any-moment nature) of Christ's coming and the catalog of signs and events that supposedly lead up to that coming can thus coexist. The rapture could happen at any moment without any necessary warning signs while the later return/"revelation" seven years or so after the rapture will be anticipated by numerous "biblical" signs.

The downside is that, as with the rest of the NT, it is difficult to find support for such a rapture in the text of Revelation. John being summoned up to heaven (4:1) can scarcely be seen as a depiction of the rapture of the church, while the narrative vision of Christ's birth and ascension to heaven followed by Satan's persecution of the woman and "the rest of her offspring" (12:17) offers no justification for skipping over the entire church age between 12:5 and 12:6. Unless one is looking through dispensational lenses, the picture is actually quite clear. The woman's offspring being persecuted following Christ's ascension are the NT church.

In addressing the seven churches of Asia, John identifies himself as "your brother and partner in the tribulation and the kingdom" (1:9). The tribulation martyrs depicted in various scenes of worship before God's throne in heaven are NT saints: "church saints," not post-rapture "tribulation saints"! Dispensational premillennialism does a great disservice to the meaning and message of the book of Revelation in that it minimizes the importance of the NT church in the Bible.

As well, modern students of Revelation who must encounter dispensational commentators are forced to navigate the confusing terminology and distinctions generated by the dispensational "rapture system." Embedded in the enterprise are multiple comings, numerous resurrections, various judgments, unwarranted "fast-forwards," etc. And of course the underlying core belief that millions will be able to repent and get right with God following the church's rapture is a dangerous example of "second chance theology." Where can we find that doctrine in the Bible?

The heart of classic dispensationalism, as already documented, is the unbending distinction between Israel and the church: promises to Israel are not fulfilled by the church but by a later phase of Israel after the church has been raptured out of the world. The impact of this approach upon the hope of one's achieving any coherent interpretation of Revelation has been shown in the present work to be debilitating. How could things get more complicated or confusing? By this time I think you know the answer...

(2) The Hyper-Preterist Alternative

On the opposite end of the spectrum from dispensationalism is preterism, or, to be more precise, full or hyper-preterism. Also a great source of confusion for students of Revelation, hyper-preterism claims that the second coming of Christ has already happened, having occurred with the AD 70 destruction of Jerusalem. Partial preterists, to be clear, also view the AD 70 fall of Jerusalem as a major part of Bible prophecy, especially of the book of Revelation, but they then also conclude that there will still be a future return of Christ.

With preterism, the best explanation for the promise of Jesus that He would come "soon" is that, in fact, He did! Within a single generation, Jerusalem was destroyed by the armies of Rome, just as Jesus had predicted. Preterists, both full and partial, view the AD 70 destruction of Jerusalem as the "coming in the clouds of the Son of Man" that Jesus prophesied.

For partial preterists, this coming in judgment upon Israel and Jerusalem was a coming separate from the second coming of Christ that is described by the apostle Paul and other NT authors. Thus the second coming still awaits. For hyper-preterists, however, the second coming has already transpired: it occurred in AD 70.

Unlike most interpreters, preterists envision promises of Christ's return in judgment in the book of Revelation as being references to the fall of Jerusalem. These references are understood as predictions provided in the visions entrusted to John the seer. Most preterists connect these visions found in Revelation to the time of the reign of the Roman Emperor Nero, probably close to the year of his death (total reign AD 54-68). As well, preterists would contend that the Great Harlot of Revelation 16-18, labeled as "Babylon the great" (14:8; 16:19; 17:5; 18:2), was in fact Jerusalem, the "great city" that was destroyed by Rome (the beast and the ten horns; 17:16-17). Her demise at the hands of the Romans fulfilled the purposes of God regarding her judgments (17:17).

(3) The Proposed Alternative

As will be revisited now, I do accept the view that Babylon the Harlot represents Jerusalem and not, as many contend, Rome, in part because of the difficulty in seeing how the beast, Rome, destroys the harlot, Rome (Chapter XVIII). However, I do not view the angel's words in the vision John experienced as being predictive of Jerusalem's demise but rather as being descriptive of what has happened and, importantly, informative as to why and by whose authority it has happened.

To the point, a word from heaven that God was in control would have been a welcome message for the churches of Asia. The unceasing propaganda from Rome at the time concerning its perceived unfettered dominion and eternal destiny would have been psychologically impactful for early Christians, as many modern researchers have concluded. Rome's crushing defeat of the Jews and the god of the Jews prompted the royal refrain that resonated for years after the fact as the ancient world "marveled" at the success of the beast after recovering from its "mortal wound" (13:3; 17:8).

Revelation offered a corrective. The vision John received from heaven portraying the rejoicing of the heavenly hosts following Jerusalem's fall and the subsequent preparations for the marriage supper of the Lamb with His bride (Revelation 19) would have held rich meaning for the saints whose "fine linen" represented their righteous deeds (19:8). The fact that the bride of the Lamb and the glorious New Jerusalem are later equated (21:2, 9-10) makes the contrast here even starker if the condemned harlot "Babylon" was actually ancient, apostate Jerusalem.

Need to Know Basis: The Questions

As I found myself drawn deeper and deeper into producing a book on John's Apocalypse, several key issues surfaced that I knew I must seek to resolve for my own satisfaction if not for that of others. Overarching concerns like how the second coming fits within the book's message and how the vivid imagery of the book factors into the book's interpretation have been addressed within the following topics. The questions generally are multi-faceted and probe for detailed answers. They represent areas of inquiry that demand careful consideration.

Question 1. What do we make of the various cycles of seven in Revelation? For me, at least three main issues came to the fore here. Regarding the seven seals, seven trumpet plagues, and seven bowl plagues, how are these related to the second coming? Further, how are they related to each other? Finally, how are they related to the rest of the visions of the book? Lots to ponder here, for sure.

Question 2. How are the setting and the date of the book related to its message? How does the answer aid the interpretation of the various visions and symbols in the book? One of the important findings of modern researchers on first-century developments pertaining to the Roman Empire and its relationship to Judaism and Christianity has been the extent to which the Flavian Dynasty (Vespasian, Titus, Domitian) used its defeat of Israel (Judea) and Jerusalem as propaganda to bolster its dynastic claims following a bloodied, disastrous civil war in the aftermath of Nero's suicide AD 68.

As one of several prominent Roman military leaders who had vied for power during the frightful Roman Civil War (or "The Long Year") and the one who ultimately prevailed, how did Vespasian leverage his status as the "conqueror of the Jewish nation" (which Rome actually had long controlled!) to solidify his dynastic status and ambitions? For Christians and Jews within the empire, the continued claim that Rome and its gods had bested the god of the Jews would have been unsettling, as would have been the pressure to conform to the will of the pagan powers in charge in ways that impacted important aspects of their lives.

Question 3. How can we best understand the significance and nature of the Cosmic Conflict depicted in Revelation beginning with Revelation 12-14, resurfacing in connection with various visions and cycles (Revelation 11, 16-17), and culminating with the defeat of the beast and the false prophet (Revelation 19) and of Satan himself (Revelation 20)? Who or what are the beast and the false prophet, i.e., the sea beast and the land beast (Revelation 13)? How do the parallel features of Revelation 12 and 20 regarding Satan and his efforts help in the interpretation of each? What role does battle imagery play in the depiction of the conflict and how does that imagery relate to the theme of divine judgment in the book?

Question 4. With respect to the controversial millennium of Revelation 20, what are the key factors that tip the scale regarding its interpretation? Included topics here are the use of symbolic numbers in the book, the arguments for recapitulation, the issue of the nature of the "first resurrection," the fulfillment of Satan's imprisonment and release, and the employment of battle imagery to describe final judgment.

Question 5. How should John's use of the OT guide our thinking concerning what the millennial kingdom of Revelation 20 and the new heavens, new earth, and New Jerusalem of Revelation 21-22 represent? Where does the "golden age" of OT prophecy fit in?

Question 6. In what sense is John the seer a "new Ezekiel" and how does the answer facilitate our understanding of the imagery and message of Revelation as well as that of the book of Ezekiel itself?

Question 7. What is at stake regarding the identification of the Great Harlot "Mystery Babylon"? What are the implications for choosing the ancient Rome or ancient Jerusalem option? What tips the scales? What are problems with either option?

Question 8. What is next according to Revelation's message to the church? How does the book employ the notion of "soon" regarding Jesus' return and how does that fit with the message of the rest of Scripture?

Question 9. Finally, what special significance does my subtitle for this book convey? The wording "Hope, Wisdom, and Mystery in John's Apocalypse" requires some explanation, yet what has been said already should have shed some light upon the significance of the terms.

Need to Know Basis: The Answers

The answers to these "need to know" topics, topics that have charted the course of the present work, are summarized below.

(Answer 1) The Cycles of Seven and the Second Coming

Throughout the NT the second coming is depicted as a singular, climactic event at which time final judgment will be rendered. At that time, according to the book of Revelation, the condemned will be cast into the lake of fire while the saved will dwell forever in (or as) the New Jerusalem. In the Gospels, Jesus told parables concerning that judgment and the separation of the wicked from the righteous that would occur, parables involving the wheat and the tares (weeds), the dragnet, the unrighteous steward, the foolish virgins, the talents, the ten minas, the wicked tenants, etc.

He also described His coming on the clouds with the angels to mete out punishment for the wicked and rewards for the righteous (esp. in the Olivet Discourse: Matthew 24; Mark 13; Luke 21; cf. Appendix B). The end would be accompanied by fearful disturbances in the created order (Lk 21:25-28, 35), culminating in the removal (or transformation) of the present heavens and earth to make way for God's new creation: the new heavens and new earth (2Pet 3:7, 10-13) featuring the New Jerusalem (Revelation 21-22).

The epistles of Paul focus primarily upon the state of the righteous in connection with these developments. Christ's return will indeed be a day of wrath (1Th 1:10; 5:2-3; 2Th 1:6-9), but Paul's emphasis is upon the accompanying salvation and glory for the redeemed (Rom 8:18-25; 1Cor 15:51-57; 1Th 3:13; 4:14-17; 5:9-10; 2Th 1:10;

2Tm 4:1, 8; Tts 2:13-14). In Revelation, however, the fate of the wicked plays a significant role throughout.

Since three cycles of seven (seals, trumpets, bowls) each lead up to the arrival of the second coming, challenges face the interpreter (Chapters X, XVI). What I have concluded in my research presented above includes the following.

The trumpet plagues (Revelation 8-9, 11) and bowl plagues (Revelation 16) are parallel but marked by increasing intensity. I am less concerned about sequences or timing involved in that I view the trumpets and bowls as each leading up to the second coming. At times in Revelation we are brought to the edge of the precipice and then the scene abruptly shifts as additional descriptions of divine wrath and judgment are introduced. Since the trumpets cycle concludes with final judgment ("your wrath came and the time for the dead to be judged"; Rev 11:18), what can follow chronologically? Nothing, really.

To complicate matters, the verses immediately following present a vision depicting the Messiah's birth and ascension to heaven followed by Satan's persecution of the church (Rev 12:1-6, 11-17). The end is not yet, at least for John's message. Much more to be said by him.

Like the trumpet plagues, most of the bowl plagues are loosely patterned after the disasters described in the plagues against Egypt in Exodus. The plagues generally increase in intensity but are closely parallel sequentially.

The second plague for both the trumpets and bowls involves disaster for the sea (8:8-9; 16:3), while the sixth plague for both involves the Euphrates River as the eastern border restraining a different kind of disaster: invasion (9:13-19) or the threat of it—the impending Armageddon conflict (16:12-16). The parallels and patterns stand out. The careful, complex literary imagery employed by John suggests that the specifics presented are often not to be taken *literally*.

God's outpoured wrath is described in terrifying scenes of suffering and destruction. Although it seems that all of creation is affected ("a third of the sun darkened," etc.), the targeted recipients of wrath are the wicked, or those who follow the beast (9:4). Fierce heat, darkness, and suffering are their lot as the beast's kingdom is thrust into total darkness (16:2, 8-11). Prior to the unleashing of the trumpet and bowl plagues, however, God's servants had been sealed from wrath (7:1-8). This did not mean they were spared from persecution or even death at the hands of the beast's followers (7:9-17; 12:11; 13:7-8; 14:1-5, 12-13; 16:6), but it did mean that the trumpet plagues and bowl plagues were non-issues for them.

Those end-times judgments were reserved for the wicked. For those who will enjoy God's new heavens and earth the demolition of the present order, whatever and however long that will entail, will be of no concern, while the frightful process may truly be horrific for those outside of Christ (2Pet 3:7-13).

The trumpet and bowl plagues are not warnings designed to convince the wicked to repent, contrary to what commentators have frequently suggested. Once these terrifying events commence (whatever they literally end up being like and however long they might last), no repenting, no "second chance," is possible. The visions clearly spell it out. Those who are not among the ones immediately slain, even those who are among individuals plunged into great suffering, do not repent of their evil deeds (9:20-21; 16:9, 11). Instead they curse God's name (16:9). Their judgment is deserved.

The trumpet and bowl plagues present several challenges for making things fit into a coherent package.

One problem is the way the cycles are broken up by additional visions. After six trumpets are sounded, we encounter the vision of the angel with the little scroll (10:1-11) and of the two faithful witnesses (11:1-13). Following the latter the seventh trumpet at last sounds and final judgment is proclaimed (11:15-18). But wait.

Following the statements regarding final judgment a new "chapter" of the book unfolds describing the conflict between Christ and His kingdom and Satan and his. The beast and the false prophet are enlisted by the dragon and the war intensifies (Revelation 12-14). The 144,000 "redeemed from the earth" worship and follow the Lamb in heaven (14:1-5), while believers on earth are challenged to faithfulness (14:7-13). Believers who die for their faith are said to have "conquered the beast" (15:2).

I believe that the destruction of Jerusalem in AD 70 is described several times in the book, most likely at 11:2, 13, and very possibly at 14:18-20; 16:17-21; 17:16-18; and 18:1-19:3. From my study of Jesus' Olivet Discourse (Appendix B) and of Paul's teaching on the man of lawlessness at 2 Thessalonians 2:1-12 (Appendix A), I conclude that once the promised desolation of Jerusalem occurs, nothing remains to be fulfilled before Christ returns. His second coming then is imminent; it could happen at any moment. I am convinced that Revelation supports such an approach.

In connection with this, in my understanding Jerusalem's fall in Revelation is first mentioned just before the sounding of the seventh trumpet signaling final judgment (11:13, 15-18). Nothing happens in between. Which might mean nothing specific needs to happen in between. All is ready.

The pouring out of the seventh bowl is perhaps a bit more complex. It is accompanied by the proclamation, "It is done!" (16:17) and describes the demolition of "the great city" by a great earthquake, the worst ever (16:18). As the following lines in the text show, this does *not* describe the second coming—it describes a disaster prior to that coming (16:19-19:5). Probably AD 70.

But after the lengthy description of the fall of "Babylon the great" (likely Jerusalem), what immediately follow are second coming events: the Marriage Supper of the Lamb and the arrival of the Divine Warrior from heaven who defeats the beast and his followers (19:6-21).

The demise of the Great Harlot at the hands of the beast brings rejoicing in heaven. That rejoicing morphs into an announcement of the Marriage Supper of the Lamb that then triggers the depiction of Christ's return. Immediately following descriptions of Jerusalem's ("Babylon's") doom, we find rejoicing in heaven over that and over the arrival of the Marriage Supper of the Lamb. Out with the old (Jerusalem) and in with the new!

That marriage is noted later as well (21:2, 9-10; 22:17), but what follows immediately is the dramatic arrival of the King of Kings and Lord of Lords in divine judgment (19:11-21). What must transpire on earth between Jerusalem's fall and eternity's call? Nothing.

The identification of Jerusalem as the harlot destroyed by the beast (Rome) and its armies supports the general NT depiction of a second coming that is imminent following the early days of the church (Jesus' "this generation"). Jesus had predicted Rome's destruction of Jerusalem within a generation. After that His return was imminent and He would arrive when unexpected, like a "thief in the night."

On the other hand, the view that Rome is the harlot destroyed by the beast (that is *also* Rome?) is problematic for the doctrine of Christ's imminent return. Rome fell in the fifth century AD (410 or 476?) and if that event needed to serve as a precursor of the second coming then imminence must be boxed up and put on the shelf (Chapter XVII).

Scholars who promote the Rome identification for "Babylon the great" do not seem to find the problem for imminence here to be an issue. Puzzling. But to be fair, note the later discussion regarding the millennium and the doctrine of imminence as it relates to the "thousand-year" reign of the saints and the binding of Satan.

The opening cycle of the seven seals in Revelation 6 seems different from the trumpets cycle and the bowls cycle. To be sure, the opened sixth seal does appear to refer to the second coming: the great day of the wrath of the One who sits on the throne and of the Lamb (6:12-17). This wrath is in response to the petitions of the martyrs under the heavenly altar who are displayed with the opening of the fifth seal (6:9-10). However, more fellow Christians would be killed before that day of God's avenging them (6:11). Christ would come at the appointed time ("soon"!).

The first four seals opened by the Lamb involve Revelations' renowned "Four Horsemen of the Apocalypse." Likely these scenes describe the perilous conditions of life for many under first-century Rome rather than end-times disasters. Conquest, warfare, famine, pestilence, and death make gruesome bedfellows as the horsemen are "given authority over a fourth of the earth to kill with sword and with famine and with pestilence and by wild beasts of the earth" (6:8).

Notice the difference between the horsemen given authority over a fourth of the earth to kill and the massive army of troops mounted upon fire-breathing horses that "actually" kill a third of mankind (9:15-19). The former represents potential widespread disasters, while the latter realizes unfathomable devastation and death. With the former scene, we may assume that the martyrs under the altar described in the verses immediately following were some of the victims of the violence described in the seals visions, while with the latter those slain in the plague of the sixth trumpet are clearly a massive cohort of the wicked designated as those who do not have God's seal on their foreheads (7:2-4; 9:4).

It is a mistake to mix and mingle the plagues of the seals, trumpets, and bowls as all being part of the "great tribulation." Great tribulation (confusion) has resulted from such an approach (Chapters X, XIII-XVI).

In summary, the seven seals describe much of what has already happened and continues to happen for God's people near the end of the first century. The faithful martyrs under the throne in heaven must wait until the full number of martyrs is finally attained. Final judgment for the wicked will then be enacted. The opening of the seventh seal triggers the sounding of the first trumpet and the next cycle ensues.

This cycle is of a different nature. Ruinous end-times catastrophes are unleashed with the sounding of each trumpet. Many are tormented while a third of mankind is killed! Yet those not yet killed refuse to repent. Their doom is deserved (9:20-21). The arrival of final judgment with the sounding of the seventh trumpet (11:15) is delayed by several visions involving John's own commission to proclaim God's message and the proclamation of the gospel by God's two faithful witnesses (10:1-11:14). The delay involved is literary drama, not a chronological pause.

The signaling of the "end" by the seventh trumpet, however, comes to seem premature. We are just getting started! A sign in heaven initiates the visionary drama pitting Satan and his forces against Christ and His people (12:1-13:18).

Following a string of brief judgment scenes involving a series of angelic pronouncements and harvest images (14:6-20), the seven bowls of wrath are emptied (16:1-21). The judgments closely parallel those of the seven trumpets but exhibit increased intensity. The scene following the pouring out of the sixth bowl leaves us in limbo: utilizing demonic spirits the dragon, the beast, and the false prophet have assembled the forces of evil at Armageddon for the final battle.

But in connection with the impending battle, Jesus proclaims, "Behold, I am coming like a thief!" (16:15). His declaration clarifies the true nature of the confrontation. No bloodshed. No physical weapons employed. The battle metaphor in the book here stands for final judgment for Satan's followers. The lake of fire awaits.

Prior to the upcoming final "battle," the seventh bowl of wrath describes one bit of unfinished business before the end: the destruction of the harlot "Babylon the great." Revelation 17-18 makes it clear that Babylon's demise precedes and is unconnected with the second coming. Once more: Babylon's demise is prior to and unconnected with the second coming.

The declaration "It is done!" (16:17) probably addresses this climactic act of judgment upon the harlot Jerusalem (Chapter XVIII). After this all is ready: the battle lines are drawn; the "eighth head of the (seven-headed!) beast" exists in some form; Christ's return is now imminent following the harlot's demise.

(Answer 2) Setting, Date, and So What

An accurate determination of the setting of the book is critical for a proper understanding of the imagery and message of Revelation. The majority of scholars hold to the late or Domitian date for the book (AD 95) and that seems to be the best option, all things considered. Those who have focused on the contents of the letters to the seven churches (e.g., Hemer) have found it hard to date what is found there being as early as the mid-sixties, like the preterist view would suggest (Chapters VI, IX).

As well, external evidence, including the important statement from Irenaeus, points us toward a Domitian date. Most attempts that understand the descriptions of the "seven rulers" in Revelation 17 from an early date perspective end up viewing the message as a failed prophecy or a very convoluted one.

Although the persecution of Christians under Nero is described in horrific terms by ancient historians, it was a localized (Rome) and short-lived (ca. AD 65) episode. For the Christians in western Roman Asia, the later dire circumstances under Domitian and those rulers who followed (e.g., Trajan) were more widespread, more ongoing, and more ominous with respect to the prospects of continued difficulties with the ruling regimes. Relevant here was the troubling correspondence between Pliny and Trajan regarding how to deal with Christians who refused to deny their faith (ca. AD 112).

If Revelation was penned circa AD 95 then any references to the AD 70 destruction of Jerusalem are looking back as reflections of what transpired and deliberations as to why rather than being predictions of what lies immediately ahead.

This is what I have argued for above and I have tried to make it clear that I do not hold these accounts in Revelation to be artificial prophecies rendered after the fact (*ex eventu*, "out of the event") but rather parts of divine visions given to John for theological and apologetic purposes. God Himself was on trial here!

It was important for God's people to reject the widespread dynastic propaganda of the Flavian rulers (Vespasian, Titus, and Domitian) who hitched their legitimacy and authority to their victory over the Jews and their holy city Jerusalem. For Flavian Rome, the destruction of the Jewish temple signified the superiority of Rome and its gods over Jerusalem and its peculiar deity. This was part of the reason why the Jerusalem temple was never rebuilt. But was there a different explanation available for what had transpired? Revelation strives to answer "Yes."

Two troubling facts about Rome surface in the last half of the first century. Rome not only survived its traumatic civil war but it emerged stronger than ever. In addition, the destruction of Jerusalem and God's temple there seemingly served to verify Rome's dominance in the world and especially its superiority over the Jewish people and their distinctive religion.

Recent studies of the era have emphasized the extremes to which Vespasian and his sons went to immortalize their conquest of the Jewish nation and thus to solidify their status as the legitimate rulers going forward. Coins depicting that conquest continued to be issued more than a decade after the fact. The new Temple of Peace in Rome prominently displayed artifacts from the Jerusalem temple while the Arch of Titus depicted Jewish captives carrying equipment from their temple for display in Rome. Additionally, the great wealth of Jerusalem and its temple was repurposed for the building of Rome's enormous Colosseum (Flavian Amphitheater).

Rome is never mentioned by name in Revelation, but "those with wisdom" are invited to identify key players and developments in John's drama. In Revelation 13, the survival from the mortal wound to the head would seem to point to Rome's emergence from its bloody civil war AD

68-69. The enigmatic "666" (13:18) is often linked by gematria or isopsephism (Chapter XIV) to the name Nero and this may be the best approach in light of his role in the massacre of numerous Christians in Rome who were blamed (by Nero) for the great fire in AD 64.

As well I have suggested a possible connection with Rome's economic system that was characterized by a novel numerical array that enlisted the six primary symbols DCLXVI for much of the calculation done throughout the empire. Doing business with the beast depended upon utilizing them. In descending order these ubiquitous symbols, D (500), C (100), L (50), X (10), V (5) and I (1) when placed together (DCLXVI) give us 666. Worth a mention? A few have thought so (e.g., Bruins, Sanders, Watt).

In Revelation 17, one of the angels with the bowls of plagues promises to explain the mystery of the harlotrous figure named "Babylon the great." But virtually all of the explanation is dedicated to describing the scarlet beast with seven heads and ten horns upon which the Great Harlot sits! That is because the key to understanding the reason for and nature of the harlot's demise is in understanding what the beast represents and how and when it interacts with the harlot.

The "was" stage of the beast points to the time leading up to Nero's death and the resultant civil war. The "is not" stage speaks of the civil disorder in connection with the "Long Year" following Nero's death. The "is" stage refers to Vespasian's ascension to power and this stage is described in two opposing ways: (1) the beast's rise to power will lead to its own destruction or (2) the fact that it "is to come" signifies future success (17:8).

The latter is assumed by those who at the time "marvel." However, the description of the "eighth head" that "belongs to the seven" then "goes to destruction" speaks of the ultimate demise of the beast and his kingdom in ways that make unclear the immediate days ahead for the church (17:11). That the beast (in some form or phase) is destroyed at Christ's return (Chapters XIV, XVIII) complicates the picture (17:14; 19:20).

Domitian, the emperor ruling when this is communicated, is that eighth head and this seems to express something beyond the "seven heads" that the beast was originally said to possess. As with the initial description of the beast, "wisdom" is called for in the interpreting what the vision describes (13:18; 17:9).

Since Vespasian was the ruler when Jerusalem was destroyed and the ruler who ended the "is not" civil unrest stage following Nero's death, the angel's vision purposed to show the judgment of the Great Harlot with a focus upon him, Vespasian, and thus located his activity in the present tense, the "is" tense, following the great recovery from the "Long Year" or "is not" stage, a recovery that caused the world to "marvel" (13:3; 17:8).

As explained in Chapters XVI and XVIII, Nero was the fifth "fallen" head who preceded the "is not" period and Vespasian the sixth head, the "one who is." The latter would be succeeded by Titus (AD 79-81) who "had not yet come" and who, when he did, would "remain only a short while" (17:10).

It was Vespasian who would fulfill God's purposes in destroying Jerusalem (17:16-17). He was "the one who is" in Rome when Jerusalem fell, even though it was his son, the general Titus, who led the final military assaults. So what are the key points for the churches of Asia (and us)? Rome was God's instrument of judgment against His people much like Assyria and Babylon had been before. God's will, not Rome's, was supreme. The beast had undergone a perilous episode of civil uncertainty and had survived, but its eventual doom was assured.

The harlot Babylon had also received her just due. As argued previously, it makes the best overall sense to view ancient Jerusalem as the harlot, "Mystery Babylon," desolated by the Romans as Jesus had predicted (Chapter XVIII). In its place the church looks forward to the arrival of the New Jerusalem from heaven.

(Answer 3) The Cosmic Conflict

Revelation is a book of conflict and the struggle is seen from the beginning lines. Christ, when He returns, will be viewed by "those who pierced him" (1:7) while in the first century He appears to John with a sharp two-edged sword protruding from His mouth (1:16). The future, final battle is here anticipated. Those in the churches of Asia who emerge as "conquerors" in the struggle are repeatedly lavished with eternal rewards (2:7 ff.). Jews who persecute the church are labeled a "synagogue of Satan" (2:9; 3:9) and Satan seems to be tied to the death of the martyr Antipas in Pergamum (2:13). The devil will cast some of the church at Smyrna into prison for "ten days" but those who suffer so are promised the crown of life and escape from the "second death" (2:10-11).

Revelation 20 seems to depict the other side of this conflict: Satan himself is imprisoned for a thousand years and then will experience eternal destruction, the "second death" (20:2-3, 10).

Not all those involved in the seven churches of Asia are described as being on the right side of the conflict. Calls to repentance abound in Revelation 2-3. Christ warns that He will "come like a thief" if they do not spiritually awaken (3:3).

The throne room scene in Revelation 4-5 depicts Jesus, the Lion of Judah and the Root of David, as a Lamb standing looking as if He had been slain. Christ's sacrificial atoning death is never far from the surface in John's Apocalypse. The fifth of the seven seals opened portrays martyrs under the altar in heaven crying out for divine justice and vengeance. However, they must wait a little while until the full number of fellow martyrs has been reached (6:9-11).

In preparation for the sounding of the seven trumpets of wrath, God's servants are sealed on their foreheads: 144,000 representing 12,000 from each of the twelve tribes of Israel (for the uniqueness of this listing see Chapter X). It is likely that these same servants are then described as a great multitude from every tribe and nation who come out of the "great tribulation" as faithful overcomers who, after their martyrdom, now worship before the throne of God and the Lamb (7:1-17).

Torments and woes directed toward those who do not have God's seal on their foreheads and toward those who do not repent of their evil works characterize the six initial trumpet plagues (8:6-9:21). Following a visionary interlude (10:1-11:14), the seventh trumpet sounds and final judgment is rendered: rewards for God's servants and wrath "destroying the destroyers of the earth" (11:15-18).

With Revelation 12 the Cosmic Conflict comes into clearer focus as Christ's entrance into the world is described in a vision and the great red dragon's attempts to destroy Him and those who follow Him are depicted. Israel's Messiah King Jesus ascends to His heavenly throne as His ("already") kingdom is established, while Satan is defeated by Michael and his forces. Satan is cast down from heaven to earth where his hostilities with the church bring about the death of many of Christ's followers even as they conquer him by the blood of the Lamb and their faithful testimony.

The conflict continues in the next chapter with the arrival of the beast and the false prophet. These entities represent, at least initially, the blasphemous Roman Empire with its power-hungry emperors and their supporters, including the imperial cult that promoted and even demanded the worship of these emperors and their images. The near collapse ("mortal wound") of that empire following the death of Nero was "healed" as Vespasian ended Rome's frightful civil war and soon after crushed Judea and Jerusalem in their revolt against Rome. The righteousness of Christ's followers and the wickedness of those controlled by the beast are depicted in stark contrast throughout.

The church age is depicted throughout the book of Revelation as a time of continuous conflict, a period of tribulation and persecution that is described numerically as a "half of seven (years)" period by several equivalent measurements: "forty-two months," "1,260 days," and "a time, and times, and half a time." Critical to a proper understanding of the book of Revelation is the recognition that these numerical symbols represent the entire church age and not an alleged end-times "three-and-a-half-year" period of intensified struggle and conflict. See Chapters VII, XI, and XIII.

We must distinguish between the ongoing war or conflict throughout the church age and the special end-times "battle" between God and the forces of evil that represents final judgment. Jesus Himself clarifies the symbolic nature of this final battle when He says that in connection with it, He will come like a thief (16:15). This final battle occurs on "the great day of God the Almighty" and will involve the destruction of Satan, the beast, and the false prophet. This battle is anticipated at Revelation 16:12-16 ("Armageddon"), and is described in Revelation 19:11-21 with a focus upon the beast and the false prophet and their followers, as well as in Revelation 20:7-10 where Satan and his hordes ("Gog and Magog") are singled out. Those "defeated" in this conflict are cast into the lake of fire after which the new home of the redeemed, one involving the new heavens and new earth and New Jerusalem, is put on display.

(Answer 4) The Millennium

Much has been said throughout regarding the nature and significance of the "millennium," the thousand-year period initially mentioned at virtually the end of the Bible, at Revelation 20. For every point there is a counterpoint, and checklists have been assembled to illustrate the validity of a number of approaches. It is hard to escape the conclusion that our approaches to such a controversial passage generally rely heavily upon the exegetical edifice previously constructed in our encountering key eschatological issues.

Conclusions regarding Israel's relationship to the church, literal versus figurative language, the Bible's teaching on life after death, the identity of the recipients of the new covenant of Hebrews 8-10, the point at which Christ's kingdom is established, etc., all play a role in the unpacking of the literary masterpiece we call the book of Revelation.

Several big-picture conclusions from our study are appropriate here, results that can be garnered above especially from Chapters XIX to XXIII, although the evidence from throughout John's Apocalypse comes to bear. The figurative nature of the duration "a thousand years" would seem to be evident in light of figurative uses of the number elsewhere in Scripture and the abundance of symbolic numbers found throughout Revelation (e.g., Chapters V, VII, X).

Both the binding of Satan and the reigning of the martyrs for Christ are linked to that duration. Either this time frame describes a period never addressed in the Bible until the very end, or it broadly relates to the space of time in view throughout the NT: the church age following Christ's atoning death and establishment of a new covenant for His people.

This timeframe that can also be referred to as "the present evil age" (Gal 1:4) is depicted in Revelation as an era of intense conflict perpetrated by Satan and his followers, both demonic and human. John's message to the church also describes the present age as a time of "great tribulation" for the people of God (Rev 7:14). Beginning with the incarnation of Christ figuratively described in Revelation 12, John's visions chronicle the efforts of the great red dragon to destroy all that is precious in God's eyes.

In the amillennial approach, Revelation 20 offers a highly condensed recapitulation of the church age and presents the triumphal aspects of that (thousand-year) period which, when presented elsewhere as a time of persecution and tribulation, is portrayed as a "three-and-a-half-year" period of Satanic opposition. During the millennium, the binding of Satan, a metaphor shown to be present in popular intertestamental Jewish writings then (e.g., Jubilees), vividly depicts in Revelation the reality of Satan's limitations made more restrictive since Christ's atoning death, conquest of the grave, and inauguration of "already" aspects of His kingdom rule.

The reigning of the saints with Christ involves those on thrones with "authority to judge," including martyrs and likely others who died in faithful obedience to Christ. The three-and-a-half years and the thousand years, then, represent the church age from opposing vantage points: the church in tribulation and the church triumphant.

The "first resurrection" was described earlier as probably referring to the intermediate state for the saved, a period described elsewhere in Revelation with scenes of the redeemed worshiping and praising God the Father and Jesus the Lamb. If so, this "resurrection to life" begins at physical death and involves entering into the immediate presence of God upon death. The "thousand years" then represent possibly different *literal* time spans experienced by the various believers who have died in the Lord. But this should not be troubling. The number is symbolic—qualitative, rather than quantitative—and speaks to the blessed existence of the redeemed in heaven whenever they may have arrived.

The symbolic nature of the number also speaks to the issue regarding the imminence of Christ's return. I have argued above that the belief in the imminence of the second coming is strained if that coming must be preceded by the destruction of ancient Rome (allegedly as the Great Harlot). However, it is fair to ask that, if a predicted fall of Rome centuries later calls into question the notion of Christ's imminent return, would not the belief in the church age lasting "a thousand years" also be a challenge to the idea of imminence? I believe that there is a reasonable response to be offered here.

As noted above, the symbolic nature of the number "a thousand" allows for the view that the timeframe technically can begin at different points along the way for those who experience martyrdom and the "first resurrection." The martyrs under the altar in heaven are told that they would be joined by others at some point before the end (6:9-11). Viewed crudely, the millennial "clock" would seem to start over and over at different times as followers of Christ conquer the dragon through their devotion and sacrificial deaths. Yet at the time of the writing of Revelation many disciples of Christ are described as already enjoying the presence of God in heaven. The thousand years, closely aligned to the duration of the church age, are already marching on.

Regarding how this all relates to imminence, it would seem to follow that a symbolic number like that used here could denote perfection or completeness without indicating an exact duration or even an approximate duration. If the millennium of Revelation 20 were to have lasted only a few Christian centuries or were to persist for several millennia and beyond (it is now 2025!), no problems would arise from such a state of affairs. We remember Peter's "A day is with the Lord..."

I have concluded from what both Jesus and Paul taught that once the AD 70 fall of Jerusalem had occurred the return of Christ could be viewed as truly imminent—it could happen at any moment. With the temple's destruction all signs relating to that first generation of disciples by then had transpired, including the martyrdom of Peter and the spread of the gospel throughout the Roman world. Christ was now coming "soon."

With the book of Revelation, we are at a slightly different juncture. Some twenty years or so had elapsed since the fall of Jerusalem and Christians had been martyred both before and after that event, and possibly during that event, at the hands of both Jews and Romans. As John wrote, a full century had elapsed since the birth of Christ in Bethlehem. Jerusalem the Harlot had now been judged. How much longer until Jesus would return? The esoteric nature of the "eighth head" (out of seven!) in Revelation 17 gives one pause. The beast was present and active when Jerusalem fell. In some form or fashion it will still be present and active when Christ comes back.

The so-called millennium will end with final judgment culminating in the lake of fire for the wicked and the new heavens and new earth for the redeemed. Christ's return will initiate judgment that is described as a great battle in which Satan and his followers are defeated.

Again, battle imagery in Revelation and in prophetic texts elsewhere in Scripture is generally metaphoric for judgment itself. Now we see that Satan's release from prison after the thousand years is a non-starter. Any hopes for a Satan-led revolt and victory are short-lived as fire from heaven destroys his forces (as happened in Ezekiel's end-times "Gog and Magog" episode) and the devil himself joins the beast and the false prophet, along with their followers, in the lake of fire, the second death.

The fact that Satan was released from prison but not unbound may suggest a parallel with the well-known Roman Triumph of John's day in which vanquished enemy leaders were held in chains as captives awaiting their ultimate execution in a carefully orchestrated reenactment of Rome's conquest over its enemies. That Satan remains bound or chained even as he is "released" for a short time might suggest such a re-enactment, one in which Satan's fiery fate is now sealed (Chapter XXII).

The well-worn alternate path for interpreters is that Satan is released for a short time to wreak havoc upon the earth before God destroys him at the second coming of Christ. This approach has always been problematic. Yet the belief in a last-days apostasy or multiple apostasies in the end times persists (before an alleged rapture? before the second coming? before both? after the rapture but before a subsequent second coming ["the revelation"]? after the millennium after the second coming?). The topic has always generated more heat than light (see Chapters XIII, XXII).

The depiction of a thousand-year reign of the saints and binding of Satan reinforces the "already and not yet" pattern elsewhere in the NT. Satan is a defeated foe even as he wreaks havoc upon the church. Believers who are faithful unto death "conquer" him. His effective influence (both as the "accuser" and the "deceiver") is diminished as God's kingdom expands and flourishes. As the next section emphasizes, the use of the OT by John furnishes ample evidence that the "golden age" promised for God's people is eternal and that it is fulfilled in the new heavens and new earth of Revelation 21-22, not in Revelation 20 and its millennium.

(Answer 5) The OT Golden Age and Revelation 20-22

One of the most inconvenient truths confronting the premillennial persuasion is that at Revelation 21 the New Jerusalem descends to the new earth after the millennial reign is over, not before it begins. Even more troubling, the OT "golden age" passages (e.g., in Isaiah 60, 65) that allegedly speak of the millennial kingdom for a restored "Israel" are cited in Revelation 21-22 as being fulfilled in the eternal state following the millennium of Revelation 20, and not in the so-called millennium itself.

The parallel texts cited in Chapter XXIII ("The Isaiah Connection Again") make it clear that Isaiah 60 and 65 are fulfilled in the language of Revelation 21-22 and not in that found in Revelation 20. Whatever the millennium of Revelation 20 describes, it is not the fulfillment of the language of Isaiah here.

Also clear is that the close parallels between the promises to the seven churches (Revelation 2-3) and their fulfillments in the later chapters of Revelation support the view that the NT church, not some later post-rapture, post-tribulation remnant, is the focus of Revelation's closing scenes. See especially "The End from the Beginning" in Chapter IX.

Plenty of OT prophecies point ahead to the church age (now part of the "already") while others envision the future eternal state, the "not yet" (along with Isaiah 60 and 65 note Isaiah 25:6-12). All tears will be wiped away. Death will be swallowed up for all time. Eternal promises, not millennial ones.

(Answer 6) John as the New Ezekiel

One of the important distinctions of the present work is the recognition of the numerous parallels between John the seer and the OT's Ezekiel the prophet. I have gone so far as to label John the "new Ezekiel" (Chapters VIII, XI). The list of parallels earlier documented is quite astounding, yet the implications of such numerous connections remain a source of confusion and disagreement. Once again, which parallels we choose to place emphasis upon are likely directly related to our eschatological preferences. Unfortunately, the principle of working from the known to the unknown falters somewhat here: both Ezekiel and Revelation are hotbeds of controversy and interpretive struggles! A few observations are made below.

Revelation clearly borrows terminology and imagery directly from Ezekiel in connection with John's recounting of the visions he experiences. His call is similar and his opening throne room scene is closely parallel (e.g., the four living creatures) although, since God is departing from Jerusalem in Ezekiel's day because of its rampant wickedness and the impending destruction by the Babylonians, we find a throne *chariot* in Ezekiel and not simply a throne (Ezekiel 1; 10-11). God will join His people in exile!

Later in the two books, Ezekiel's restored temple (Ezekiel 40-48) becomes John's restored city (Revelation 21-22), but involved with each is the river of life flowing from God's throne with fruit trees bearing fruit each month. Both Ezekiel and John eat a (sweet and sour!) scroll in connection with the descriptions of their calls (Eze 3:1-3, 14; Rev 10:9-10). The Gog and Magog invasion of Ezekiel 38-39 is utilized by John in describing the final battle ("Armageddon") of Revelation (Rev 16:12-16; 19:11-21; 20:7-10). Quite significant, I believe, is Ezekiel's stark, graphic language in connection with his prolonged descriptions of Jerusalem as a lewd, lustful whore (Ezekiel 16, 23), descriptions that may help with interpreting the Great Harlot or Babylon the Harlot in Revelation 16-19. To that complex task we now return.

(Answer 7) Mystery Babylon

Apart from those who insist upon an important future role for Iraq's modern-day Babylon (as with dispensationalism) and those who view Revelation's Great Harlot as the Roman Catholic Church or as a version of a liberal, apostate modern Christendom, the bulk of discussion surrounding the topic comes from those who view imperial Rome as Babylon the Harlot or ancient Jerusalem as that harlot. Both views have garnered strong support (Chapters XVII, XVIII).

As the present work unfolded, the identification of the Great Harlot became more and more a key issue to resolve. The topic is tightly intertwined with the complex and controversial questions surrounding the identification of the various heads of the beast, the designations "is not," "is," and "is to come" regarding certain heads, and the connections between the beast and the great prostitute. Revelation 17 is the key chapter, one to which, surprisingly, many commentators give short shrift.

Quite telling is the fact that in Revelation 17 the angel's offer to explain all about the great prostitute, "Babylon the great," whose violent demise was just described (Rev 16:17-20), results instead in a detailed description of the nature of the seven-headed beast. We read of its five fallen heads, its near demise and remarkable recovery (cf. 13:3, 12, 14), its extensive interactions with the Great Harlot, and its brutal destruction of that harlot—a city with which it had enjoyed a profitable, if problematic, relationship. The beast upon which the harlot had ridden comes to hate the harlot and brings about her complete desolation.

I find it difficult from the language here to conclude that Rome can be both the beast and the harlot whom the beast brutally destroys!

What is much more fitting, however, is the interpretation that the "mortal wound" of the beast, the recovery from that wound, the Jewish revolt that erupted during Nero's abusive reign, Rome's conquest and destruction of Jerusalem and the Jewish state, and the Flavian Dynasty's propagandistic uses of the victory over Jerusalem and its people *all form a neat package* that makes perfect sense in addressing the concerns of the early church represented in Revelation's "Seven Churches of Asia." If the above topics represent a major concern of John the seer, then Jerusalem most likely is the harlot in mind.

The evidence for Jerusalem being the Great Harlot (Rev 17:2) or Babylon the Great (Rev 17:5) is considerable. Early on in Revelation the Jews harassing the church are described as a "synagogue of Satan" (Rev 2:9; 3:9). Jerusalem is singled out as the place where Christ had been crucified and is labeled symbolically "Sodom and Egypt"

(Rev 11:8). Isaiah centuries earlier had referred to unfaithful Jerusalem as a whore (Isa 1:21) and had given it the name "Sodom" (Isa 1:10).

I have briefly reviewed the justification for labeling John the "new Ezekiel." Ezekiel's graphic language regarding Jerusalem's spiritual whoredom and resultant punishment is well documented (Ezekiel 16, 23). Once we consider the gravity of Jerusalem's eventual rejection of Jesus as the Messiah, the notion that Revelation could represent that city as Babylon the Great, the Great Harlot, is not out of line. This is even more so when we consider how Jerusalem became an oppressive city from which Jesus' followers were warned to flee in light of its deserved impending destruction.

We find eight references to "the great city" in Revelation, seven of which clearly refer to the harlot Babylon (Rev 11:8; 16:19; 17:18; 18:10, 16, 18, 19, 21). However, the book's initial reference to "the great city" speaks of Jerusalem, "where their Lord was crucified" (Rev 11:8). Also, interestingly, both "the great city" of Revelation 11 and that of Revelation 16 are ravaged by a "great earthquake," no doubt figurative (Rev 11:13; 16:18). The same city? The same metaphoric earthquake? I think so.

The problems with identifying Rome with Babylon the Great have been discussed above (esp. Chapter XVII). Three major points have been made.

1. The Great Harlot is said to ride upon the beast before it is eventually destroyed by the beast and its forces. How then can both the harlot and the beast be identified as Rome?

2. The fall of ancient Rome occurred in the fifth century, a full century after the conversion of Constantine and the subsequent conversion of

much of the Roman Empire. By the time Rome fell, it had become a leading center for Christian activity in the Mediterranean World. If the fall of Rome was the fulfillment of Revelation 16-18, its timing was odd, to say the least.

3. A fifth-century fulfillment for the demise of Babylon the Great would seem to conflict with the biblical teaching of the imminence of Christ's second coming. If Rome's fall were a precursor of Christ's return, it would be confusing to allege that Jesus' coming will be like that of a thief in the night. The view that ancient Rome was the Babylon of Revelation makes the notion of an any-moment or imminent return of Christ during the early Christian centuries a challenge.

In sum, the idea that the fall of Revelation's Babylon is a yet-future event depends upon a highly futuristic approach to the book that must be rejected, especially if it presumes that the church will have been raptured out of the world. The fall of Babylon in Revelation has nothing to do with what most refer to as the end times!

On the other hand, the idea that the fall of Rome in the fifth century is in mind in Revelation would be in contradiction with the Bible's teaching of Christ's imminent return, even if one were to accept the unlikely proposition that both the beast and the harlot are symbols of Rome as one destroys the other. The conclusion with the least theological dissonance is that ancient Jerusalem, viewed as apostate and as in opposition to God's new Israel, the church, is graphically portrayed in Revelation as the abominable harlot whose unholy alliances ultimately bring about her fitting destruction.

(Answer 8) Coming Soon

Important discussions regarding the imminent return of Christ can be found in Chapters V, VII, and XXIV (also in Appendix A). I have contended that all relevant signs and promises needing to be fulfilled preliminary to Christ's return *have* been fulfilled and in fact *were* fulfilled in events connected with the first generation of believers, e.g., Jesus' prediction regarding Peter's martyrdom in old age, His proclamation regarding the Great Commission, and His predictions concerning the destruction of Jerusalem and the temple.

A major stumbling-block in the discussion is removed with the identification of Paul's "man of lawlessness" as an antagonist in connection with the Jewish Revolt that culminated in the destruction of Jerusalem, rather than as an end-times "antichrist" figure (Appendix A).

Revelation concludes with the promise of the imminent return of Jesus ("the time is near," Rev 1:3; "I am coming soon," Rev 3:11; 22:7, 12, 20). Again, this promise is a main pillar for the strict preterist view that the AD 70 fall of Jerusalem was the "second coming" of Jesus, a view that must be rejected, although I do believe that certain aspects of Revelation relate to events and individuals in the first century AD, e.g., the arrival of the beast and likely the AD 70 destruction of Jerusalem. Throughout the present work, however, I have also argued for a future return of Christ, regardless of what degree of importance might be placed upon several key first-century events. However, if the imminent or any-moment return of Christ is a reality, how are the "soon" promises regarding Jesus' return in Revelation to be understood now, centuries later?

Jesus Himself acknowledged that as the Son of the Father He did not know the day or the hour of His own coming (Mt 24:36). His return would be sudden, unexpected, and imminent. It could happen at any moment, as the rest of the NT contends.

In connection with Luke 18:6-8, Darrell Bock discusses the term "soon," what could be labeled the "eschatological 'soon'"(my words). In Bock's words, Jesus' coming is soon "in that it is next on the eschatological calendar." He also explains, "Until the vindication comes, it seems a long way away, especially in the midst of persecution, but after it comes and is established for eternity, it will not seem so delayed" (*Luke*, 295).

What is next on the eschatological calendar, to use Bock's wording? Christ's return in glory! See Chapter XXIV: Still Coming "Soon."

The best approach? The "eschatological soon" is a "soon" made possible by the fulfillment of all signs and promises that were given regarding events needing to occur before the second coming of Christ. If such fulfillments have already occurred, then the return of Jesus is truly "imminent," it could happen at any moment. Some have spoken of possible or potential imminence versus necessary imminence, what could happen versus what must happen.

Numerous scenes in Revelation may have depicted events that had already occurred by the end of the first century. What events then still remain that will unfold "soon?" They are those events occurring in connection with the second coming of Christ, e.g., His visible coming with the clouds in judgment (Rev 1:7); His victory in the great Last Battle (Rev 19:11-21); His Great White Throne Judgment (Rev 20:11-15); and His casting of Satan, the beast, and the false prophet into the lake of fire (Rev 19:20; 20:10).

The highly figurative and stylized trumpet plagues and bowl plagues may figure in here as well, although their figurative nature clouds any clear sense of timing we might seek to establish. Most agree that key aspects of these two cycles involve repetition or recapitulation. The specific events described in one cycle may be paralleled in the other. Also, many have noted that the cyclical parallels play out with increasing intensity. Timing and sequence are thrown out the window for the most part.

Apart from the preterist approach, whether the second coming is a two-stage event (dispensationalism) or, as more traditionally understood, one single stage (historic premillennialism, postmillennialism, and amillennialism), the mainstream views all wrestle with applying the word "soon" to Jesus' return in light of the lengthy lapse in time thus far.

Again, I believe the most helpful answer is in the concept of imminence and that Christ's return is "soon" in that it could happen at any moment: no signs or prophecies still need be fulfilled before He comes back. This is a commonly held explanation among evangelical scholars and would seem to be the best option (see also Chapter XXIV).

As described in Jesus' Olivet Discourse (Matthew 24; Mark 13; Luke 21), the fall of ancient Jerusalem was foreshadowed by signs (e.g., "the abomination of desolation"), unlike Jesus' subsequent return in which He would come like a "thief in the night" (Mt 24:43).

My approach to Revelation harmonizes well with the rest of the NT in envisioning a second coming devoid of warning signs. For the notion of imminence regarding Christ's return I have suggested the label "the eschatological 'soon.'"

The warning signs that Jesus gave in the Olivet Discourse concerned the fall of first-century Jerusalem in AD 70, not the second coming (also Mt 23:37-39; Lk 19:41-

44; 23:26-31). His teaching that did relate to His subsequent coming in glory in the Discourse, however, emphasized that no warning signs would occur in connection with that later event. His declarations regarding "this generation" and "those standing here" related to promises for the first generation of believers (Mt 16:24-28; Mk 8:34-9:1; Lk 9:23-27). See Appendix B.

Other teachings of Jesus involving that initial generation of believers included His prophecy regarding the death of Peter in his old age (Jn 21:18-19) and the promise of the universal spread of the gospel (Mt 28:18-20; Acts 1:8). Once the first generation of the church age essentially culminated with Jerusalem's fall (AD 70—roughly forty years after the church's birth at Pentecost), no further prophecies remained needing to be fulfilled before Christ's return. His return then would be "imminent." He could come at any moment and in that sense His return would be impending, unpredictable—"soon."

In 1999, on the eve of "Y2K," Vernard Eller offered a number of helpful insights as he discussed the "two-part affirmation" regarding Christ's return: the claim that "the time is short" and the warning that Jesus would come as "a thief in the night" (78-80). Both terms "soon" and "sudden" clearly described that return. Eller rejects the notion that "soon" or "the time is short" involves a "calendar claim." He wisely contends, "Somehow the idea that 'Jesus wants to come like a thief, but here are the data you need to calculate the time of his coming' doesn't work" (78).

Eller suggests that in a sense the claim that "the time is short" or "the end is at hand" is not made by the NT writer (esp. Paul) looking ahead but rather looking back—"looking back to see all that God already has done in the way of bringing his promise to fulfillment: the coming of

God's Messiah, his atoning death and victorious resurrection, the coming of the Holy Spirit, the creation of the new faith community and its missionary outreach. Seeing this, he says, 'The day is far gone, and the time is short'" (79-80). A great insight! And certainly, in view of the expanse of eternity, "the time is short."

As well, Eller notes that the immensity of that glorious future event naturally carries with it the sense that it is coming "soon" as it looms massively on the horizon (79). Such language, then, becomes a subjective description rather than an objective claim. No "calendar claim" here.

We have contended that Revelation itself offers no signs needing to be fulfilled prior to Christ's return. A late-first-century original audience of the book would have recognized many pointers to events that had already transpired. They may have understood themselves as living after the time of the "seven rulers" of Revelation 17:7-11, but during the time of the "eighth beast" or "eighth head" who "belonged to the seven" (17:11).

For them the nature of future dealings with the beast remained a mystery. So for us. For them, Armageddon, the trumpet and bowl plagues, and the Gog and Magog encounter lay in wait. The same is true for us today. But things will change. Soon.

(Answer 9) Hope, Wisdom, and Mystery

Finally, the subtitle of the present work deserves mention. The terms involved have significance on different levels regarding their role in the study of Revelation. Both "wisdom" (*sophia*) and "mystery" (*mystērion*) occur four times in the book (wisdom: Rev 5:12; 7:12; 13:18; 17:9; mystery: Rev 1:20; 10:7; 17:5; 17:7). Surprisingly the term "hope" (*elpis*) does not occur at all in John's Apocalypse! However, the theme is all-pervasive.

The Cosmic Conflict, front and center in the book, culminates in glorious victory for the saints (Chapter XIII). The crown of life awaits those who are faithful unto death. I have argued that the "thousand years" of Revelation 20 refers to the intermediate state of believers who have died and now are in the presence of God (Chapter XXI). That period will end with the second coming and final judgment at which time Satan and his followers will be cast into the lake of fire.

For the redeemed, the New Jerusalem will then descend as part of the eternal new heavens and new earth. Those within it will enjoy direct access to the throne of God and of the Lamb. Revelation, therefore, concludes with one of the greatest portrayals of hope realized that can be found in all of Scripture. Even if the word itself does not occur!

The confluence of the terms "wisdom" and "mystery" in Revelation, especially at Revelation 17, took on special significance in my examination of the message of the book. On a broad level, wisdom is one of the attributes credited to the Lamb in Revelation (5:12; 7:12), while the seven stars and the seven lampstands introduced at the opening of the book are a "mystery" presented by the glorious risen Christ. The lampstands, He explains, are the seven churches while the stars are the angels (or messengers) of those churches (1:20).

Calls for wisdom seem to express a challenge in Revelation as they often do elsewhere. Follow the clues! The label "mystery" refers to that which is initially hidden or unknown, but which eventually is made known or revealed. In the NT and related literature, a mystery is that which is hidden by God from human reason and therefore must be revealed by God to those for whom it is intended (see, e.g., Bauer, 530). In Revelation 10 the expression "the mystery of God" seems to describe the entire revelation of

God and His purposes (10:7). When God's mystery is finished, the seventh angel will sound his trumpet (10:15-18).

Twice in Revelation we find the call for wisdom in interpreting what John is describing in highly figurative language. The identity of the beast is of key concern in Revelation 13 and no other specific names or labels are provided (apart from the "seven hills" and the "seven rulers" in Revelation 17).

Some level of designed murkiness would be expected within John's first-century work, of course, if the beast in fact is a designation for Rome or the Roman emperor as most interpreters now conclude. Here wisdom involves the challenge for one with understanding to calculate the number of the beast, the famous "666" (13:18).

I have investigated the options that this mysterious number (requiring wisdom) may refer to the Emperor Nero specifically or perhaps to the Roman imperial socio-political system in general with all its economic intricacies. These would include its novel, unique array of symbols for various calculations, noting that the representative sequence DCLXVI, a listing of Roman numerals in their natural descending order, gives us $500 + 100 + 50 + 10 + 5 + 1 = 666$ (Chapter XIV).

The "mortal wound" of the beast and the remarkable recovery from that wound become key pieces of the puzzle (13:3, 12, 14). In John's earliest audiences, readers (or, better, hearers!) with wisdom could have identified the mortal wound as the demise of Nero and the resulting bloody civil war that nearly toppled the entire Roman Empire.

The tie-in of Revelation 13 with Revelation 17 becomes crucial here. Early readers could also have recognized that the fifth fallen ruler (17:10) was indeed

Nero who, after the chaos of the Year of the Four Emperors, was followed by the Flavian Emperor Vespasian who then established a fledgling dynasty and was succeeded first by his son Titus and then by his younger son Domitian (17:10-11).

Finally, John's initial audiences might have readily concluded that the Great Harlot, who for a time had ridden on the beast (Rome) and who was subsequently devastated by the beast and its allies (17:3-7, 16-17), was in fact Jerusalem, as various clues in the book might suggest ("the great city" where Christ was crucified; hostile Jews in their "synagogue of Satan"; Babylon the Harlot and the intense OT harlotry parallels involving wicked Jerusalem of the past, etc.) cf. *(Answer 7) Mystery Babylon.*

The events of the Roman Civil War along with the contemporary circumstances involving the Jewish Revolt and the subsequent destruction of Jerusalem in AD 70 seem a suitable match for the language of Revelation 17. What to make of all this?

John's original audience stood at the entrance of a passageway that many have traversed in the years following. We are now at the far end of that passageway, at least many of us feel that we are. How much time must yet elapse is not told us even as it was not told to the saints under the heavenly altar in Revelation 6. They were told to "rest a little longer" (6:11). That vagueness must suffice for us as well.

By the end of the first century much of "eschatology" had already transpired! The coming of the Messiah, His call to Israel, His willing atoning sacrifice for the sins of the world, His resurrection from the dead, His mandate to evangelize the known world, His pronouncement of doom upon apostate Jerusalem—the churches John addressed in Revelation were well aware of such previous developments. To varying degrees the seer emphasized these truths so that the churches then and there (and later and afar) could be comforted and encouraged in the face of intensely formidable opposition. The hour of trial with the beast was dark, but Christ had won the day!

We have featured the popular "already and not yet" paradigm and utilized it throughout (starting with Chapter II). Its value for interacting with Revelation should be obvious. John joined the host of prophetic voices that proclaimed the unveiling and the culmination of "the mystery of God" (10:7).

One of the convictions in the present work is that key aspects of Revelation that often have been relegated to the future, both John's future and ours, instead speak to meaningful and pivotal events that lay in the past—likely, for John's initial audience, in the recent past.

Throughout John's message the accomplished once-for-all atoning work of Christ is ever present (e.g., 1:5-7, 17-18; 3:4, 21; 5:5-6, 9-12; 7:13-14; 11:8; 12:10-11; 13:8). Martyrdom at the hands of the dragon, the beast, and the harlot Babylon is a recurring theme (e.g., 1:9; 2:10-11, 13; 3:21; 6:9-11; 7:13-14; 11:7-12; 12:10-12; 13:7-10; 14:12-13; 16:6; 17:6; 19:2; 20:4). Also key for John would likely have been the topic of the AD 70 fall of Jerusalem, a display of divine wrath for which God employed the despised Roman occupying forces, much as He had done with Babylon's might against Jerusalem and Judah centuries previous.

The prophetic significance of past fulfilled events merges in Revelation with the important promises of what lies ahead. Both supply hope and assurance for the future.

God is in control. His promises cannot fail. Reminders from the past provide encouragement for what lies ahead. He is not done. Revelation begins and ends with the promise that Christ will indeed return to establish an eternal new order (1:7; 19:11-16; 22:7, 12, 20). A glorious future is on the horizon. And when will that be?

Soon.

Appendices

APPENDIX A

THE MAN OF LAWLESSNESS

I. Wrath at Last
II. The Man of Lawlessness Revealed
    A. A Pivotal Text—A Problem Text
    B. The Pre-trib Dispensational Dilemma
    C. Posttribulational Options
    D. The Antichrist Question
    E. The BIG Question
    F. The Unexpected Answer
    G. A New Paradigm: Rethinking Verse 8
    H. Seated in God's Temple
    I. Abominations That Desolate
    J. The Lawless One and the Restrainer
    K. With the Breath of His Mouth
    L. Finally the Right Focus

The importance of Paul's contribution to the Bible's teaching on the second coming cannot be overstated. And of all his NT epistles, the Thessalonian letters take center stage. The two letters to the church at Thessalonica represent the most extensive teaching of Paul on the subject of the second coming. These are probably among the earliest letters that Paul wrote and they illustrate the common understanding that Paul's letters represent *ad hoc* communications, documents addressing specific issues, needs, or questions that arose in the various congregations with which Paul labored.

The discussion below involves two major sections, the key one dealing with the controversial figure labeled the "man of lawlessness" (2Th 2:1-12), with the other describing God's wrath being poured out upon the Jews who had rejected Christ and were hindering the spread of the gospel (1Th 2:14-16). Because of the alleged difficulties involved, many scholars have viewed the account at 1 Thessalonians 2:14-16 as an "interpolation," a passage inserted here by another author.

I believe that it is fair to say, however, that the majority of NT scholars today continue to hold these verses as genuinely Pauline. It is difficult to extract arbitrarily the wording involved in this passage from its immediate context. The results are unsatisfying from both a text-critical and a literary standpoint.

Likewise, a substantial cadre of scholars has excluded 2 Thessalonians from the corpus of genuine Pauline epistles. Two of the more interesting reasons for this exclusion are: the lack of conformity of the "man of lawlessness" passage with other writings of Paul; and the overly similar wording and subject matter observed when comparing 1 Thessalonians with 2 Thessalonians. The latter, in other words, is not trusted because it is too similar to what Paul has said elsewhere! It must be the work of a clumsy imitator. Conclusion: Some people are never satisfied.

These two key texts in Paul's Thessalonian correspondence are examined below, texts that are vitally connected to the topic of the "antichrist"/"man of lawlessness"/"beast" and to the understanding of the book of Revelation in general the earlier passage from Paul speaks of wrath that will come upon the Jewish nation because of their rejection of Christ and persecution of His servants (1Th 2:14-16). The subsequent text describes events surrounding the manifestation of "the man of lawlessness," an enigmatic figure whose deception and destructive activity will spell doom for those who follow him (2Th 2:1-12).

Both passages are hotly debated and decidedly problematic. Both passages have been denied as Pauline by numerous critics who cannot harmonize the content of these texts with what they think Paul should or would have said. Perhaps the questions and doubts could be better addressed if one could establish that the two passages in question are directly related. This relationship is not generally recognized or even hinted at in the analyses of the vast majority of commentators. And yet this relationship may be a key that helps unlock the centuries-old mystery of Paul's "man of lawlessness" and helps clarify that figure's connection to the topic of the second coming. Surprises await.

I. Wrath at Last

For you, brothers, became imitators of the churches of God in Christ Jesus that are in Judea. For you suffered the same things from your own countrymen as they did from the Jews, [15]who killed both the Lord Jesus and the prophets, and drove us out, and displease God and oppose all mankind [16]by hindering us from speaking to the Gentiles that they might be saved—so as always to fill up the measure of their sins. But wrath has come upon them at last! (1Th 2:14-16)

The above verses are among some of the most controversial in Paul's letters. Because of that, a number of commentators have concluded that the verses represent a later interpolation and thus are not original with Paul. This finding is not on the basis of any textual evidence in the manuscripts but is simply from a dislike of what is found in the wording here. Modern sensitivities have raised the question of anti-Semitism and Paul, but that accusation has been well handled in the literature. How could Paul be called anti-Semitic?

Instead, his sharp language here is not at all untypical of ongoing internecine debate and disagreement. In Paul's day verbal barbs between Pharisees and Sadducees were commonplace. The anti-Jerusalem rhetoric from the Qumran community is well documented in the Dead Sea Scrolls. Strong feelings often produce striking language, but one need only look at another early epistle from Paul, the book of Galatians, to see further harsh and accusatory tones, in this case toward the Judaizers who were undermining his work among the churches in Galatia (Gal 4:17; 5:12; 6:12-13).

Post-holocaust sentiment engenders appropriate caution for any discussion in which Jews, ancient or modern, seem to bear the brunt of strident criticism. The theologically liberal participants ("Fellows") of the infamous "Jesus Seminar" erased any such harsh wordings from Jesus' lips, voting them out of existence, but students of an authoritative, fully inspired Scripture must seek to deal with such utterances appropriately.

The persecution of early Christians by first-century Jews is well documented in the NT. Paul says here that the members of the churches in Judea suffered at the hands of their countrymen, the Jews. Was this persecuting true of all Jews?

Paul himself was an earlier example of a Jewish leader bent on stamping out this worrisome Christian heresy. The translators of the ESV supply here an explanatory footnote: "The Greek word *Ioudaioi* can refer to Jewish religious leaders, and others under their influence, who opposed the Christian faith in that time." The point is noted.

369

Paul's frustrations from the fierce Jewish opposition to
the gospel are evident. The problem did not end in Judea.
The descriptions in Acts flesh out Paul's accusations here.
Jewish opponents not only drove him out of various cities
but also pursued him during his attempts to evangelize
other destinations (Acts 14:19; 17:13). His criticisms of his
fellow Jews sound like those of pagan authorities such as
the Roman historian Tacitus and others.

According to Tacitus, the Jews felt "hostility and hatred
toward all people" (*Histories* 5.5.2). Such harsh accusations,
however, were racially and culturally motivated; Paul's were
religious in nature. Not only had the Jews rejected salvation
for themselves, but they were fervent in hindering the
preaching of the gospel to other Jews, as well as to Gentiles,
in the Mediterranean world. In some fashion, however,
God's punishment of them has been made manifest.

When Paul states that God's wrath (*orgē*) has come
upon the Jews, to what historical event might he be
referring? Jeffrey Weima notes eight options that have been
suggested:

1. God's wrath resulting from the crucifixion of Christ

2. The recent expulsion of Jews from Rome in AD 49
    by Claudius (Acts 18:1-13; Suetonius, *Claudius* 25.4)

3. The massacre of thousands of Jews in Jerusalem in
    AD 49 because of Jewish nationalistic violence
    (Josephus, *Antiquities* 20.102, 105-15, 118-210)

4. A great famine in AD 47 (Acts 11:28; Josephus,
    Antiquities 20.51, 101)

5. The violent crushing of a revolt led by Theudas in
    AD 44-46 (Acts 5:36; Josephus, *Antiquities* 20.98)

6. The sudden death of Herod Agrippa I in AD 44 (Acts 12:23)

7. The fall of Jerusalem and the destruction of the temple in AD 70

8. God's wrath resulting from the rejection of the gospel (Weima, 177)

Paul claims that "wrath has come upon them at last." The aorist tense form of *phthanō* (*ephthasen*) is best translated "has come" here even though some want to give it the sense of "is about to come," seeking to link it to an impending event such as the destruction of Jerusalem. Yet Jerusalem's demise may be in view either way.

Disturbing events linked to AD 49, those immediately prior to Paul's writing this, events such as (2 above) the expulsion of the Jews from Rome because of turmoil stemming from a certain "Chrestus" (according to the Roman biographer Suetonius—no doubt a garbled reference to violent Jewish resistance to Christians preaching about Christ) and (3 above) the Roman massacre of thousands of Jews in Jerusalem were very likely seen by Paul as precursors to the ultimate demise: the fall of Jerusalem and the destruction of the temple.

Regarding the expulsion of the Jews from Rome, Paul no doubt received a vivid firsthand account from Aquila and Priscilla upon meeting them in Corinth (Acts 18:1-3). Paul likely had already heard details from others.

In addition, the massacre of Jews at Jerusalem certainly became known quickly throughout the Jewish Diaspora. If Paul believed that God's wrath would soon be poured out upon Jerusalem in fulfillment of Jesus' previous warnings, these dire recent downturns with regard to Roman-Jewish relations could have served as a signal and confirmation to the apostle regarding the certainty of Jerusalem's doom.

The connection between Paul's vituperation and Jerusalem's fate is reinforced by a comparison of Paul's words here with Jesus' woes directed against the Jewish leaders of His day. Especially similar are the words at Matthew 23:29-36. Paul's mention of the killing of Jesus and the prophets (1Th 2:15; cf. Mt 23:30-31, 34), the pursuit and persecution of Jesus' followers (1Th 2:15-16; cf. Mt 23:34), and the "filling up of the measure of their sins" (1Th 2:16; cf. Mt 23:32-33, 35-36) closely mirror Jesus' accusations and warnings against the scribes and Pharisees of Jerusalem.

These words in Matthew immediately precede Jesus' foretelling the destruction of Jerusalem and the temple (Mt 24:1-35). God's vengeance being poured out upon Jerusalem because of the rejection of its Messiah is especially noted in Luke (Lk 19:41-44; 21:20-24; 23:27-31).

More simply, one could follow Gordon Fee here and just view Paul's words as prophetic (102). Judgment upon Jerusalem was an accomplished fact in the mind of God and its certainty could thus be expressed in a past tense (here the Greek aorist). Paul's concluding words raise a final question.

The words "at last" are a rendering of the Greek *eis telos*. Literally these words could be said to represent something like "unto an end" or "unto a goal." Idiomatically the phrase could be translated as "at last" (ESV, NIV), "fully" (NAS), "to the uttermost" (KJV, NKJV, ASV), and "completely" (NET).

The translation "until the end" suggested by several commentators is less satisfactory. Motivated by their views concerning the ultimate conversion and salvation of the Jews ("all Israel"), views based on a misunderstanding of Romans 11:26, some suggest that God's wrath will be poured out upon the Jews *until* the end, meaning until the events surrounding Christ's return.

What will happen then to the Jews is not stated in 1 Thessalonians. By this approach, room is left for the miraculous salvation of the Jewish people or nation in the future.

A better approach, however, might be to see the fulfillment of this oracle of doom as being the destruction of Jerusalem. Paul's language here matches statements by Jesus in the Gospels in stating that God's wrath poured out upon Jerusalem was deserved judgment. If the views below about the "man of lawlessness" be accepted, God's condemnation of Jerusalem and the temple are even more pronounced in Paul's mind than most have realized. If this is so, it may have some bearing on the identification of the "great harlot" of Revelation 17-18 being Jerusalem, not Rome as many contend.

II. The Man of Lawlessness Revealed

If you are well versed in the Scriptures on the end times and have studied much of what has been said about the "man of sin"/"antichrist"/"beast" in the NT, the presentation here will likely go against most, if not all, of what you have been led to believe about the "man of lawlessness" in 2 Thessalonians 2. Most would agree that 2 Thessalonians 2:1-12 is one of the most critical and difficult passages of all regarding the end times.

All eschatological traffic passes through this checkpoint. For many it seems to be the foundation for the idea that the church will someday go through a worldwide "great tribulation" led by some monstrous ruler out to destroy God's people. This idea may be true, but it may not. If my understanding of this passage is correct, 2

Thessalonians 2 may, in the final analysis, have little or nothing to say about the subject!

> *Now concerning the coming of our Lord Jesus Christ and our being gathered together to him, we ask you, brothers, ²not to be quickly shaken in mind or alarmed, either by a spirit or a spoken word, or a letter seeming to be from us, to the effect that the day of the Lord has come. ³Let no one deceive you in any way. For that day will not come, unless the rebellion comes first, and the man of lawlessness is revealed, the son of destruction, ⁴who opposes and exalts himself against every so-called god or object of worship, so that he takes his seat in the temple of God, proclaiming himself to be God. ⁵Do you not remember that when I was still with you I told you these things? ⁶And you know what is restraining him now so that he may be revealed in his time. ⁷For the mystery of lawlessness is already at work. Only he who now restrains it will do so until he is out of the way. ⁸And then the lawless one will be revealed, whom the Lord Jesus will kill with the breath of his mouth and bring to nothing by the appearance of his coming. ⁹The coming of the lawless one is by the activity of Satan with all power and false signs and wonders, ¹⁰and with all wicked deception for those who are perishing, because they refused to love the truth and so be saved. ¹¹Therefore God sends them a strong delusion, so that they may believe what is false, ¹²in order that all may be condemned who did not believe the truth but had pleasure in unrighteousness. (2 Th 2:1-12)*

A. A Pivotal Text—A Problem Text

Paul's words here are viewed as weighty and decisive by many Bible scholars. They are certainly relevant to any end-times discussion. But there may be a slight problem. It is possible, and, I believe, likely that, at some point early along the way, the church outside Thessalonica missed the exact point of Paul's rather cryptic prophecy (or "oracle"). Most would agree that this is among Paul's most difficult teachings to understand. Because of it, some critics have denied that Paul wrote the book.

Second Thessalonians 2 just does not fit with what else we know about Paul, many allege. Others have suggested that 2 Thessalonians was written before 1 Thessalonians, a not uncommon view. Still others, even some who accept Pauline authorship and the traditional ordering of the books, become very vague and uncertain in their unraveling of the specifics of the text. Perhaps some things were just not meant to be understood, we are told!

Why do commentators struggle so with this chapter? I contend that it is because we have lost the key to unlock the rather vague, perhaps "veiled," terminology that Paul employs. I believe that a series of false assumptions has led us far from the original intention of the oracle. If I am right, the implications for NT eschatology are significant.

B. The Pre-trib Dispensational Dilemma

Second Thessalonians 2 opens with a controversy disrupting the church. Some in the church apparently were being led to believe that the "day of the Lord" had already occurred or was immediately upon them. If so, they obviously had missed it or had misunderstood what "it" was all about (2Th 2:1-2)! Paul wants to reassure them that the "day of the Lord" has not taken place, as some deceivers had claimed, and that it would not take place until certain events transpired.

These events involving the "man of lawlessness" and the "rebellion" had been a frequent topic of discussion when Paul had been with them, as he now reminds them (2Th 2:5). The Greek word *elegon* is an imperfect tense verb that often denotes continuous past action ("I used to tell you..." as NIV well renders).

If we are to believe the dispensational take on this passage, this ongoing topic of conversation between Paul and the Thessalonians concerned the career of the end-times antichrist following the rapture of the church and preceding the second coming (which would follow the rapture by seven years). This whole approach is really quite bewildering in view of the much more pressing matters at hand for the beleaguered Thessalonian Christians.

First and 2 Thessalonians emphasize the struggles, the many "tribulations," of Paul's converts at Thessalonica. The challenges were great. Why would Paul devote extensive time warning about the dark days ahead after the church is taken out of the world? It makes no sense. Even more so in light of a common view that Paul had only spent several weeks or possibly months with the fledgling congregation! (The language of Philippians 4:15-16 would suggest at least several months.)

If the Thessalonian Christians were concerned that somehow they had missed the "day of the Lord" and if Paul, by dispensational reckoning, had indeed proclaimed a pre-trib rapture that would inaugurate the day of the Lord, wouldn't the fact that the rapture itself hadn't occurred yet be an obvious corrective? Why bother to discuss the so-called great tribulation, along with the alleged antichrist's career, when the key event that enables the church to "escape" all of that obviously had not occurred? Why go into detail about a series of events that the rapture would precede and would in fact preclude Christians from having to experience?

If indeed Paul's teaching in 2 Thessalonians 2 is in response to the confusion some are in because false teachers have claimed that the "day of the Lord" has already happened, the dispensational interpretation of Paul's words makes no sense. The dispensational premillennial understanding of the role of the man of lawlessness in prophecy forces its adherents into a completely illogical line of reasoning here.

Of course, desperate circumstances often require desperate measures. Some attempt to save the day here at all costs by holding to an extremely unlikely meaning for the Greek word *apostasia* (2Th 2:3). This word is variously rendered as "falling away" or "rebellion" by most translators (note our English derivative "apostasy" in the religious sense). In light of the inherent difficulties of holding the view that Paul here skips over an alleged rapture and begins discussing a post-rapture antichrist, some have tried to argue that the very word *apostasia* itself refers to the rapture of the church. They try to interpret the term in the sense of "departure" and give it a positive sense.

By doing so, they now can have Paul making reference to the rapture in his response to the Thessalonians' concern. Paul is saying here, according to them, that the day of the Lord (featuring the second coming) will not come until the "departure" (rapture) occurs and the man of lawlessness (antichrist) is at some point revealed. This makes sense to some dispensationalists since it fits their system, but it does not correspond to the best understanding of the word *apostasia*. The basic sense of "rebellion" for this term is now recognized by some of our more recent, popular translations (ESV, NIV, NRSV).

We will see that this meaning is the one that Josephus gives it as well in his various uses of the term. To argue that *apostasia* refers to the "blessed hope" of the church lacks credibility, and top dispensational scholars, including John Walvoord, have rejected the identification of *apostasia* with their "rapture" (Walvoord, *Blessed*, 125).

C. Posttribulational Options

The alternative to the above unlikely approach is, rather, that Paul is explaining that certain events must transpire before Christ's coming for His church. The "day of the Lord" had not yet arrived and would not occur until the man of lawlessness had come on the scene.

Those premillennialists who are "posttribulational" see this very clearly and argue it persuasively. They see the so-called "great tribulation" as something the church will go through rather than escape. The second coming is after ("post") the great tribulation. Their approach better explains Paul's line of reasoning in 2 Thessalonians 2.

Amillennialists would agree with the post-trib premillennialists at this point. There is no separate rapture of the church followed by a seven-year period in the middle of which begins the great tribulation, etc. Amillennialists teach that Christ will return in glory and triumph for his church (1Th 4:13-18; 2Th 1:10) while at the same time dealing out retribution to the wicked (1Th 5:2-3; 2Th 1:7-9).

However, one of the great challenges Paul's teaching on the man of lawlessness presents is that seemingly Jesus cannot return until the drama Paul cryptically outlines here unfolds. This drama would seem to contradict the picture Paul is painting elsewhere of a return of Christ that could happen at any time. A discussion concerning the man of lawlessness, then, becomes a discussion concerning the doctrine of imminence, the belief that Christ could come at any moment.

Paul's language would indicate that the Thessalonian believers could be expected to properly identify the events surrounding the appearance of the man of lawlessness when he arrives on the scene. Such an identifiable event would seem to eliminate the possibility that Christ could come at any time.

It is one thing to maneuver around much of the symbolic imagery in the book of Revelation with its elusive visions, flashbacks, fast-forwards, and cycles of judgment for the wicked. It is another thing to make sense of the activities of the man of lawlessness as it relates to Paul's teaching concerning the second coming.

Will the man of lawlessness be an end-times figure who will persecute the church? Or perhaps someone or some institution that has been around for a long time? Protestants and others have pointed to the pope for years, while Catholics have fingered heretics and apostates. Neither of these identifications is likely what Paul was describing. The answer lies in a different direction.

D. The Antichrist Question

Interpreters who are convinced that there is an end-time individual who will cruelly orchestrate a worldwide persecution of the church are heavily influenced by Paul's teaching on the man of lawlessness in 2 Thessalonians 2. The fact is that the use of the term "antichrist" in 1 and 2 John can be explained in various ways. John himself claimed that many antichrists had already come (1Jn 2:18). He also defined the spirit and teaching of "antichrist" in terms of false claims being made in his own day (perhaps "Gnostic" teachings), namely that Christ had not "come in the flesh" (1Jn 4:3; 2Jn 7).

As well, the career of the "beast" in Revelation 13, 17, etc. (also Daniel 7), can be interpreted as something that spans the entire church age. The apocalyptic style of the book of Revelation creates uncertainty as to how literally one should take the "outline of events" depicted in that book. The image of the "beast" goes through several transitions, sometimes describing a kingdom or empire, sometimes a specific king or individual. Alleged portrayals of the antichrist's career in the book of Daniel are quite dubious and certainly cannot form the basis of a convincing profile (e.g., Dan 7:19-27; 9:25-27; 11:36-45)

We are left, then, with Paul's man of lawlessness as an "unmistakable" antichrist looming on the future horizon. Or are we? Without this ominous personage, the belief in the certainty of such an end-times figure who will persecute the church worldwide is on much shakier ground. If antichrist = beast = man of lawlessness, then at least something of substance can emerge from Scripture regarding an end-times scenario involving this figure. But if antichrist ≠ beast ≠ man of lawlessness, then we are left with another situation entirely. And that is where I am. I find little similarity in the descriptions of these three figures that would suggest that they are referring to the same entity.

A quick glance at any number of treatments on the subject of the great tribulation and the antichrist makes clear how big a role 2 Thessalonians 2 really plays in the discussion. The vast majority of scholars links Paul's descriptions here with the descriptions of the antichrist in 1 and 2 John and with the beast of Revelation.

What is especially troubling is that at the same time commentators mightily struggle with what in the world Paul is actually describing here they invariably offer it as the showcase passage on the Bible's teaching on the antichrist and then in turn link it to Revelation's "beast." By so doing they handily equate the three figures.

E. The BIG Question

But what if 2 Thessalonians 2 *isn't* describing a future antichrist figure? What if the man of lawlessness *isn't* slain at Christ's return and *doesn't* immediately precede that return, as virtually everyone assumes? Such conclusions would have far-reaching ramifications for the antichrist issue.

I am convinced these surprising alternatives in fact describe the true situation. Paul's teaching on the man of lawlessness may have an entirely different focus from what we have been led to believe. By a series of mistaken assumptions and translators' misdirections, we have been led down the wrong path. That path has produced consternation for just about every interpreter of this crucial text. No one I have read appears to be very convinced or convincing regarding attempts to decipher it. I have not found a single author who seemed particularly happy regarding his or her product.

Many bemoan the difficulty of the passage and join the chorus that laments that, while the original audience understood clearly what Paul meant, we pretty much have no clue! Perhaps that is because these scholars are on the wrong track. The passage does not make sense because interpreters are trying to place it into a time frame and context where it simply does not belong.

The analysis below will re-examine certain terms and expressions with which commentators and translators have struggled to the end that, in my estimation, outside of the arguments below no persuasive presentation of this text currently exists. The following analysis will pave the way for a surprising new understanding of Paul's teachings in 2 Thessalonians 2.

Terms under renewed scrutiny include: "rebellion" (*apostasia*; 2:3); "lawlessness" (*anomia*, 2:3); "God's temple" (*naos*; 2:4); "the restrainer" or "that which restrains" (2:6-7); the "Lord (Jesus)" (2:8); "by" (2:8); ESV "appearance" or NIV "splendor" (*epiphaneia*; 2:8); "his coming" (*parousia autou*; 2:8); "the lie" or "what is false" (2:11); and "condemned" (2:12). Surprises await.

F. The Unexpected Answer

Assuming that the basic content of the Olivet Discourse was known by Paul, and it almost certainly was, something important is missing here. Paul writes 2 Thessalonians in AD 50 or so, and the Thessalonians are at that time worried about missing the day of the Lord. Paul must have known that Jesus had given one clear sign that would transpire before He would return: the AD 70 destruction of Jerusalem! How could the second coming, the day of the Lord, occur when Jerusalem's fall, God's unmistakable sign for that generation, had not yet happened?

Why have scholars missed this? Answers vary. Of course, some outright reject the notion that the Gospel writers accurately conveyed what Jesus taught and therefore such teachings were not available to Paul. Still others debate whether Paul had written accounts before him or only oral traditions and wonder how extensive any of those would have been. Was the complete Olivet Discourse available to Paul, or did he just have key nuggets of Jesus' teachings that had been delivered to the disciples on the Mount of Olives (and elsewhere)? How much of the Olivet Discourse in the Synoptics can we in fact assume was available to the apostle Paul?

Few would assume that Paul had the complete manuscripts of Matthew, Mark, and Luke before him, but some have concluded that Matthew was available and others have suggested that earlier forms of Mark and several assumed sources for Luke were at Paul's disposal (Lk 1:1-4).

Importantly, we should note that numerous scholars *have* documented the parallels between Paul's letters to the Thessalonians and the Olivet Discourse, especially Matthew 24. Such parallels would seem to indicate Paul's awareness of these teachings. And yet interpreters have missed the potentially revolutionary conclusion from such parallels. If Paul's language concerning the second coming is tied to Jesus' teachings recorded in the Olivet Discourse, his content regarding the man of lawlessness may also be—more strongly, may likely be.

In Matthew 24 in particular, we find reference to the "abomination of desolation," the persecution of Christians, the increase of "lawlessness," wholesale deception, the destruction of the temple, and the subsequent return of Christ in glory to gather his elect from the four winds of heaven (Mt 24:2, 4, 9-12, 15, 30-31). In writing to the Thessalonians, Paul spoke of the persecution of believers at the hands of the Jews (1Th 2:14-16), of Christ's return in glory—using the same term, *parousia*, "coming," found in the Olivet Discourse (2Th 2:1; Mt 24:3, 27, 37, 39)—and of a "lawless one" who would be associated with a "rebellion" or "revolt," *apostasia*, that would result in the deception and destruction of many (2Th 2:3, 8-12).

I think it likely that Paul received even further revelation about the monumentally important fall of Jerusalem and destruction of the temple, and that 2 Thessalonians 2:1-12 is a kind of "AD 70 oracle." The political ramifications of writing about this ominous future event would have been problematic. Such a document would hint of subversion or sedition. But Paul could have spoken about it more freely, even if his written communication were more guarded ("I told you these things"; 2Th 2:5). Again, the Greek verb *elegon* here is imperfect tense and as such suggests continuous action;

therefore, the NIV rendering (also NET) is to be preferred: "I used to tell you these things." This seems to have been an ongoing topic of discussion.

The impending fall of Jerusalem is not mentioned elsewhere in Paul's writings except perhaps for his mention of the wrath that would come upon the Jews because of their rejection of Christ and mistreatment of His followers—also written to the Thessalonians (1Th 2:16). Perhaps these two highly controversial texts, 1 Thessalonians 2:14-16 and 2 Thessalonians 2:1-12, may offer mutual assistance in our coming to grips with what Paul actually teaches here (for 1 Thessalonians 2:14-16 see above).

G. A New Paradigm: Rethinking 2 Thessalonians 2:8

The first order of business is to rethink 2 Thessalonians 2:8 since it seems to say that Jesus will destroy the man of lawlessness at His second coming. This is what just about everyone I have read teaches. I believe they are likely wrong. Instead of the common approach, I hold that the man of lawlessness was a first-century figure present at the destruction of Jerusalem in AD 70. It needs to be noted that preterists also teach a connection with the destruction of Jerusalem in AD 70. But don't forget, strict preterists believe that the fall of Jerusalem *was* the second coming! That is a view that must be rejected. But how do we avoid such a conclusion and still view this as an AD 70 oracle?

The ESV reads (extending into 2:9),

And then the lawless one will be revealed, whom the Lord Jesus will kill with the breath of his mouth and bring to nothing by the appearance of his coming. ⁹The coming of the lawless one is by the activity of Satan with all power and false signs and wonders... (2Th 2:8-9)

Most translations read pretty much the same, so we are about to break some new ground.

1. At 2:8 there is a manuscript difference between "Lord" and "Lord Jesus." The shorter reading "Lord" is attested less, but it is found in every major manuscript family. Many English translations have the shorter reading "Lord" (KJV, NKJV, NAS, NET). The significance? The shorter term "Lord" does not necessarily point to Christ and His second coming, but could easily signify God's judgment upon Jerusalem.

The Jewish historian Josephus said that, through the Roman armies, God sent down fire from heaven upon the Jews and the city. Even if "Lord Jesus" were the original reading, it should be noted that this would not disqualify the wording from being a reference to the fall of Jerusalem. No one is an expert on the Trinity (!), and Jesus could be viewed as the divine representative who orchestrates Jerusalem's destruction. This is especially so in light of Paul's practice of applying OT *kyrios*, "Lord," references to Jesus within his NT epistles. (Throughout the Greek OT *kyrios* regularly translates the Hebrew name *Yahweh*.)

2. At 2:8, the term "appearance" (*epiphaneia*) could refer to the man of lawlessness, and not to the Lord (Jesus). The translation "appearance" (ESV, NAS) or even "manifestation" (NET) is much to be preferred over the rendering "splendor" (NIV) or "brightness" (KJV). A strong grammatical argument can be made for the notion that *epiphaneia*, "appearance," here refers to the man of lawlessness and not to Jesus. How?

3. "Everyone understands" that the *parousia* of 2:8 refers to the Lord, while the *parousia* of 2:9 refers to the man of lawlessness. However, our translators always "fix" the word order or add a few words for us because the Greek word order as it stands could be understood to indicate that the "his coming" of 2:8 and the "whose coming" of 2:9 refer to the same individual: the man of lawlessness! Translators seem to be convinced that this understanding would create a problem. Instead, I believe that this is the solution.

Here is my proposed translation: "And then the lawless one will be revealed, whom the Lord will overthrow with the breath of His mouth and will overpower at (the time of) the appearance of his coming, (9) whose coming is according to the working of Satan..." Follow carefully here. The Greek words go something like: "...the appearance of his coming (9) whose coming is according to the working of Satan..."

Translators of this passage have universally assumed that the "his coming" of 2:8 must refer to Jesus even though the following "whose coming" of 2:9 must by context refer to the man of lawlessness. Commentators are eager to point out that both Jesus and the man of lawlessness have their own *parousia*, their own "coming," the latter in imitation of the former. Such detailed observations, however, may miss the point.

Translators have bent over backwards to "help" the English reader understand that the "his coming" and the "whose coming" refer to entirely different individuals, the former referring to Jesus and the latter referring to the man of lawlessness. This "guidance" is accomplished by inserting at 2:9 the additional words: "of the man of lawlessness." These words do not exist in the original Greek text! Instead we simply find the genitive (possessive) pronoun "whose" (*hou*), a pronoun that clearly refers to the man of lawlessness since his coming is "by the activity of Satan!" To be crystal clear: The Greek "whose coming" (*hou ... parousia*) at 2:9 is uniformly rendered by "helpful" translators instead as "the coming of the man of lawlessness."

The upshot of all of this is that when the Greek is translated more literally, as I would advocate here, the possibility exists that the "his coming" of 2:8 and the "whose coming" of 2:9 refer to the same individual, namely the man of lawlessness. To repeat, "his coming" at 2:8 could refer either to the man of lawlessness or to Jesus, but a major theological hurdle is cleared with the improved understanding that in fact it, along with the "whose coming" of 2:9, refers to the man of lawlessness.

To analyze more fully, we should also note that the Greek possessive (genitive) pronoun "whose" (*hou*) at the beginning of 2:9 ("whose coming is") parallels the objective (accusative) pronoun "whom" (*hon*) earlier in 2:8 ("whom the Lord will overthrow"). The case is made by some that since the pronouns "whom" and "whose" in 2:8-9 are parallel, both referring to the man of lawlessness, therefore the abrupt "whose coming" immediately following the "his coming" (Jesus' they surmise) is understandable if awkward. The alleged "danger" is that since one could contend that the "his coming" immediately followed by the "whose coming" refer to the same individual, confusion might set in.

Our numerous English translations have "fixed the problem." However, the *real* danger, perhaps, is that by failing to recognize that the "his" and "whose" do in fact refer to the same individual, namely the man of lawlessness, interpreters, including mainstream translators, have long relegated this text to the trash heap of unintelligibility. A longtime professor of distinction once told me regarding this text that perhaps some Bible passages are not meant to be understood! Perhaps. But why not?

The all-important words "his coming" at 2:8 could go either way, referring either to Jesus or the man of lawlessness, but the above proposed understanding restores this text to one that now makes perfect sense. The Greek dative case of the word "appearance" (*epiphaneia*) could either be dative of "means," as has been generally understood, therefore "by (means of) the appearance of His coming," or dative of "time when," as I have taken it here—"at (the time of) the appearance of his coming." The change potentially transforms the text. Note that now the man of lawlessness is described by three eschatological "coming" terms: *apokalyptō*, *epiphaneia*, and *parousia*, instead of just the two that most recognize: *apokalyptō* and *parousia*. He is "revealed" (*apokalyptō*, 2:3, 8); he experiences a "manifestation" or an "appearing" (*epiphaneia*, 2:8); and he experiences a "coming" (*parousia*, 2:8, 9).

As a further note on the notion of a Greek dative of "time when" at 2:8, this passage is almost universally rendered in English translations by utilizing the word "by," thus indicating a dative of "means." And yet a number of prominent NT commentators, even when basing their comments upon a standard English translation reading "by" (e.g., NIV), regularly and repeatedly supply the preposition "at" in their interpretive comments (e.g., Fee, *Thessalonians*, 291-292; Wanamaker, 257-258). The term "at" suggests occasion while "by" would imply manner or means. It conveys a matter of timing more than a matter of instrumentality. We see this clearly in the rendering by the prominent NT scholar James D. G. Dunn:

> "[8]And then the lawless one will be revealed, whom the Lord Jesus will do away with by the breath of his mouth and destroy at the appearance of his coming (*parousia*), [9]whose coming (*parousia*) is by the activity of the Satan, in every miracle and sign and wonder that is false." (302)

Again, "at," not "by." Note also that Dunn translates the beginning of 2:9 more literally, not adding the phrase "of the man of lawlessness," contrary to most English translations. He does not take the next step, however, and identify the "his coming" at 2:8 as referring to the man of lawlessness as I have done here.

In spite of what our standard translations have uniformly done, a number of careful interpreters instinctively see what they understand as the manifestation of Christ's coming as being the occasion for the man of lawlessness' destruction rather than the instrument or means for his destruction. The key take-away for us, however, is that this understanding of "time when"—therefore "at"—also makes possible a radically different understanding of the text. The Lord will render powerless the man of lawlessness "at" the manifestation of the lawless one's coming. This will take place in connection with the defeat of the "rebellion" and the resultant destruction of Jerusalem and the temple.

4. But what about the idea of the "apostasy," Greek *apostasia* (2:3)? Both ESV and NIV got it right when they rendered it "rebellion," rather than "falling away," but maybe not for the right reasons. Commentators are generally united in seeing the "rebellion" described here as a spiritual rebellion and therefore embrace the translation "falling away," referring to religious apostasy. That is, in fact, the sense of the only other occurrence of *apostasia* in the NT. Paul was accused of leading Jews into "apostasy" or "falling away" (*apostasia*) from Moses (Acts 21:21).

However, it is important to note that the term *apostasia* and its twin *apostasis* are the words regularly used by Josephus to describe the Jewish revolt against Rome! They occur dozens of times in Josephus, especially in his War of the Jews, as evidenced in Karl H. Rengstorf's important concordance on Josephus. Most commentators have missed or ignored the possibility that the term is being used here in its political, not religious, sense.

For the sake of completeness, we should note that the related verb *aphistēmi*, "to revolt, withdraw, fall away," is found in the NT in both the religious sense (1Tm 4:1) and political sense (Acts 5:37). In Acts, Judas the Galilean is offered as an example of one who drew people away to follow him and, as a result, he was killed and his followers scattered.

But what about the context of persecution regarding Paul's words here? Would not that fit the idea of religious "apostasy" better? Perhaps, but look again at the passage. Where is the notion of persecution in the man of lawlessness section? I cannot find it. Even more, try to find Christians or believers mentioned there. They are not there.

Unbelievers are deceived and suffer destruction because of the man of lawlessness, not believers. Things are starting to look at least a little suspicious.

H. *Seated in God's Temple*

One of the problems with viewing the temple (*naos*) of God (2:4) as symbolic of the church, as some try, is that the deceptive efforts of the man of lawlessness do not seem to be directed toward believers. There is no anti-Christian sentiment expressed, no mention of the persecution of followers of Christ. The targets of this despot's lies are those who *already* have rejected the truth of God (2:10-12). These individuals likely refer to the Jewish nation in its rejection of their Messiah.

The activities of the lawless one seem to involve self-exaltation over God's laws, standards, and worship regulations. They are in opposition to "every so-called god or object of worship." Paul also refers to "so-called gods" in describing idols and other objects of pagan worship (1Cor 8:5). The man of lawlessness will set himself up against every authority or divine standard. In effect he proclaims himself as the divine standard.

The OT prophets at times singled out human rulers as boasting of having divine attributes, including the king of Babylon and the king of Tyre (Isa 14:12-14; Eze 28:2-10). Of the king of Babylon Isaiah wrote, "You said in your heart, 'I will ascend to heaven; above the stars of God I will set my throne on high...'" (Isa 14:13). Similarly, Ezekiel records God's condemnation of the boastful king of Tyre:

"Because your heart is proud, and you have said 'I am a God, I sit in the seat of the gods, in the heart of the seas,' yet you are but a man, and no god, though you make your heart like the heart of a god. ..." (Eze 28:2). "Because you make your heart

like the heart of a god, therefore behold, I will bring foreigners
upon you, the most ruthless of the nations…" (Eze 28:6-7)

God mockingly asks the king of Tyre, "Will you still
say, 'I am a god,' in the presence of those who kill you,
though you are but a man, and no god, in the hands of those
who slay you?" (Eze 28:9). The exaggerated, poetic
language of the OT prophets may serve as the basis here
for Paul's description of the ultimate arrogance of the man
of lawlessness in his despotic attempt to control Jerusalem
and its inhabitants.

Both religious regulations and the laws of the land are
under the merciless control of the man of lawlessness.
Using the Jerusalem temple as his base of operation and
claiming divine authority, "he takes his seat in the temple
of God, proclaiming himself to be God" (2Th 2:4).

The oracular nature of this prophecy and the
apocalyptic significance Paul attaches to Jerusalem's fall
may account for some of the lofty language regarding the
claims of the lawless one. According to James D. G. Dunn,

> …in 2 Thessalonians Paul speaks with the voice of an
> apocalyptic visionary. The language is exaggerated,
> and the feelings it both expresses and provokes are
> powerful, echoing similar frustrations and longings of
> the past. As with so much apocalyptic imagery, it has
> an element of the grotesque about it… (305).

As to the realities involved regarding the Jewish Revolt
of AD 66-70, Josephus accused John of Gischala and his
fellow rebels of polluting the temple and abusing God (see
"J. The Lawless One and the Restrainer"). The Romans
themselves gave greater respect to the house of God than
these Jewish renegades (*War* 5.402-403). Josephus records
that, as the situation deteriorated, John melted down

various sacred utensils donated to the temple. He also emptied the vessels of sacred wine and oil that the priests utilized in their offering of sacrifices and then distributed the contents to his followers (*War* 5.562-565).

According to Josephus, John told those with him that "it was proper for them to use divine things while they were fighting for the Divinity, without fear, and that such whose warfare is for the temple, should live of the temple" (*War* 5.564). For John, his "noble" cause made him a law unto himself. Josephus' contempt for "these villains" was unrestrained. In his mind, if the Romans had delayed their efforts God would have destroyed the city Himself by means of earthquake, flood, or the kind of disaster that overtook Sodom (*War* 5.566).

For the best understanding of our passage, one should set Paul's words in the context of first-century events and in the genre of Jewish apocalyptic literature. Too often they are viewed in the context of modern geo-political struggles with such a view guided by the employment of crudely literalistic exegesis. Here is a key question. What would have made sense to Paul's original audience? What kind of world event would have given the Thessalonians assurance that the sign of the arrival of the man of lawlessness had in fact occurred? The fall of Jerusalem and destruction of its temple check all the boxes for an event that Paul insists they would clearly recognize.

I. Abominations That Desolate

A number of Bible scholars have suggested a connection between the language of this chapter and that of several other key texts, namely the "abomination of desolation" reference in Matthew 24:15 and the language of Daniel 9:24-27 involving the coming of a "desolator." The first-century Jewish historian Josephus understood the language of Daniel 9 as being fulfilled in the horrible events of AD 70 when the murderous Zealots took over the temple mount in Jerusalem and slaughtered thousands, even many as they were coming to worship.

The huge temple mount structure became the rebels' fortress and the sight of unimaginable atrocities. Describing the scene, Josephus quotes the high priest Ananus as saying, "Certainly it had been good for me to die before I had seen the house of God full of so many abominations, or these sacred places, that ought not to be trodden upon at random, filled with the feet of these blood-shedding villains" (*War* 4.162-163).

I have become more and more convinced that Jesus' use of "abomination of desolation" (Mt 24:15; Mk 13:14) had reference to the future actions of the Jews themselves bringing on the desolations at the hand of the Romans (note, e.g., Stein, 90-93). Jesus viewed the event He was describing as being in fulfillment of Daniel's words (Mt 24:15). As well, later Josephus seems to have understood Daniel 9 in this way as he recounts prophetic oracles concerning the destruction of the city and sanctuary (cf. Dan 9:26-27).

> These men, therefore, trampled upon all the laws of men, and laughed at the laws of God; and for the oracles of the prophets, they ridiculed them as the tricks of jugglers; yet did these prophets foretell many things concerning [the rewards of] virtue, and [punishments of] vice, which when these zealots violated, they occasioned the fulfilling of those very prophecies belonging to their own country; for there was a certain ancient oracle of those men, that the city should then be taken and the sanctuary burnt, by right of war, when a sedition should invade the Jews, and

their own hand should pollute the temple of God. Now while these zealots did not [quite] disbelieve these predictions, they made themselves the instruments of their accomplishment (*War* 4.386-388).

And who is there that does not know what the writings of the ancient prophets contain in them, and particularly that oracle which is just now going to be fulfilled upon this miserable city? For they foretold that this city should be then taken when somebody shall begin the slaughter of his own countrymen. And are not both the city and the entire temple now full of the dead bodies of your countrymen? It is God, therefore, it is God Himself who is bringing on this fire, to purge that city and temple by means of the Romans, and is going to pluck up this city, which is full of your pollutions (*War* 6.109-110).

These amazing statements deserve careful study. It is hard to imagine a more likely fulfillment of what Paul is describing in 2 Thessalonians 2 than the incredible scenes that unfolded in Jerusalem during the times Josephus describes. But who was the "lawless one," and what about the "restrainer" who had to be removed (2Th 2:6-7)? At this point, only brief comments can be made. For more, consult my upcoming *The Man of Lawlessness: Recovering Paul's Jerusalem Apocalypse.*

J. The Lawless One and the Restrainer

Josephus describes the Jewish Zealot leader John of Gischala as being the primary individual responsible for the horrible fate of Jerusalem (see "H. Seated in God's Temple"). Regarding John's actions in fleeing his hometown in Galilee and coming to Jerusalem, Josephus writes that John, trapped in Gischala, bought time through deception and engineered an escape to Jerusalem.

> Thus did this man put a trick upon Titus, not so much out of regard to the seventh day as to his own preservation, for he was afraid lest he should be quite deserted if the city should be taken, and had his hopes of life in that night, and in his flight therein. Now this was the work of God, who therefore preserved this John, that he might bring on the destruction of Jerusalem... (*War* 4.103-104).

Remarkably Josephus viewed John's escape from Gischala and role in Jerusalem's fall as the work of God! Later, after John's arrival in Jerusalem,

> These harangues of John's corrupted a great part of the young men, and puffed them up for the war; but as to the more prudent part, and those in years, there was not a man of them but foresaw what was coming, and made lamentation on that account, as if the city was already undone; and in this confusion were the people... (*War* 4.128-129).

John's destructive activity caused the older, wiser, more prudent in the city to realize that Jerusalem's fate was sealed. Josephus records much about John's arrogance and deception as well as his sacrilege of the temple and the things of God. Hundreds of thousands died directly because of his lawless, despotic behavior.[11]

Regarding the "mystery of lawlessness" already at work in Paul's day and the future arrival of the "man of lawlessness," Paul speaks of one "who now restrains it" (2Th 2:7) and "what is restraining him now" (2Th 2:6). Commentators are quick to note Paul's language here as involving both a personal restrainer and an impersonal restraining force. Notably, one of the earliest Christian interpretations of this distinction was that it referred to the Roman emperor and to the empire in general. In the minds of some later Christians, including the church father Jerome, the fall of Rome in the fifth century signaled the imminent arrival of the so-called "antichrist." Rome's political role as restrainer supposedly ended at that point. Chaos would now ensue as the "end" drew near. Another approach regarding this overall view may be more fruitful, however.

In Paul's day, at the time when he wrote to the church at Thessalonica, the Roman emperor was Claudius (AD 41-54). I would suggest that in fact Paul has Claudius specifically in mind. Historians of the first century have often depicted Claudius as a "law and order" emperor

---

[11] For details concerning John of Gischala, consult my upcoming work mentioned above. Josephus scholars are quick to point out, and rightly so, that Josephus and John were mortal enemies, fierce rivals in the power struggles in Galilee prior to Josephus' capture and John's flight to Jerusalem. Debates continue as to the veracity of Josephus' reports concerning John's activity, but his record is by far our most important source regarding what transpired, and the end result of the conflict would suggest the kinds of activities attributed by Josephus to John and his followers.

One might argue that the term "man of lawlessness" could have referred to several individuals in connection with Jerusalem's fall, including Simon bar Gioras, the eventual primary military leader of the Jewish forces against the Roman assault. For more on the rebel leadership, consult Steve Mason (*A History of the Jewish War A.D. 66-74* [2016]), Martin Goodman (*Rome and Jerusalem* [2007]), Martin Hengel (*The Zealots* [1989]), Mireille Hadas-Lebel (*Flavius Josephus* [1993]), and others.

especially when his activities and deliberations are compared to the irrational excesses of both his predecessor, Gaius Caligula (AD 37-41), and his successor, Nero (AD 54-68). No close friend of the Jews, Claudius still exercised a fairness and orderliness that was displayed in several of his edicts for the eastern provinces.

These actions provided a stark contrast to the megalomaniacal attempts of young Caligula to have his statue placed inside the temple in Jerusalem! Only his assassination prevented that horrendous sacrilege and accompanying massacres. Also, upon Nero's later rise to power the Jews in their homeland increasingly bore the brunt of greedy, predatory, and often violent Roman procurators whose actions helped foment social instability and political sedition.

I propose that Paul received revelation of the fact that Jerusalem's demise would not occur as long as the current regime (Claudius) was in control. Once the restrainer was gone, however, what Paul calls the "mystery of lawlessness" would degenerate into the circumstances that produced the "man of lawlessness" and Jerusalem's resultant demise. It is noteworthy that of the two NT references to the emperor Claudius (Acts 11:28; 18:2), the initial one involves a prophecy regarding a disaster (famine) that, as Luke relates, transpired during his reign.

K. With the Breath of His Mouth

Another argument against Paul's referring to Jesus' glorious return in 2:8 is that nothing else in the remainder of 2 Thessalonians refers to it. After what I view as a Greek dative of "time when"—"at the appearance of his coming"—everything that follows speaks of the coming (*parousia*) of the lawless one and the deception that will be wrought upon those who have *already* rejected the truth of the gospel. There is nothing after 2 Thessalonians 2:3 that even hints at a description of the second coming except the language at 2:8.

We are told earlier that the second coming will not occur unless the man of lawlessness previously arrives on the scene (2: 3). When he arrives, he will be removed by the breath of the Lord's mouth (2:8). This could very naturally be interpreted as God's overthrow of Jerusalem and the rebellion by the hands of the Romans. God's breathing fire down upon the enemy is not an image found elsewhere in the NT regarding the second coming. However, it is found commonly in the OT in reference to God's punishment of a people or city.

Regarding the Ammonites, God decreed through Ezekiel, "And I will pour out my indignation upon you; I will blow upon you with the fire of my wrath, and I will deliver you into the hands of brutish men, skillful to destroy" (Eze 21:31). Further, because of Jerusalem's great wickedness, God warns her inhabitants, "I will gather you and blow on you with the fire of my wrath, and you shall be melted in the midst of it" (Eze 22:21). The context of these verses in Ezekiel 21-22 shows that Babylon will be God's instrument of judgment, the deliverer of His fiery wrath.

Josephus repeatedly connected Rome's attack upon the city with the exercising of God's wrath. The city and the temple were being consumed by the very "fire of God" (*War* 6.110). If my understanding of Paul's "his coming" at 2 Thessalonians 2:8 is to be accepted, the entire chapter then makes perfect sense. It offers a very natural answer to the Thessalonians' question in light of what Jesus had taught about the one "sign" or event that would precede His return in glory: Jerusalem's fall.

L. Finally the Right Focus

Understood as outlined above, 2 Thessalonians 2 does not describe the second coming, only the necessary events that would precede that coming. As Jesus had taught, once the judgment upon Jerusalem had transpired, no further signs would be given to warn of His return. Clearly the events of AD 70 and the later occasion of His personal return were portrayed as distinct and distinctive occurrences in Jesus' descriptions. The desolations of AD 70 would be preceded by specific warning signs; His glorious return would not.

Two additional pieces of the puzzle need to be added here. It is assumed by most that the man of lawlessness will arrive immediately before Christ returns in light of the assumed connection with the second coming. However, the text does not say this. It just says Christ will not return until the man of lawlessness has been manifested. Christ's return could come immediately following or, as my view permits, in the distant future. No timeframe is actually given by Paul, just as none is given in Jesus' Olivet Discourse between the events of AD 70 and His second coming.

Another piece of the puzzle relates to the "signs and wonders" wrought in connection with the arrival of the man of lawlessness. It is generally assumed that these phenomena are end-times displays of Satanic power meant to deceive believers and turn them away from Christ. But there is another approach. Again, a major source here is Josephus, who vividly describes a variety of remarkable, seemingly supernatural events that transpired in connection with the Jewish revolt and Jerusalem's fall: a bright star, a comet, a light inside the temple at night, the massive temple gate opening on its own, a great voice booming from within the temple, "Let us depart from here," and even visions of chariots and troops running among the clouds (*War* 6.285-300).

Some of these signs seemed to be warnings, but, as Josephus points out, certain signs admitted of several interpretations and those bent on revolt and violence chose the interpretation best suited for their purposes. Even the Roman historian Tacitus records remarkable phenomena that accompanied the fall of Jerusalem, e.g., a vision of armies waging war in the sky, with Josephus as his possible source (*Histories* 5.13). Both the Gospels and the book of Acts record ample evidence of Satanic activity in connection with attempts to hinder the spread of the gospel. The outpouring of Satanic influences in connection with Jerusalem's fall should not be particularly surprising.

The verses following 2:8 tell us the following. The lawless one's coming would be according to the working of Satan (2:9). Satan's work would involve miracles, lying wonders, and wicked deception (2:9-10). This deception would be directed toward those who had already rejected the truth of the gospel (2:11). God Himself would be the One who sends them a "delusion" that would result in their believing "the lie" (2:11). Satan serves as the unwitting instrument of God's judgment. The result of their believing "the lie" would be that all those who had not believed might be condemned (2:12).

The term "all" used by Paul at 2:12 need not be viewed in an absolute sense and thus does not need to refer to final judgment. The use of "all" (*pas*) in this section seems to indicate emphasis (2:9, 10, 12). The man of lawlessness comes by the activity of Satan "with all power" (2:9), "with all wicked deception" (2:10). "All" who rejected the truth and took pleasure in unrighteousness are "condemned" by the delusion God (through Satan) sends (2:12). In each case limitations seem inherent: not all, but much or many.

At this point Paul expresses his gratitude for the faith and sanctification of the Thessalonian Christians (2:13), but there is no further reference to Christ's return: no flaming fire, no coming in glory, no deliverance of the saints, no attending angels—nothing. If 2 Thessalonians 2:8 is a second coming reference, it is a remarkably abrupt one! Instead, everything that follows 2:8 focuses upon the disastrous results of the coming (*parousia*) or appearing (*epiphaneia*) of the man of lawlessness.

This supports the previous arguments given that 2 Thessalonians 2 is not a second coming passage at all. Rather it is a passage describing in rather veiled, cryptic, and, some might argue, apocalyptic language the scene that is about to be played out in Jerusalem. Jesus' predictions about Jerusalem's destruction would certainly unfold before "the coming of the Son of Man" occurred. The Thessalonians had forgotten that one paramount sign. No *parousia* of Christ would take place until all the things prophesied about "this generation" had come about, until the Jewish *apostasia* against Rome had run its fatal course.

One puzzle that can now be better addressed is why it is necessary for the unbelieving wicked to believe "the lie." Are they not already under God's condemnation? What further lie would be necessary to be believed in order for the unrighteous to be "condemned" (*krinō*, "judge, condemn")? If this refers to eternal punishment, the sense of the text is unclear. However, if the wording refers to the events in connection with AD 70, it makes perfect sense. That evil generation would need to buy into the seditious rebellion against Rome in order for it to be utterly devastated.

One prominent lie that John of Gischala and his followers promoted was that God would never allow the city and temple to fall to the Romans. No matter what brand of evil these wicked Jews practiced (and Josephus documents their horrors in detail), God would protect them from enemy hands since they were, after all, God's chosen covenant people. John commissioned false prophets to propagate that lie, while drawing more and more victims to the temple mount (*War* 6.285-286).

As a result of this monstrous deception, hundreds of thousands met their violent end. Josephus gives the figure at 1,100,000 dead and 97,000 prisoners (*War* 6.420; see also 5.567-569). Many scholars question such high numbers, but the notion that hundreds of thousands died would be hard to dispute convincingly. Josephus mentions the vast multitude who came for Passover but then found themselves trapped in the city (*War* 6:422-429).

As noted previously, Paul may have alluded to the upcoming horrors of AD 70 in his other letter to the Thessalonians:

> *For you, brothers, became imitators of the churches of God in Christ Jesus that are in Judea. For you suffered the same things from your own countrymen as they did from the Jews, [15]who killed both the Lord Jesus and the prophets, and drove us out, and displease God and oppose all mankind [16]by hindering us from speaking to the Gentiles that they might be saved—so as always to fill up the measure of their sins. But wrath has come upon them at last! (1Th 2:14-16)*

Jesus himself had earlier said to the corrupt Jewish leaders of his day,

> *... so that on you may come all the righteous blood shed on earth, from the blood of righteous Abel to the blood of Zechariah the son of Berechiah, whom you murdered between the sanctuary and the altar. [36]Truly I say to you, all these things will come upon this generation. [37]O Jerusalem, Jerusalem, the*

*city that kills the prophets and stones those who are sent to it!
How often would I have gathered your children together as a
hen gathers her brood under her wings, and you were not willing!
³⁸See, your house is left to you desolate.(Mt 23:35-38)*

In Matthew, these words immediately precede Jesus'
prophecy concerning the destruction of Jerusalem. Clearly
this destruction would be the result of the wickedness of
the generation that rejected their Messiah upon His
visitation to them.

It was fitting that the desolation wrought upon
Jerusalem was prompted by that wicked generation itself,
as the descriptions by Josephus so vividly portray. The man
of lawlessness and his accomplices played their role to the
hilt in a deadly drama orchestrated by God in fulfillment of
our Lord's tearful words.

The fateful "lie" was believed. The destruction was
complete—a horrific desolation wrought in connection
with the unspeakable abominations committed by the man
of lawlessness and his followers.

Appendix B

The Olivet Discourse:
Jesus' "Little Apocalypse"

The Olivet Discourse provides a key component of the teaching of the NT regarding Christ's return. Found in Matthew 24-25, Mark 13, and Luke 21, this important Discourse points to the future fall of Jerusalem (AD 70) and to the subsequent return of Christ to judge the world. Matthew, Mark, and Luke are often designated the "Synoptic Gospels" since they all view Christ's life and ministry is similar ways (thus, from Greek, they "look alike" at things). The Gospel of John is understood to stand apart in many ways regarding content selected from Jesus' life and ministry. The Olivet Discourse in the Synoptics has been referred to at times as the "Little Apocalypse."

With respect to the Olivet Discourse, it is essential to recognize that Matthew 24-25, Mark 13, and Luke 21 all report Jesus' teachings about the same topics: the many persecutions facing the early church, the AD 70 destruction of Jerusalem, continued persecutions after that destruction, and the return of Christ—a return at times referred to as the *parousia* ("coming, presence"). One guiding feature offered in the Discourse was that Jerusalem's destruction would be preceded by warning signs, in particular one designated "the abomination of desolation" (Mt 24:15; Mk 13:14; cf. Luke 21:20 speaking of armies surrounding the city), while Jesus' return, His *parousia*, would be without warning, like "a thief in the night" (Mt 24:43; Rev 16:15

"like a thief"), and would be both sudden and universally seen, like the lightning flashing across the sky (Mt 24:27; Lk 17:24). The sharp distinction between warnings and lack of warnings is an element featured throughout the Discourse and aids in the determination of whether or not Christ was referring to prophesied first-century events or to promised end-times events.

Prominent terms repeated throughout the Discourse offer challenges, especially to those espousing the dispensational end-times approach. When His disciples proclaimed admiration for the magnificent Herodian temple before them, Jesus prophesied its total destruction within a generation. This prompted questions regarding when this would transpire and what additional signs might accompany Christ's return and the end of the age.

Confusion on the part of Jesus' disciples has unfortunately created confusion among those attempting to interpret the answer Jesus gave to what was a (misspoken) question posed by His immediate followers. Their question actually involved two future events, not one, and Jesus dealt with both: the AD 70 destruction of Jerusalem and His subsequent return, a return that, following Jerusalem's fall, would be imminent, i.e., it could happen at any moment— a return for which no clear signs would be given in anticipation. A return that Jesus' church still awaits.

Throughout, the "you" that Jesus addresses clearly refers to an immediate first-century audience. The dispensational attempt to locate the "you" of Luke's version in the first century while instead inserting the "you" into the end times following an alleged rapture of the church in both Matthew and Mark's version is unconvincing and quite remarkable. With such an approach sound exegetical methodology becomes a lost cause.

Less clear, perhaps, is Jesus' utilization of the term "the end." I have concluded that Jesus actually never uses this term in the Olivet Discourse as a reference to the second coming but rather as one either to the end of the life of a faithful disciple, "the one who endures to the end" (Mt 24:13), or to the end or fall of Jerusalem (Mt 24:14). His disciples referred to "the end of the age" in their questioning Him (Mt 24:3), but Jesus does not happen to use that label in His answer even when describing His return (Mt 24:27-31, 36-25:46).

Matthew 24:14 deserves further comment since it is probably misapplied by most: "And this gospel of the kingdom will be proclaimed throughout the whole world as a testimony to all nations, and then the end will come." Many believe that this verse teaches that the evangelization of the entire world must be accomplished before Jesus can return. I have good friends who believe that and teach that. I just do not happen to agree with them in this instance. Countless questions arise from such an interpretation. What needs to happen, exactly? Are the many thousands of people groups and languages all involved here? If a movie about Jesus gets broadcast over a certain geographical region, does that count? Must the Bible be presented in the "heart language" of each specific tribe or people group or will the regional "trade language" suffice? Missions organizations will often promote this passage as a primary motivation to reach the world's unreached and thereby "hasten the Lord's return."

The approach above is a lot to hang on the shoulders of Matthew 24:14. I remain unconvinced by that line of reasoning, even though the worldwide spread of the gospel is the true hope of the world. While teaching in Brazil a series concerning the end times, I presented the alternate ideas below to a highly receptive group of missionary preachers and teachers. They had never heard the approach before, but it made a lot of sense to them.

What was Jesus actually saying here in the context of His teaching concerning the destruction of Jerusalem? The "end" likely refers to Jerusalem's demise, the subject of the disciples' question, not to the end of the world or the gospel era. Jesus was indicating that by the time Jerusalem fell, Christianity would not be a localized Jewish sect, but a "worldwide" movement, one unhindered by whatever catastrophe might befall the Jewish capital.

The word at Matthew 24:14, *oikoumenē*, meaning "inhabited earth," is used in similar ways elsewhere, not necessarily indicating the entire globe. The census mentioned in Luke 2:1 was for the entire *oikoumenē*, "the entire Roman world." The NIV adds "Roman" here to help us properly limit the scope involved. ESV simply reads "all the world."

Jews at Pentecost came "from every nation under heaven"(Acts 2:5). More than a dozen locales or people groups outside Judea are listed by Luke (Acts 2:9-11). If just some from each nation went back home with the gospel following their conversion, that saving message would have quickly reached "every nation under heaven"! Also consult especially Romans 1:8; 16:26; Colossians 1:6, 23. Phrases in connection with the church's first-century evangelizing efforts are found in these passages, phrases like "in all the world" (Rom 1:8); "in the whole world it is bearing fruit and growing" (Col 1:6); and "proclaimed in all creation under heaven" (Col 1:23). If these words from Paul are not to be taken absolutely literally, then why must Jesus' words?

In Paul's .day, the gospel had spread throughout the known world, even to eastern regions beyond the control of the Roman Empire. By the time Jerusalem fell, the early church was a worldwide, not a localized, entity. The Jewish disaster of AD 70 had minimal impact upon the ongoing spread of the gospel throughout the inhabited world, the *oikoumenē*. I am convinced that this is what Jesus was alluding to in His reference to the coming "end." This finds support several ways. In Matthew, mention of the "end" at Matthew 24:14 is followed by reference to the "abomination of desolation" at Matthew 24:15. In Luke, rumors of wars and claims of false messiahs will not be signs that the end will immediately follow (Lk 21:8-9), but when they see the Roman armies surrounding the city, they will know that Jerusalem's end, its "desolation," has come (Lk 21:20).

The expressions "great tribulation" (Mt 24:21) and "abomination of desolation" (Mt 24:15; Mk 13:14) both refer to events surrounding the fall of Jerusalem. Josephus describes in great detail the abominations enacted by the radical Jewish Zealots and "robbers" who took control of Jerusalem's Temple Mount and plundered much of the beleaguered populace of the city. The bloody warfare engaged in by various Jewish factions struggling for control ended when the Romans finally broke through the Jewish fortifications protecting the city and the Temple Mount. A great slaughter ensued.

To use Jesus' (and Daniel's) terminology, the "abominations" perpetrated by rebel Jewish forces resulted in the "desolations" attending Rome's destruction of Jerusalem and its temple. None of what Jesus predicted had to do with what some today foresee as a post-rapture destruction of an end-times rebuilt Jerusalem temple!

The expression "great tribulation" (*thlipsis megalē*) appears four times in the NT and each time refers to something totally different from the other occurrences (Mt 24:21; Acts 7:11 [ESV "great affliction"]; Rev 2:22; 7:14). In Revelation 7 it describes persecution of the church through which many martyrs have proved themselves faithful. In Stephen's sermon in Acts 7 it refers to the great famine in the time of Joseph. In Revelation 2 Jesus warns of the great punishment (tribulation, death) awaiting the followers (or "children") of the false teacher "Jezebel."

In Matthew's version of Jesus' words in the Olivet Discourse the term refers to the events in connection with the destruction of first-century Jerusalem (as does simply "tribulation," Mk 13:19). Again, there is nothing in the discourse that speaks of a post-rapture "tribulation period" as envisioned by most premillennial dispensationalists.

A major challenge is presented by Matthew's use of the word "immediately" in connection with Christ's return. That return will occur "immediately after the tribulation of those days" (Mt 24:29). How can one argue that in fact Jesus predicted that His return would come immediately after the fall of Jerusalem? Clearly another approach is needed.

My suggestions rely on the fact that Jesus utilized the term "tribulation" in the Discourse in several ways. (1) Tribulation was suffered by Christ's followers leading up to Jerusalem's fall (Mt 24:9-14). He speaks of hatred toward the disciples, of apostasy and betrayal, of many false prophets, and of an increase in lawlessness. Such things transpired in the years leading up to Jerusalem's AD 70 demise. (2) Jesus then refers to the circumstances surrounding Jerusalem's destruction as "great tribulation" of an unparalleled nature, so destructive that had it not been cut short (by the Roman armies in a surprisingly sudden fashion, as described by Josephus) no one would have survived (Mt 24:15-22). (3) I propose that the "then" that follows (Mt 24:23) refers not to the events involving Jerusalem's fall but to what transpires *after* the fall: further deception and opposition ("false christs and false prophets," deceptive "great signs and wonders"; Mt 24:24). Further "tribulation."

Much found in the various NT epistles sounds similar warnings against false prophets and teachers seeking to deceive the elect (1Tm 4:1-3; 2Tm 3:1-9; 4:3-4; 2Pet 2:4-22; 3:3-13, 15-17; 1Jn 2:18-23, 26-27; 3:7-10; 4:1-6; 2Jn 7-11; Rev 2:2, 14-15, 20-24). These warnings were relevant to challenges for Christians both before and after Jerusalem's demise.

My suggestion, then, is that when Jesus speaks in Matthew of "the tribulation of those days," He is not speaking of the fall of Jerusalem specifically but of the tribulation Jesus' followers will face after that fall (Mt 24:23-26). Any claim that Jesus has been spotted somewhere by His people will be false. The sudden coming of the Son of Man will be a universal experience witnessed by all (Mt 24:27-28).

He will come "immediately" in the sense that His coming will be without warning or signs. It may not be a coincidence that within the Discourse itself this description directly follows Matthew's analogy involving the flashing lightning, a vivid description only used by Matthew in the Discourse and only by Luke elsewhere (Lk 17:24).

Although the Parable (or Lesson) of the Fig Tree follows a brief description of the second coming in all three accounts, its focus in Matthew, Mark, and Luke seems to be the fall of Jerusalem. Jesus speaks of signs that the key event is near and that it will transpire within "this generation," the generation involving Jesus' immediate audience.

In the parable, we find repeated the terminology "these things" and "all these things" (Mt 24:33-34; Mk 13:29, 30; Lk 21:21), language harkening back to the opening of the Discourse where the disciples ask about "(all) these things"

Jesus has just described, namely things involving the destruction of the temple (Mt 24:3; Mk 13:4; Lk 21:7). The translation "it is near, right at the door"(NIV) is preferable to "he is near, at the very gates" (ESV) at Matthew 24:33 since Jerusalem's fall, and not the second coming, seems to be the topic here.

Attempts to connect "this generation" with the generation that is remaining when Christ returns are unsatisfactory. Likewise, efforts to translate "this generation" instead as "this race" (the Jewish race) have found little acceptance. When context is fairly factored in, terms like "you" and "this generation" clearly relate to Jesus' first-century audience, not a far distant one.

The parables found especially in Matthew's recording of the Olivet Discourse round out the picture of Christ's return. In them is emphasized its unexpected and sudden nature. Judgment then rendered will be just and final. Key concepts emphasized are the church's anticipation and preparation. Be ready! Comparisons with the days of Noah ("eating and drinking, marrying and giving in marriage") leave little room for the notion of a great tribulation following the secret rapture of the church, a tribulation that ends with Christ's second coming (the coming that allegedly initiates an earthly millennium).

Leading dispensationalists have conceded that the Synoptic Gospels contain no mention of a pretribulational rapture. They must find that somewhere else and, in my view, such further efforts have not offered persuasive results. Meanwhile, the Olivet Discourse is particularly unfriendly to searches that comb through the Gospels. Those who seek to link the "abomination of desolation" and the "great tribulation" to future post-rapture days have tried to argue that Matthew 24 and Mark 13 are describing events following the rapture of the church—a rapture nowhere mentioned in those books! What is puzzling is that an account as oft-cited as the Olivet Discourse is so detrimental to the views espoused within the dispensational approach. Dispensational scholars should steer clear away. And yet, we are constantly reminded of Jesus' "warnings" concerning "wars and rumors of wars"! And, of course, we are supposed to know what those mean…

No one has argued that the Olivet Discourse is a simple text to understand. The assumptions of Jesus' disciples and the questions those assumptions prompted necessitated a complex answer, one that has challenged the church throughout the years. However, I do believe that a careful analysis of the language found in the Synoptic Gospels can provide reasonable answers to the questions often posed concerning this influential portion of Jesus' teachings.

The importance of Jesus' teachings in the Gospels concerning the fall of Jerusalem has often been unrecognized or minimized in the church. Complicating the matter is the debate as to whether or not this monumental event is addressed elsewhere in the NT. This issue is formative for the study of the book of Revelation and scholars of various persuasions have been convinced that portions of that book indeed address the fall of Jerusalem in AD 70.

In addition, I have proposed (e.g., Appendix A) that Paul may have addressed this topic as well in his two letters to the Thessalonians (1Th 2:14-16; 2Th 2:1-12). Often, NT scholars list parallels between Matthew 24 and 1 and 2 Thessalonians but, in my view, fail to see the full implications from such connections. Again, careful study of Jesus' end-times teachings, teachings involving both the fall of Jerusalem in AD 70 and the second coming, demands close attention to Jesus' Olivet Discourse, His "Little Apocalypse." Through the years many scholars have devoted their efforts to the Discourse. If pressed to recommend just one essential treatment covering the Olivet Discourse, I would land on Robert H. Stein's excellent study based on Mark's version, *Jesus, the Temple and the Coming of the Son of Man: A Commentary on Mark 13* (2014).

APPENDIX C

BASIC PRINCIPLES FOR INTERPRETING PROPHECY

The examination of basic guidelines for interpreting prophecy, poetry, and other literary categories (genres) is an essential prelude to studying a topic like the book of Revelation. In contrast, starting with the latest popular book on the end times and the most recent news clipping about the Middle East can end badly for those seeking God's plans for the future.

Years ago I received a call from a large, mature adult Bible School class in southern Ohio. The class involved elders and other leaders in the church who wanted me to come and share a series of lessons with them. The problem was they wanted to study the book of Revelation. Convincing them to begin with a six-week study on "principles of Bible interpretation" was a nonstarter. It was Revelation or bust!

As great and motivated a group as we had, the lack of general background needed for the challenge was frustrating. We could not get where I wanted to go with the format we had. In my opinion, it did not end well, certainly not as well as I had hoped. For readers who have not already dug deeply into the subject, the outline of interpretive principles in this appendix should serve as a helpful tool as we make the journey toward understanding what the book of Revelation has to say. May the journey end well.

Six Principles for Interpreting Prophecy

Many valuable tools have been produced to help us in our study of Bible prophecy. Some user-friendly works with helpful suggestions and clear explanations would include Gordon Fee and Douglas Stuart's *How to Read the Bible for All It's Worth* (1982), Tremper Longman III's *Reading the Bible with Heart and Mind* (1997), and Mark Moore's *Seeing God in HD* (2008). For special attention on apocalyptic literature see, e.g., D. Brent Sandy, *Plowshares & Pruning Hooks: Rethinking the Language of Prophecy and Apocalyptic* (2002), and for a more in-depth general treatment consult William W. Klein, et al., *Introduction to Biblical Interpretation* (1993).

There are important guidelines to consider as we study the interpretation of prophecy in the Bible and in Revelation specifically. Once we start looking at the language in Revelation and some of the individual prophecies relating to Jesus' second coming in particular, it will be helpful to refer back to these basic guiding principles for insight and direction for interpretation.

Principle One: The NT Serves as Our Inspired Guide for the OT.

Which comes first, the OT or the NT? Be careful how you answer; we are not thinking chronologically here. A key issue in interpreting prophecy today is whether we should start with the OT and decide upon the interpretation of fulfillments based upon our notions of how the OT should be interpreted (literally, symbolically, typologically), or start with how the NT uses the OT in making our determination. Our starting point may have a great impact upon where we land. The unity of inspired Scripture would seem to suggest the latter approach above.

If we insist that certain prophecies must be fulfilled literally and yet the NT interprets them in a different way, then we are left with a choice. We may need to rethink our understanding of "literal interpretation" if the NT leads us in another direction. If Hebrews states that Jeremiah's promised "new covenant" is in effect in the church, we may need to reevaluate in what way "Israel" is to be the recipient of the promise. If the NT claims Jesus is now ruling on the throne of David, I may need to jettison my images of an earthly throne set up in the city of Jerusalem.

The NT, I believe, should serve as our guide. We should go not to the current newspapers or magazines, not to the most popular, trendy books or series of books, but rather to the NT itself. (And yes, online resources *are* important, but don't necessarily *start* with the most recent, trendy podcasts.) We should be more concerned about how the Apostle Paul understood OT prophecy than about how certain contemporary prophecy gurus understand these words. The NT writers were inspired by God. Few today make such a claim for themselves, but sometimes people treat their words as if they had or should.

Principle Two: Prophecy Is Often Symbolic or Figurative.

One of the things we must keep in mind is that there is symbolic or figurative language in the Bible. This should be no surprise, since we use metaphoric language and figurative expressions all the time. Take the sports world. Sportscasters or announcers have to dabble in symbolic, metaphoric language or they won't have a job for long. When we hear statements like "Boy, that was a real barn burner," no one is looking for flames anywhere! We know what a barn burner is—a game with a really close score. If the newspaper says that the home team "dodged a bullet tonight," no one is looking for a gunman somewhere.

Decades ago the Chicago Bears had a massive lineman known as the "refrigerator." William Perry weighed three-hundred-plus pounds back in a day when few players did. The term "refrigerator" had a certain connotation. People will desperately avoid having a refrigerator fall on them! Who wants to run full speed into a refrigerator? The metaphor was obvious.

The book of Revelation contains numerous symbols and figures of speech, as is documented extensively throughout the present book. Descriptions of the second coming throughout the NT are necessarily full of metaphoric imagery as well. The use of symbols and various figurative expressions (metaphor, simile, irony, hyperbole, synecdoche, personification, etc.) cannot be avoided as we attempt to describe the unknown (then and there) in terms of the known (here and now).

What vocabulary do we have to describe the new creation (new heavens and new earth, New Jerusalem)? Even terms like "up" and "down" become problematic when we contemplate the sphere-shaped planet we inhabit. Jesus uses the term "lightning" to depict the nature of His sudden, unexpected, yet visible-to-all return. The simile "like a thief in the night" regarding the second coming has suggested to some scholars that such language coming from the mouth of Jesus must be authentic. No devout first-century Christian author would have originated such a derogatory comparison to describe Jesus' return! Our Lord Himself took advantage of this powerful imagery in describing His future coming.

It is virtually impossible to live our lives without the use of symbolism in our speech. We should not be surprised that the OT and the NT both supply a hefty dose of symbolic or figurative language, even more so when we consider our third point.

Principle Three: Much of Prophecy Is in Poetic Form.

Hebrew poetry is not characterized by rhyming and, as such, is not like typical English poetry. If ancient biblical Hebrew does rhyme it is either an accident or maybe it has to do with certain grammatical endings of words that just happened to sound alike. The concept of rhyming like we have in our language really is not the primary thing.

Instead, Hebrew poetry is characterized by parallelism in which the thoughts and vocabulary of one or more lines are paralleled in the next line or lines. Much of parallelism is such that the first line and the second line basically say the same thing employing varied expressions. That is known as *synonymous parallelism.*

The book of Proverbs is full of *antithetic parallelism,* where the first line is in contrast to the second line. We might have references to the good son or righteous son as opposed to the evil or wicked son. "A wise son makes a glad father, but a foolish son is a sorrow to his mother" (Prov 10:1). We see that certain things are favored by God and blessed by God while other things are an abomination to the Lord: "...for the righteous falls seven times and rises again, but the wicked stumble in times of calamity" (Prov 24:16). Hebrew poetry often features symbolic numbers. Here the number "seven" indicates completeness or fullness.

Synthetic parallelism may to some extent serve to represent everything else. Often the second line will simply build on the first line in varying ways. One example: "The Lord is my shepherd; I shall not want" (KJV). A cause-effect relationship may be involved here at times. Also, words that may expand or explain the meaning of the first line can be found in the second line of synthetic parallelism.

Important for any study of Bible prophecy is the fact that the OT prophets are full of Hebrew parallelism and poetry. Here is a summary:

1. Most of Isaiah, Jeremiah, Hosea, Joel, and Amos are poetry.

2. All but a few verses of Nahum are poetry.

3. Obadiah and Micah are entirely poetry except for the introductory title.

4. Zephaniah is all poetry except for the first verse.

5. Habakkuk and Lamentations are entirely in poetry.

This represents a rather extensive body of literature! The first point regarding "most of" Isaiah, Jeremiah, Hosea, Joel, and Amos demands further qualification. Those books contain a number of narrative or historical sections. Those portions, not the prophetic sections, are what provide the non-poetic, prose elements. In essence, virtually all the prophetic content of these books is poetic.

If we add in here the various prophetic portions found in the Pentateuch, Psalms, and historical books, we come to recognize that almost all of OT prophecy is in poetic form. We read poetry differently than we read the front page of the newspaper. Recognizing that OT prophecy is generally poetic ought to caution us against the extreme interpretations or hyper-literalism that we find with some of our modern interpreters.

Principle Four: At Times Prophecy Is Obscure, Paradoxical, or Fragmentary.

Admittedly, without the coming of Christ into the world, certain OT passages would not really make a lot of sense. Some ancient Jews viewed that there would be two Messiahs: one would become a conquering king, the other a suffering servant. They could not really see how those two images found in the OT could dovetail.

Sometimes, I have had students work on Isaiah 53 with me, actually reading from the Greek Septuagint (LXX), which dates from around 250 BC. The Jewish translators in 250 BC who rendered the Hebrew OT into Greek obviously struggled with this passage, one that foretold the crucifixion of Jesus by which He became the bearer of sins, not only for the Jews, but for the whole world. Somehow this intense suffering and horrible death ended up in a note of triumph and victory.

The translators struggled with the poetry, the vocabulary, etc., and, even more difficult, they had no point of reference from which to understand what was being described. For those standing on this side of the cross, things are now much clearer. For translators centuries before Christ, the obscurity was a real hindrance.

In 586 BC Jerusalem fell to the Babylonians and its king Zedekiah was led into captivity with thousands of other prisoners. Zedekiah had attempted to escape the city but was captured. Ezekiel records a rather enigmatic prediction about this king (called here "prince") and his fate:

> *And the prince who is among them shall lift his baggage upon his shoulder at dusk, and shall go out. They shall dig through the wall to bring him out through it. He shall cover his face, that he may not see the land with his eyes. ¹³And I will spread my net over him, and he shall be taken in my snare. And I will bring him to Babylon, the land of the Chaldeans, yet he shall not see it, and he shall die there. (Eze 12:12-13)*

According to Ezekiel, Zedekiah would be brought to Babylon but, in his words, "he shall not see it." What is involved here? Another prophet, Jeremiah, provides the gruesome answer to the mystery. After capturing Zedekiah,

> *The king of Babylon slaughtered the sons of Zedekiah before his eyes, and also slaughtered all the officials of Judah at Riblah.* [11]*He put out the eyes of Zedekiah, and bound him in chains, and the king of Babylon took him to Babylon, and put him in prison till the day of his death. (Jer 52:10-11)*

Blinded Zedekiah indeed lived and died in a land of exile he never saw! Sometimes the pictures in the prophets are fragmentary and it takes looking at several passages together to acquire a complete picture. Some texts are paradoxical, joining images of suffering and conquering, death and victory. Simply put, we have to recognize some of the interpretive problems that are connected with studying prophecy and this obscurity is one of the problems we face.

Principle Five: There Is Prophetic Blending, Foreshortening, or Telescoping.

When the prophets looked ahead and predicted certain events to come, they were generally not granted the ability to pinpoint precisely the elements of time and sequence. Their experience would have been like looking at a mountain range, seeing the mountain peaks in the distance, but really having no way of discerning how far apart they actually were. Many of us have had those disorienting kinds of moments.

Years ago, while helping lead a backpacking trip for Bible college students along the Continental Divide, I thought it might be fun to take an hour or so to tackle a nearby slope. Three hours later, I was not close to my intended destination, and so I headed back before nightfall became an issue. My sense of distance had been way off.

At times, reading the Bible can become a bit disorienting as one tries to match known past historical events with the prophetic claims and descriptive content of the OT prophets. So what are some events that might be blended together in prophecy?

Certainly the Jews' return from the Babylonian captivity was one of these great future events the prophets anticipated (Jer 25:12; 29:10, after "seventy years"). No doubt the first coming of Christ was one of these events. I think the destruction of Jerusalem in AD 70 is also part of the mix here—one of those events that would take place for the generation that would reject the coming of the Messiah (Dan 9:24-27; Lk 21:20-24).

Of course the second coming belongs to this collage of future events, especially since the OT makes no clear distinction between the Messiah's first and second comings (see the discussion in Chapter II regarding the "already and not yet" paradigm). This blending or telescoping of events, therefore, is a critical, if not welcome, aspect of "decoding" Bible prophecy.

Importantly, we need to look to the NT to begin a process of establishing reliable guidelines for the task. Unfortunately, some use the concepts described above, referring to them as matters of "prophetic perspective," to distort what are some relatively clear chronological clues from the NT itself.

I question several of the conclusions based on the excessive application of the "prophetic perspective" model. For example, the Olivet Discourse (Matthew 24; Mark 13; Luke 21) contains predictions concerning both the AD 70 destruction of Jerusalem and the second coming. Instead of carefully distinguishing which verses refer to which, as I believe must be done, some scholars will toss them all into the blender of "prophetic perspective" and relegate the soupy mix to Jesus' Jewish "prophetic consciousness."

Like all good Hebrew prophets, Jesus had no clear idea as to the timelines involved with the events he foresaw, so it is claimed. Descriptions of the fall of Jerusalem are blended in with those of the end of the world. Who can tell what's what? Jesus couldn't, some assert, and we are left with the confusing results. At times, the notion of "prophetic perspective" has been an excuse for not digging deeper to make the difficult, but often evident, distinctions. As well, the murky result may come from scholars who reject the attempts of more conservative scholars to harmonize passages in which wording may vary at times. Some give up on any harmonization efforts way too soon.

To make things worse, the notion of "double fulfillment" gets thrown into the mix. Certain prophecies, it is claimed, actually point ahead to more than one fulfillment. Prophecy students have found this idea helpful when confronted with a fulfillment that does not suit their notion of appropriate literalness. Although Jesus claimed that John the Baptist fulfilled the promises of Elijah's future coming (Mal 4:5-6; Mt 11:7-15), since that coming was not literally accomplished, a later literal fulfillment is expected by some, especially dispensationalists, who expect Elijah himself to return after the "rapture."

As another example, Jesus' prophecy of the destruction of Jerusalem and its temple in the Gospels contains language that some claim points to two temples being desolated: Herod's first-century structure that was destroyed by the Romans and an alleged future temple to be built by Israel in connection with the final days. This alleged future temple will then be destroyed by the efforts of the "antichrist" during the "great tribulation." Two

Elijahs, two temples destroyed—conclusions prompted by instances where the degree of literalness of a fulfilled promise does not pass muster for all interested parties.

As well, the antichrist is found by some in Isaiah where the prophet speaks of a "harsh taskmaster" (Isa 19:4—possibly an Assyrian ruler instead) and in Daniel where Antiochus IV Epiphanes (second c. BC) is actually being described (Dan 8:9-14, 23-26). Is such doubling up of references and fulfillments what the Bible really says? I deem it highly doubtful.

Principle Six: Prophecy Often Utilizes Typology.

Many students of Bible prophecy have a fascination with typology, so a brief word about that pursuit needs to be included here. Typology involves certain people, things, or events in the OT that have a correspondence in the NT, a divinely intended correspondence. We can speak of "types" (Greek *typos* = "pattern, model") in the OT and their corresponding "antitypes" in the NT. (The Greek preposition *anti* could mean either "against" or, as it does here, "instead of.") For example, Moses, Joshua, David, the Passover lamb, and the ark of the covenant's mercy seat all functioned as types of Christ. The flood served as a type of both baptism (1 Peter 3) and the second coming (2 Peter 3). Elijah prefigured John the Baptist as a type.

Often unrecognized is the fact that this phenomenon of typology can relate to the interpretation of symbols and metaphors found in specific prophecies as well. In Isaiah 11 we read that the "new David," the one who would come in the future, will conquer certain kingdoms, and Isaiah, near the end of the chapter, actually refers to kingdoms by name: the Philistines, the Edomites, the Ammonites, and the Moabites (Isa 11:14). These are all nations that will be conquered by this new ruler to come. However, most modern readers would recognize that there are no Edomites, Ammonites, Philistines, or Moabites today!

Instead, these are the very nations that David had conquered (2 Samuel 8, 10). I would suggest that since David was a type of Christ the future victorious reign of Christ—the future "conquest" of the Messiah—is described in terms of David's accomplishments.

The new David, then, will do "David-like things." He will be a conqueror of the nations. The key to understanding a passage like Isaiah 11 is to recognize that, in view of further NT revelation, this is not a physical or military victory that the new David will win, but rather a spiritual one. The messianic conquest will involve hearts and minds, not swords and spears.

Among Jeremiah's restoration prophecies we find promises of a future Davidic kingdom and Levitical (!) priestly kingdom that will be forever. Once again, the solution for understanding what is involved comes back to typological language in prophecy.

> *"Behold, the days are coming, declares the Lord, when I will fulfill the promise I made to the house of Israel and the house of Judah. 15In those days and at that time I will cause a righteous Branch to spring up for David, and he shall execute justice and righteousness in the land. 16In those days Judah will be saved, and Jerusalem will dwell securely. And this is the name by which it will be called: 'The Lord is our righteousness.' 17"For thus says the Lord: David shall never lack a man to sit on the throne of the house of Israel, 18and the Levitical priests shall never lack a man in my presence to offer burnt offerings, to burn grain offerings, and to make sacrifices forever...*

> *22As the host of heaven cannot be numbered and the sands of the sea cannot be measured, so I will multiply the offspring of*

David my servant, and the Levitical priests who minister to me." (Jer 33:14-18, 22)

The "righteous Branch" will establish an eternal kingdom, especially since the Messiah Himself will reign forever. His followers who will sit on the throne with Him will share in that eternal rule (Eph 2:6; Col 3:1; 2Tm 2:12; Rev 2:26-27; 3:21; 20:4). In addition, the OT Levitical sacrificial system served as a type of the atoning sacrifice that would be made by the coming Davidic-Melchizedekian priest-king (Zec 6:12-13; Heb 8:1-2; 1Pet 2:5-10). "New Covenant Israel" will *all* be priests to their God, the antitype to the limited pool of priestly worshipers under the Old Covenant.

We read in 1 Peter, "But you are a chosen race, a royal priesthood, a holy nation, a people for his own possession, that you may proclaim the excellencies of him who called you out of darkness into his marvelous light" (1Pet 2:9). Centuries earlier Jeremiah used typological language in prophesying concerning a future people of God who would function as priest-kings.

Three Helpful Guidelines: We Should Interpret the Bible Literally Unless...

Three helpful guidelines are offered by Floyd Hamilton in his book *The Basis of Millennial Faith* (1952). His useful statement here has been quoted by many from the amillennial persuasion as well as by historic premillennial and dispensational proponents. We should note that there will be differences among students of the Bible on exactly how to apply these three guidelines, but Hamilton's statement is valuable:

In fact a good working rule to follow is that the literal interpretation of the prophecy is to be accepted unless (a) "the passages contain obviously figurative language," or unless (b) "the New Testament gives authority for interpreting them in other than a literal sense," or unless (c) "a literal interpretation would produce a contradiction with truths, principles or factual statements contained in non-symbolic books of the New Testament." (53)

a. "The literal interpretation of the prophecy is to be accepted unless the passages contain obviously figurative language…"

What may be obvious to you or me may not be obvious to someone else, but at least we can use this as a basic point of reference. Symbols and figures that are not tied to passages dear to particular millennial convictions are more readily agreed upon by the majority of interpreters. Jesus calls (the clever) Herod Antipas a "fox" (Lk 13:32) and refers to Himself as a "door" (Jn 10:9). These uses of figurative language are not under scrutiny.

However, when Ezekiel speaks of the coming of "David their king" (Eze 37:24) and Malachi predicts the coming of "Elijah" to turn the hearts of Israel back to God (Mal 4:5-6), interpreters may differ widely regarding the nature of fulfillment involved, depending on their overall prophetic views. Some who do not recognize obvious figurative language here envision the future resurrections of both David and Elijah to fulfill certain leadership roles in an alleged earthly millennial kingdom. And one misstep leads to another.

b. "The literal interpretation of the prophecy is to be accepted unless the New Testament gives authority for interpreting them in other than a literal sense…"

The mention of the "fallen booth of David" in Acts 15:15-17 is taken from Amos 9:11-12 and is applied to the reign of Christ following His resurrection and ascension. The booth (or "tent") imagery describes the earlier demise of David's dynasty and its later rebirth in Jesus, the eternal son of David. A key component of the rebuilding of David's booth (or "hut") is the inclusion of the Gentile nations, the very theme of the council at Jerusalem during which James quotes from Amos 9.

In Hebrews 8, 10 the "New Covenant" promised to "the house of Israel and the house of Judah" in Jeremiah 31:31 is clearly fulfilled in the present high-priestly ministry of Christ and is enjoyed by the "New Israel" made up of both Jews and Gentiles. The Northern Kingdom of ancient Israel had become so apostate in the years leading up to its captivity that it was viewed as "Gentile" in the mind of God (Am 9:7; Rom 9:24-26). For Paul, the expression "not my people," earlier applied to the Northern Kingdom of Israel by the prophet Hosea, in his day could be used for the Gentile world as a whole.

Psalm 22 is rightly considered to be the "crucifixion psalm." The opening line takes us to the foot of the cross: "My God, my God, why have you forsaken me? Why are you so far from saving me, from the words of my groaning?" (Ps 22:1). Yet many of the images found in the psalm are not remotely duplicated in the NT in its descriptions. Notably in Psalms we find animal imagery regarding the suffering of the afflicted one:

Many bulls encompass me; strong bulls of Bashan surround me;
¹³they open wide their mouths at me, like a ravening and
roaring lion. (Ps 22:12-13)

Deliver my soul from the sword, my precious life from the power
of the dog! ²¹Save me from the mouth of the lion! You have
rescued me from the horns of the wild oxen! (Ps 22:20-21)

Bulls, lions, wild oxen? What is happening here? The best option, I believe, is to view the animal imagery as symbolic of the vicious human assailants who brutalize Israel's Messiah, the Suffering Savior. Here the NT, in its substantial use of Psalm 22, supports the symbolic nature of the animal imagery in Psalm 22 by not citing any of it in connection with the crucifixion (Mt 27:35, 39, 46; Jn 19:23-24; Heb 2:11-12).

Since David was an OT "type" of Christ, his personal sufferings, perhaps depicted in this psalm, naturally serve also to depict the sufferings of Jesus, the "antitype." In whatever crises David himself may have been experiencing, the literal presence of the vicious animals outlined was also unlikely.

As a side note, we find here a rejoinder to the oft-made claim that prophecies about Jesus' second coming must be fulfilled literally since the prophecies concerning His first coming were all fulfilled literally. Not true. The animal imagery of Psalm 22 would suggest a measure of poetic license that should be given to the OT authors who prophesied about the life and work of Israel's future Messiah.

Many of the messianic promises in the OT are found in poetic sections, so the claim for a strictly literal understanding of these passages is suspect from the outset.

A careful, case by case study of the language of promise and fulfillment is needed, not arbitrary, rigid assumptions.

c. *"The literal interpretation of the prophecy is to be accepted unless a literal interpretation would produce a contradiction with truths, principles or factual statements contained in non-symbolic books of the New Testament."*

This last guideline would suggest that we use the Gospels to interpret the book of Revelation and not the other way around. We should allow clearer texts to illuminate those less straightforward. Acts and the NT Epistles should take precedence over Daniel, Ezekiel, and Zechariah regarding the process of allowing Scripture to interpret Scripture. The narratives and speeches in the book of Acts can help give us the meaning of various OT prophetic, poetic passages.

Similarly, if Jesus claimed that John the Baptist fulfilled the promise of the coming of "Elijah" (Mt 11:14; 17:10-13), then that statement should not be rejected, as it often is, by interpreters who insist on a "literal" fulfillment of the return of Elijah promised in Malachi 4:5-6. This rejection is regardless of what the Gospels say Jesus said!

Hamilton himself goes on to offer:

Another obvious rule to follow is that the clearest New Testament passages in non-symbolic books are to be the norm for the interpretation of prophecy rather than obscure or partial revelations contained in the Old Testament. In other words, we should accept the clear and plain parts of Scripture as a basis for getting the true meaning of the more difficult parts of Scripture (53-54).

And that makes a lot of sense. The study of Bible prophecy is plagued by the misguided explaining away of clear texts and their obvious meanings in order to make room for overly literalistic conclusions from less clear, often highly figurative, stylistic passages.

In two chapters in the present work (III, IV) we investigate the various mainstream views proposed for understanding what the Bible says about prophecy, the end times, and, in particular, Revelation. A key consideration is how symbolic and non-symbolic texts are evaluated in particular systems and why certain conclusions are drawn. How best can the whole body of Scriptural evidence be understood?

No doubt we are best served by an approach to Revelation that recognizes clear connections with the rest of Scripture and does not attempt to introduce numerous new, distinctive teachings in a book that may well have signaled the end of inspired literature from the apostolic age.

BIBLIOGRAPHY

Barker, Margaret. *The Revelation of Jesus Christ.* Edinburgh: T&T Clark, 2000.

Barr, David L. *Tales of the End: A Narrative Commentary on the Book of Revelation.* Santa Rosa, California: Polebridge Press, 1998.

Bateman IV, Herbert W., ed. *Three Central Issues in Contemporary Dispensationalism.* Grand Rapids, Michigan: Kregel Publications, 1999.

Bauckham, Richard. *The Climax of Prophecy: Studies on the Book of Revelation.* London: T&T Clark, 1993.

————. *The Theology of the Book of Revelation.* Cambridge, UK: Cambridge University Press, 1993.

Bauer, W., Wm. F. Arndt, F. W. Gingrich and F. Danker. *A Greek-English Lexicon of the New Testament and Other Early Christian Literature.* Chicago: University of Chicago Press, 1979, 2nd ed.

Beale, G. K. *The Book of Revelation.* The New International Greek Testament Commentary. Grand Rapids: Wm. B. Eerdmans Publishing Company; Carlisle: The Paternoster Press, 1999.

————. *Handbook on the New Testament Use of the Old Testament.* Grand Rapids: Baker Academic, 2012.

————. "Eden, the Temple, and the Church's Mission in the New Creation," *Journal of the Evangelical Theological Society* 48:1 (March 2005), 5-31.

Blackwell, Ben C., John K Goodrich, and Jason Maston, eds. *Reading Revelation in Context: John's Apocalypse and Second Temple Judaism.* Grand Rapids: Zondervan Academic, 2019.

Blaising, Craig A. and Darrell L. Bock. *Progressive Dispensationalism*. Wheaton, Illinois: Bridgepoint, Victor Books, 1993.

———, eds. *Dispensationalism, Israel and the Church: The Search for Definition*. Grand Rapids: Zondervan, 1992.

Blomberg, Craig L. *Matthew. The New American Commentary Vol. 22*. Nashville, TN: Broadman Press, 1992.

———. "The Posttribulationism of the New Testament," in *A Case for Historic Premillennialism: An Alternative to "Left Behind" Eschatology*, pp. 61-87. Ed. by Craig L. Blomberg and Sung Wook Chung. Grand Rapids: Baker Academic, 2009.

——— and Sung Wook Chung, eds. *A Case for Historic Premillennialism: An Alternative to "Left Behind" Eschatology*. Grand Rapids: Baker Academic, 2009.

Bock, Darrell L. *Luke*. The IVP New Testament Commentary Series. Downers Grove, Illinois: InterVarsity Press, 1994.

———. ed. *Three Views on the Millennium and Beyond*. Counterpoints. Grand Rapids: Zondervan Publishing House, 1999.

Bruins, Evert M. "The Number of the Beast," *Nederlands Theologisch Tijdschrift* 23 (1969), 401-407.

Caird, G. B. *A Commentary on the Revelation of St. John the Divine*. New York: Harper & Row, Publishers, 1966.

Carrington, Philip. *The Meaning of the Revelation*. London: SPCK, 1931.

Chilton, David. *The Days of Vengeance: An Exposition of the Book of Revelation*. Ft. Worth, Texas: Dominion Press, 1987.

Clement. trans. Grant, Robert M. and H. H. Graham. *First and Second Clement*. Vol. 2 of The Apostolic Fathers: A New Translation and Commentary, ed. Robert M. Grant. Camden, NJ: Thomas Nelson, 1965.

Clouse, Robert G., ed. *The Meaning of the Millennium: Four Views.* Downers Grove, Illinois: InterVarsity Press, 1979.

Collins, John J. *The Apocalyptic Imagination: An Introduction to Jewish Apocalyptic Literature.* 2nd ed. Grand Rapids: Wm. B. Eerdmans Publishing Company; and Livonia, Michigan: Dove Booksellers, 1998 (Crossroad, 1984).

Cullmann, Oscar. *Christ and Time.* Philadelphia, PA: The Westminster Press, 1950.

Dunn, James D. G. *The Theology of Paul the Apostle.* Grand Rapids: Wm B. Eerdmans Publishing Company, 1998.

Edersheim, Alfred. *The Life and Times of Jesus the Messiah.* Grand Rapids: Wm B. Eerdmans Publishing Company, 1971, first printing one volume edition (1883).

Ehrman, Bart D. *The Triumph of Christianity: How a Forbidden Religion Swept the World.* New York: Simon & Schuster Paperbacks, 2018.

Eller, Vernard. "STOP the Dating Game: Don't waste your time doing what Jesus said can't be done," *Christianity Today* 43:12 (October 25, 1999), 75-80.

Erdman, Charles R. *The Revelation of John: An Exposition.* Philadelphia: The Westminster Press, 1966.

Eusebius. Cruse, C. F., trans. *Eusebius' Ecclesiastical History.* Complete and Unabridged. New Updated Edition. Peabody, Massachusetts: Hendrickson Publishers, 2004.

Fee, Gordon D. *The First and Second Letters to the Thessalonians.* The New International Commentary on the New Testament. Grand Rapids: William B. Eerdmans Publishing Company, 2009.

———— and Douglas Stuart. *How to Read the Bible for All It's Worth.* Grand Rapids, Michigan: Zondervan, 1982.

Ford, J. Massyngberde. *Revelation: Introduction, Translation and Commentary.* The Anchor Bible Vol. 38. Garden City, New York: Doubleday & Company, Inc., 1975.

Friesen, Steven J. *Imperial Colts and the Apocalypse of John: Reading Revelation in the Ruins*. New York: Oxford University Press, 2001.

Gentry, Kenneth L., Jr. *Before Jerusalem Fell: Dating the Book of Revelation*. Powder Springs, Georgia: American Vision, 1998.

Goodman, Martin. *Rome and Jerusalem: The Clash of Ancient Civilizations*. New York: Alfred A. Knopf, 2007.

Goulder, M. D. "The Apocalypse as an Annual Cycle of Prophecies," *New Testament Studies* 27:3 (April 1981), 342-367.

Gregg, Steve, ed. *Revelation, Four Views: A Parallel Commentary*. Nashville: Thomas Nelson Publishers, 1997.

Grenz, Stanley J. *The Millennial Maze: Sorting Out Evangelical Options*. Downers Grove, IL: InterVarsity Press, 1992.

Hadas-Lebel, Mireille. Trans. Richard Miller. *Flavius Josephus: Eyewitness to Rome's First-Century Conquest of Judea*. New York: Macmillan Publishing Company, 1993.

Hamilton, Floyd E. *The Basis of Millennial Faith*. Grand Rapids: William B. Eerdmans Publishing Company, 1952.

Heiser, Michael S. *The Old Testament in Revelation: Notes from the Naked Bible Podcast*. Naked Bible Press, 2021.

Hemer, Colin J. *The Letters to the Seven Churches of Asia in Their Local Setting*. Grand Rapids: Wm. B. Eerdmans Publishing Company, 2001 (Sheffield 1986).

Hendriksen, William. *More Than Conquerors: An Interpretation of the Book of Revelation*. Grand Rapids: Baker Book House, 1967 (1939).

Hengel, Martin. Trans. David Smith. *The Zealots: Investigations Into the Jewish Freedom Movement in the Period from Herod I Until 70 A.D.* Edinburgh: T. & T. Clark, 1989.

Hill, Charles E. *Regnum Caelorum: Patterns of Millennial Thought in Early Christianity*, 2nd ed. Grand Rapids: Wm. B. Eerdmans Publishing Company, 2001.

Hoekema, Anthony A. "Amillennialism." In *The Meaning of the Millennium: Four Views*, pp. 155-189. Ed. by Robert G. Clouse. Downers Grove, Illinois: InterVarsity Press, 1979.

Ice, Thomas and Timothy J. Demi, eds. *The Return: Understanding Christ's Second Coming and the End Times*. Grand Rapids: Kregel Publications, 1999.

Ice, Thomas and Kenneth L. Gentry Jr. *The Great Tribulation: Past or Future? Two Evangelicals Debate the Question*. Grand Rapids, Michigan: Kregel Publications, 1999.

Josephus. Whiston, William, A. M., trans. *Josephus: The Complete Works*. Nashville, TN: Thomas Nelson Publishers, 1998 (1737).

Kistemaker, Simon J. "Hyper-Preterism and Revelation." In *When Shall These Things Be? A Reformed Response to Hyper-Preterism*, pp. 215-254. Ed. by Keith A. Mathison. Phillipsburg, New Jersey: P&R Publishing Company, 2004.

Klein, William W. et al. *Introduction to Biblical Interpretation*. Grand Rapids: Zondervan Academic, 2017, 3rd ed.

Ladd, George Eldon. *The Blessed Hope*. Grand Rapids: William B. Eerdmans Publishing Company, 1956.

————. *A Commentary on the Revelation of John*. Grand Rapids: William B. Eerdmans Publishing Company, 1972.

————. *Crucial Questions about the Kingdom of God*. Grand Rapids: William B. Eerdmans Publishing Company, 1952.

————. *The Gospel of the Kingdom*. Grand Rapids: William B. Eerdmans Publishing Company, 1959.

———. *Jesus and the Kingdom*. Waco, TX: Word Books, 1964.

———. *The Last Things: An Eschatology for Laymen*. Grand Rapids: William B. Eerdmans Publishing Company, 1978.

———. *The Pattern of New Testament Truth*. Grand Rapids: William B. Eerdmans Publishing Company, 1968.

———. *The Presence of the Future*. Grand Rapids: William B. Eerdmans Publishing Company, 1974 (revision of *Jesus and the Kingdom* [1964]).

———. *A Theology of the New Testament*. Grand Rapids: William B. Eerdmans Publishing Company, 1974.

Lewis, Arthur H. *The Dark Side of the Millennium: The Problem of Evil in Rev. 20:1-10*. Grand Rapids: Baker Book House, 1980.

Lindsey, Hal with C. C. Carlson. *The Late Great Planet Earth*. Grand Rapids: Zondervan Publishing House, 1970.

———. *Satan Is Alive and Well on Planet Earth*. Grand Rapids: Zondervan Publishing House, 1972.

Longman, Tremper, III. *Revelation Through Old Testament Eyes: A Background and Application Commentary*. Grand Rapids: Kregel Academic, 2022.

———. *Reading the Bible with Heart and Mind*. Colorado Springs, Colorado: NavPress, 1997.

Lowery, Robert A. *Revelation's Rhapsody: Listening to the Lyrics of the Lamb: How to Read the Book of Revelation*. Joplin, Missouri: College Press Publishing Company, 2006.

Lumpkin, Joseph B. *The Book of Jubilees; The Little Genesis; The Apocalypse of Moses*. Fifth Estate, Incorporated, 2011.

Mason, Steve. *A History of the Jewish War A.D. 66-74*. New York: Cambridge University Press, 2016.

Mathison, Keith A. *Postmillennialism: An Eschatology of Hope*. Phillipsburg, NJ: P & R Publishing, 1999.

————. "The Eschatological Time Texts of the New Testament." In *When Shall These Things Be? A Reformed Response to Hyper-Preterism*, pp. 155-213. Ed. by Keith A. Mathison. Phillipsburg, NJ: P&R Publishing Company, 2004.

————, ed. *When Shall These Things Be? A Reformed Response to Hyper-Preterism.* Phillipsburg, NJ: P&R Publishing Company, 2004.

McKenzie, Duncan W. *The Antichrist and the Second Coming: A Preterist Examination.* Volume I: Daniel and 2 Thessalonians. Xulon Press, 2009.

————. *The Antichrist and the Second Coming: A Preterist Examination.* Volume II: The Book of Revelation. Xulon Press, 2012.

McKnight, Scot with Cody Matchett. *Revelation for the Rest of Us: A Prophetic Call to Follow Jesus as a Dissident Disciple.* Grand Rapids: Zondervan Reflective, 2023.

Menninger, Karl. *Number Words and Number Symbols: A Cultural History of Numbers*, trans. (from German) Paul Broneer. Mineola, New York: Dover Publications, 1992.

Metzger, Bruce M. *Breaking the Code: Understanding the Book of Revelation.* Nashville: Abingdon Press, 1993.

Michaels, J. Ramsey. "Revelation 1:19 and the Narrative Voices of the Apocalypse," *New Testament Studies* 37 (1991), 604-620.

Moore, Mark E. *How to Dodge a Dragon.* Joplin, Missouri: College Press, 1998.

————. *Seeing God in HD.* Joplin, Missouri: College Press, 2008.

Murphy, Frederick J. *Apocalypticism in the Bible and Its World: A Comprehensive Introduction.* Grand Rapids: Baker Academic, 2012.

Noē, John. *Beyond the End Times: The Rest of The Greatest Story Ever Told.* Bradford, PA: International Preterist Association, 1999.

————. *Shattering the 'Left Behind' Delusion.* Bradford, PA: International Preterist Association, 2000.

North, James B. *From Pentecost to the Present: A Short History of Christianity.* Joplin, Missouri: College Press Publishing Company, 1983.

Osborne, Grant R. *Revelation.* Baker Exegetical Commentary on the New Testament. Grand Rapids: Baker Academic, 2002.

Pechawer, Larry. *Leaving the Rapture Behind.* Joplin, Missouri: MIREH Publishers, 2003.

Philo. *The Embassy to Gaius.* Trans. F. H. Colson. Loeb Classical Library: Philo Vol. 10. Cambridge, Massachusetts: Harvard University Press, 1962.

Provan, Iain. "Foul Spirits, Fornication and Finance: Revelation 18 from an Old Testament Perspective," *Journal for the Study of the New Testament* 64 (1996), 81-100.

Rengstorf, Karl H., ed. *A Complete Concordance to Flavius Josephus.* 4 vols. Leiden: E. J. Brill, 1973.

Russell, D. S. *The Method and Message of Jewish Apocalyptic.* The Old Testament Library. Philadelphia: The Westminster Press, 1964.

Sanders, Henry A. "The Number of the Beast in Revelation," *Journal of Biblical Literature* 37:1 (1918), 95-99.

Sandy, D. Brent. *Plowshares & Pruning Hooks: Rethinking the Language of Prophecy and Apocalyptic.* Lisle, Illinois: IVP Academic, 2002.

Saucy, Robert L. *The Case for Progressive Dispensationalism.* Grand Rapids, Michigan: Zondervan Publishing House, 1993.

Scobie, Charles H. H. "Local References in the Letters to the Seven Churches," *New Testament Studies* 39 (1993), 606-624.

Scofield, C. I. *The Scofield Reference Bible*. New York: Oxford University Press, 1917.

Smalley, Stephen S. *The Revelation to John: A Commentary on the Greek Text of the Apocalypse*. Downers Grove, Illinois: IVP Academic, 2005.

Stein, Robert H. *Jesus, the Temple and the Coming of the Son of Man: A Commentary on Mark 13*. Downers Grove, Illinois: InterVarsity Press, 2014.

Stone, Michael E. and Matthias Henze. *4 Ezra and 2 Baruch: Translations, Introductions, and Notes*. Minneapolis: Fortress Press, 2013.

Storms, Sam. *Kingdom Come: The Amillennial Alternative*. Geanies House, Fern, Ross-shire IV20 1TW, Scotland, UK: Mentor Imprint of Christian Focus Publications Ltd., 2019 (2013).

Tacitus. *The Histories*. trans. Kenneth Wellesley. New York: Penguin Books, 1972 (1964).

Thayer, Joseph Henry. *A Greek-English Lexicon of the New Testament*. Grand Rapids: Zondervan Publishing House, 1962 (1889).

Thompson, Leonard L. *The Book of Revelation: Apocalypse and Empire*. New York: Oxford University Press, 1990.

Toussaint, Stanley D. "Are the Church and the Rapture in Matthew 24?" In *The Return: Understanding Christ's Second Coming and the End Times*, pp. 121-136. Ed. by Thomas Ice and Timothy J. Demi. Grand Rapids: Kregel Publications, 1999.

Walvoord, John F. *The Blessed Hope and the Tribulation*. Grand Rapids: Zondervan Publishing House, 1976.

———. *The Millennial Kingdom*. Grand Rapids: Zondervan Publishing House, 1959.

————. *The Return of the Lord.* Grand Rapids: Zondervan Publishing House, 1955.

Wanamaker, Charles A. *The Epistles to the Thessalonians: A Commentary on the Greek Text.* The New International Greek Testament Commentary. Grand Rapids, Michigan: Wm. B. Eerdmans Publishing Co., 1990.

Watt, W. C. "666," *Semiotica* 77:4 (1989), 369-392.

Weima, Jeffrey A. D. *1-2 Thessalonians.* Baker Exegetical Commentary on the New Testament. Grand Rapids: Baker Academic, 2014.

Witherington, Ben, III. *Jesus, Paul and the End of the World: A Comparative Study in New Testament Eschatology.* Downers Grove, IL: InterVarsity Press, 1992.

————. *Revelation.* The New Cambridge Bible Commentary. Cambridge: Cambridge University Press, 2003.

————. *Revelation and the End Times: Unraveling God's Message of Hope.* Nashville: Abingdon Press, 2010.

Wood, Shane J. *The Alter-Imperial Paradigm: Empire Studies and the Book of Revelation.* Biblical Interpretation Series 140. Leiden: Brill, 2016.

————. "An Alter-Imperial Reading of the Release of Satan (Rev 20:7-10)." In *Dragons, John, and Every Grain of Sand: Essays on the Book of Revelation in Honor of Dr. Robert Lowery*, pp. 181-191. Ed. by Shane J. Wood. Joplin, Missouri: College Press Publishing Company, 2011.

————. *Thinning the Veil: Encountering Jesus Christ in the Book of Revelation.* Downers Grove, IL: InterVarsity Press, 2025.

————, ed. *Dragons, John, and Every Grain of Sand: Essays on the Book of Revelation in Honor of Dr. Robert Lowery.* Joplin, Missouri: College Press Publishing Company, 2011.

Wright, N. T. *Jesus and the Victory of God.* Christian Origins and the Question of God, Volume 2. Minneapolis: Fortress Press, 1996.

———. *Surprised by Hope: Rethinking Heaven, the Resurrection, and the Mission of the Church.* New York: Harper One, 2008.

About the Author

Dr. Larry Pechawer taught Bible and Biblical Languages for over forty years before his retirement from Ozark Christian College in Joplin, MO.

Previously he had taught at Cincinnati Bible College and Seminary and at Central Christian College of the Bible (Moberly, MO), where he also served as Academic Dean. Larry regularly ministered to churches in Kentucky, Ohio, and Missouri while he taught in the college classroom. He also offered college and seminary-level courses on eighteen cross-cultural trips in ten countries.

He attended The Ohio State University and graduated from Cincinnati Bible College and Seminary (BA, MA). His PhD degree from Hebrew Union College-Jewish Institute of Religion, Cincinnati, OH, was in the field of Semitic Languages.

The three appendices in this work offer support for a variety of research for the book's argumentation. The first, "The Man of Lawlessness," will be further addressed in Pechawer's forthcoming book *The Man of Lawlessness: Recovering Paul's Jerusalem Apocalypse*.

Among other publications, Dr. Pechawer has produced *The Lost Prayer of Jabez* and *Leaving the Rapture Behind* and compiled *Poetry and Prophecy, Vol. III* of Standard Publishing's Through the Bible Commentary.

www.ingramcontent.com/pod-product-compliance
Lightning Source LLC
Chambersburg PA
CBHW021209090426
42740CB00006B/172